I0868580

# Advanced Image Processing and Video Intelligence Applications

Edited by


**Ravinder M.**

*Department of Computer Science and Engineering, Indira Gandhi Delhi Technical University for Women (IGDTUW) New Delhi, Delhi, India*

**Arti Ranjan**

*Department of Computer Science and Engineering, Niels Brock Copenhagen Business College, Copenhagen, Denmark, Department of Computer Science and Engineering, Indira Gandhi Delhi Technical University for Women (IGDTUW) New Delhi, Delhi, India*

&

**Youddha Beer Singh**

*Department of Computer Science and Engineering, Galgotias College of Engineering and Technology, Greater Noida, Uttar Pradesh, India*

# Advanced Image Processing and Video Intelligence Applications

Editors: Ravinder M., Arti Ranjan and Youddha Beer Singh

ISBN (Online): 979-8-89881-591-2

ISBN (Print): 979-8-89881-592-9

ISBN (Paperback): 979-8-89881-593-6



Published by Bentham Science Publishers Pte. Ltd. Singapore,

in collaboration with Eureka Conferences, USA. 

First published in 2026.

need for a court order if at any point you breach any terms of this License Agreement. In no event will any delay or failure by Bentham Science Publishers in enforcing your compliance with this License Agreement constitute a waiver of any of its rights.

3. You acknowledge that you have read this License Agreement, and agree to be bound by its terms and conditions. To the extent that any other terms and conditions presented on any website of Bentham Science Publishers conflict with, or are inconsistent with, the terms and conditions set out in this License Agreement, you acknowledge that the terms and conditions set out in this License Agreement shall prevail.

**Bentham Science Publishers Pte. Ltd.**
No. 9 Raffles Place
Office No. 26-01
Singapore 048619
Singapore
Email: subscriptions@benthamscience.net

BENTHAM SCIENCE

# CONTENTS

# FOREWORD

We are living through a silent visual revolution in the digitally-first world of today. Previously merely capturing memories or information, images have evolved into rich, dynamic data sources that impact decisions, mold industries, and enhance the human experience. The strong, and frequently unseen, engine of image processing technologies, a field that has developed quickly and now affects almost every part of our lives, is responsible for this change.

Insightful and up to date, "Advanced Image Processing and Video Intelligence Applications" delves into this fascinating topic. From the basic ideas of image processing to its most advanced uses, which include smart surveillance, immersive entertainment, healthcare diagnostics, and even satellite imagery-based climate monitoring, it takes readers on an educational trip.

This book is unique because it carefully strikes a balance between technical complexity and readability. Both beginners and experts can relate to the authors' deft demythologizing of difficult subjects like machine learning, statistical techniques, and huge language models by placing them in relatable real-world scenarios. By doing this, they make it possible for a wide range of people to interact with one of the most influential technologies of our day, including students, teachers, business professionals, and inquisitive minds.

The book also seeks to delve deeper into the sociological and ethical ramifications of image processing, moving beyond the algorithms and mechanics. It is our duty to employ automated visual systems responsibly and equitably as our reliance on them increases. Because of this contemplation, Image Intelligence is more than just a technical guide; it is a credo for ethical innovation. I recommend this book with a great deal of gratitude and excitement. Image Intelligence will enlighten, inspire, and challenge you to view the world both literally and figuratively from a different perspective, regardless of whether you are new to image processing or looking to expand your knowledge.

**Rashmi Rathi Upadhyay**
Department of Computer Science and Engineering
Sharda University, Greater Noida, Uttar Pradesh
India

# PREFACE

In today's digital era, both images and videos dominate how we communicate, learn, and interpret the world around us. From social media and entertainment to healthcare, agriculture, security, and scientific research, the ability to create, enhance, and analyze visual content has become indispensable. ***"Advanced Image Processing and Video Intelligence Applications"*** is a comprehensive exploration of the technologies that empower this visual transformation, offering readers insights into the methods and innovations that are shaping modern life. This book emerges from the recognition of a profound shift: the move from simple image enhancement techniques to advanced, AI-driven frameworks capable of extracting knowledge, detecting patterns, and enabling real-time decision-making from massive streams of visual data. It highlights the dual dimensions of progress: image processing, which refines and restores static visuals, and video intelligence, which unlocks dynamic understanding from continuous frames. Together, these fields are redefining automation, efficiency, and intelligence across industries.

The primary aim of this book is to make advanced concepts in image and video intelligence accessible to a wide readership. It is designed for students, researchers, and professionals in computer science, engineering, and related disciplines, as well as practitioners in fields where visual technologies play a critical role. Each chapter balances technical rigor with practical application, beginning with foundational principles and advancing to deep learning–based approaches, transformer architectures, and emerging multimodal methods. Case studies drawn from domains such as healthcare, transportation, agriculture, and disaster management illustrate how these technologies are solving real-world challenges.

## KEY FEATURES

- This book is designed to offer a panoramic view of the current state and future prospects of image processing technologies, emphasizing their transformative power across various domains. The book aims not only to educate its readers on the technical aspects but also to provoke thoughtful consideration of the broader impacts of these technologies on society.

- The aims of this book are to demystify the complex field of image processing and showcase its profound impact on modern society. This book intends to bridge the gap between the intricate technical concepts of image processing and their practical applications across various aspects of everyday life, using image processing technologies such as statistical methods, Machine Learning/Deep Learning Methods, Transformers, and Language Models, including Large Language Models and Small-scale models.

- This book targets a broad audience, ranging from students and educators in the field of computer science and engineering to industry professionals and technology enthusiasts keen on understanding how image processing technologies are revolutionizing the way we live, work, and interact with the world around us. Further, the book aims to not only educate its readers on the technical and practical aspects of image processing but also to inspire them to consider the future possibilities and ethical dimensions of this rapidly evolving field.

This book certainly motivates the reader to work in the field of Image and Video Intelligence using computer vision. This book may also be used as a reference book for graduates/postgraduate students studying computer science, information technology, and electronics and communication engineering.

**Ravinder M.**
Department of Computer Science and Engineering
Indira Gandhi Delhi Technical University for Women (IGDTUW)
New Delhi, Delhi
India

**Arti Ranjan**
Department of Computer Science and Engineering
Niels Brock Copenhagen Business College
Copenhagen, Denmark
Department of Computer Science and Engineering
Indira Gandhi Delhi Technical University for Women (IGDTUW
New Delhi, Delhi
India

&

**Youddha Beer Singh**
Department of Computer Science and Engineering
Galgotias College of Engineering and Technology
Greater Noida, Uttar Pradesh
India

# List of Contributors

| | |
|---|---|
| **Abhijeet Gajanan Chimankar** | Department of Computer Science, Radhai Mahavidyalaya, Chhatrapati Sambhajinagar, Maharashtra, India |
| **Ajeet Kumar Bhartee** | Department of Computer Engineering, National Institute of Technology (NIT), Uttarakhand, Srinagar, India |
| **Akshansh Mishra** | Department of Computer Science and Engineering (Artificial Intelligence), ABES Institute of Technology, Ghaziabad, Uttar Pradesh, India |
| **Akshay Dheeraj** | ICAR-Indian Agricultural Statistics Research Institute, New Delhi, Delhi, India |
| **Aneesh Kumar Mishra** | Department of Computer Science and Engineering, JECRC University, Jaipur, Rajasthan, India |
| **Anita Shukla** | Department of Basic Sciences and Humanities, Pranveer Singh Institute of Technology, Kanpur, Uttar Pradesh, India |
| **Ankit Jain** | Department of Electronics and Communication Engineering, Pranveer Singh Institute of Technology, Kanpur, Uttar Pradesh, India |
| **Ankush Patil** | Department of Mathematics, Research Centre, L.V.H ASC College, Nashik & MIT Academy of Engineering, Pune, Maharashtra, India |
| **Annu Mishra** | Department of Computer Science and Engineering, Sharda School of Engineering and Technology, Greater Noida, Uttar Pradesh, India |
| **Anshul Khanna** | Department of Computer Science and Engineering, JIMS Engineering Management Technical Campus (JEMTEC), Greater Noida, Uttar Pradesh, India |
| **Anuradha Pillai** | Department of Computer Science and Engineering, Symbiosis Institute of Technology, Pune, Maharashtra, India |
| **Aryan Vashisth** | Department of Computer Science and Engineering (Artificial Intelligence), ABES Institute of Technology, Ghaziabad, Uttar Pradesh, India |
| **Ashutosh C Kakde** | Department of Agricultural Engineering, Nehru Institute of Technology, Coimbatore, Tamil Nadu, India |
| **Atowar Ul Islam** | Department of Computer Science, University of Science and Technology, Baridua, Meghalaya, India |
| **Ayushi Godiya** | School of Engineering, Ajeenkya DY Patil University, Charholi Buduruk, Pune, Maharashtra, India |
| **Deepika Punj** | Department of Computer Science and Engineering, J.C. Bose University of Science and Technology, Faridabad, Haryana, India |
| **Dler Salih Hasan** | Department of Computer Science and Information Technology, Salahaddin University - College of Science, Erbil, Iraq |
| **Ela Kumar** | Department of Computer Science and Engineering, Ajay Kumar Garg Engineering College, Ghaziabad, Uttar Pradesh, India |
| **Harsimran Singh** | Department of Electrical Engineering, Guru Kashi University, Talwandi Sabo, Punjab, India |
| **Imran Ullah Khan** | Department of Electronics and Communication Engineering, Integral University, Lucknow, Uttar Pradesh, India |

| | |
|---|---|
| **Inderpreet Kaur** | Department of Computer Science and Engineering, The Sharda School of Engineering and Technology, Sharda University, Greater Noida, Uttar Pradesh, India |
| **Isha Sood** | School of Engineering, Ajeenkya DY Patil University, Charholi Buduruk, Pune, Maharashtra, India |
| **Kirti Seth** | School of Computer and Information Engineering, Inha University, Tashkent, Uzbekistan |
| **L. Karthick** | Department of Mechanical Engineering, Hindusthan College of Engineering and Technology, Coimbatore, Tamil Nadu, India |
| **M. Babu** | Department of Mechanical Engineering, SRM Easwari Engineering College, Chennai, Tamil Nadu, India |
| **M. Masilamani** | Department of Artificial Intelligence and Data Science, Dr. Mahalingam College of Engineering and Technology, Pollachi, Tamil Nadu, India |
| **Madhu** | ICAR-Indian Agricultural Statistics Research Institute, New Delhi, Delhi, India |
| **Mayank Dixit** | Department of Computer Science and Engineering, Galgotias College of Engineering & Technology, Greater Noida, Uttar Pradesh, India |
| **Meena Kumari** | Department of Computer Science and Engineering (Internet of Things), ABES Institute of Technology, Ghaziabad, Uttar Pradesh, India |
| **Mohammad Mudassir** | Support Engineer, Algorand Foundation, New York, USA |
| **Mohd Shaliyar** | Department of Computer Science and Applications, Sharda School of Engineering and Technology, Greater Noida, Uttar Pradesh, India |
| **Poorva Nayyar** | Software Developer, Carry more hoists Pvt. Ltd, Faridabad, Haryana, India |
| **Prateek Kumar Yadav** | Department of Computer Science and Engineering, Galgotias College of Engineering & Technology, Greater Noida, Uttar Pradesh, India |
| **Preeti Yadav** | Department of Computer Science and Information Technology, Mahatma Jyotiba Phule Rohilkhand University, Bareilly, Uttar Pradesh, India |
| **Punam Dattatray Gawali** | School of Humanities and Engineering Sciences, MIT Academy of Engineering, Pune, Maharashtra, India |
| **Rajneesh Kumar Singh** | Department of Computer Science and Applications, Sharda School of Engineering and Technology, Greater Noida, Uttar Pradesh, India |
| **Rajni Jain** | ICAR-National Institute of Agricultural Economics and Policy Research, New Delhi, Delhi, India |
| **Ravi Prakash Chaturvedi** | Department of Computer Science and Applications, Sharda School of Engineering and Technology, Greater Noida, Uttar Pradesh, India |
| **Rekha Baghel** | Department of Computer Science, Indira Gandhi Delhi Technical University for Women, New Delhi, Delhi, India<br>Department of Computer Science and Engineering, Ajay Kumar Garg Engineering College, Ghaziabad, Uttar Pradesh, India |
| **Sameer Asthana** | Department of Computer Science and Applications, Greater Noida Institute of Technology (GNOIT), Greater Noida, Uttar Pradesh, India |
| **Sandeep Vishwakarma** | Department of Computer Science and Engineering, J.C. Bose University of Science and Technology, Faridabad, Haryana, India |

| | |
|---|---|
| **Sanjay Kumar** | Department of Computer Science and Engineering, Galgotias College of Engineering and Technology, Greater Noida, Uttar Pradesh, India |
| **Sapna Nigam** | ICAR-Indian Agricultural Statistics Research Institute, New Delhi, Delhi, India |
| **Seema Shukla** | Department of Computer Science & Engineering, Sharda University, Greater Noida, Uttar Pradesh, India |
| **Shivam Shukla** | Department of Computer Science and Engineering, Galgotias College of Engineering & Technology, Greater Noida, Uttar Pradesh, India |
| **Shradhanwita Mukherjee** | Department of Computer Science and Engineering, Haldia Institute of Technology, Haldia, West Bengal, India |
| **Subhajit Ghosh** | Department of Computer Science and Engineering Artificial Intelligence and Machine Learning, Meerut Institute of Engineering and Technology, Meerut, Uttar Pradesh, India |
| **Sudeep Marwaha** | ICAR-Indian Agricultural Statistics Research Institute, New Delhi, Delhi, India |
| **Sulaxan Jadhav** | Symbiosis School of Economics, Symbiosis International (Deemed University), Pune, Maharashtra, India |
| **Sumanta Kuila** | Department of Computer Science and Engineering, Haldia Institute of Technology, Haldia, West Bengal, India |
| **Surendra Singh** | Department of Computer Science and Engineering, Maulana Azad National Institute of Technology, Bhopal, Madhya Pradesh, India |
| **Surrya Prakash DilliBabu** | Department of Mechanical Engineering, Vel Tech Rangarajan Dr. Sagunthala R&D Institute of Science and Technology, Chennai, Tamil Nadu, India |
| **T. Prabhu** | Department of Mechatronics Engineering, Hindusthan College of Engineering and Technology, Coimbatore, Tamil Nadu, India |
| **T Sivamani** | Department of Electronics and Communication Engineering, Hindusthan Institute of Technology, Coimbatore, Tamil Nadu, India |
| **V. K. Choudhary** | ICAR-Directorate of Weed Research, Jabalpur, Madhya Pradesh, India |
| **V N Shukla** | Information Technology, Election Commission of India, New Delhi, Delhi, India |
| **Vipul Kumar Mishra** | Department of Artificial Intelligence and Data Science, Gati Shakti Viswavidyalaya, Vadodara, Gujarat, India |

# CHAPTER 1

# Integrating Image Processing and Deep Learning for Effective Image Dehazing

**Sandeep Vishwakarma**[1,*], **Anuradha Pillai**[2], **Deepika Punj**[1] and **Preeti Yadav**[3]

[1] *Department of Computer Science and Engineering, J.C. Bose University of Science and Technology, Faridabad, Haryana, India*

[2] *Department of Computer Science and Engineering, Symbiosis Institute of Technology, Pune, Maharashtra, India*

[3] *Department of Computer Science and Information Technology, Mahatma Jyotiba Phule Rohilkhand University, Bareilly, Uttar Pradesh, India*

**Abstract:** This chapter delves into the cohesive integration of conventional image processing methods with deep learning techniques to address the complex problem of image dehazing. Atmospheric haze often degrades the quality of outdoor imagery, reducing clarity and obscuring scene details. While conventional image processing techniques have historically been employed to mitigate haze effects, recent advancements in deep learning present promising prospects for enhancing the efficacy and resilience of dehazing algorithms. Within this chapter, an overview is provided encompassing both traditional image processing methodologies and deep learning architectures tailored for dehazing tasks, encompassing discussions on their respective strengths and limitations. Furthermore, strategies for amalgamating these methodologies are explored with the objective of achieving superior dehazing performance. The adverse effects of haze, fog, and smoke on outdoor image quality significantly impede various tasks, including computer vision and visual perception. This chapter meticulously examines the fusion of image processing techniques and deep learning models to effectively combat image haze. Commencing with an examination of the atmospheric scattering physics underlying haze formation and the ensuing challenges, the chapter proceeds to evaluate conventional image processing techniques for dehazing, highlighting their inherent limitations. Subsequently, a comprehensive exploration of deep learning-based dehazing methodologies ensues, encompassing diverse convolutional neural network (CNN) architectures and their respective advantages. The chapter elucidates how deep learning capitalizes on image processing principles to acquire haze-relevant features, thereby achieving enhanced dehazing outcomes. Finally, the chapter addresses existing challenges and future prospects within this dynamic research domain.

[*] **Corresponding author Sandeep Vishwakarma:** Department of Computer Science and Engineering, J.C. Bose University of Science and Technology, Faridabad, Haryana, India;
E-mail: ersandeep.jnp@gmail.com

**Ravinder M., Arti Ranjan, Youddha Beer Singh (Eds.)**

**Keywords:** Convolutional neural network, Deep learning, Image dehazing, Polarization, Vision in bad weather.

## INTRODUCTION

This chapter explores the fusion between traditional image processing methodologies and the burgeoning realm of deep learning (DL) techniques, all in pursuit of mitigating the pervasive challenge posed by atmospheric haze in outdoor imagery. Atmospheric haze, caused by the scattering and absorption of light due to airborne particles and moisture, poses a significant challenge to capturing clear and visually appealing outdoor images. These haziness effects not only obscure fine details but also diminish overall visibility, significantly impeding tasks ranging from computer vision applications to human visual perception [1].

Historically, traditional image processing techniques have served as the bedrock for addressing the issue of image haze. These methods, like dark channel prior (DCP), atmospheric scattering model (ASM), and guided image filtering, operate on established principles of image manipulation to enhance clarity and contrast in hazy scenes. While effective to a certain extent, these conventional approaches often exhibit limitations in handling complex scenes, varying lighting conditions, and may introduce undesirable artifacts or loss of image details [2].

In recent years, deep learning has rapidly emerged as a revolutionary force in computer vision. Convolutional neural networks (CNNs), in particular, have shown exceptional ability in capturing complex patterns and representations directly from data. By utilizing the vast information contained in large-scale datasets, deep learning models can identify intricate relationships between hazy and clear images, significantly advancing dehazing performance [3].

Against this backdrop, the chapter provides a comprehensive overview of both traditional image processing techniques and deep learning models for image dehazing. By elucidating the strengths and limitations of each approach, the chapter sets the stage for a nuanced exploration of strategies for integrating these methodologies to achieve synergistic improvements in dehazing performance. Through this integrated lens, the chapter aims to unlock new insights and avenues for advancing the state-of-the-art (SOTA) in image dehazing research and practice [4].

Visual information is the cornerstone of many applications that shape our world. From the autonomous vehicles navigating our streets to the robotic arms assembling intricate machinery in factories, clear and accurate vision is fundamental for successful operation. Surveillance systems rely on it to monitor public spaces, while medical imaging allows doctors to diagnose and treat diseases. In the realm of remote sensing, clear visuals are essential for monitoring environmental changes and managing natural resources [5].

However, adverse weather conditions like haze, fog, and smoke can significantly disrupt this visual clarity. Haze, a widespread phenomenon, arises from tiny particles suspended in the atmosphere. These particles scatter light, reducing visibility and obscuring crucial scene details within captured images. This not only hinders the performance of the aforementioned applications but can also lead to safety hazards and inaccurate decision-making [6].

Imagine an autonomous car struggling to navigate through a hazy landscape, its sensors failing to distinguish between road markings and blurred surroundings. Or picture a medical professional unable to discern subtle details in a hazy X-ray, potentially delaying a critical diagnosis [7]. These scenarios highlight the urgency of developing robust methods to counteract the effects of haze and restore clarity to images shown in Fig. (**1**).

**Fig. (1).** Hazy image and ground truth image.

This chapter delves into the fascinating realm of image dehazing, exploring how image processing techniques and deep learning models together are shaping the future of this field. We will begin by unravelling the scientific principles behind haze formation and the challenges it presents. We will then embark on a journey through traditional image processing methods for dehazing, understanding their strengths and limitations. Subsequently, we will witness the rise of deep learning as a game-changer in this domain, exploring the potential of convolutional neural networks (CNNs) to achieve superior dehazing performance. We will unveil how deep learning leverages the wisdom of image processing to extract meaningful features from hazy images and recover the hidden scene with exceptional clarity. Finally, we will cast our gaze towards the horizon, discussing the exciting challenges and promising future directions that lie ahead in this captivating research area [8].

## Scientific Principles behind Haze Formation and the Challenges

Haze formation is a captivating interplay of physics and atmospheric conditions. Let's delve deeper into the scientific principles behind this phenomenon and the challenges it presents for image acquisition. We can represent a hazed image as a combination of one clear image, a scene transmission map, and global atmospheric light, as described in a study and presented in Eq. (1) [9].

$$P(t) = Q(t)\,a(t) + Z(1 - a(t)) \tag{1}$$

Here P(t): hazy image

Q(t): clear image,

Z: Global atmospheric light,

a(t): scene transmission

The formation of haze in the atmosphere is primarily governed by the physical phenomenon of atmospheric scattering, which involves the interaction of light with airborne particles and molecules, as shown in Fig. (**2**). Understanding the scientific principles used in haze formation is crucial for developing effective strategies. This section delves into the key principles and mechanisms involved in haze formation, as well as the challenges posed by haze in image processing and computer vision applications [10].

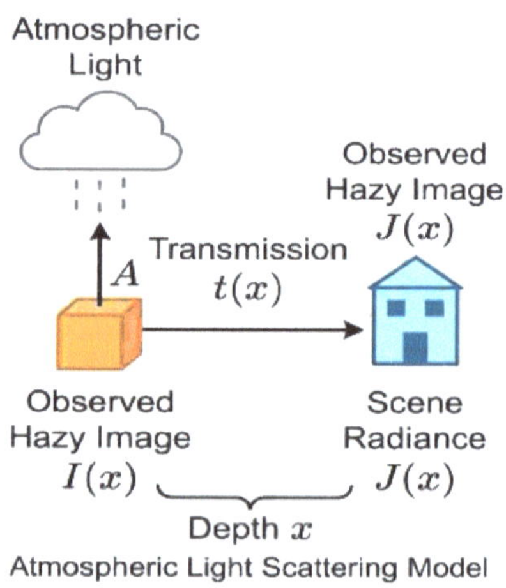


**Fig. (2).** Interaction of light with airborne particles and molecules.

1. *Atmospheric Scattering:*

Atmospheric scattering refers to the process by which particles and molecules in the Earth's atmosphere deflect and scatter sunlight in various directions. There exist two main types of scattering: Rayleigh scattering and Mie scattering [11].

- *Rayleigh scattering*: This arises when the scattering particles, such as air molecules or tiny dust particles, are much smaller than the wavelength of light. It is more effective at shorter wavelengths, like blue and violet, which explains why the sky appears blue during the day.
- *Mie Scattering:* This takes place when the scattering particles are similar in size or larger than the wavelength of light. It is responsible for the white or gray appearance of clouds and haze.

2. *Aerosols and Particulate Matter:*

Haze consists of tiny airborne particles, known as aerosols, suspended in the atmosphere. These aerosols can include various types of particulate matter, such as dust, smoke, pollutants, and biological particles. The size, shape, composition, and concentration of aerosols play crucial roles in determining the extent of light scattering and the degree of haziness in the atmosphere [12].

3. *Light Attenuation and Visibility Reduction:*

As light travels through the atmosphere, it undergoes scattering, absorption, and attenuation by aerosols and molecules. This leads to a reduction in the intensity of light reaching an observer and a decrease in visibility, particularly over long distances [13, 14]. The scattering of light by haze particles also contributes to the diffusion of light rays, resulting in a loss of contrast and sharpness in outdoor imagery [15, 16]. Various challenges involved are as follows:

- Haze poses significant challenges for image processing and computer vision applications, including:
- Reduced Visibility: Haze reduces the visibility of outdoor scenes, making it difficult to discern fine details and objects at a distance.
- Low Contrast: Hazy images often exhibit low contrast and poor visibility of scene elements, hindering tasks such as object detection and recognition.
- Color Distortion: Haze can introduce color shifts and alterations in the appearance of objects, complicating color-based image analysis and interpretation.
- Complex Lighting Conditions: Haze can exacerbate the effects of complex lighting conditions, such as glare and uneven illumination, further complicating image processing tasks.

Addressing these challenges requires the development of sophisticated dehazing algorithms, which can effectively mitigate the adverse effects of haze and restore the clarity and quality of outdoor imagery. By leveraging insights from the principles of atmospheric scattering and aerosol physics, researchers can devise innovative approaches to enhance visibility and improve the performance of image processing and computer vision (CV) systems in hazy environments.

## Overview of Dehazing Method

Haze removal, also known as dehazing, aims to recover a clear scene image (Q) from its hazy counterpart (P). Traditional and deep learning methods tackle this challenge using different approaches. Let's look into both methods with mathematical formulas to understand their core principles.

### *Traditional Image Processing Methods*

Conventional approaches utilize image processing techniques and predefined assumptions about clear images, which estimate the transmission map (Z) and atmospheric light (A) based on the atmospheric scattering equation, given as Eq. (2).

$$\mathbf{P(t) = Q(t) * Z(t) + N(1 - T(t))} \tag{2}$$

Here, t represents a pixel location in the image.

### *Dark Channel Prior (DCP)*

DCP exploits the observation that outdoor images without haze often have low intensity in at least one color channel (typically blue) in regions without sky. This forms the basis for estimating the transmission map (T). Here's the mathematical breakdown: Dark Channel (Dc): Define the Dark Channel (Dc) for each pixel location (x) as the minimum intensity value across all color channels (RGB), presented in Eq. (3):

$$\mathbf{Dc(t) = min(R(t), G(t), B(t))} \tag{3}$$

Refining Dark Channel: To account for sky regions that might have low intensity values, a small opening operation is applied to the Dark Channel, given in Eq. (4):

$$\mathbf{T'(t) = min(Dc(t), W^* \; ones(image\_size))} \tag{4}$$

Here, W is a small window size, and ones(image_size) represents a matrix filled with the size of the image.

Transmission Map (T): Further refine T' using atmospheric light estimation (A), as given in Eq. (5):

$$\mathbf{T(t) = 1 - \omega * min(T'(t), 1)} \quad (5)$$

Where ω is a weighting factor between 0 and 1.

### *Guided Filtering*

Guided filtering leverages the guidance of a haze-free reference image (usually estimated) to refine the transmission map. The methods offer reasonable results but struggle with complex haze variations and color distortions, and they have limitations in handling real-world scenarios.

### *Deep Learning for Image Dehazing (ImDe)*

Deep learning approaches utilize convolutional neural networks (CNNs) to learn complex image features and relationships for dehazing [17]. Unlike traditional methods, they do not rely on manual features or prior assumptions. Here's the basic concept: Deep Learning (DL) Model, presented in Eq. (6).

$$\mathbf{F(I) = J} \quad (6)$$

The model F takes the hazy image (I) as input and directly predicts the dehazed image (J). Here's a breakdown of two common architectures:

DehazeNet [18]:

This early deep learning model uses a CNN architecture with several convolutional and deconvolutional layers. It learns to estimate the transmission map (T) from the hazy image and then recovers the scene radiance (J) using the following formula in Eq. (7):

$$\mathbf{P(t) = (Q(t) - A) / T(t) + A} \quad (7)$$

### *U-Net-based architectures*

These architectures utilize a U-shaped network with the encoder-decoder structure. The network learns to perform dehazing implicitly, without explicitly estimating the transmission map. Deep learning methods offer several advantages over traditional approaches: Automatic Feature Extraction: CNNs learn haze-relevant features directly from large datasets, eliminating the need for hand-crafted features [19, 20].

End-to-End Learning: These models can be trained end-to-end, directly predicting the dehazed image from the hazy input, thereby simplifying the dehazing pipeline. While the provided formulas offer a basic understanding, the actual implementation of deep learning models involves complex optimization techniques and loss functions beyond the scope of this explanation.

## LITERATURE REVIEW

Unveiling the Mysteries of Single Image Dehazing (ImDe) Haze, fog, and smoke act like unwelcome curtains, obscuring the beauty and clarity of outdoor scenes in captured images. These atmospheric phenomena significantly degrade image quality, hindering the performance of many applications in computer vision (CV) and visual perception. Fortunately, the field of single-image dehazing has emerged to combat this challenge, offering a range of techniques to restore the hidden details and unveil the true essence of hazy images. This review delves deep into the realm of single-image dehazing, exploring both traditional image processing methods and the groundbreaking advancements brought forth by deep learning.

### Traditional Image Processing Techniques: Pioneering Efforts

The early days of single-image dehazing were marked by the ingenuity of traditional image processing methods. These techniques rely on mathematical models and well-established image processing principles to estimate the key factors influencing hazy image formation: the transmission map and atmospheric light.

Boundary Constraints: Recognizing the inherent characteristics of haze, techniques like boundary constraints incorporate spatial information into the dehazing process. Haze often exhibits smooth variations across an image, and boundary constraints leverage this knowledge. By employing tools like bilateral filtering, these methods enforce smoothness in the transmission map, leading to more natural-looking dehazed images [21, 22]

While these traditional methods laid the foundation for image dehazing, they have undeniable limitations. Complex variations in haze characteristics, color distortions arising during dehazing, and the inability to handle real-world scenarios with prominent sky regions or non-uniform haze distributions are among the challenges faced by these techniques.

## Deep Learning Revolution: A New Era of Dehazing

The emergence of deep learning has revolutionized numerous domains, and single-image dehazing is no exception. (CNNs). The workhorses of deep learning possess the remarkable ability to learn complex image features and relationships. This translates to significant advantages for dehazing tasks.

The entire dehazing process can be learned in a single step, directly predicting the dehazed image from the hazy input. This streamlines the dehazing pipeline and eliminates the need for the intermediate steps required by traditional methods.

Popular CNN architectures have emerged as powerful tools for single-image dehazing. Here are some prominent examples:

DehazeNet: This pioneering deep learning model stands as a testament to the early efforts in this field. DehazeNet employs a CNN architecture specifically designed to estimate the transmission map, a crucial parameter for successful dehazing.

U-Net-based architectures: Inspired by the U-Net architecture, these models leverage encoder-decoder structures. The encoder captures high-level features from the hazy image, while the decoder refines those features and meticulously reconstructs the dehazed image. This approach has proven highly effective for dehazing tasks [23].

Attention Mechanisms: Recognizing the importance of focusing on crucial image regions, attention mechanisms have been incorporated into deep learning models for dehazing. These mechanisms enable the model to learn which parts of the image require greater attention for haze removal, resulting in better dehazing while preserving essential scene details.

The integration of deep learning has undoubtedly pushed the boundaries of single-image dehazing (ImDe), achieving superior performance compared to traditional methods. However, challenges remain that require further exploration and innovative solutions.

This literature review covers the most important developments in the field of video dehazing. One of the early techniques for video dehazing was based on the dark channel (DC). According to this approach, the hazy image has a black channel that can be used to estimate the scene transmission and then be used to remove the haze. However, this technique has drawbacks, such as color distortion and halo artifacts.

Researchers suggested using additional data, such as depth maps and polarization information, to overcome these restrictions. To determine the transmission map, the exact distance between the camera and the scene's objects was estimated using depth information. The transmission map was estimated using the polarisation information to determine the polarisation angle.

Another strategy involved combining distinct photographs from the same scene that were taken from various perspectives using image fusion techniques. This method enabled increased scene detail and haze removal. But in real-world circumstances, taking many pictures of the same scene was only sometimes practicable. CNNs have been used in recent years to improve the effectiveness of video dehazing approaches. To remove haze from video frames, these techniques employ CNNs to learn the underlying mapping between hazy and clear frames. These technologies significantly outperform conventional ones in terms of efficiency and processing speed.

The reported SSIM and PSNR values represent average scores across the respective test sets in Table **1** and Table **2**. The field of video dehazing is evolving rapidly, propelled by deep learning architectures that enhance performance and efficiency. Researchers are venturing into innovative areas, from robust transmission estimation to attention-based refinements, to restore vibrancy and clarity in hazy videos. Further studies could focus on real-time applicability.

**Table 1. Comparison of various approaches.**

| Ref. No. | Title | Technique Used | Dataset Used | Parameter | Result |
|---|---|---|---|---|---|
| [24] | "Single Image Dehazing using A New Color Channel" | "Dark Channel, New Color Model" | "I-HAZE,O-HAZE, BSDS500, RESIDE, FRIDA, And Google Dataset" | Atmospheric Light, Transmission Map, Radiance | Good And Acceptable |
| [25] | "Single Image Dehazing based on Learning of Haze Layers" | "Convolutional Neural Network" | "Middlebury Stereo Datasets, NYU Depth Datasets, Hazerd Datasets and RESIDE Datasets" | Feature Extraction, Multi-Convolutional Layers , Reconstruction Decon V | Better Than DCP, SCDCP, And CAP; Dehazenet, MSCNN, |

*(Table 1) cont.....*

| Ref. No. | Title | Technique Used | Dataset Used | Parameter | Result |
|---|---|---|---|---|---|
| [26] | "Single Image Dehazing for a variety of Haze Scenarios Using Back Projected | "Genera- Tive Adversarial Network Architecture" | "I-Haze And O- Haze Datasets of NTIRE 2018, NTIRE 2019, NTIRE 2020" | Atmospheric Light, Transmission Map, | Average Running Time Of 0.0311 S I.E. 31.1 Ms Per Image. SSIM: 0.8994 PSNR: 22.56 |
| [27] | "Deep Residual Haze Network For Image Dehazing And Deraining" | "Drhnet (Deep Residual Haze Network), Reverse Parametric Rectified Linear Unit" | Self-Dataset Created | Atmospheric Light, Transmission Map, | 7 Layer Transformation Component is the best Choice for the Proposed Drhnet. |
| [28] | "Single Image Dehazing *via* Multi-Scale Convolutional Neural Networks With Holistic | "Multi-Scale Deep Neural Network" | "NYU Depth Dataset" | Atmospheric Light, Transmission Map, | PSNR: 21.27 SSIM: 0.85 |
| [29] | "Single Remote Sensing Multispectral Image dehazing Based On A Learning Framework" | "Novel And Effective Algorithm Based On A Learning Framework" | "Google Earth and nasa Earth observatory website" | Atmospheric Light, Transmission Map, | PSNR: 27.28 SSIM: 0.812 MSE: 2.137 FADE: 0.761 |
| [30] | "Real-Time Video Dehazing *via* Incremental Transmission Learning and Spatial- Temporally Coherent Regularization" | "Transmission Map Frame- By- Frame by A Boundary Constrained Open Dark Channel Model" | "Five Real-World Video Sequences, I.E., 'Hazeroad', 'Bali',Playground', 'City1' And 'City2'" | Visible Edge Ratio E And The Average Gradient Ratio R | E: 0.73 R: 2.39 |
| [31] | "Fast Video Dehazing Using Per-Pixel Minimum Adjustment" | "New Quad- Tree Method To Estimate The Atmospheric Light" | "NYU Depth V2 Dataset" | Atmospheric Light, Transmission Map, | $\varepsilon = 0.95$, $K$=35, $\mu$ =0.9, $\delta\ell = 15$) |

*(Table 1) cont.....*

| Ref. No. | Title | Technique Used | Dataset Used | Parameter | Result |
|---|---|---|---|---|---|
| [32] | "Underwater Image And Video Dehazing With Pure Haze Region Segmentation" | "Novel Method for Hazy Images | "PKU-EAQA Dataset" | White Balancing | Subjective Evaluation (SE% 43.67 |
| [33] | "Video Dehazing Based On Convolutional Neural Network Driven Using Our Collected | "Convolutional Neural Networks" | "NYU Depth V2 Dataset" | Atmospheric Light, Transmission Map, | PSNR:20.4987 SSIM: 0.9683 |
| [34] | "Real-time Dehazing for Image and Video" | "dark channel prior; bilateral filter" | "RESIDE, NYU Depth" | Atmospheric Light, Transmission Map | Good and Acceptable |
| [35] | "End-to-End United Video Dehazing and Detection" | "End-to-End Video Dehazing Network " | "ILSVRC1015 VID dataset" | Atmospheric Light, Transmission Map | PSNR: 20.9908 SSIM: 0.9087 |
| [36] | "Generic Model-Agnostic Convolutional Neural Network for Single Image | "Generic Model-Agnostic Convolutional Neural | "RESIDE" | Atmospheric Light Intensity, Transmission Map, Haze Pixel Density | PSNR: 20.53 SSIM: 0.8081 |
| [37] | "Cycle-Dehaze: Enhanced CycleGAN for Single Image Dehazing" | "CycleGAN" | "NYU-Depth, D-HAZY, I-HAZE & O-HAZE" | Atmospheric Scattering, Transmission Map, and Atmospheric | PSNR: 15.41 SSIM: 0.66 |
| [38] | "FFA-Net: Feature Fusion Attention Network for Single Image Dehazing" | "Feature Fusion Attention Network" | "RESIDE, NYU Depth V2" | Atmospheric Light, Transmission Map, and Perpetual Loss | PSNR: 36.39 SSIM: 0.9886 |

*(Table 1) cont.....*

| Ref. No. | Title | Technique Used | Dataset Used | Parameter | Result |
|---|---|---|---|---|---|
| [39] | "Single Image Dehazing using a New Colour Channel" | "Dark Channel, New Color Model" | "I HAZE, O- HAZE, RESIDE, FRIDA, and Google Dataset" | Atmospheric Light, Transmission Map, and Radiance | Good and Acceptable |
| [40] | "Contrastive Learning for Compact Single Image Dehazing" | "Contrastive Learning" | "RESIDE, Dense-Haze, NH-HAZE | Contrast, Atmospheric Light | PSNR:37.17 SSIM:0.9901 |

**Table 2. Comparative analysis of various methods and datasets for video dehazing.**

| Ref. No. | Method | Year | Dataset | SSIM | PSNR |
|---|---|---|---|---|---|
| [41] | Non-local Means Filtering | 2016 | NYU Depth | 0.8658 | 27.2 |
| [42] | Multi-scale CNN | 2018 | NYU Depth | 0.9044 | 29.2015 |
| [43] | Spatio- temporal CNN with residual connections | 2018 | NTIRE2018, RESIDE, And O-HAZE | 0.9008 | 24.4322 |
| [44] | Spatio- Temporal CNN | 2018 | Self- Captured | 0.984 | 39.888 dB |
| [45] | Fusion-based CNN | 2020 | Self- Captured | 0.969 | 37.187 dB |
| [46] | Dynamic | 2021 | Online | 0.9136 | 32.1147 |
| [47] | CNN Filter Bank | 2020 | Self- Captured | 0.967 | 35.802 dB |
| [48] | CNN-based method with multi- scale fusion and temporal coherence | 2020 | NTIRE2020 and RESIDE | 0.9684 | 31.5681 |
| [49] | Dynamic Transmission Map Estimation for Video Dehazing *via* Spatio- Temporal Fusion Network | 2022 | DehazeVideo-500, HazeCity- 500 | 0.913 | 28.91 |
| [50] | A Lightweight and Efficient Video Dehazing Network with Channel Attention | 2022 | DehazeVideo-500, HazeCity- 500 | 0.908 | 28.54 |
| [51] | Efficient Video Dehazing with Adaptive Transmissio n Estimation and Multi-scale Fusion | 2023 | DehazeVideo-500, MIT Indoor 7 Scenes | 0.91 | 28.76 |

## PROPOSED FRAMEWORK

We are proposing a Generative Adversarial Network (GAN) based model for image dehazing, as shown in Fig. (**3**). This involves the use of two major elements: a generator and a discriminator. Here, the generator aims to remove haze from images, while the discriminator distinguishes between dehazed images and real haze-free images. This adversarial setup not only improves the realism of the dehazed images but also enables the model to handle complex and diverse hazing effects encountered in real-world scenarios.

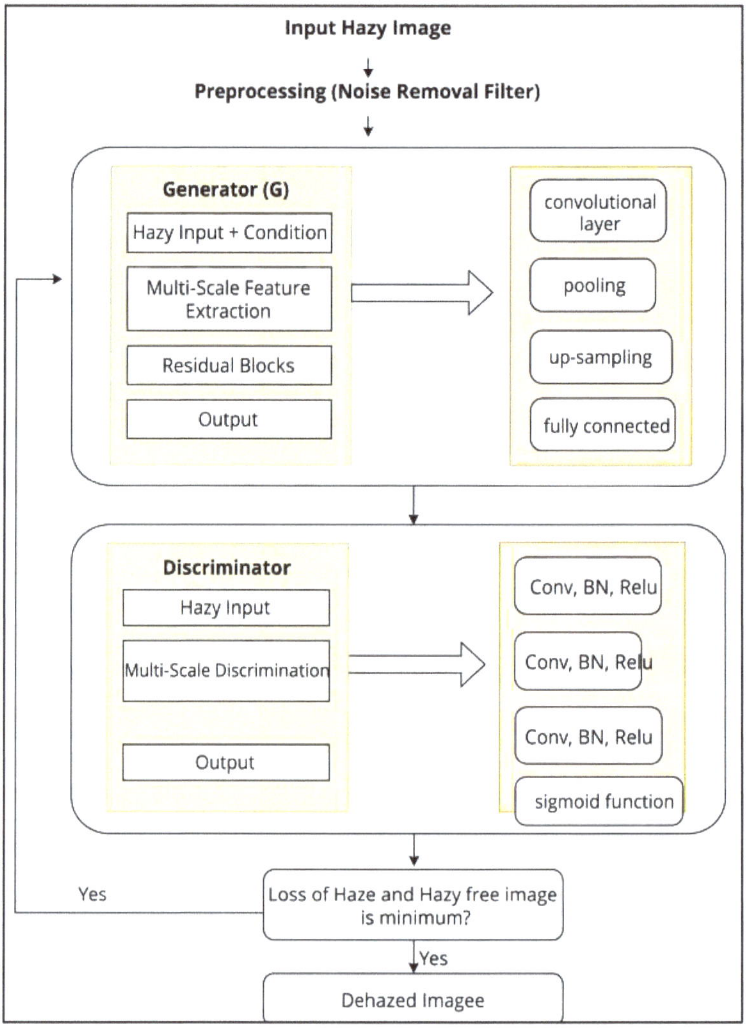


**Fig. (3).** Proposed framework.

## ARCHITECTURAL DETAILS

### Generator (G) Architecture

- Input Layer: Takes hazy images.
- Convolutional Layers: Multiple layers with varying kernel sizes to extract and learn features at different scales.
- Intermediate Normalization and Activation Layers: Batch normalization and ReLU activation for stable training.
- Residual Connections: This helps in training deep networks using gradients to flow through.
- Deconvolutional Layers: For upscaling the feature maps to the original image size.
- Output Layer: Produces the dehazed image, typically using a sigmoid or tanh activation function to normalize the pixel values.

### Discriminator (D) Architecture

- Input Layer: Takes either real haze-free images or dehazed images from the generator.
- Convolutional Layers: Designed to progressively downsample the input, extracting features that are crucial for distinguishing real images from generated ones.
- Output Layer: Dehazed Image.

## EXPERIMENTS AND RESULTS

The model was trained using an NVIDIA TITANX GPU and developed in Python using the TensorFlow framework. The implementation was performed in PyCharm, with PyTorch used for the Conditional Generative Adversarial Network (CGAN). The CGAN was specifically designed to eliminate fog and haze from images and required approximately 6 hours of training. The experiments were conducted using two widely recognized datasets, RESIDE [52] and DENSE [53].

For evaluating the performance of the proposed approach, we compared it with leading dehazing techniques such as MSBDN [54], Dehamer [55], DCP [56], and FD-GAN [57].

### Evaluation Metrics

To assess the effectiveness of our approach, we utilized Peak Signal-to-Noise Ratio (PSNR) and Structural Similarity Index (SSIM), both of which are widely used for image quality evaluation in dehazing tasks. The proposed method was benchmarked against prior-based dehazing techniques (DCP) as well as physical model-based approaches, including MSBDN, Dehamer, DCP, and FD-GAN.

The formula for SSIM is given in Eq. (8):

$$SSIM\ (p,q) = \frac{(2\mu_p\mu_q+C_1)(2\sigma_{pq}+C_2)}{(\mu_p^2+\ \mu_q^2+C_1)(\sigma_p^2+\sigma_q^2\ +C_2)} \tag{8}$$

p and q are the compared images.

μp and μq are the means of p and q.

σp2 and σq2 are the variances of p and q.

σpq is the covariance of x and y.

c1 and C1 are constants for stabilizing the division with a weak denominator.

The calculation of SSIM involves several intermediate steps and functions. Here is a simplified representation given in Eq. (9):

$$\mathbf{SSIM = L(o, p) * C(o, p) * S(o, p)} \tag{9}$$

L(o, p) measures luminance similarity. C(o, p) measures contrast similarity. S(o, p) measures structural similarity.

Each of these functions considers the local means, standard deviations, and covariances of pixel neighborhoods in the original and processed images.

PSNR is a common metric that measures the peak signal-to-noise ratio. A higher PSNR generally indicates better image quality.

Here's the formula for PSNR, given in Eq. (10):

$$\mathbf{PSNR = 10 * log_{10}(MAX\_I^2 / MSE)} \tag{10}$$

MAX_I: highest possible pixel value,

MSE (Mean Squared Error): It can be calculated using the formula given in Eq. (11):

$$\mathbf{MSE = 1 / (MN) * \Sigma\ (x - y)^2} \tag{11}$$

M and N represent the dimensions (width and height) of the image.

x and y represent the corresponding pixel values in the original and processed images at a specific location.

We have applied the proposed algorithm to both the Outdoor (Fig. **4**) and Indoor Fig. (**6**) RESIDE dataset [52], encompassing diverse environmental conditions. The algorithm's performance was rigorously evaluated against a spectrum of existing approaches. Using the Structural Similarity Index (SSIM) and Peak Signal-to- Noise Ratio (PSNR), I quantified the quality of the dehazed images and meticulously documented the results in a tabular format (Tables **3** and **4**). Table **3** shows outdoor images, and Table **4** shows indoor images. This comprehensive comparison not only elucidates the efficacy of the proposed algorithm but also provides insights into its relative performance compared with other methodologies. To enhance the interpretability of the findings, a comparison is drawn in graphical form as shown in Figs. (**5** and **7**), facilitating a holistic understanding of the algorithm's strengths and areas for improvement across different datasets and scenarios.

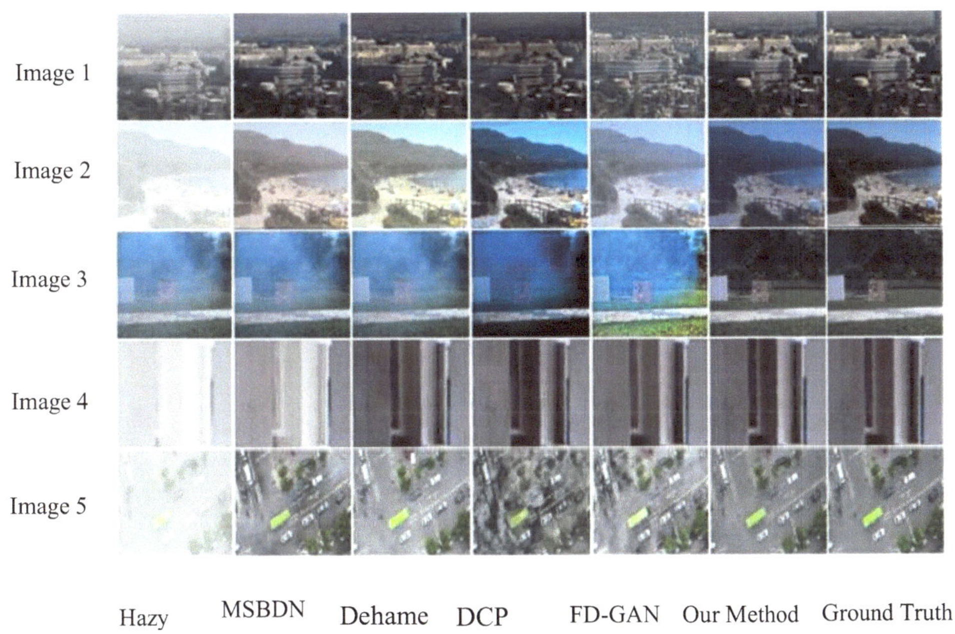


**Fig. (4).** Comparison of various methods on DENSE data.

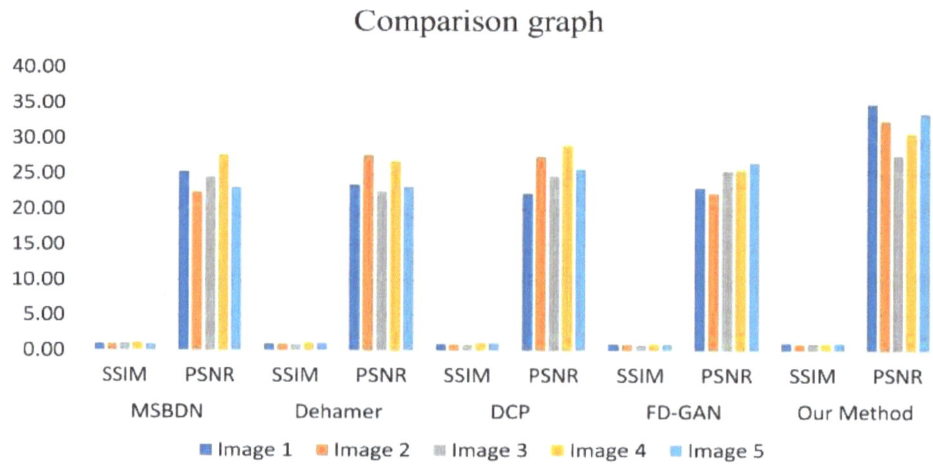


**Fig. (5).** Comparison graph MSBDN, Dehamer, DCP, FD-GAN, Our Method.

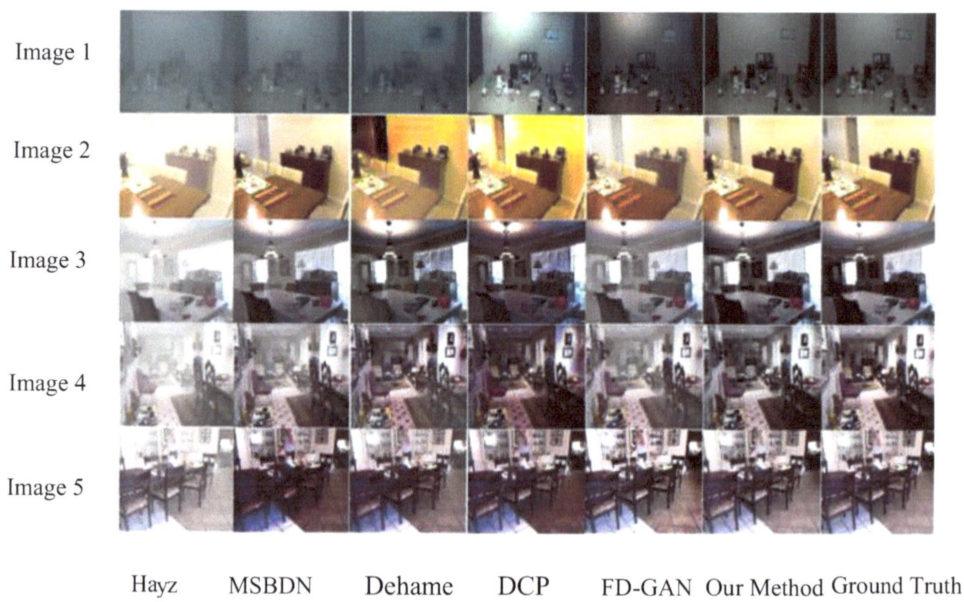


**Fig. (6).** Comparison of various methods on ITS Indoor data.

**Table 3. Comparative analysis comparison on SSIM and PSNR.**

| Image | MSBDN | | Dehazer | | DCP | | FD-GAN | | Our Method | |
|---|---|---|---|---|---|---|---|---|---|---|
| | SSIM | PSNR | SSIM | PSNR | SSIM | PSNR | SSIM | PSNR | SSIM | PSNR |
| Image 1 | 0.91 | 23.76 | 0.87 | 25.37 | 0.98 | 27.23 | 0.93 | 22.6 | 0.93 | 25.6 |

*(Table 3) cont.....*

| Image | MSBDN | | Dehazer | | DCP | | FD-GAN | | Our Method | |
|---|---|---|---|---|---|---|---|---|---|---|
| Image 2 | 0.91 | 24.57 | 0.92 | 25.43 | 0.96 | 26.62 | 0.98 | 25.92 | 0.95 | 34.6 |
| Image 3 | 0.89 | 23 | 0.99 | 26.63 | 0.85 | 23.69 | 0.88 | 22.23 | 0.96 | 28.6<br>5 |
| Image 4 | 0.96 | 23.07 | 0.9 | 22.73 | 0.91 | 27.89 | 0.89 | 27.45 | 0.97 | 33.4<br>8 |
| Image 5 | 0.89 | 22.23 | 0.89 | 26.6 | 0.89 | 26.71 | 0.91 | 24.85 | 0.92 | 32.7 |
| **Average** | **0.91** | **23.33** | **0.91** | **25.35** | **0.918** | **26.43** | **0.92** | **24.61** | **0.95** | **31.01** |

**Table 4. Comparison on SSIM and PSNR.**

| Image | MSBDN | | Dehamer | | DCP | | FD-GAN | | Our Method | |
|---|---|---|---|---|---|---|---|---|---|---|
| | SSIM | PSNR | SSIM | PSNR | SSIM | PSNR | SSIM | PSNR | SSIM | PSNR |
| Image 1 | 0.89 | 25.23 | 0.85 | 23.48 | 0.88 | 22.23 | 0.86 | 23.07 | 0.97 | 34.98 |
| Image 2 | 0.87 | 22.46 | 0.91 | 27.70 | 0.89 | 27.45 | 0.88 | 22.23 | 0.87 | 32.48 |
| Image 3 | 0.92 | 24.70 | 0.89 | 22.62 | 0.91 | 24.85 | 0.86 | 25.37 | 0.99 | 27.73 |
| Image 4 | 0.99 | 27.70 | 0.93 | 26.74 | 0.97 | 28.98 | 0.92 | 25.43 | 0.90 | 30.81 |
| Image 5 | 0.90 | 23.08 | 0.98 | 23.20 | 0.95 | 25.60 | 0.90 | 26.63 | 0.94 | 33.71 |
| Average | 0.91 | 24.63 | 0.91 | 24.75 | 0.92 | 25.82 | 0.88 | 24.55 | 0.93 | 31.94 |

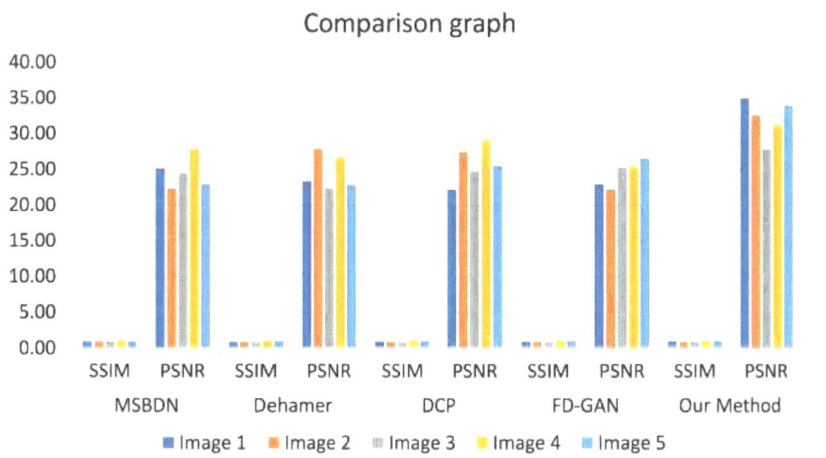


**Fig. (7).** Comparison graph MSBDN, Dehamer, DCP, FD-GAN, Our Method.

Table **3** provides a comparative analysis of five image dehazing techniques on the DENSE dataset: MSBDN, Dehazer, DCP, FD-GAN, and Our Method. The evaluation is typically based on two primary metrics: (SSIM) and (PSNR). Among the five tested images, Our method consistently achieves competitive results, with SSIM scores ranging from 0.89 to 0.97 and PSNR values between 22.6 and 34.6 dB. Notably, Image 3 highlights the superior performance of Our Method, attaining an impressive SSIM of 0.96 and a PSNR of 28.65 dB, outperforming the other approaches.

On average, our method demonstrates strong performance, achieving an SSIM of 0.946 and a PSNR of 31.006 dB, establishing itself as a promising solution for image dehazing tasks. These results emphasize the effectiveness of our method in improving image clarity and quality across various conditions, reinforcing its potential as a valuable tool in image processing and computer vision applications.

Table **4** presents a comparative analysis for the ITS indoor image of different image dehazing algorithms, including MSBDN, Dehazer, DCP, FD-GAN, and our proposed method, based on the evaluation metrics (SSIM) and (PSNR). Each row corresponds to a specific image, while the last row represents the average performance across all images. For Image 1, our method demonstrates superior performance compared to other algorithms, achieving an impressive SSIM of 0.97 and PSNR of 34.98, indicating a significant enhancement in image clarity and fidelity. Similarly, for Image 3, our method outperforms other algorithms with a near-perfect SSIM of 0.99 and a competitive PSNR of 27.73. Conversely, some images, such as Image 2, exhibit varied performance across algorithms. While Dehazer achieves the highest SSIM of 0.91 for Image 2, our method still maintains competitive performance with an SSIM of 0.87 and a commendable PSNR of 32.48. To represent the advantages of our method, we evaluate our method on the RESIDE against several competitive image dehazing methods Table **5**: MSBDN, Dehamer, DCP, and FD-GAN.

**Table 5. Comparison on SSIM and PSNR for the Outdoor and Indoor datasets.**

| RESIDE (Dataset) | MSBDN | | Dehamer | | DCP | | FD-GAN | | Our Method | |
|---|---|---|---|---|---|---|---|---|---|---|
| | SSIM | PSNR | SSIM | PSNR | SSIM | PSNR | SSIM | PSNR | SSIM | PSNR |
| Outdoor | 0.91 | 23.33 | 0.91 | 25.35 | 0.918 | 26.43 | 0.92 | 24.61 | 0.95 | 31.01 |
| Indoor | 0.91 | 24.63 | 0.91 | 24.75 | 0.92 | 25.82 | 0.88 | 24.55 | 0.93 | 31.94 |
| Average | 0.91 | 23.98 | 0.91 | 25.05 | 0.92 | 26.13 | 0.90 | 24.58 | 0.94 | 31.48 |

In the end, we can say that the average performance across all images reaffirms the efficacy of our proposed method, with an average SSIM of 0.93 and PSNR of 31.94, surpassing or matching the performance of other algorithms in most cases. This comprehensive analysis underscores the effectiveness and reliability of our proposed dehazing approach in enhancing image quality across diverse datasets and scenarios.

The Table **5** presents a comparative analysis of several dehazing algorithms, including MSBDN, Dehazer, DCP, FD-GAN, and Our Method, across both Outdoor and Indoor datasets. The evaluation metrics employed are the Structural Similarity Index (SSIM) and Peak Signal-to-Noise Ratio (PSNR), which are widely used to assess image quality. In terms of SSIM, Our Method consistently outperforms other algorithms across both datasets, achieving the highest SSIM scores of 0.95 for Outdoor and 0.93 for Indoor images. Similarly, in terms of PSNR, Our Method demonstrates superior performance, with the highest PSNR scores of 31.01 for Outdoor and 31.94 for Indoor images. These results indicate that Our Method excels in preserving structural information and minimizing distortion compared to other algorithms. Overall, the average SSIM and PSNR scores further corroborate the effectiveness of Our Method, establishing it as a promising approach for image dehazing tasks in diverse environmental conditions.

## CONCLUSION

In conclusion, this chapter highlights the potential of integrating image processing and deep learning techniques for enhancing the effectiveness of image dehazing. By combining the complementary strengths of traditional methods and deep learning models, it is possible to develop more robust and efficient dehazing algorithms capable of handling diverse real-world scenarios. Future advancements in this direction are expected to yield significant improvements in the quality and applicability of dehazed images across various domains. We have developed an efficient framework for image dehazing and defogging using a Conditional Generative Adversarial Network (CGAN).

Experimental results show that the proposed framework excels over the state-of-the-art techniques, achieving a higher image restoration rate. In the future, this framework can be further enhanced to handle thick, nighttime, and extreme haze conditions. During winter, heavy haze significantly reduces visibility, leading to accidents for automobile drivers. An advanced automated system with improved efficiency could assist drivers by providing clearer vision in hazy weather conditions.

## REFERENCES

[1] J. Kopf, B. Neubert, B. Chen, M. Cohen, D. Cohen-Or, O. Deussen, M. Uyttendaele, and D. Lischinski, "Deep photo: model-based photograph enhancement and viewing", *ACM Trans. Graph.*, vol. 27, no. 5, pp. 1-10, 2008. [http://dx.doi.org/10.1145/1409060.1409069]

[2] Y.Y. Schechner, and Y. Averbuch, "Regularized image recovery in scattering media", *IEEE Trans. Pattern Anal. Mach. Intell.*, vol. 29, no. 9, pp. 1655-1660, 2007. [http://dx.doi.org/10.1109/TPAMI.2007.1141] [PMID: 17627052]

[3] M Anitharani, and S. I. Padma, "Literature survey of haze removal of secure remote surveillance system", *Int. J. Eng. Res. Technol.,* vol. 2, 2013.

[4] G Kadian, and R Kumar, "A comprehensive study on haze detection techniques", vol. 13, no. 6, pp. 588–593, 2018.

[5] L Bisen, and M. A. Dravid, "Survey on haze removal techniques", *Int. J. Mod. Trends Eng. Res.*. vol. 1, no. 4, pp. 202–206, 2014.

[6] S.G. Narasimhan, and S.K. Nayar, "Vision and the Atmosphere", *Int. J. Comput. Vis.,* vol. 48, no. 3, pp. 233-254, 2002.
[http://dx.doi.org/10.1023/A:1016328200723]

[7] D Wu, Q Zhu, J Wang, Y Xie, and L Wang, "Image haze removal: status, challenges and prospects", In: *2014 4th IEEE international conference on information science and technology*. IEEE, Apr 26, 2014, pp. 492-497.
[http://dx.doi.org/10.1109/ICIST.2014.6920524]

[8] K. Nishino, L. Kratz, and S. Lombardi, "Bayesian Defogging", *Int. J. Comput. Vis.,* vol. 98, no. 3, pp. 263-278, 2012.
[http://dx.doi.org/10.1007/s11263-011-0508-1]

[9] S Sun, W Ren, T Wang, and X Cao, "Rethinking image restoration for object detection", *Advances in Neural Information Processing Systems (NeurIPS),* 2022.

[10] T. Treibitz, and Y.Y. Schechner, "Polarization: Beneficial for visibility enhancement?", *Proc. IEEE Comput. Soc. Conf. Comput. Vis. Pattern Recognit. Workshops,* pp. 525-532, 2009.

[11] J.H. Kim, W.D. Jang, J.Y. Sim, and C.S. Kim, "Optimized contrast enhancement for real-time image and video dehazing", *J. Vis. Commun. Image Represent.,* vol. 24, no. 3, pp. 410-425, 2013.
[http://dx.doi.org/10.1016/j.jvcir.2013.02.004]

[12] S.G. Narasimhan, and S.K. Nayar, "Contrast restoration of weather degraded images", *IEEE Trans. Pattern Anal. Mach. Intell.,* vol. 25, no. 6, pp. 713-724, 2003.
[http://dx.doi.org/10.1109/TPAMI.2003.1201821]

[13] Y. Jin, W. Yan, W. Yang, and R. T. Tan, WangL.GallJ.ChinT.-J.SatoI.ChellappaR."Structure representation network and uncertainty feedback learning for dense non-uniform fog removal", *in Computer Vision – ACCV 2022*, L. Wang, J. Gall, T.-J. Chin, I. Sato, and R. Chellappa, Eds. Cham, Switzerland: Springer, 2023, pp. 154–171.

[14] P. Morales, T. Klinghoffer, and S.J. Lee, "Feature forwarding for efficient single image dehazing", *Proc. IEEE Comput. Soc. Conf. Comput. Vis. Pattern Recognit. Workshops,* pp. 2078-2085, 2019.
[http://dx.doi.org/10.1109/CVPRW.2019.00260]

[15] R. Younis, and N. Bastaki, "Accelerated fog removal from real images for car detection", *Proc. IEEE GCC Conf.,* 2017.
[http://dx.doi.org/10.1109/IEEEGCC.2017.8448075]

[16] A. Ranjan, and M. Ravinder, "VAEWGAN-NCO in image deblurring framework using variational autoencoders and Wasserstein generative adversarial network", *Signal Image Video Process.,* vol. 18, no. 5, pp. 4447-4456, 2024.
[http://dx.doi.org/10.1007/s11760-024-03085-5]

[17] B. Cai, X. Xu, K. Jia, C. Qing, and D. Tao, "DehazeNet: An end-to-end system for single image haze removal", *IEEE Trans. Image Process.,* vol. 25, no. 11, pp. 5187-5198, 2016.
[http://dx.doi.org/10.1109/TIP.2016.2598681] [PMID: 28873058]

[18] K. He, J. Sun, and X. Tang, "Guided image filtering", *IEEE Trans. Pattern Anal. Mach. Intell.,* vol. 35, no. 6, pp. 1397-1409, 2013.
[http://dx.doi.org/10.1109/TPAMI.2012.213] [PMID: 23599054]

[19] M. Ravinder, V. Gupta, K. Arora, A. Ranjan, and Y.C. Hu, "Video-captioning evaluation metric for

segments (VEMS): A metric for segment-level evaluation of video captions with weighted frames", *Multimedia Tools Appl.,* vol. 83, no. 16, pp. 47699-47733, 2023. [http://dx.doi.org/10.1007/s11042-023-17328-z]

[20] Ranjan and M. Ravinder, "Deep learning based image deblurring: A comparative survey", *Proc. IEEE ICAC3N,* pp. 996-1002, 2022.

[21] W. Ren, and X. Cao, "Single image dehazing", *Pacific Rim Conf. Multimedia,* pp. 14-24, 2017.

[22] Z. Luan, H. Zeng, Y. Shang, Z. Shao, and H. Ding, "Fast video dehazing using per-pixel minimum adjustment", In: *Math. Probl. Eng.* vol. 2018. , 2018, pp. 1-8. [http://dx.doi.org/10.1155/2018/9241629]

[23] Q. Chen, R. Liao, M.Y. Shalaginov, and T.H. Zeng, "Scoliosis detection with convolutional neural networks", *Proc. IEEE BIBM,* pp. 3785-3787, 2022.

[24] J. Xiao, M. Shen, J. Lei, J. Zhou, R. Klette, and H. Sui, "Single image dehazing based on learning of haze layers", *Neurocomputing,* vol. 389, pp. 108-122, 2020. [http://dx.doi.org/10.1016/j.neucom.2020.01.007]

[25] A. Singh, A. Bhave, and D. K. Prasad, "Single image dehazing for a variety of haze scenarios using back projected pyramid network", *arXiv preprint arXiv:2012.01188,* 2020.

[26] C. Wang, Z. Li, J. Wu, H. Fan, G. Xiao, and H. Zhang, "Li, J. Wu, H. Fan, G. Xiao, and H. Zhang, "Deep residual haze network for image dehazing and deraining,"", *IEEE Access,* vol. 8, pp. 9488-9500, 2020. [http://dx.doi.org/10.1109/ACCESS.2020.2964271]

[27] W. Ren, J. Pan, H. Zhang, X. Cao, and M.H. Yang, Single image dehazing *via* multi-scale convolutional neural networks with holistic edges, *Int. J. Comput. Vis.,* vol. 128, no. 1, pp. 240-259, 2020. [http://dx.doi.org/10.1007/s11263-019-01235-8]

[28] S. Shao, Y. Guo, Z. Zhang, and H. Yuan, "Single remote sensing multispectral image dehazing based on a learning framework", *Math. Probl. Eng.,* vol. 2019, no. 1, 2019. [http://dx.doi.org/10.1155/2019/4131378]

[29] S.J. Peng, H. Zhang, X. Liu, W. Fan, B. Zhong, and J.X. Du, "Real-time video dehazing via incremental transmission learning and spatial-temporally coherent regularization", *Neurocomputing,* vol. 458, pp. 602-614, 2021. [http://dx.doi.org/10.1016/j.neucom.2020.02.134]

[30] C. Wang, Z. Li, J. Wu, H. Fan, G. Xiao, and H. Zhang, "Deep residual haze network for image dehazing and deraining", *IEEE Access,* vol. 8, pp. 9488-9500, 2020. [http://dx.doi.org/10.1109/ACCESS.2020.2964271]

[31] W. Ren, J. Pan, H. Zhang, X. Cao, and M.H. Yang, "Single image dehazing via multi-scale convolutional neural networks with holistic edges", *Int. J. Comput. Vis.,* vol. 128, no. 1, pp. 240-259, 2020. [http://dx.doi.org/10.1007/s11263-019-01235-8]

[32] S. Shao, Y. Guo, Z. Zhang, and H. Yuan, "Single remote sensing multispectral image dehazing based on a learning framework", *Math. Probl. Eng.,* vol. 2019, no. 1, 2019.4131378 [http://dx.doi.org/10.1155/2019/4131378]

[33] M. Ju, Z. Gu, and D. Zhang, "Single image haze removal based on the improved atmospheric scattering model", *Neurocomputing,* vol. 260, pp. 180-191, 2017. [http://dx.doi.org/10.1016/j.neucom.2017.04.034]

[34] P. Rao, S. Shirgire, S. Sanganwar, K. Vyawhare, and S. R. Vispute, "Agriculture data analysis using ML and DL", *Proc. 2022 2nd Int. Conf. Intell. Technol. (CONIT),* Hubli, India, pp. 343-355, 2022.

[35] S. Emberton, L. Chittka, and A. Cavallaro, "Underwater image and video dehazing with pure haze

region segmentation", *Comput. Vis. Image Underst.*, vol. 168, pp. 145-156, 2018. [http://dx.doi.org/10.1016/j.cviu.2017.08.003]

[36] X. Zhang, T. Wang, W. Luo, and P. Huang, "Multi-level fusion and attention-guided CNN for image dehazing", *IEEE Transactions on Circuits and Systems for Video Technology,* vol. 31, no. 11, pp. 4162-4173, 2021.

[37] X. Lv, W. Chen, and I-Fan Shen, "Real-time dehazing for image and video", In: *18th Pacific Conference on Computer Graphics and Applications*, 2010, pp. 62-69.

[38] B. Li, X. Peng, Z. Wang, J. Xu, and D. Feng, End-to-end united video dehazing and detection in *AAAI*, 2018, pp. 7016–7023. [http://dx.doi.org/10.1609/aaai.v32i1.12287]

[39] Z Zheng, and X Jia, "4K-HAZE: A dehazing benchmark with 4K resolution hazy and haze-free images", 2023.

[40] D. Engin, A. Genc, and H.K. Ekenel, "Cycle-dehaze: Enhanced CycleGAN for single image dehazing", *Proc. IEEE CVPR Workshops,* pp. 938-946, 2018. [http://dx.doi.org/10.1109/CVPRW.2018.00127]

[41] X. Qin, Z. Wang, Y. Bai, X. Xie, and H. Jia, "FFA-Net: Feature Fusion Attention Network for Single Image Dehazing", *Proceedings of the AAAI Conference on Artificial Intelligence,* vol. 34, no. 07, pp. 11908-11915, 2020. [http://dx.doi.org/10.1609/aaai.v34i07.6865]

[42] G. Sahu, A. Seal, O. Krejcar, and A. Yazidi, "Single image dehazing using a new color channel", *J. Vis. Commun. Image Represent.,* vol. 74, 2021.103008 [http://dx.doi.org/10.1016/j.jvcir.2020.103008]

[43] H. Wu, Y. Qu, S. Lin, J. Zhou, R. Qiao, Z. Zhang, Y. Xie, and L. Ma, "Contrastive learning for compact single image dehazing", *Proc. IEEE/CVF CVPR,* pp. 10551-10560, 2021. [http://dx.doi.org/10.1109/CVPR46437.2021.01041]

[44] D. Berman, "Non-local image dehazing", *Proc. IEEE CVPR,* pp. 1674-1682, 2016.

[45] S. Zhang, F. He, W. Ren, and J. Yao, "Joint learning of image detail and transmission map for single image dehazing", *The Visual Computer,* vol. 36, no. 2, pp. 305-316, Feb 2020. [http://dx.doi.org/10.1007/s00371-018-1612-9]

[46] S. P. Yadav, S. Zaidi, C. D. S. Nascimento, V. H. C. de Albuquerque, and S. S. Chauhan, "Analysis and design of automatically generating for GPS based moving object tracking system", *Proceedings of the International Conference on Generative AI Issues Facing Society (GAIFS),* pp. 1-6, 2023.

[47] K. Purohit, S. Vats, R. Saklani, V. Kukreja, V. Sharma, and S.P. Yadav, "Improvement in K-means clustering for information retrieval", *Proc. IEEE ICESC,* pp. 1239-1245, 2023. [http://dx.doi.org/10.1109/ICESC57686.2023.10193031]

[48] Qingsong Zhu, Jiaming Mai, and Ling Shao, "A fast single image haze removal algorithm using color attenuation prior", *IEEE Trans. Image Process.,* vol. 24, no. 11, pp. 3522-3533, 2015. [http://dx.doi.org/10.1109/TIP.2015.2446191] [PMID: 26099141]

[49] S.H. Gao, M.M. Cheng, K. Zhao, X.Y. Zhang, M.H. Yang, and P. Torr, "Res2Net: A new multi-scale backbone architecture", *IEEE Trans. Pattern Anal. Mach. Intell.,* vol. 43, no. 2, pp. 652-662, 2021. [http://dx.doi.org/10.1109/TPAMI.2019.2938758] [PMID: 31484108]

[50] S. Emberton, L. Chittka, A. Cavallaro, J. Mao, A. Kumari, S. Sahdev, S. K. Sahoo, B. Li, X. Peng, Z. Z. Wang, J. Xu, D. Feng, H. Lu, Y. Li, S. Nakashima, S. Serikawa, Z. Luan, H. Zeng, Y. Shang, and J. I. Guo, "Study on image dehazing with the self-adjustment of the haze degree", *Mathematical Problems in Engineering,* vol. 2018, pp. 1-8, 2018.

[51] J. Gui, X. Cong, C. Peng, Y. Y. Tang, and J. T. Kwok, "Adversarial attack and defense for dehazing networks", *arXiv preprint arXiv,* vol. 2303, p. 17255, 2023.

[52] B. Li, W. Ren, D. Fu, D. Tao, D. Feng, W. Zeng, and Z. Wang, "Benchmarking single-image dehazing and beyond", *IEEE Trans. Image Process.,* vol. 28, no. 1, pp. 492-505, 2019. [http://dx.doi.org/10.1109/TIP.2018.2867951] [PMID: 30176593]

[53] Y.B. Singh, A.D. Mishra, and P. Nand, "Use of machine learning in the area of image analysis and processing", *Proc. ICACCCN,* pp. 117-120, 2018. [http://dx.doi.org/10.1109/ICACCCN.2018.8748338]

[54] H. Dong, J. Pan, L. Xiang, Z. Hu, X. Zhang, F. Wang, and M.H. Yang, "Multi-scale boosted dehazing network with dense feature fusion", *Proc. IEEE CVPR,* pp. 2157-2167, 2020. [http://dx.doi.org/10.1109/CVPR42600.2020.00223]

[55] C.L. Guo, Q. Yan, and S. Anwar, "Image dehazing transformer with transmission-aware 3D position embedding", *Proc. IEEE/CVF CVPR,* pp. 5812-5820, 2022. [http://dx.doi.org/10.1109/CVPR52688.2022.00572]

[56] S. Lee, S. Yun, J.H. Nam, C.S. Won, and S.W. Jung, "A review on dark channel prior based image dehazing algorithms", *EURASIP J. Image Video Process.,* vol. 2016, no. 1, p. 4, 2016. [http://dx.doi.org/10.1186/s13640-016-0104-y]

[57] Y. Dong, Y. Liu, H. Zhang, S. Chen, and Y. Qiao, FD-GAN: Generative adversarial networks with fusion-discriminator for single image dehazing in *AAAI*, 2020, pp. 10729–10736. [http://dx.doi.org/10.1609/aaai.v34i07.6701]

## CHAPTER 2

# Deep Learning-based Approaches for Addressing Imbalance in Breast Cancer Image Datasets: Challenges, Opportunities, and Open Issues

**Rekha Baghel**[1,2,*] and **Ela Kumar**[1]

[1] *Department of Computer Science, Indira Gandhi Delhi Technical University for Women, New Delhi, Delhi, India*

[2] *Department of Computer Science and Engineering, Ajay Kumar Garg Engineering College, Ghaziabad, Uttar Pradesh, India*

**Abstract:** Breast cancer detection is a critical area in healthcare where deep learning has shown remarkable promise in assisting medical professionals with early diagnosis. However, the effectiveness of these models is often limited by the imbalance present in medical datasets, where negative (non-cancerous) cases vastly outnumber positive (cancerous) cases. This disproportionate distribution leads to biased learning, as deep learning models tend to prioritize the majority class while neglecting the minority class, which is clinically most important. Consequently, false negatives—cases where cancer goes undetected—pose significant risks to patient outcomes. Addressing this imbalance is therefore essential to ensure accurate and trustworthy predictions in breast cancer detection systems. In this chapter, we propose a comprehensive framework that directly tackles the imbalance problem through a combination of innovative data-level and model-level strategies. At the data level, our approach employs advanced augmentation techniques and synthetic image generation methods designed specifically for medical data, ensuring that positive class samples are enriched without compromising clinical authenticity. At the model level, we integrate cost-sensitive learning and adaptive weighting mechanisms within deep neural networks, encouraging the model to focus more on minority cases. Furthermore, we enhance robustness by employing ensemble strategies that reduce bias and improve generalization. Unlike existing solutions that address imbalance in isolation, our framework emphasizes a holistic integration of sampling, augmentation, and model optimization to create a balanced learning environment. This proposed approach not only mitigates dataset imbalance but also improves sensitivity and specificity, providing a more reliable decision-support tool for healthcare professionals.

**Keywords:** Breast cancer, Data analysis, Deep learning, Imbalanced dataset, Machine learning.

* **Corresponding author Rekha Baghel:** Department of Computer Science, Indira Gandhi Delhi Technical University for Women, New Delhi, Delhi, India; Department of Computer Science and Engineering, Ajay Kumar Garg Engineering College, Ghaziabad, Uttar Pradesh, India; E-mail: Rbaghel2022@gmail.com

**Ravinder M., Arti Ranjan, Youddha Beer Singh (Eds.)**

## INTRODUCTION

In the contemporary era, the significance of data has attained a paramount status, as the prosperity and advancement of a company or organization are predominantly contingent upon the adept comprehension and effective utilization of the amassed data. Every organization and corporation nowadays produces vast amounts of data across several industries, including commercial, finance, banking, and the health sector . Medical data collection can be sourced from various entities within the healthcare ecosystem, including hospitals, healthcare professionals, care providers, and insurance agencies. Upon acquiring the necessary medical datasets, the next step would be to meticulously examine and develop appropriate modeling techniques. These techniques are employed to extract valuable insights that can facilitate accurate predictions.

When a dataset exhibits an unbalanced distribution, a significant percentage of cases are associated with a single class referred to as the dominant class, and comparatively fewer belong to another class known as the dormant class, it is commonly referred to as data imbalance. Within the domain of machine learning, data imbalance emerges as a noteworthy concern. It is observed that the distribution of classes within a dataset could be more equitable, with a majority of datasets exhibiting a long-tail distribution [1]. The challenge associated with high-imbalance datasets arises from the disproportionate distribution of instances across different classes. Consider a scenario where there are 90 cases from the dominant class and only 10 cases from the minority class. In this case, a classification model that assigns all 100 inputs to the majority class would achieve an accuracy of 90%, completely disregarding the dormant class. This observation highlights a common trend: the classification performance of machine learning models decreases with imbalanced datasets [2]. In various domains, including the medical field, the minority class is often considered more significant. Nevertheless, it often faces the challenge of being overshadowed by the majority class, leading to overfitting. To address the curse of data imbalance, preprocessing techniques, including "random oversampling" and "undersampling," have been employed [3]. It is imperative to employ these techniques to develop precise classifiers [4].

The exponential growth of data has been observed in various industries, with the healthcare sector experiencing a significant surge due to digitalization. The available data exhibits a significant imbalance, necessitating the implementation of various methodologies to address this concern. The healthcare sector exhibits a notable disparity in data distribution, with a substantial preponderance of data about individuals with normal or healthy conditions compared to those afflicted with an illness. Consequently, the classifier exhibits a bias favoring the dominant class, thereby diminishing the accuracy of predictions about the minority class [5].

## IMBALANCED MEDICAL DATASETS: AN OVERVIEW

Data imbalance is a common phenomenon in datasets used for various machine learning and mining tasks [6]. Imbalanced datasets can manifest in different ways and for various reasons. Binary Class Imbalance is the simplest form of data imbalance, with only two classes. One class is significantly more prevalent than the other. For example, detecting a rare disease in medical diagnosis might lead to a binary class imbalance if the disease cases are a small fraction of the total instances. In multi-class datasets, there are more than two classes. An imbalance occurs when some classes are heavily overrepresented while others are underrepresented. Specific labels might be assigned to only a few instances in datasets with multiple labels, leading to multi-label imbalance. An example is document categorization, where some topics are less common than others [7]. Various types of data imbalance and factors causing data imbalance are shown in Fig. (**1**) and **2**, respectively.

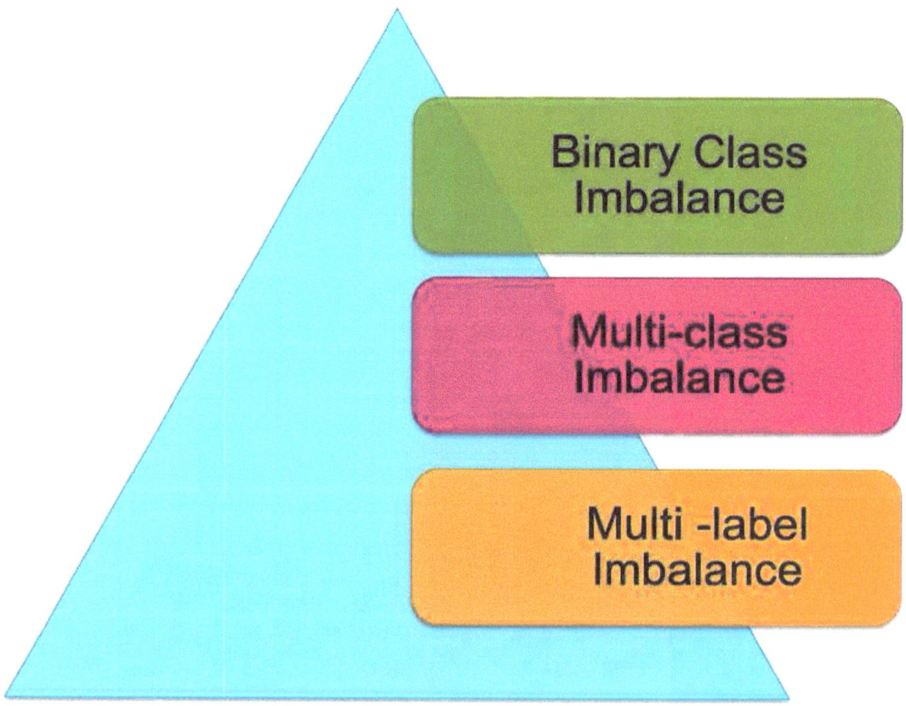


**Fig. (1).** Types of data imbalance.

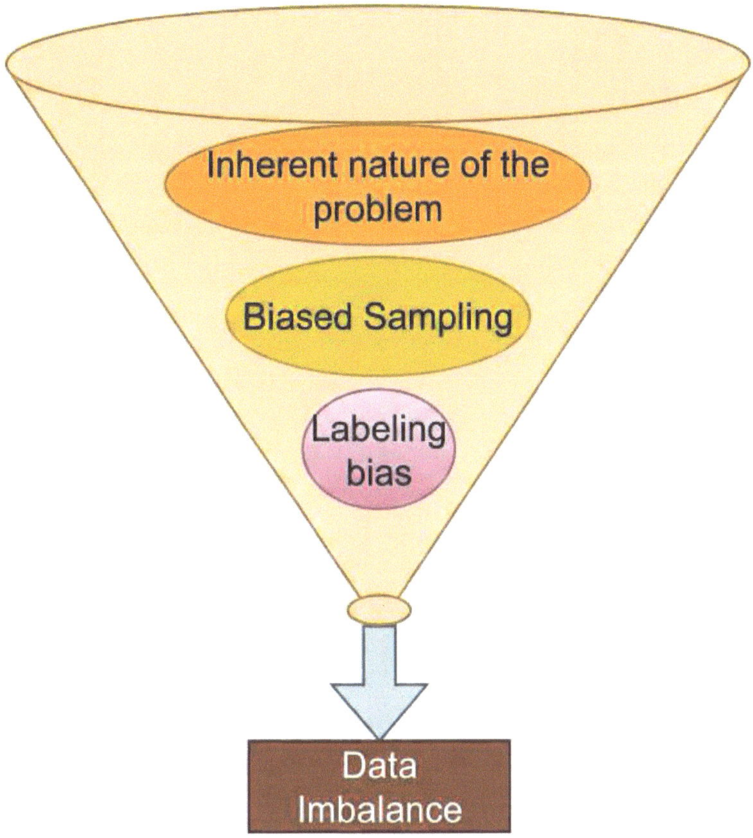


**Fig. (2).** Factors causing data imbalance.

There is a possibility that models constructed using imbalanced data will appear biased in favour of the dominant class, resulting in less than ideal performance for the dormant class. Conventional accuracy metrics employed to gauge the performance of models can sometimes be misleading. It is not uncommon for a model to achieve high accuracy even when the minority class performs poorly, as long as it correctly predicts the majority class. Imbalanced datasets can lead to suboptimal decision boundaries, thereby affecting a model's ability to classify instances correctly.

Handling imbalanced data in machine learning poses several significant challenges affecting predictive models' performance, generalization, and reliability. These challenges are crucial to understanding and effectively addressing the issues arising from data imbalance.

## REVIEW OF DEEP LEARNING-BASED IMAGE PROCESSING FOR IMBALANCED DATASETS

Data imbalance techniques aim to rectify this, making the dataset more suitable for training and improving the model's performance. Popularly used techniques include "Data-Level Techniques", "Algorithm-Level Techniques", and "Cost-Sensitive Algorithms", as shown in Fig. (**3**).

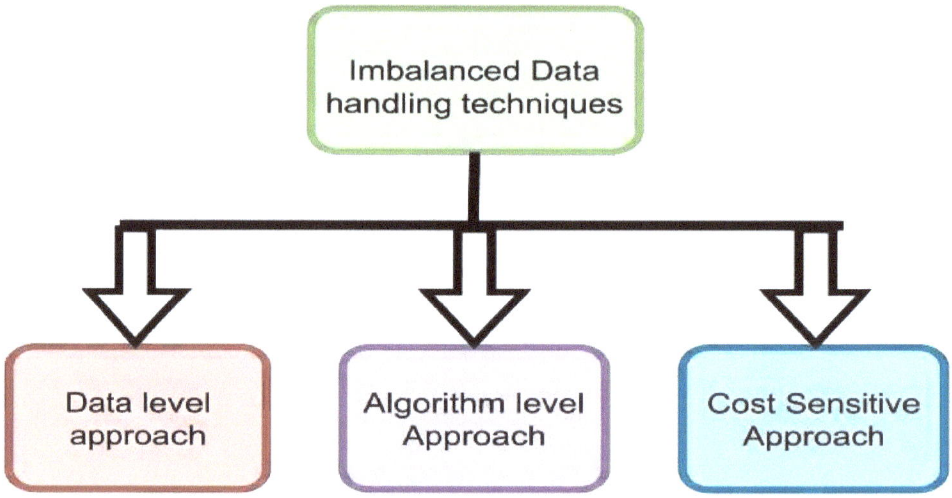


**Fig. (3).** Various imbalanced data handling techniques.

Data-level-based sampling methods often deal with imbalanced datasets by altering the distribution of sample instances within the dataset. These strategies optimize the distribution of classes, making the minority class instances more accessible for learning. "Oversampling" and "undersampling" methods are based on the Data level approach [7].To match or come close to the number of examples in the dominant class, oversampling entails increasing the quantity of cases in the dormant class.

It can be challenging to collect data for the minority class when the available data is limited. Oversampling Might introduce noise, leading to overemphasis on minority-class outliers. Under-sampling involves reducing the number of instances in the majority class to achieve a balanced dataset.

Undersampling is suitable when most class instances are redundant, and there is a need to reduce training time and complexity. However, it might lead to a loss of information and reduced model accuracy, especially if the dataset is already tiny.

The cost-sensitive approach is used to address imbalanced datasets by incorporating the costs associated with misclassification into the learning process. Traditional machine learning methods strive to minimize the total classification error, which can result in skewed models that favour one particular class in situations when the distribution of classes is uneven. Cost-sensitive learning prioritizes underrepresented classes or classes of higher importance. Popularly used deep learning algorithms for breast cancer detection are depicted in Fig. (**4**).

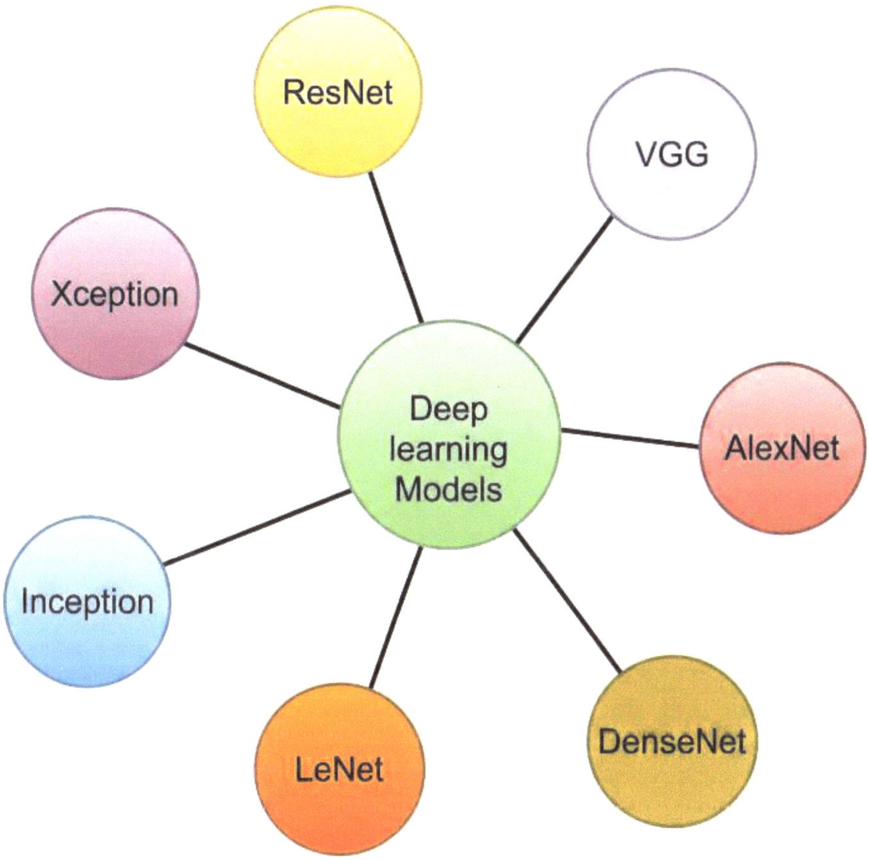


**Fig (4).** Various deep learning models.

Table **1** presents a literature review of various ML/DL models for breast cancer detection. Table **2** shows the recent work done on GANs. Fig. (**5**) shows the connection graph of recent work done on breast cancer detection.

**Table 1. Literature review of various ML/DL models for breast cancer detection.**

| S.No | Year | Deep learning models | Model architecture | Image augmentation method |
|---|---|---|---|---|
| 1 | 1998 | CNN(LeNet) | The system includes several hidden layers, in addition to an input and an output layer. Convolutional layers, RELU activations, pooling layers, and fully connected layers make up the hidden layers. | Random horizontal flipping translations |
| 2 | 2015 | ResNet | ResNet comprises convolutional layers, skip connections, residual blocks, batch normalisation, and ReLU activations as its primary components. | Crop, flip |
| 3 | 2014 | VGG | Convolutional layers (ConV layers) with modest 3x3 filters, max-pooling layers (MPL), and fully connected layers (FCL) comprise the Visual Geometry Group (VGG). | Random horizontal flipping, random cropping, random resizing |
| 4 | 2014 | Inception | Inception primarily comprises inception modules composed of parallel convolutional branches with varying filter sizes, pooling layers, and dimensionality reduction techniques like 1x1 convolutions. | Random cropping, Random horizontal flipping, Random resizing, scaling, Colour augmentation, rotation shearing |
| 5 | 2012 | AlexNet | The main components of AlexNet include local response normalization (LRN), conV layers, MPL, ReLU activations, FCL, and dropout regularization. | Flip, Translate, Intensity Changing |
| 6 | 2017 | Xception | One of the primary elements of Xception is depthwise separable convolutions, which effectively eliminate parameters while separating spatial and channel-wise convolutions for efficient feature extraction. | Random cropping, Random horizontal flipping, Random resizing scaling, Color augmentation, rotation shearing |
| 7 | 2017 | DenseNet | It includes densely connected blocks, transition layers, final fully connected layer, pooling layers, batch normalization<br>ReLU Activation | Flip, Crop, Translate |

**Table 2. Recent Work done on GANs.**

| Methods | Advantages | Disadvantages |
|---|---|---|
| **GAN** | One benefit of GANs is that they do not require the input to be based on an anticipated data distribution. To enhance the genuineness of the generated samples, random noise Z can be input via direct sampling. | The samples generated are too uncontrolled to concentrate on the specified samples, which is a drawback; therefore, constraints must be added to the GAN. |

*(Table 2) cont.....*

| Methods | Advantages | Disadvantages |
|---|---|---|
| CGAN | In addition to generating samples with particular identifiers, CGAN is also capable of enhancing the quality of the samples produced. | Conditional Generative Adversarial Networks (CGANs) encounter several constraints, including mode collapse (where the generator fails to produce diverse outputs), training instability, reliance on labeled data, sensitivity to hyperparameters, varying output quality, high computational requirements, complex evaluation metrics, the risk of overfitting, challenges in interpreting conditional spaces, and potential ethical and bias concerns. |
| AGGAN | To enhance the generator's perception of the necessary sample structure, it not only incorporates tags into the input but also appends tags to the actual sample. | The constraints of this model encompass mode collapse, difficulties in balancing generator and auxiliary classifier objectives, challenges in achieving diverse outputs, and the possibility of propagating biases from the training data. |
| DCGAN | Due to inefficiency, DCGAN removed the hidden layer of full connection in GAN training. Batch Normalisation supports model convergence and prevents generator collapse, enabling deeper gradient propagation. | DCGANs generally produce images with lower resolution in comparison to more advanced models. |

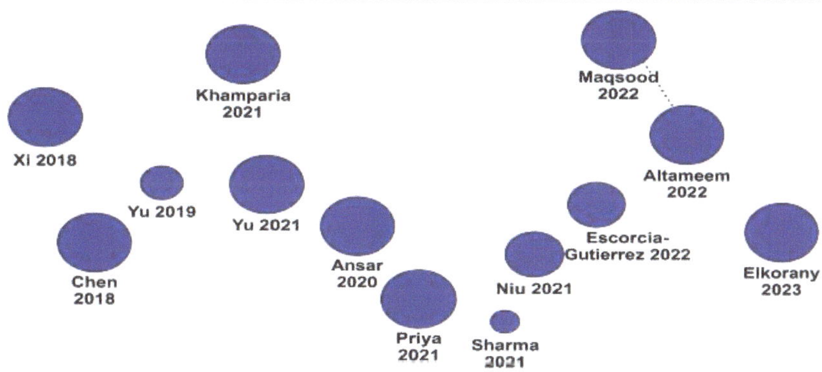


**Fig. (5).** Connection graph of recent work done on Breast cancer detection.

This chapter [8] explores the issue of breast cancer diagnosis and suggests a deep DL-based approach for extracting significant features from the imagery. Authors have used the ResNet50 model for feature extraction (FE) and then ensemble-based learning methods for classification tasks. Through rigorous experimentation on an IDC dataset, the hybrid model has proven to be incredibly robust and high-performing. It has attained an impressive recall of 94.32%, an accuracy rate of 95%, a precision of 94.86%, and an F1 score of 94.57%. These results outperform the existing models. The Light Boosting-based Classifier (LGB) is widely acknowledged as the optimal machine learning approach to complement ResNet50V2.

This chapter [9] addresses the urgent need for enhanced breast cancer detection methods due to its high mortality rate globally. The proposed method utilises a deep learning-based feature selection technique to enhance both the sensitivity and accuracy of computer-aided diagnostic systems in detecting early breast cancer. The model integrates transfer learning and CNNs to mine relevant features from mammograms. The features were optimized using the Butterfly Optimisation and the Gaussian function to choose the most pertinent ones. The Deep Belief Network classifier was provided with the optimized features (OpFe) to differentiate between healthy and cancerous images. The proposed model achieves significant improvements in accuracy, achieving 98.6% and 98.85% on the breast and MIAS datasets, respectively, compared to existing methods. Fig. (**6**) shows the general architecture of the Convolutional Neural Network model.

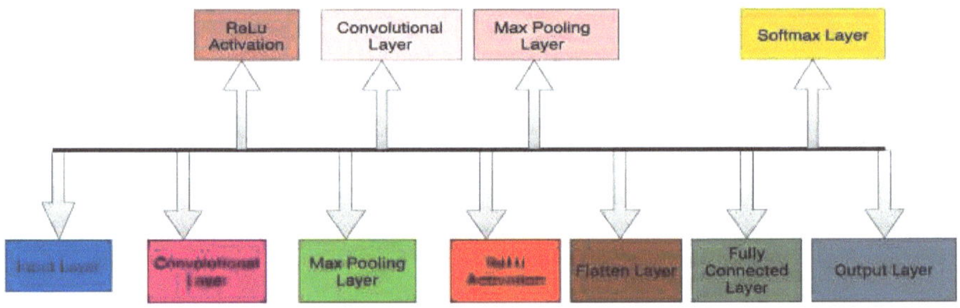


**Fig. (6).** Convolutional neural network model architecture.

The study [10] proposes a CAD-based approach to classify and localize masses and calcifications in mammographic images, aiming to reduce radiologists' workload and costs. Deep CNNs are employed for the process of automatically acquiring and developing features, as well as constructing a classifier. Due to limitations in training the CNNs directly on full mammogram images, training of classifiers is done on labelled image patches, after which they are adapted for full image analysis. VGGNet achieves the highest overall classification accuracy at 92.53%, while ResNet is chosen for its ability to compute class activation maps without further training, demonstrating remarkable localization capabilities of deep CNN classifiers despite no supervised information on abnormality locations.

The study [11] addresses the challenge of accurately identifying malignant regions in biopsy images, crucial for early breast cancer diagnosis. It proposes a pixel categorization approach utilizing principal component analysis (PCA) and genetic algorithm (GA) to extract spatial characteristics from the imagery. These features are selected using GA and input into the ensemble classifiers for pixel-level categorization. The suggested model, with a particular emphasis on GA, PCA, and DT, obtains high accuracies of 0.99 to 1.0 on a compact feature set, demonstrating its effectiveness in image annotation and tumor identification.

Further validation of the method's excellent results is provided by the utilization of the universal image quality index (UIQI) and the structural similarity index (SSI). The CAD system proposed in a study [12] aims to classify and localize abnormalities in mammogram images, including calcifications and masses. The classifiers in the CAD system were trained on labeled image patches and then applied to complete mammographic images to accurately localize anomalies. VGGNet is identified as the most accurate classifier with an overall accuracy of 92.53% among various advanced CNN architectures. Deep CNNs, including ResNet, have excellent localization qualities even when there is no control on the location of abnormalities. Computing class activation maps are created using ResNet due to their deployability without further training or structural changes.

The detection of calcium salts in breast tissue, known as micro-calcifications, is challenging because of the limited efficacy of current methods like Haralick-based feature extraction. The novel Hybrid LOOP Haralick FE [13]combines Local Optimal Oriented Pattern and Haralick texture features to achieve 3.83% accuracy over Haralick. Deep CNNs can localize abnormalities without supervision using this method. Class activation maps use ResNet owing to their deployability.

In a study [14], the authors constructed a Deep Belief Network (DBN) that facilitates four key phases: pre-processing, segmentation, FE, and classification. Pre-processing focuses on noise removal and gland enhancement in mammogram images, followed by fuzzy c-means segmentation aided by masking. FE utilizes techniques such as Speeded Robust Transform (SURF) and Scale Invariant Feature Transform (SIFT), applied alongside gradient boosting tree and AdaBoost classifiers. The classification process is evaluated using measures such as recall, precision, accuracy, and F1 score.

In another study [15], the authors developed an approach to address the challenge of FE using the improved Grey-Level Co-occurrence Matrix (AGLCM) method, coupled with machine learning algorithms for image classification. The proposed four-step process involves image acquisition, pre-processing using Contrast Limited Adaptive Histogram Equalization (CLAHE), FE *via* AGLCM for texture, intensity, and shape-based features crucial for anomaly detection, and classification. The study utilizes the eXtreme Gradient Boosting (XGBoost) classifier on mammograms. It compares the results of this classifier with those of various classifiers, including RF, K-NN, ANN, and SVM, using the MIAS dataset. Findings suggest that the XGBoost, CLAHE, and AGLCM classifier outperforms existing methods, indicating potential for future experimentation on larger datasets and a focus on optimal feature selection to enhance classification accuracy.

The authors [16] developed an innovative method for profound FE in the diagnosis of breast cancer subtypes, leveraging TL with the BreaKHis dataset. Five components make up the methodology: selection, categorization, concatenation, conversion, and FE. 19 Pre-trained CNN models are employed in the FE phase to extract features from the input dataset, and SVM is used to evaluate each feature's incorrect classification rate. Two networks achieve the highest accuracy and are combined to form the DRNet model, using DenseNet201 and ResNet50. To divide the obtained features into five sub-sets of low-level features, a hierarchical discrete wavelet transform is applied to them. Feature selection is performed using an iterative neighbourhood component analyser to determine the least necessary features for classification. A cubic support vector machine serves as the classifier, achieving average classification accuracies of 97.71%, 97.68%, 98.04%, and 98.61% for magnification levels of 400×, 200×, 100×, and 40×, respectively.

Methods like ultrasound, mammography, and MRI are impractical for frequent mass screenings. Thermography emerges as a potential solution due to its non-invasive nature and low cost, suitable for routine self-screening. Utilizing AI techniques and data from 306 images, the research presented [17] implements transfer learning with pre-trained models and Bayesian Networks (BNs) for diagnostic interpretability. A novel FE method focusing on temperature-related images enhances diagnostic accuracy. Results reveal MobileNet as the top-performing model with 93.8% accuracy, followed by BN at 90.20%, and an expert model combining CNN and BN, achieving 90.85% accuracy despite limited data availability.

Another approach [18] involves FE from several pre-trained CNN models, followed by feature concatenation and selection constructed on mutual information using the objective variable. Nominated features are then categorized using neural network (NN), random forest (RF), KNN, and SVM. The newly developed RSNA dataset is analyzed with a remarkable 92% accuracy by the NN-based classifier, which includes additional features such as age, thereby improving performance. A comparison with contemporary methods demonstrates the superiority of the proposed algorithm, particularly in terms of sensitivity and accuracy. The MIAS dataset was evaluated and found to have a precision rate of 94.5%, whilst the DDSM dataset achieved an accuracy rate of 96%.

The chapter [19] developed a method that utilizes FE and deep learning methods-based classification. During pre-processing, the input image is subjected to edge smoothing to eliminate noise and scaling. This is followed by feature extraction using a 3D Convolutional Neural Network. Extracted deep features are then fed into the Stochastic Diffusion Kernel based on RNN (SDKRNN) for classification.

This model effectively integrates the advantages of convolutional and kernel blocks, demonstrating superior performance stability in comparison to current methodologies. Experimental results evaluate various performance measures, including accuracy, precision, F-1 score, AUC, and specificity, achieving impressive scores of 98%, 93.8%, 89%, 70%, and 80%, respectively. The method outperforms current breast cancer detection methodologies, emphasizing its efficacy in the diagnosis of breast cancer.

This research [20] developed an innovative DL approach integrating convolutional neural networks (CNN) with UNet and encoder architectures. Classification accuracy rates and enhanced performance measures are achieved for the suggested RF-KNN and DT-KNN models. The research utilizes the EfficientNet model, known for its durable architecture with attention components. Each image undergoes augmentation methods such as shifts, flips, rotations, and brightness modifications before being processed individually by the EfficientNet model. Augmentation ensures the diversity of input features for ensemble classifiers, including Decision Tree, Random Forest, and K-Means Nearest Neighbor. This model surpasses the performance of established models like DenseNet121, EfficientNet-B3, and ResNet50, and when applied to a similar dataset, showcases its effectiveness in classifying breast cancer images.

In this work, a novel deep CNN architecture was suggested for the ultrasound image classification of breast tumors, which achieved promising results in data analysis, and they used deep CNNs as a DL procedure [21]. The authors of this article investigated the application of DL-based techniques to mammogram analysis by enhancing the analysis results and exhibited the significance of augmenting and processing data to attain high classification precision [22].

In this article, the authors evaluated the performance of numerous pioneering CNN architectures in contrast to a comparatively innovative model called the Vision Transformer (ViT) [23]. In this article, the authors suggested an architecture incorporating the pre-trained CNN of VGG16 with spatial pyramid pooling (SP layer) and network in the network (NiN) [24].

In a study [[25], a simple ANN model was used to handle the class imbalance problem in real-life imbalance datasets in which the majority class contains 500 samples, and the minority class contains 268 samples. WBCD is a breast cancer dataset that contains 458 samples of the majority class, while 241 samples of the minority class [25].

The imbalanced dataset encountered the issue of less data in the minority classes. Therefore, due to the unavailability of a sufficient amount of data belonging to minority classes, various deep learning models face the problem of overfitting.

Many authors have proposed various data augmentation approaches as a solution to this problem, such as oversampling the instances of the minority class and undersampling the instances of the majority class. But these approaches just remove or replicate the existing data; they do not consider the vicinity distribution properties of the minority or majority classes. In supervised-based approaches, a function f Ɛ F is found that imitates the relationship between the input variable i and the output j in a joint distribution P (i, j). For this purpose, loss is calculated to understand the difference between predicted f(i) and expected output i for all examples in P(i,j). In the vicinity distribution, for models, it is not required to remember all the instances of the dataset; therefore, these models give higher performances [26]. To consider this issue, the Generative Adversarial Network (GAN) was proposed for creating synthetic data that is very similar to existing data. Since its introduction by Goodfellow in 2014, GAN has emerged as a prominent area of investigation within the domains of artificial intelligence. Few-shot learning (FSL) [27] addresses supervised learning with limited training samples. Transfer learning is used in FSL to adapt pretrained models to new tasks, but overfitting is a challenge due to insufficient data. A study proposes using Conditional Generative Adversarial Networks (CGAN) for data augmentation in Handwritten Character Recognition tasks. CGAN generates realistic additional samples, enhancing transfer learning performance for models like GoogleNet, VGG-16, and AlexNet. Results demonstrate improved fine-tuning with fewer epochs, increased F1-score, and reduced Generalization Error.

This study [28] introduces a novel hybrid framework aimed at effectively tackling the challenges associated with imbalanced sample distribution in the field of machine learning. RGAN-EL combines generative adversarial networks (GANs) with ensemble learning methods to enhance classification performance. It employs a training sample selection strategy and generator training loss to improve sample quality and oversamples minority class samples. Experiments on 41 real imbalanced datasets show that RGAN-EL outperforms six typical ensemble learning methods and RGAN improves upon three classical GAN models in terms of F1-score and AUC evaluation indexes.

This study [29] addresses the challenge of limited datasets in healthcare by proposing a novel K-CGAN method for generating synthetic data in the breast cancer domain. The study uses non-image Wisconsin Breast Cancer data to evaluate five classification methods and feature selection techniques. Synthetic data generated by K-CGAN are assessed using recall, precision, accuracy, and F1 Score metrics, demonstrating its effectiveness in classification tasks. Empirical results reveal K-CGAN's superior stability compared to other GAN variants, suggesting that the synthetic data accurately represent the original dataset and hold promise for improving breast cancer detection models.

This work [30] proposes a novel hybrid sampling method based on GAN to address class overlap issues in oversampling. The approach combines GAN-based oversampling with an adaptive weighted undersampling method. This method generates a balanced dataset and effectively reduces the impact of class overlapping. Results on synthetic and real customer datasets demonstrate the superiority of this method over benchmark methods, evaluated using both profit-based and accuracy-based metrics.

One of the limitations of GANs is that they require a huge amount of a balanced dataset to generate synthetic samples. Authors in [30] developed an approach to create synthetic images of the minority class of the imbalanced dataset. They have used the CIFAR-10 and MNIST fashion datasets for training and testing the model.

## UNDERSTANDING THE ARCHITECTURE OF DEEP LEARNING MODELS

Deep learning has become increasingly crucial in our daily lives and has already had a significant impact on various industries, including the detection of cancer, precision healthcare, predictive forecasting, and speech recognition [30]. Some of the latest trends in the field involve deep convolutional networks, residual networks, RNN, reinforcement learning, the incorporation of Transformer architecture into computer vision, and variational autoencoders. Current trends and innovations in breast cancer detection involve the utilization of various convolutional neural network (CNN) architectures to enhance accuracy and efficiency. Researchers have explored architectures like DenseNet-201, ResNet-50, Inception-V3, InceptionResNet-V3, MobileNetV2, NASNetMobile, and NASNetLarge [21]. These models aim to improve tumor detection from reconstructed images of microwave imaging scan data, achieving high accuracies of up to 88.41% with NASNetLarge [31]. Additionally, studies have focused on applying CNN and Vision Transformer (ViT) architectures to mammogram analysis, incorporating data augmentation techniques for improved performance [23]. The integration of deep learning models into computer-aided diagnosis systems shows promise in enhancing breast cancer detection and diagnosis, especially in resource-constrained settings.

### CNN

Many authors proposed approaches based on neural networks. Neural networks suffer from high dimensionality. If there is only one hidden layer and the input layer consists of a 100*100 pixel image, then it requires millions of weights. To overcome this issue, authors proposed the Convolutional neural network (CNN) shown in Fig. (**6**). A CNN is comprised of several layers, such as the Input, convolutional, hidden, pooling, and fully connected layers. The input layer consists of image data such as the width of the image, the height of the image, and the color channels of the image. 16x16x3 image consists of 16 widths, 16 heights, and 3 colors: Red, Green, and Blue. For detecting the various features of the image, such as texture, edge, and pattern, convolution filters or kernels are applied to the input. These filters are the learnable parameters that create the feature maps by applying the convolution operation. Stride determines the number of filter movements across the input matrix. A small feature map requires a larger stride and vice versa. Padding is applied to control the spatial size of the feature map. Padding can be applied in two ways: valid padding and same padding. In the valid padding, the feature maps are smaller than the input. Same padding is a technique for adding padding to an input so that the output feature map has the same spatial dimensions as the input.

Activations are applied to learn the non-linearity. Pooling layers are used to diminish the less important spatial features to decrease the computational complexity. Max Pooling and Average Pooling can be used. Max pooling proceeds with the maximum value from each square of the feature map, while Average pooling continues with the average value of each square. The pooling size is used to decide the size of the square.

The architecture of a 16x16x3 image is represented in Table **3**.

**Table 3. CNN architecture of 16x16x3 image.**

| S.No. | Layer | Layer functions | Output Dimensions |
|---|---|---|---|
| 1 | Input Layer | 16x16x3 | 16x16x3 |
| 2 | Convolutional layer +Activation function (ReLU) | 32 filters of 3x3,<br>stride 1,<br>padding same-16x16x32 | 16x16x32 |
| 3 | Max Pooling | 2x2 pooling size, stride 2 → 8x8x32 | 8x8x32 |
| 4 | Convolutional layer+ Activation function (ReLU) | 64 filters of 3x3, stride 1, padding same → 8x8x64 | 8x8x64 |
| 5 | Max Pooling | 2x2 pooling size, stride 2 → 4x4x64 | 4x4x64 |
| 6 | Flatten | 4x4x64 → 1024 | 1024 |
| 7 | Fully Connected + ReLU | 128 neurons | 128 |
| 8 | Output Layer (Softmax) | 10 neurons for classification(if there are 10 classes) | 10 |

## RESNET

ResNet, the improved architecture of CNN, was developed by Kaiming *et al.* in 2015. When the gradients become very low during propagation, the deep learning model converges slowly and shows poor performance. As the number of layers increased, the deep learning model suffered from the vanishing gradient problem. The ResNet model was proposed to solve the issue of the Vanishing Gradient problem. The concept of residual learning is used here to overcome the vanishing gradient problem. In this, the model learns the transformations between the input layer and the output layer with the help of residual mappings. This residual connection is created by allowing the connection between the input layer and the output layer with the help of skip connections. Skip connections are used to skip the layer that has produced the high loss.

The ResNet model consists of many layers, each comprising a residual block. ResNet architecture consists of five phases. Each phase is made of several residual blocks. The first phase consisted of a convolutional layer and a max pooling layer. The second phase consists of two ConV layers and skip connections. There are three residual blocks in the second phase. There are four, six, and three residual blocks in the third, fourth, and fifth phases. The last stage output is given to the global average pooling layer. The output of this layer is given to the fully connected layer to produce the final output.

This architecture comes with several variants comprising ResNet-18, ResNet-34, ResNet-50, ResNet-101, and ResNet-152. The number associated with each ResNet corresponds to the total number of layers in the architecture. In ResNet-18, there are a total of 18 layers. Fig. (7) shows the ResNet model Architecture and Table **4** shows the ResNet-50 Architecture of a 16x16x3 image.

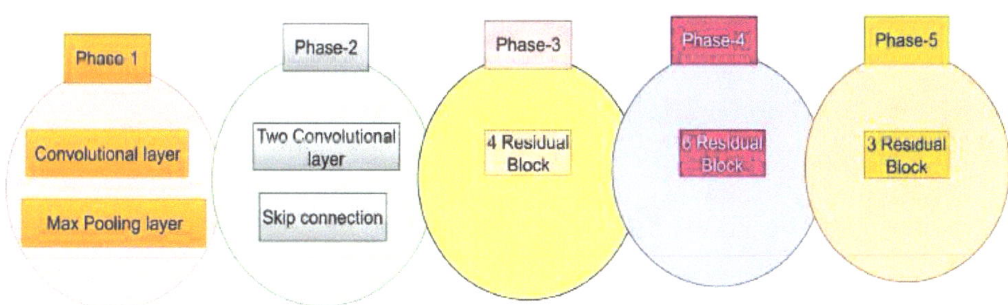


**Fig. (7).** ResNet model architecture.

**Table 4. ResNet-50 Architecture of 16x16x3 image.**

| S.No. | Layer | Layer functions | Output Dimensions |
|---|---|---|---|
| 1 | Input Layer | 16x16x3 | 16x16x3 |
| 2 | Convolution layer-1 | 7x7, 64 filters, stride 2, padding same → 8x8x64 | 8x8x64 |
| 3 | Max Pooling | 3x3, stride 2, padding same → 4x4x64 | 4x4x64 |
| 4 | Residual Block Layer 1 (Conv2_x) | 1x1, 64 filters → 3x3, 64 filters → 1x1, 256 filters → 4x4x256<br>Repeat 3 times | 4x4x256 |
| 5 | Residual Block Layer 2 (Conv3_x): | 1x1, 128 filters, stride 2 → 3x3, 128 filters → 1x1, 512 filters → 2x2x512<br>Repeat 4 times | 2x2x512 |
| 6 | Residual Block Layer 3 (Conv4_x) | 1x1, 256 filters, stride 2 → 3x3, 256 filters → 1x1, 1024 filters → 1x1x1024<br>Repeat 6 times | 1x1x1024 |
| 7 | Residual Block Layer 4 (Conv5_x) | 1x1, 512 filters, stride 2 → 3x3, 512 filters → 1x1, 2048 filters → 1x1x2048<br>Repeat 3 times | 1x1x2048 |
| 8 | Global Average Pooling | 2048 | 2048 |
| 9 | Fully Connected Layer | Softmax → Number of classes | Number of classes |

## AlexNet

Authors in [32]came up with the idea for AlexNet, which is a CNN. Among its twenty-five layers, eight of them are learnable. In addition to three completely connected layers, five ConV layers make up these eight layers. The utilization of the RELU activation function occurs throughout each of the learnable layers, except for the final layer. The ConV layers are associated with a variety of kernel sizes, which include four strides with no padding, one stride with two paddings, and one stride with one padding. AlexNet performs nonlinear downsampling and utilizes three max-pooling functions to decrease computational complexity. Every single function makes use of filters that have two strides and no padding. Following the first two layers of the final fully linked layers, which have a total of 4096 channels, a dropout layer is placed to prevent overfitting. This final group contains one thousand channels, equivalent to the total output classes.

## VGG-16

The VGG structure comprises 47 layers, 16 of which are trainable. Thirteen Conv layers and three completely connected layers comprise the 16 levels. Five blocks comprise the ConV layers, which are succeeded by an MPL. Filters with a consistent size, stride, and padding of 1 are employed in each block's conV layer. Additionally, a Rectified Linear Unit activation is implemented at the conclusion. VGG-16 utilizes concise and unchanging conV kernels to reduce the number of parameters and to generate a more unique decision function. The MLP that has been implemented employs filters with two strides and no padding. Consequently, the activation map from the preceding layer has each spatial dimension reduced by half. The FCL in VGG-16 is identical to that in AlexNet [27].

## CHALLENGES IN DEEP LEARNING-BASED IMAGE PROCESSING FOR IMBALANCED DATASETS

Deep learning models have provided approaches to unlocking information to address the imbalance issue. GANs are very popular for accomplishing this task, and synthetic images are developed to resemble real images. When applying GANs in various areas, such as disease prediction, it is necessary to identify the right proportion of real and synthetic images. Fake images can be utilized to increase sample size, but they cannot replace real images.

For generating synthetic samples, GANs always need a balanced dataset. If the dataset is imbalanced and samples are insufficient, GANs cannot guarantee better performance. More improvements are needed to generate high-quality synthetic samples of the minority classes in small, imbalanced datasets.

Deep learning models have shown very effective performance in handling data imbalance, but due to limited data samples, they may suffer from overfitting. These models require large amounts of data for training, but when data is limited, they exhibit generalization errors and become overfit.

Many approaches have been proposed for inter-class data imbalance handling, but very little work has been done for intra-class data imbalance handling. Therefore, there is a need for approaches that can address intra-class data imbalance issues.

## CONCLUSION

This study reviewed the comprehensive range of deep learning approaches for breast cancer detection in the imbalanced dataset, including three categories: data-level, algorithm-based, and cost-sensitive approaches. Various algorithm-based approaches based on deep learning algorithms are proposed by the authors, and these algorithms gain attention due to their performance. ResNet and VGG are the most popular deep-learning models for breast cancer detection. Data augmentation is found to be very effective in reducing the effect of data imbalance. We found that the various improved versions of GANs significantly improve the model's performance on imbalanced datasets. Based on this study, we argue that new approaches can be encouraged by new challenges, as applicable approaches can be selected based on the challenges faced by the dataset used for breast cancer detection. Furthermore, we discussed the current state of various approaches to breast cancer detection based on imbalanced data and the opportunities for deep learning techniques to handle them. Our research will yield an exhaustive understanding of image-processing techniques based on deep learning.

## REFERENCES

[1] J. M. Johnson, and T. M. Khoshgoftaar, "Survey on deep learning with class imbalance", *J Big Data,* vol. 6, 2019. [http://dx.doi.org/10.1186/s40537-019-0192-5]

[2] J. H. Joloudari, A. Marefat, M. A. Nematollahi, S. S. Oyelere, and S Hussain, "Effective class-imbalance learning based on SMOTE and convolutional neural networks", *Applied Sciences*. vol. 13, no. 6, p. 4018, 2023.

[3] I. H. Sarker, "Machine learning: Algorithms, real-world applications and research directions", *SN Computer Science,* vol. 2, no. 3, pp. 1-21, 2021. [http://dx.doi.org/10.1007/s42979-021-00592-x]

[4] S. S. Kim, and H. Sohn, "Structural damage detection using limited information", *Mech. Syst. Signal Process.,* vol. 170, p. 108765, 2022.

[5] N Norori, Q Hu, F. M. Aellen, F. D. Faraci, and A Tzovara, "Addressing bias in big data and AI for health care: A call for open science", *Patterns,* vol. 2, no. 10, p. 100347, 2021. [http://dx.doi.org/10.1016/j.patter.2021.100347]

[6] H Kaur, H. S. Pannu, and A. K. Malhi, "A systematic review on imbalanced data challenges in machine learning: Applications and solutions", *ACM Computing Surveys,* vol. 52, no. 4, pp. 1-36, Aug 2019.

[7] K. Ghosh, C. Bellinger, R. Corizzo, P. Branco, B. Krawczyk, and N. Japkowicz, "The class imbalance problem in deep learning", *Machine Learning,* vol. 113, no. 8, pp. 4845-4901, 2024. [http://dx.doi.org/10.1007/s10994-022-06268-8]

[8] S Sharmin, T Ahammad, M. A. Talukder, and P Ghose, "A hybrid dependable deep feature extraction and ensemble-based machine learning approach for breast cancer detection", *IEEE Access,* vol. 11, pp. 87694-87708, 2023. [http://dx.doi.org/10.1109/ACCESS.2023.3304628]

[9] A. A. Malibari, M. K. Nour, A. S. Mehanna, M. A. Hamza, A. S. Zamani, I Yaseen, and A Motwakel, "Gaussian optimized deep learning-based belief classification model for breast cancer detection", *Computers, Materials & Continua,* vol. 73, no. 2, 2022.

[10] D Ribli, A Horváth, Z Unger, P Pollner, and I Csabai, "Detecting and classifying lesions in mammograms with deep learning", *Scientific Reports,* vol. 8, no. 1, pp. 1-7, 2018. [http://dx.doi.org/10.1038/s41598-018-22437-z]

[11] N Behar, and M Shrivastava, "Pixel-level feature extraction model for breast cancer detection", *Computers, Materials & Continua,* vol. 74, no. 2, pp. 3371-3389, 2023. [http://dx.doi.org/10.32604/cmc.2023.031949]

[12] Xi P, Shu C, Goubran R, "Abnormality detection in mammography using deep convolutional neural networks", In: *Proc. IEEE Int. Symp. Medical Measurements and Applications (MeMeA),* 2018, pp. 1-6.

[13] N Rao, and P Pullaiah, "Detection of breast cancer on magnetic resonance imaging using hybrid

feature extraction and deep neural network techniques", *Int J Intel Eng Sys,* vol. 13, no. 6, pp. 229-240, 2020.
[http://dx.doi.org/10.22266/ijies2020.1231.21]

[14] S. P. A. Surendhar, and R. Vasuki, "Breast cancer detection using deep belief network by applying feature extraction on various classifiers", *Turkish J. Comput. Math. Educ.,* vol. 12, no. 1, pp. 471-487, 2021.

[15] L. K. Kumari, and B. N. Jagadesh, "A robust feature extraction technique for breast cancer detection using digital mammograms based on advanced GLCM approach", *EAI Endorsed Transactions on Pervasive Health and Technology,* vol. 8, no. 30, pp. 1-10, 2022.
[http://dx.doi.org/10.4108/eai.11-1-2022.172813]

[16] B Muhammad, F Ozkaynak, A Varol, and T Tuncer, "A novel deep feature extraction engineering for subtypes of breast cancer diagnosis: A transfer learning approach", In: *Proc. Int. Symp. Digital Forensics and Security (ISDFS).* Istanbul, Turkey, 2022, pp. 1-7.
[http://dx.doi.org/10.1109/ISDFS55398.2022.9800813]

[17] N Aidossov, V Zarikas, A Mashekova, Y Zhao, E. Y. Ng, A Midlenko, and O Mukhmetov, "Evaluation of integrated CNN, transfer learning, and BN with thermography for breast cancer detection", *Applied Sciences,* vol. 13, no. 1, p. 600, 2023.

[18] Z Jafari, and E Karami, "Breast cancer detection in mammography images: A CNN-based approach with feature selection", *Information,* vol. 14, no. 7, 2023.
[http://dx.doi.org/10.3390/info14070410]

[19] B Buvaneswari, J Vijayaraj, and B Satheesh Kumar, "Histopathological image-based breast cancer detection employing 3D-convolutional neural network feature extraction and stochastic diffusion kernel recursive neural networks classification", *Imaging Science Journal,* vol. 69, no. 5–8, pp. 350-363, 2021.
[http://dx.doi.org/10.1080/13682199.2022.2161148]

[20] S. P. A. Surendhar, R. K. Kanna, and R Indumathi, "Ensemble feature extraction with classification integrated with Mask RCNN architecture in breast cancer detection based on deep learning techniques", *SN Computer Science,* vol. 4, no. 5, p. 121, 2023.
[http://dx.doi.org/10.1007/s42979-023-01893-z]

[21] U Ilhan, K Uyar, and E. I. Iseri, "Breast cancer classification using deep learning", In: *Advances in Intelligent Systems and Computing* vol. 1306. , 2021, pp. 709-714.
[http://dx.doi.org/10.1007/978-3-030-64058-3_88]

[22] M Prodan, E Paraschiv, and A Stanciu, "Applying deep learning methods for mammography analysis and breast cancer detection", *Applied Sciences,* vol. 13, no. 7, 2023.
[http://dx.doi.org/10.3390/app13074272]

[23] B Maistry, and A. E. Ezugwu, "Breast cancer detection and diagnosis: A comparative study of state-of-the-art deep learning architectures",

[24] C. S. R. Sannasi, and H Rajaguru, "Deep learning-based breast cancer detection using VGG-NiN architecture", *AIP Conference Proceedings,* vol. 2725, p. 16, 2023.
[http://dx.doi.org/10.1063/5.0125243]

[25] M Shrinidhi, T. K. K. Jegannnathan, and R Jeya, "Classification of imbalanced datasets using various techniques along with variants of SMOTE oversampling and ANN", *Advances in Science and Technology,* vol. 124, pp. 504-511, 2023.
[http://dx.doi.org/10.4028/p-338i7w]

[26] M Xu, S Yoon, A Fuentes, and D. S. Park, "A comprehensive survey of image augmentation techniques for deep learning", *Pattern Recognition,* vol. 137, p. 109347, 2023.
[http://dx.doi.org/10.1016/j.patcog.2023.109347]

[27] P Yadav, and S Yadav, "Image fusion using hybrid methods in multimodality medical images",

*Medical & Biological Engineering & Computing,* vol. 58, pp. 669-687, 2020.
[http://dx.doi.org/10.1007/s11517-020-02136-6]

[28] S. P. Yadav, D. P. Mahato, N. T. Linh, Ed., *Distributed Artificial Intelligence: A Modern Approach* CRC Press, Dec 2020.

[29] E Strelcenia, and S Prakoonwit, "Improving cancer detection classification performance using GANs in breast cancer data", *IEEE Access,* vol. 11, pp. 71594-71615, 2023.
[http://dx.doi.org/10.1109/ACCESS.2023.3291336]

[30] A Ranjan, and M Ravinder, "AEWGAN-NCO in image deblurring framework using variational autoencoders and Wasserstein generative adversarial network", *Signal, Image and Video Processing,* vol. 18, pp. 4447-4456, 2024.
[http://dx.doi.org/10.1007/s11760-024-03085-5]

[31] L Shen, L. R. Margolies, J. H. Rothstein, E Fluder, R McBride, and W Sieh, "Deep learning to improve breast cancer detection on screening mammography", *Scientific Reports,* vol. 9, no. 1, pp. 1-12, 2019.
[http://dx.doi.org/10.1038/s41598-019-48995-4]

[32] N. L. W. Keijsers, "Neural networks", In: *Encyclopedia of Movement Disorders*, 2010, pp. V2-25--V2-259.
[http://dx.doi.org/10.1016/B978-0-12-374105-9.00493-7]

# CHAPTER 3

# Ancient Indian Scripts Identification: A Machine Learning and NLP Approach

**Subhajit Ghosh**[1,*]

[1] *Department of Computer Science and Engineering – Artificial Intelligence and Machine Learning, Meerut Institute of Engineering and Technology, Meerut, Uttar Pradesh, India*

**Abstract:** Understanding of ancient script is linked to the discovery of our past heritage and cultural evolution. The task of deciphering such texts, often eroded by time, presents significant challenges. Recent advancements in Machine Learning (ML) and Natural Language Processing (NLP) offer transformative tools to automate and enhance the interpretation of these historical artifacts. This chapter introduces the application of ML and NLP techniques in identifying and analyzing ancient Indian scripts, throwing light on their complexities, cultural context, and linguistic variations. The chapter provides a comprehensive review of existing methodologies and the obstacles inherent in deciphering historical documents. Challenges associated with scripts like Brahmi, Devanagari, and others are explored, which highlight their linguistic intricacies and historical depth, and also their cultural specificity. Traditionally, transcription by experts has been the primary approach. This method is time-intensive and prone to errors. By contrast, recent advancements in ML and NLP have enabled automated processes, achieving notable improvements in accuracy and efficiency. The key techniques, which include image preprocessing, feature extraction, and classification algorithms, are assessed to determine their suitability in addressing the complexities of ancient scripts. Additionally, the chapter investigates the integration of domain-specific knowledge, such as epigraphy and palaeography, with ML and NLP frameworks. This interdisciplinary approach utilizes historical corpora, linguistic resources, and computational algorithms to enhance accuracy and contextual understanding. The chapter emphasizes the need for collaboration among historians, linguists, and computer scientists to develop robust systems for deciphering ancient texts. Case studies and a literature review demonstrate the potential of ML and NLP in revolutionizing the study of Indian scripts. The chapter concludes with a discussion on future research directions, underscoring the importance of innovation and interdisciplinary collaboration in unravelling the secrets encoded in these invaluable relics of the past.

**Keywords:** Ancient scripts, Brahmi, Epigraphy, Historical documents, Indian texts, Machine learning, Natural language processing, Text identification.

* **Corresponding author Subhajit Ghosh:** Department of Computer Science and Engineering – Artificial Intelligence and Machine Learning, Meerut Institute of Engineering and Technology, Meerut, Uttar Pradesh, India; E-mail: subhajit.ghosh@miet.ac.in

**Ravinder M., Arti Ranjan, Youddha Beer Singh (Eds.)**

## INTRODUCTION

We need to know about our ancient scripts. The identification and interpretation of ancient texts have long been a cornerstone of historical and linguistic research. They are a window to our understanding of our ancient history. The lack of knowledge and understanding of Pali, Maratha, and even the ancient scripts used by the Moghuls will hinder the accurate comprehension of historians to arrive at conclusions regarding the history associated with those earlier periods. Understanding ancient scripts is critical for estimating the history and societal structures, as well as the languages in prevalence, the cultures of past civilizations, and their origins [1, 2]. Numerous scripts have been used over the centuries, *viz*., Brahmi, Tamil-Brahmi, and Devanagari, each contributing to the richness of our cultural heritage. The ancient Indian scripts threw light on the socio-political and religious practices in vogue, and conditions of the economy of these times. Inscriptions and manuscripts, artifacts, and currency of those times contain revelatory information. The comprehension of these texts helps historians and linguists reconstruct historical narratives and understand linguistic tradition. This is crucial in the preservation of administrative records and ancient literature [3, 4].

The manual deciphering of these scripts is time-consuming and contains errors. This study looks into the application of modern Machine Learning and Natural Language Processing techniques in the identification and interpretation of ancient scripts. Through probing the methods and challenges involved, contributions to digital humanities and computational linguistics can be made. The comprehension and digitalization of ancient texts ensure that invaluable cultural information is not lost forever. This enables easy access for those seeking information, including researchers as well as the general public. The identification and assessment of these texts are labour-intensive when done manually and prone to errors. This necessitates the development of automated solutions.

Some of the major Ancient Indian Scripts include Brahmi, Tamil-Brahmi, Kharosthi, Devanagari, and others. Brahmi is considered one of the earliest antiquated writing systems prevalent in ancient India, and a few such inscriptions date back to the 3rd century BCE. It is widely accepted that several South and Southeast Asian scripts originated from Brahmi. Languages like Sanskrit and Hindi are derived from the Brahmi script and are recognized by the horizontal line at the top of the letters. Tamil-Brahmi uses the features of the Brahmi script adapted for the Tamil language. It was used in inscriptions from the early centuries CE. These scripts, in addition to documenting historical events, also reflect the linguistic diversity and cultural richness of ancient India. They are crucial for our understanding of pre-modern historical literature and for assessing administrative records and religious texts that were prevalent several centuries ago.

Deciphering ancient scripts involves challenges such as the availability of complete data, fading of inscriptions, and the need for expert knowledge in historical linguistics and paleography. Ancient scripts often exhibit variations and evolutions over time and across regions [5].

Some of the important tasks in the analysis would include aspects of image preprocessing and feature extraction, as well as the use of classification algorithms to address the complexities of understanding ancient documents, besides the utilization of resources that contain linguistic and historical collections, and techniques of inferencing contextuality to improve the accuracy of text identification [6].

To improve the readability of ancient texts, a combination of domain knowledge and modern technologies can go a long way. Domain knowledge in fields such as epigraphy and paleography, coupled with knowledge of technology related to ML and NLP, can help the process of decipherment. In fact, a team consisting of linguists, computer scientists, and historians working together, sharing their expertise, can enable the building of effective systems for text identification [7].

The evolution of languages dates back several centuries, bringing with it changes and complexities of its own. Literature [8] provides a detailed review that examines the application of machine learning in the study of ancient texts, covering a wide range of languages, scripts, and media across more than three and a half millennia of global civilizations. In the case of Indian scripts like Brahmi and Devanagari, the challenges of unravelling their meanings are immense [9]. An attempt is being made in this write-up to summarize the existing literature and the possibilities of using modern technologies – NLP and ML – in the identification and transcription of historical documents, and to posit future research directions.

## HISTORICAL BACKGROUND OF ANCIENT INDIAN SCRIPTS

### Brahmi Script

Brahmi script has been traced back to the 3rd century BCE. Several modern Indian scripts like Tamil and Devanagari have inherited some of their characteristics. The discovery of Inscriptions written using the Brahmi script on rock edicts, coins, and other artifacts reveals its wide usage in ancient times. Text identification of Brahmi script and its variability pose enormous challenges in historical documents and artifacts. Contemporary techniques use CNNs trained on annotated Brahmi datasets, which have been found to be significantly accurate in character identification [10 - 12].

### Devanagari Script

Devanagari has its origin in the Brahmi script around the 7th century CE and is used in many Indian languages like Sanskrit and Marathi. It has gained wide popularity owing to its structured character set and grammar rules, and its script finds usage across India. For the identification of text, Deep learning models, such as LSTMs and Transformers, have been used to transcribe and translate ancient historical manuscripts. Recent Deep Learning systems that use CNNs and RNNs exhibit high accuracy in the identification of Devanagari script in text and OCR systems [13].

### Tamil-Brahmi Script

The Tamil script, derived from Brahmi, is one of the oldest scripts in the world. The discovered inscriptions on stones and palm-leaf using the Tamil script are believed to be around 5th century BCE. The challenges of reading old Tamil texts owing to deterioration and stylistic changes over time have been addressed appreciably through the use of modern techniques, including developments in image pre-processing and noise reduction, and CNN-based character recognition. Recently, collaborative digitalization projects are underway that combine the power of ML & NLP to facilitate the comprehension of ancient Tamil-Brahmi script [14, 15].

### Kharosthi Script

The ***Kharosthi Script*** originated from present-day northern Pakistan around the 4th and 3rd century BCE [16, 17]. It was essentially a form of Prakrit, a language from the Indo-Aryan family of languages, and its prevalence was along northern Pakistan, parts of north-western India, Central Asia and Afghanistan. Inscriptions bearing the Kharosthi script were found in the Gandhara region in northern Pakistan, and in the Ashokan edicts around the mid-3rd century BCE. It did not spawn other scripts [18].

### Bengali Script

The Bengali script, Kutialipi, originated from an eastern variety of the Brahmi script, characterised by a distinguishing feature sometime around the 7th century.

The Bangla (a.k.a. Bengali) script has undergone changes over the centuries and has culminated in the cursive pattern we see now, with its unique horizontal line and circular shapes. This makes the identification of Bangla text a complex task.

Historians have investigated changes in letter style since ancient times. In the epigraphic records, they have pointed out a curious species of palaeographic chronometer for dating otherwise undatable inscriptions. R.D. Banerji and D.N. Chakravarty studied Bengali palaeography that revealed a similar tendency of morphology usage of script as a helpful device for history [19]. Bengali has a rich literary tradition. Significant works in Bengali literature, especially those by Rabindranath Tagore, Sarat Chandra Chattopadhyay & Bankim Chandra Chattopadhyay, are of high cultural value.

### Assamese Script

The present form of the Assamese script, which traces its origin to the Brahmi script, has evolved from the Kamarupi script during the early medieval period. The script draws on the Bengali script, but it also has distinguishing features that demonstrate the uniqueness of the linguistic and cultural tradition of Assam and its people.

Among the many ancient Indian scripts, the Bengali and Assamese scripts are striking for their intricate structures and for the wealth of historical documents they preserve, necessitating their preservation. The comprehension of these documents is critical for the progress of historical research and the preservation of these two old cultures.

## MACHINE LEARNING AND NLP TECHNIQUES

Comprehension of ancient scripts is fundamental to understanding specific cultures and their evolution over the years. Deriving semantics from ancient texts has great challenges owing to varied linguistic structures, destruction that occurs over time, and a very limited supply of trained experts. India, with its plethora of languages and spanning several centuries, has to encounter a significant challenge.

The methodology has the following stages. A dataset is prepared at the beginning with the samples of different ancient scripts that contain several linguistic characteristics and periods harking back to the primeval. **Preprocessing techniques** are used to improve data quality and uniformity. These pre-processing techniques would mostly consist of normalization, segmentation, and noise reduction. Techniques like ML and NLP are used for the interpretation of ancient texts [20].

Machine Learning (ML) algorithms learn from data that enables them to make predictions. For historical documents, ML can be used for character recognition and modelling languages. Natural Language Processing (NLP) deals with the interaction between computers and human languages, and requires performing tasks such as tokenization, morphological and syntax analysis, semantic interpretation and others. In cases where annotated data is available, Supervised Learning Techniques [21] can be used, including Neural Networks, SVMs, and others. Supervised learning techniques such as Convolutional Neural Networks (CNNs) have been effective in recognizing characters in olden texts. Training script identification can happen on large labelled datasets to learn characteristic features, which has been successful in the identification of characters from manuscripts that have been subjected to degradation over the years.

For unlabelled data, we use **Unsupervised Learning techniques** [22] like Clustering and Dimensionality Reduction. Clustering algorithms like K-means and Dimension Reduction methods like PCA are popular. Unsupervised learning helps in clustering and pattern recognition. Deep Learning techniques like Convolutional Neural Networks (CNNs) and Recurrent Neural Networks (RNNs) are effective in image recognition and sequence prediction. Autoencoders and Generative Adversarial Networks (GANs) are used for reconstruction of missing sections from illegible texts and for finding structures in script data. Autoencoders are neural networks used for efficient coding of input data. They can also be used for reconstructing and denoising old, degraded manuscript images, thus improving their readability.

Use of techniques like **Transfer learning** [23] is common in the absence of adequate annotated datasets. Pre-training a model on a big dataset and thereafter customizing it for a smaller dataset. This technique has been effective in script identification in a constrained environment where annotated datasets are not readily available, as per the needs of training. Such pre-trained models applicable to similar scripts can be a basis for fine-tuning, just as in the case of similar languages like Bengali and Assamese.

The method of reading ancient texts consists of tasks such as image preprocessing and feature extraction, followed by the use of classification algorithms, the utilization of linguistic resources and historical corpora, and the consideration of text context. This process has proved effective in handling complexity and increasing the accuracy of historical documents.

# PROPOSED METHODOLOGY

## Data Collection and Preprocessing

Firstly, there is a need to collect good-quality images of historical documents. These may be obtained from manuscripts, archaeological discoveries, epigraphical databases, and others, necessitating data specialists, archeologists, and historians to work jointly. The process of digitalization requires the conversion of physical texts through high-resolution scanning into their digital versions. There is a need for experts to annotate, i.e., label the data precisely in case of supervised learning. Preprocessing steps include the reduction of noise, binarization and normalization, segmentation, and enhancement of images to increase the readability of the text. In the case of textual data, preprocessing would include steps such as tokenization, stemming, and lemmatization. Optical Character Recognition (OCR) technologies require customized models due to the varied shapes of historical characters when recognizing old manuscripts. Besides feature extraction and representation, Morphological analysis is used to analyse the structure of words, including their roots, prefixes, and suffixes, which is essential for understanding inflected languages. Semantic analysis examines the meanings of words and phrases. Syntactic analysis investigates the structure of sentences. The above steps are needed for the translation of text and its interpretation [24]. Fig. (**1**) provides the details about the proposed methodology step by step.

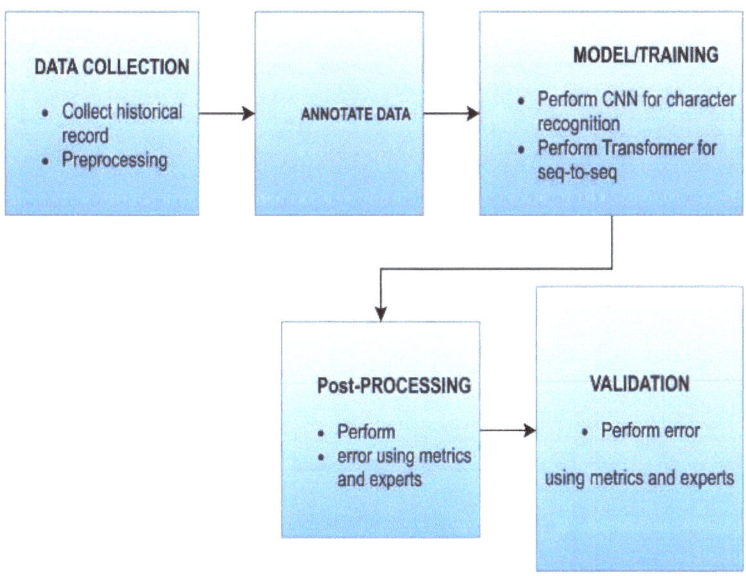


**Fig. (1).** Proposed methodology.

## Model Selection and Training

The task of Model Selection is crucial. Some models use multiple CNNs for character recognition, and the task of translating sequence-to-sequence is entrusted to Transformer-based models. Adaptation of Transfer learning techniques to the characteristics of historical manuscripts can be used in conjunction with pre-trained models.

## Post-processing and Validation

Error correction as per the rules of the language and cross-referencing digital archives form the core of post-processing work. Validation is done using metrics and expert evaluations. This has proved to be helpful in providing accurate and reliable identification of the ancient text.

# ML ALGORITHMS FOR TEXT IDENTIFICATION

With technological developments, a newer approach to reading ancient scripts is needed. With the advancement in Machine Learning (ML) and Natural Language Processing (NLP), a framework has evolved that integrates ML and image processing techniques, from preprocessing techniques [25, 26] like noise reduction and normalization to ensure data quality, feature extraction, and classification of images to quickly decipher ancient texts, successfully recognizing characters and symbols. Feature extraction techniques like Histogram of Oriented Gradients (HOG) and Scale-Invariant Feature Transform (SIFT) aid in mapping the salient characteristics of the scripts. Table **1** provides the steps and types of Machine Learning algorithms used in an appropriate perspective [27, 28].

**Table 1. Steps & types of machine learning.**

| Steps | Supervised Learning | Unsupervised Learning | Deep Learning |
|---|---|---|---|
| PRE-PROCESSING | Noise Reduction, Normalization for Data Quality<br>Feature Selection – HOG, SIFT | Dimensionality reduction | Scanning and Resolution adjustment, Image denoising, Contrast enhancement, Binarization, Background Removal ... |
| TRAINING | Support Vector Machines, Decision Trees ... | Clustering Algorithms – K-Means, ... | CNN, RNN, Transformer, Transfer Learning |
| TESTING | Evaluated on metrics like Precision and Recall, F1 score, and accuracy. | | |

Computational text analysis is not just about digitizing traditional methods; it introduces entirely new ways of exploring ancient texts and scripts. Unlike humans, computers interpret text by converting words into numbers or vectors, which allows them to analyze patterns and meanings using mathematical models [29, 30]. Although this approach is vastly different from conventional methods, it provides fresh perspectives on textual analysis. For instance, transitioning to digital tools enables large-scale interdisciplinary collaboration. In the analogue era, resources like card catalogues were only accessible to a limited number of scholars and couldn't easily connect with other collections. In a digital format, however, these can be shared, compared, and linked across disciplines through technologies like the semantic web, opening up unparalleled opportunities for collaborative research [31].

Supervised and unsupervised learning algorithms are trained on the extracted features to achieve accurate classification and clustering of the ancient text. The tuning and validation of models deliver good performance when tested with various datasets and types of scripts. Moreover, deep learning methods using Convolutional Neural Networks (CNNs) and Recurrent Neural Networks (RNNs) have been able to detect non-trivial patterns and their dependencies in texts. The choice of ML model is crucial. It has been found that CNNs are good for image recognition, and RNNs do well for sequential data analysis [32, 33]. The models and algorithms used for the identification of text belong to the following categories: Supervised learning, Unsupervised Learning and Deep Learning. In supervised learning, training occurs on labeled datasets to build models that are used in the identification of texts. CNNs have the ability to learn feature hierarchies for spatial data and are successful in the recognition of ancient scripts [34, 35]. The Supervised Learning Algorithms, SVM, Decision Trees, Convolution Neural Networks (CNNs), and Recurrent Neural Networks (RNNs) use annotated/labelled datasets during the phase of training. This results in accurate classification of ancient characters. In unsupervised learning, such as clustering and dimensionality reduction, useful when annotated data are scarce, patterns, and intrinsic structures can be identified in unlabeled data. Unsupervised learning approaches like clustering help form groups of similar words and characters, enabling the detection of latent patterns, unknown symbols and similarities in the data. Deep learning approaches such as CNNs are accurate in the recognition of image-based text, and methods like RNNs and Transformer models are strong in sequential data processing, which is an essential part in tasks such as modelling of languages and their translation [36]. Other approaches in deep learning, like Transfer Learning, use pre-trained models on big datasets to deliver good performance on small datasets, only on certain tasks, usually in the identification of historical manuscripts with limited annotated data. This is achieved through a process of knowledge transfer from training on modern scripts and allied tasks [37].

Training on any of the above selected approaches occurs on a pre-processed dataset. Thereafter, they are evaluated on metrics like precision and recall, F1-score, and accuracy. To ensure robustness, cross-validation techniques are used. The use of recent developments in ML and NLP is quite effective in the identification of texts from old manuscripts. There are stumbling blocks, though, with data scarcity and the variability in scripts; nonetheless, research has shown the effectiveness of these techniques in reading historical documents [38].

## NLP TECHNIQUES FOR TEXT IDENTIFICATION

NLP techniques are used to extract the distinguishing features of the historical scripts and synthesize linguistic and contextual understanding of recognized script samples. Multiple techniques have been presented in Table **2**. These include tasks such as character and word level embeddings, syntactic parsing, and semantic analysis, tokenization, stemming, and part-of-speech tagging. Training on ancient data yields models effective for text interpretation and facilitates translation work, thus building on insights derived from the ML approach and, in the process, aiding classification and identification and helping with a deep understanding of the content [39, 40].

**Table 2. NLP techniques for text identification.**

| SNO | Techniques | Area where used | Estimation |
|---|---|---|---|
| 1 | OCR | OCR technology is greatly used in the digitization of manuscripts, and for the conversion of scanned images of the text into a form that can be easily read by the machine. | The conventional OCR techniques are not very effective with ancient scripts. Recent advances in deep learning have greatly improved OCR accuracy. |
| 2 | Part of Speech Tagging | The need for Part-of-speech tagging is for the comprehension of grammatical structures. | Each word in a text gets associated with its corresponding parts of speech. |
| 3 | Named Entity Recognition (NER) | Named Entity Recognition (NER) is useful for the identification and classification of entities in the document. | It can extract proper names and places, and other important terms. This facilitates the right interpretation of the old manuscripts. |

*(Table 2) cont.....*

| SNO | Techniques | Area where used | Estimation |
|---|---|---|---|
| 4 | Sequence-to-Sequence Model | Based on architectures such as Recurrent Neural Networks (RNNs) and Transformers. Adaptability through learning of mappings from visual features to text allows these models to decipher ancient manuscripts. | Gives good performance in tasks like transcription and text translation. |

There are other NLP techniques like Optical Character Recognition (OCR), Part-of-Speech Tagging, Named Entity Recognition (NER), and others used for text identification. OCR technology is greatly used in the digitization of manuscripts, and for the conversion of scanned images of the text into a form that can be easily read by the machine [41, 42]. The conventional OCR techniques are not very effective with ancient scripts. Recent advances in deep learning have greatly improved OCR accuracy. Therefore, the recent OCR systems synthesize the beneficial aspects of ML and NLP techniques that are able to perform recognition and transcribe ancient scripts perfectly. However, there is a need for OCR systems to adapt to the unique characteristics of languages [43].

Named Entity Recognition (NER) is useful for the identification and classification of entities in the document. It can extract proper names and places, and other important terms. This facilitates the right interpretation of the old manuscripts. The need for Part-of-speech tagging is to comprehend grammatical structures, in which each word in a text is associated with its corresponding part of speech. Advanced NLP models can be trained to handle the abnormalities in the syntax of ancient languages, such as Bengali and Assamese [44].

There are NLP techniques such as Sequence-to-Sequence Models that give good performance in tasks like transcription and text translation. These are based on architectures such as Recurrent Neural Networks (RNNs) and Transformers. Adaptability through learning of mappings from visual features to text allows these models to decipher ancient manuscripts. Word and character embeddings contain syntactic and semantic relationships in textual data. Embeddings of words and characters in vector spaces can be used for script identification, classification, and translation.

Shad *et al.* [45] examined the role of Artificial Intelligence in the decipherment of ancient scripts, focusing on key technologies like optical character recognition (OCR), natural language processing, and machine translation. OCR digitizes and analyzes historical texts, while NLP helps decipher grammatical structures and meanings, and machine translation helps reconstruct lost languages. The chapter highlights case studies, including the application of neural networks to the undeciphered Indus script and deep learning techniques to enhance the readability of the Dead Sea Scrolls. These examples showcase the transformative potential of AI technologies in this field. Moreover, the integration of AI with traditional philological methods accelerates the decipherment process, offering valuable insights into the linguistic, cultural, and historical contexts of ancient civilizations.

## CHALLENGES AND SOLUTIONS

The Ancient Indian scripts, with their unique graphical structures and long history of development, bring immense challenges to text recognition techniques. Knowledge of such scripts is essential both for historical research and the preservation of cultural heritage.

### Script Variability

Scripts have evolved over time, which has led to differences in styles and forms of the characters. This is often due to regional and temporal differences. Owing to this variability, the task of building a good generalizable text identification model is reasonably difficult.

### Data Scarcity

There is a scarcity of annotated data for ancient scripts. This is quite a challenge for training ML models, and steps such as data augmentation and transfer learning can help in addressing this issue. Building high-quality annotations is a challenge as expert knowledge is needed, and the availability of large annotated datasets needed for recent ML approaches is limited.

### Noisy and Degraded Texts

Physical degradation owing to fading, tearing, staining, ink bleeding, and other factors makes the texts illegible and introduces noise into images, which makes the automated recognition of text difficult. Denoising and super-resolution, which are well-known image processing techniques, are often used to improve the digitized texts.

### Multilingual and Multi-script Scenarios

Historical texts are often written using multiple languages and scripts. It is therefore necessary to build a multilingual NLP model. In such cases, the use of cross-lingual transfer techniques provides good outcomes.

## Lack of Standardization

In olden days, the unavailability of standardized orthography resulted in a word or phrase being written in several ways in the manuscripts. This made the task of text identification even more difficult.

## Error Analysis

The errors in the identification of scripts stemming from inaccurate recognition of similar characters in degraded manuscripts are assessed.

Combining knowledge from fields like epigraphy and palaeography with machine learning (ML) and natural language processing (NLP) has made significant progress. These efforts address challenges such as small datasets, uneven data distribution, and the complexity of ancient writing. For example, creating synthetic data has become a key way to generate more training examples for tasks like recognizing Old Aramaic scripts. This approach helps ML models perform better despite the lack of real-world data and improves their ability to handle rare or damaged scripts.

Additionally, tools like domain-specific knowledge graphs have been used to adapt pre-trained language models for specialized tasks, such as classifying texts or answering questions. These methods capture the unique context and meaning found in ancient writings. Frameworks like KnowledgeDA show how tailored data can enhance NLP applications in specialized areas.

Efforts to study scripts like Cuneiform and Egyptian hieroglyphs often require ML techniques like convolutional neural networks (CNNs). While these methods improve tasks like identifying symbols, they still require significant human effort for labeling and verifying data.

To learn more, explore recent studies on synthetic data for ancient languages and advancements in domain-specific NLP tools, which demonstrate the importance of combining subject expertise with modern technology.

There are still several challenges remaining, even after the advancements witnessed in the field. Some of these challenges include the changeability in the scripts, the degradation of the manuscripts over time, the variations in handwriting, the complexity in the structure of the scripts, the unavailability of standardization in orthography, and a few others. The development of effective identification models is further constrained owing to the limited supply of annotated datasets.

## EVALUATION METRICS AND BENCHMARKING

Acceptability of a proposed technique is arrived at after thorough experimentation on a wide range of historical scripts. The performance metrics that include accuracy, precision and recall are used to estimate the effectiveness of the models across a wide range of script categories and variations of the language. Accuracy and Precision metrics provide the accuracy of identifying characters and words in the manuscript. Metrics like **Recall and F1-Score** estimate the ability of the model to identify scripts accurately with a desirable value for precision and recall.

There is a need to establish benchmark datasets for ancient scripts. This is needed for evaluating a model and for providing comparative estimates of different models and approaches. Significant improvements over baseline methods where ML & NLP were used on datasets of Brahmi, Devanagari, and Tamil scripts have been reported. The efficiency of the models was estimated using measures like correctness in character recognition and transcribability, and the results prove their effectiveness.

## CASE STUDIES

The Digital Library of India project has been able to digitize several historical documents. This project has come up with good datasets for the purpose of training ML and NLP models. The Muktabodha Digital Library works on the preservation and knowledge sharing of Sanskrit and allied manuscripts. Their work in the area of digitizing and transcribing texts provides excellent knowledge of the right methodologies for dealing with historical scripts. The Indic OCR project is working on building OCR systems for Indian scripts. Their work on languages such as Bengali and Assamese OCR systems showcases the application of ML and NLP techniques in the identification of ancient text. The research is part of a bigger goal to preserve and comprehend India's cultural heritage, glimpses of which are documented in these historical documents. These projects will help scholars, historians, and allied professionals in deciphering inscriptions. It would also lead the way for the development of automated tools for digitization and the archival of historical documents.

ML and NLP have significantly advanced the study and preservation of Indian scripts. Several case studies highlight the transformative potential of these technologies: The **AI4Bharat initiative** has developed resources such as Samanantar, the largest parallel corpus for Indian languages, enabling robust machine translation across 11 Indian languages. IndicBART, another innovation, utilizes transfer learning for low-resource languages like Tamil, demonstrating enhanced translation quality by exploiting linguistic similarities between Indian languages. Efforts like the digitization of palm-leaf manuscripts utilize ML algorithms to recognize and interpret complex Indian scripts. Convolutional Neural Networks (CNNs) have been particularly effective for script recognition, enabling accurate transcription of Sanskrit, Kannada, and other ancient.

Technologies such as neural machine translation and OCR are employed in projects like the creation of digital repositories for endangered Indian languages, ensuring their preservation and accessibility. These tools also address the script diversity and non-standard orthography prevalent in Indian languages. AI models trained on Indic languages have been tailored to support applications such as chatbots and virtual assistants. For instance, language models optimized for Hindi and Dravidian languages are used in public services and education platforms, showcasing AI's ability to bridge linguistic gaps in multilingual societies.

These examples illustrate how ML and NLP are revolutionizing the study of Indian scripts by enhancing accessibility, promoting cultural preservation, and enabling new academic research paths.

Rusho *et al.* assessed the efficacy of employing digital archaeology techniques in documenting, analyzing, and preserving archaeological sites and artifacts in Bangladesh.

## FUTURE DIRECTIONS AND CONCLUSION

The past work on historical documents was based on manual transcription by the experts. This is time-consuming as well as susceptible to errors. In recent times, ML and NLP are helping to automate this process and improve the identification and interpretation of historical texts. For this, they use computational algorithms to analyse patterns and features within the script. Ancient Indian scripts, including Brahmi, Devanagari, Bengali, Assamese, and others, have a long history of evolution over centuries. Such scripts are found in historical, literary, and religious texts. The appearance of newer ML techniques such as few-shot learning and generative models is likely to advance olden script identification. Despite challenges like script variability and lack of standardization, the developments in ancient text identification hold great promise towards our understanding of the cultural and linguistic heritage of India. Working as a team along with archaeologists and historians can assist in the understanding of ancient texts. This would be possible through seamless integration of computational techniques with Archaeological and Historical expertise. This can have wider application in other areas of Digital Humanities.

Ancient Indian script identification is a non-trivial task. The use of improved ML and NLP techniques is showing promising results. A continual improvement of these technologies can provide better knowledge about our historical heritage contained in these historical manuscripts. Techniques like Convolutional Neural Networks (CNNs), Recurrent Neural Networks (RNNs), and Optical Character Recognition (OCR) are demonstrating good results in the recognition and transcription of these manuscripts. Advancements will influence the digital humanities and the preservation of ancient texts.

Further research needs to build larger, more diverse annotated datasets, include other ancient scripts, develop models that cancope with challenges such as variability and the state of decay of old manuscripts, and incorporate advanced ML techniques like Deep Learning. There is a need to use transfer learning techniques to make use of existing models in a better way. Collaboration with historians and linguists can improve matters. The symbiosis of domain-specific knowledge and interdisciplinary collaborations is probably the only answer to these multifaceted challenges involved in old text identification.

The developments in the area are likely to greatly influence the field of digital humanities. Automated text identification can help big digitization projects and quicken the process of reading and interpretation of inscriptions and manuscripts, epigraphic sources, and others. This will improve our understanding of our country's linguistic and cultural heritage.

## REFERENCES


[1] R. Salomon, *Indian Epigraphy: A Guide to the Study of Inscriptions in Sanskrit, Prakrit, and the Other Indo-Aryan Languages.* Oxford University Press, 1998. [http://dx.doi.org/10.1093/oso/9780195099843.001.0001]

[2] G.A. Grierson, *Linguistic Survey of India.* Government Printing: Calcutta, India, 1903.

[3] Q. Li, H. Peng, J. Li, C. Xia, R. Yang, L. Sun, P.S. Yu, and L. He, "A Survey on Text Classification: From Traditional to Deep Learning", *ACM Trans. Intell. Syst. Technol.,* vol. 13, no. 2, pp. 1-41, 2022. [http://dx.doi.org/10.1145/3495162]

[4] B. Lavanya, "History and Types of Script in Ancient Indian Civilization", *Humanities and Social Sciences,* vol. 10, no. 3, p. 117, 2022. [http://dx.doi.org/10.11648/j.hss.20221003.11]

[5] J. Jayanthi, and P.U. Maheswari, "Comparative study: enhancing legibility of ancient Indian script images from diverse stone background structures using 34 different pre-processing methods", *Herit. Sci.,* vol. 12, no. 1, p. 63, 2024. [http://dx.doi.org/10.1186/s40494-024-01169-6]

[6] A.C. Aioanei, R.R. Hunziker-Rodewald, K.M. Klein, and D.L. Michels, "Deep Aramaic: Towards a synthetic data paradigm enabling machine learning in epigraphy", *PLoS One,* vol. 19, no. 4, p. e0299297, 2024. [http://dx.doi.org/10.1371/journal.pone.0299297] [PMID: 38640100]

[7] S. Ferrara, and F. Tamburini, "Advanced techniques for the decipherment of ancient scripts", In: *Lang. Lang.* vol. 21. , 2022, no. 2, pp. 239-259.

[8] S. Gordin, "Optical character recognition for ancient non-alphabetic scripts", *Open Access Government,* pp. 280-281, 2022.

[9] F.M. Shiri, T. Perumal, N. Mustapha, and R. Mohamed, "A comprehensive overview and comparative analysis on deep learning models: CNN, RNN, LSTM, GRU", *arXiv preprint*, arXiv:2305.17473, 2023.

[10] S.R. Narang, M. Kumar, and M.K. Jindal, "DeepNetDevanagari: a deep learning model for Devanagari ancient character recognition", *Multimedia Tools Appl.,* vol. 80, no. 13, pp. 20671-20686, 2021. [http://dx.doi.org/10.1007/s11042-021-10775-6]

[11] K. Poornimathi, V. Muralibhaskaran, and L. Priya, "Preserving Tamil Brahmi Letters on Ancient Inscriptions: A Novel Preprocessing Technique for Diverse Applications", In: *Proceedings of the International Conference on Data Management, Analytics and Innovation (ICDMAI 2024)*. Springer: Singapore, 2024, pp. 165-177. [http://dx.doi.org/10.1007/978-981-97-3245-6_13]

[12] I. Sutskever, O. Vinyals, and Q.V. Le, "Sequence to sequence learning with neural networks", In: *Proc. 27th Int. Conf. Neural Information Processing Systems (NIPS'14)* vol. 2. MIT Press: Cambridge, MA, USA, 2014, pp. 3104-3112.

[13] M. Perino, L. Pronti, C. Moffa, M. Rosellini, and A.C. Felici, "New Frontiers in the Digital Restoration of Hidden Texts in Manuscripts: A Review of the Technical Approaches", *Heritage,* vol. 7, no. 2, pp. 683-696, 2024. [http://dx.doi.org/10.3390/heritage7020034]

[14] S.J. Pan, and Q. Yang, "A survey on transfer learning", *IEEE Trans. Knowl. Data Eng.,* vol. 22, no. 10, pp. 1345-1359, 2010. [http://dx.doi.org/10.1109/TKDE.2009.191]

[15] A. Vaswani, "Attention is all you need", *Proc. 31st Int. Conf. Neural Information Processing Systems (NIPS'17),* pp. 5998-6008, 2017. [http://dx.doi.org/10.48550/arXiv.1706.03762]

[16] M. Sokolova, and G. Lapalme, "A systematic analysis of performance measures for natural language generation", *Inf. Process. Manage.,* vol. 45, no. 4, pp. 427-438, 2009. [http://dx.doi.org/10.1016/j.ipm.2009.03.002]

[17] AF Gad, "Accuracy, precision, and recall in deep learning", *Paperspace Blog,* 2020.

[18] "Kharosthi Script," World History Encyclopedia, 2024. [Online]. Available: https://www.worldhistory.org/Kharosthi_Script/

[19] "Bangla Language and Script," Resource Centre for Indian Language Technology Solutions (RC-ILTS), Indian Statistical Institute (ISI), Kolkata. [Online]. (Accessed Oct. 14, 2022).

[20] A. Barhate, A. Tale, N. Jikar, P. Verma, P. Kumar, and P. Yesankar, "A comprehensive review of supervised learning algorithms in healthcare applications", In: *Proc. 2024 2nd DMIHER Int. Conf. on Artificial Intelligence in Healthcare, Education and Industry (IDICAIEI)* IEEE., 2024, pp. 1-6. [http://dx.doi.org/10.1109/IDICAIEI61867.2024.10842845]

[21] D. Tirthyani, S. Kumar, and S. Vats, Clustering and Unsupervised. In: Learning. *Recent Trends and Future Direction for Data Analytics.* IGI Global, 2024, pp. 119-139. [http://dx.doi.org/10.4018/979-8-3693-3609-0.ch005]

[22] A. Arya, and A. Ranjan, Beyond Syntax and Semantics: The Quantum Leap in Natural Language Processing. In: *A Handbook of Computational Linguistics: Artificial Intelligence in Natural Language Processing.* Bentham Science Publishers, 2024, pp. 255-284. [http://dx.doi.org/10.2174/9789815238488124020015]

[23] A. Ranjan, and M. Ravinder, "ROBDD-TrOCRBERTa: a novel robust-optimized blurred document text deblurring and completion with DCGAN-TrOCR and DistilRoBERTa", *Int. J. Inf. Technol.,* vol.

16, no. 7, pp. 4611-4619, 2024.
[http://dx.doi.org/10.1007/s41870-024-02073-9]

[24] A. Graves, and J. Schmidhuber, "Offline handwriting recognition with multidimensional recurrent neural networks", *Advances in Neural Information Processing Systems (NeurIPS),* vol. 21, pp. 545-552, 2009.

[25] S. Chadha, S. Mittal, and V. Singhal, "An insight of script text extraction performance using machine learning techniques", *Int. J. Innov. Technol. Explor. Eng.,* vol. 9, no. 1, pp. 2581-2588, 2019.
[http://dx.doi.org/10.35940/ijitee.A5224.119119]

[26] S.R. Gudadhe, A.A. Bardekar, and A.B. Ranit, "A novel approach using machine learning and NLP for revolutionizing pali manuscript conservation", *2024 4th International Conference on Sustainable Expert Systems (ICSES),* vol. 15, IEEE, pp. 844-848, 2024.
[http://dx.doi.org/10.1109/ICSES63445.2024.10763163]

[27] C. Wigington, C. Tensmeyer, B. Davis, W. Barrett, B. Price, and S. Cohen, "Start, follow, read: end-to-end full page handwriting recognition", *Proc. ECCV 2018,* 2018.
[http://dx.doi.org/10.1007/978-3-030-01231-1_23]

[28] B. Hauer, and G. Kondrak, "Decoding anagrammed texts written in an unknown language and script", *Trans. Assoc. Comput. Linguist.,* vol. 4, pp. 75-86, 2016.
[http://dx.doi.org/10.1162/tacl_a_00084]

[29] D. Firmani, P. Merialdo, E. Nieddu, and S. Scardapane, "In Codice ratio: OCR of handwritten Latin documents using deep convolutional networks", *Proc. 11th Int. Workshop on Artificial Intelligence for Cultural Heritage* (AICH 2017), Bari, Italy, 2017, pp. 9–16.

[30] E. Guéville, and D. J. Wrisley, "Transcribing Medieval Manuscripts for Machine Learning", *arXiv preprint arXiv:2207.07726,* 2022.
[http://dx.doi.org/10.48550/arXiv.2207.07726]

[31] M. Horton, *Deciphering ancient texts with AI.* NVIDIA Technical Blog, August 9, 2021. [Online]. Available: https://developer.nvidia.com/blog/deciphering-ancient-texts-with-ai/

[32] M. Agrawal, B. Chauhan, and T. Agrawal, "Machine learning algorithms for handwritten Devanagari character recognition: a systematic review", *J. Sci. Technol.,* vol. 7, no. 1, 2022.

[33] A.D. Mishra, and Y.B. Singh, "Big data analytics for security and privacy challenges", In: *international conference on computing, communication and automation, ICCCA* IEEE, 2016, pp. 50-53.
[http://dx.doi.org/10.1109/CCAA.2016.7813688]

[34] Y.B. Singh, A.D. Mishra, and P. Nand, "Use of machine learning in the area of image analysis and processing", In: *2018 International Conference on Advances in Computing, Communication Control and Networking (ICACCCN)* IEEE, 2018, pp. 117-120.
[http://dx.doi.org/10.1109/ICACCCN.2018.8748338]

[35] S.P. Yadav, and S. Yadav, "Image fusion using hybrid methods in multimodality medical images", *Med. Biol. Eng. Comput.,* vol. 58, no. 4, pp. 669-687, 2020.
[http://dx.doi.org/10.1007/s11517-020-02136-6] [PMID: 31993885]

[36] N. T. Linh, S. P. Yadav, D. P. Mahato, N. T. Linh, Ed., *Distributed Artificial Intelligence: A Modern Approach* CRC Press: Boca Raton, FL, 2020.

[37] R. Shad, A. Egon, and K. Potter, *Application of Artificial Intelligence in Deciphering Ancient Scripts and Languages,* 2024. Available from: https://easychair.org/publications/preprint/jNQt

[38] S. Gordin, "Reading & deciphering ancient writing systems with AI", *Open Access Government,* 2022.

[39] T. Sommerschield, Y. Assael, J. Pavlopoulos, V. Stefanak, A. Senior, C. Dyer, J. Bodel, J. Prag, I. Androutsopoulos, and N. de Freitas, "Machine Learning for Ancient Languages: A Survey", *Comput. Linguist.,* vol. 49, no. 3, pp. 703-747, 2023.

[http://dx.doi.org/10.1162/coli_a_00481]

[40] M. A. Rusho, and N. Hassan, "Pioneering the Field of Digital Archeology in Bangladesh", *OSF Registries,* 2024.

[41] R. Ding, X. Han, and L. Wang, "A Unified Knowledge Graph Augmentation Service for Boosting Domain-specific NLP Tasks", In: *Findings of the Association for Computational Linguistics: ACL 2023*, Toronto, Canada, 2023, pp. 353-369.
[http://dx.doi.org/10.18653/v1/2023.findings-acl.24]

[42] A. Ranjan, and M. Ravinder, "Data augmentation for blurred-text image deblurring using non-euclidean extrapolations", *Int. J. Inf. Technol.,* vol. 17, no. 4, pp. 2309-2320, 2025.
[http://dx.doi.org/10.1007/s41870-024-02334-7]

[43] R. Dabre, H. Shrotriya, A. Kunchukuttan, R. Puduppully, M.M. Khapra, and P. Kumar, "IndicBART: A pre-trained model for indic natural language generation", *arXiv preprint* arXiv:2109.02903, 2021.

[44] R. Shad, K. Potter, and A. Gracias, "Natural Language Processing (NLP) for Sentiment Analysis: A Comparative Study of Machine Learning Algorithms", *Preprints,* 2024.
[http://dx.doi.org/10.20944/preprints202410.2338.v1]

[45] S Bhuvaneswari, and K Kathiravan, "Enhancing epigraphy: a deep learning approach to recognize and analyze Tamil ancient inscriptions", *Neural Computing and Applications,* vol. 36, no. 31, pp. 19839-19861, 2024.

# CHAPTER 4

# A Deep Learning Approach for Geopolitical Entities Extraction from Indian Election Data

**Seema Shukla**[1,*] and **V N Shukla**[2]

[1] *Department of Computer Science & Engineering, Sharda University, Greater Noida, Uttar Pradesh, India*

[2] *Information Technology, Election Commission of India, New Delhi, Delhi, India*

**Abstract:** Named Entity Recognition (NER) is an essential task in Natural Language Processing (NLP) that enables the identification and classification of significant entities from unstructured text. In the context of Indian elections, extracting geopolitical entities such as states, districts, and parliamentary constituencies is particularly important for effective data analysis, interpretation, and decision-making. This chapter proposes a deep learning–based framework for geopolitical entity recognition in election-related textual data, combining Embeddings from Language Models (ELMo) with Bi-directional Long Short-Term Memory (BiLSTM) networks to capture both contextual semantics and sequential dependencies. To further enhance accuracy, a custom gazetteer of Indian geopolitical entities was integrated into the model, enabling it to leverage domain-specific knowledge and resolve ambiguities often encountered in election data. The framework was evaluated using a corpus of over 50,000 words derived from official documents published by the Election Commission of India. Experimental results demonstrate that incorporating deep contextual embeddings alongside gazetteer-based features significantly improves the model's ability to identify and classify entities compared to baseline approaches. This study not only highlights the importance of combining neural architectures with curated domain knowledge but also lays the foundation for more accurate text mining and information retrieval systems in the electoral domain. The proposed methodology can serve as a reliable tool for political analysts, researchers, and policymakers who seek to derive insights from large-scale electoral data. Future directions include extending the approach to recognize other domain-specific entities and refining gazetteer integration techniques to further boost generalizability and robustness across varied datasets.

**Keywords:** BiLSTM for NER, Deep learning for NER, ELMo word representation, Gazetteer, Geopolitical entities (GPEs), Indian Election domain text, Information retrieval, Named entity recognition, Natural language processing, NLP, Text mining.

* **Correspondence Author Seema Shukla:** Department of Computer Science & Engineering, Sharda University, Greater Noida, Uttar Pradesh, India; E-mail: seemashukla@gmail.com

**Ravinder M., Arti Ranjan, Youddha Beer Singh (Eds.)**

## INTRODUCTION

The standards of Indian elections are considered to be among the highest across the world. The Indian constitution elaborates Indian democracy as a federal structure, with Parliament as the central government and assemblies as provincial governments, known as State Governments in the Indian context. Some named entities that appear frequently in texts related to Indian elections include voters, candidates contesting elections, constituencies, etc. At times, NEs are not single words but chunks of words containing stop words like "Andaman and Nicobar Islands." The context of named entities in a sentence plays an important role in their appropriate understanding. It is important, since the motto of the Election Commission of India – an autonomous body responsible for the conduct and administration of elections in India – is to ensure free, fair, transparent, and inclusive elections. Therefore, besides names, the extraction of GPEs is also significant.

NER is a part of NLP that can extract named entities from a text for categorization into different types. These entities can be anything ranging from the names of people, organizations, and locations to temporal entities such as dates and times, to numerical entities like quantities and monetary values, and many more. It helps many businesses and organizations to find insights from large unstructured datasets [1]. It is one of the important steps for extracting information to facilitate the conversion of information present as unstructured text into structured data, for example, data in a relational database. NER has applications in many NLP tasks such as information retrieval [2], machine translation [2], question answering [3], and sentiment analysis [4, 5]. An NER system takes text data as input and finds and tags each entity in the text as the appropriate type of named entity, depending on the text data domain. For example, while classes such as diagnosis, disease, medicine, etc. may be appropriate for text in the medical domain [6], company names or mutual funds may be more suitable for financial documents [7]. Similarly, in the Indian context, 'New Delhi' and 'Sikkim' should be correctly recognized as GPEs. Over the past few years, advancements in deep learning have revolutionized NER systems, allowing for greater accuracy and flexibility across a range of domains.

Early NER models mostly relied on rule- and dictionary-based approaches, which required domain specialists and qualified linguists to create and maintain rule sets. However, the rules do not cover all language events, the creation process is too long, and this technique is less likely to be portable. NER, although being a fundamental NLP function, is hampered by the complexities that come with every natural language. Some of these challenges include ambiguity and abbreviations, the number of words or phrases written in different forms, and terms that are not often used these days or are domain-specific.

In the context of Indian elections, the need for accurate extraction of geopolitical entities (GPEs)—such as states, districts, and parliamentary constituencies—has become increasingly significant. Elections in India involve a complex interplay of geographical and political boundaries, making it essential to identify these entities correctly to facilitate data analysis. GPE extraction enables better insights into election trends, voter demographics, and constituency-level dynamics, providing valuable tools for researchers, policymakers, and election officials. However, the diversity and multilingual nature of Indian election data pose significant challenges for traditional NER systems. This chapter presents a deep learning-based approach to extract and classify geopolitical entities from Indian election-related texts. By leveraging Embeddings from Language Models (ELMo) for contextual word representations and Bi-directional Long Short-Term Memory (BiLSTM) networks for sequence encoding, the proposed model can accurately identify GPEs in election documents. Furthermore, to improve accuracy, a custom gazetteer of geopolitical entities was integrated into the model, enriching word embeddings with domain-specific knowledge about Indian locations and constituencies.

This chapter highlights useful methods for demonstrating the efficacy of combining deep learning techniques with gazetteer features to enhance NER performance in the Indian election domain. The model was evaluated on a corpus of over 50,000 words from the Election Commission of India's dataset, yielding encouraging results. By refining the NER process, this work opens new possibilities for automated text mining and information retrieval within the domain of Indian elections.

## APPROACHES FOR NER

### Rule-Based Approaches

Historically, NER systems were developed using rule-based approaches, where experts manually crafted grammars and dictionaries to recognize entities. While effective for specific tasks, these systems struggled with scalability and adaptability, especially in complex domains like elections, where named entities may include not just single words but phrases containing stop words and contextually significant terms. In a rule-based system, the programmer defines the rules based on the grammar of the language to detect named entities [8, 9]. For example, "Election Commission of India" is an organizational entity that consists of a noun phrase preposition noun phrase. Rules are defined for the recognition of named entities based on their syntactic structure. As text size increases, the rules become more complex. These rules not only need to be developed but also continuously and consistently updated, even with minor modifications in some cases, to ensure that variants are considered and identified [10, 11].

Because they make use of the features that are related to the language, rule-based NER Systems are thought to be very efficient. To achieve adequate accuracy, they rely on domain-specific characteristics. On the other hand, these systems have several disadvantages, including being extremely expensive, domain-specific, and non-portable. As a result, methods built for one domain cannot be utilised for another, causing academicians to shift their attention to machine learning-based methodologies.

**Learning Based Approaches**

As NLP evolved, the focus shifted towards machine learning methods that leverage annotated training data to automatically learn patterns for entity recognition. Early ML techniques, such as Conditional Random Fields (CRF) and SVM, provided improved accuracy by learning from labeled datasets, yet they still required extensive feature engineering, often dependent on domain expertise. These systems highlighted the importance of selecting relevant features that can effectively capture the nuances of named entities in varying contexts.

Machine learning approaches convert NER problems into classification problems [12], which are solved using supervised, semi-supervised, or unsupervised approaches. Supervised learning in artificial intelligence involves training a computer system using labeled input data to predict specific outputs. The model learns from this labeled data to recognize patterns and associations between inputs and corresponding labels, enabling it to accurately label new, unseen data. The NER problem is handled as a supervised learning problem, or more accurately, a sequence classification problem. There is a requirement for training data to enable supervised learning algorithms to work [13]. This procedure is time-consuming and labour-intensive since it requires that domain experts label NEs in text data. This labelled data is used to train the ML model, which can then detect and categorize named entities in unannotated or test data. In supervised learning-based NER systems, selecting the right features is critical. This model can discover patterns and classify positive and negative instances by recognising patterns that locate comparable data. Several approaches, such as Hidden Markov Models, Support Vector Machines [14], Maximum Entropy, and Conditional Random Fields [15] have been used for NER. Supervised learning methods are known to give good results. However, they depend on labelled data, without which these algorithms are unable to perform.

Semi-supervised learning methods deal with this deficiency of labelled data by making use of unlabeled data. This unlabeled data is selected from data that is classified with low confidence by some standard classifier proven to give high accuracy [16].

Unsupervised learning is not commonly employed in Named Entity Recognition (NER). When used, it often incorporates elements of partial supervision. Popular unsupervised methods include clustering techniques and approaches based on association rules. For instance, some models classify named entities using only unlabeled data [17], while others combine a small-scale named entity dictionary with an unlabeled corpus to achieve classification through ensemble methods [18]. Unlike rule-based techniques, these approaches are more adaptable across domains and languages. Clustering methods, leveraging distributional statistics and contextual similarity, extract named entities from unlabeled data by grouping similar items. On the other hand, association rule-based methods focus on discovering relationships within large datasets. The motivation behind unsupervised NER methods is to overcome the lack of annotated data for various domains and languages. By utilizing lexical resources, patterns, and statistical analysis on extensive corpora, clustering-based systems can identify and group named entities effectively [19].

### Hybrid approaches

Hybrid approaches leverage the strengths of both learning-based and rule-based systems to enhance performance [20]. These methods integrate the outputs of multiple machine learning techniques or handcrafted rules to produce the final results. Researchers have proposed various hybrid NER systems over time. For instance, the combination of machine learning algorithms with post-processing methods has been applied for extracting biomedical entities [21]. Some language-specific NER systems use a blend of CRF, transformation-based learning, and rule-based approaches [22]. A classifier ensemble approach has been used to process data in Indic, while a mix of lexical resources, patterns, and rote-based learning has been employed for Turkish NER [23]. Studies indicate that hybrid systems tend to outperform standalone approaches in terms of accuracy.

### Deep Learning Approaches

Earlier machine learning methods, though initially successful, are only as good as their feature extractors. They are limited in their application to NLP tasks because they require a lot of domain expertise for feature engineering. Deep learning has come to the rescue of NLP researchers because of its ability to discover patterns in high-dimensional data [24]. A deep learning framework works by adding more layers and more units in each layer of an artificial neural network, providing it the ability to represent functions of high complexity. A sufficiently deep network has the ability to give a good performance if it is provided with a large training set [25]. Deep learning models use non-linear activation functions to discover features from textual data, leading to the development of NER systems that are successfully able to identify named entities.

DL models for NER can be categorized based on the representation of input sentences, type of neural network or encoder used, and the type of decoder used [26]. Artificial Neural Networks (ANNs) require input to be in the form of numerical vectors. To achieve this, distributional similarity-based methods are commonly employed to represent words from a large corpus as low-dimensional, dense real-valued vectors, with each dimension reflecting a latent feature. These representations, learned automatically from text using unsupervised models, capture both semantic and syntactic properties of the words in the corpus [27, 28]. Such representations can be at the word or character level. Additionally, some researchers have enriched these distributed representations by incorporating features like lexical similarity [29] and linguistic dependency [30]. Including features derived from a gazetteer in word representations has also been proposed [31, 32]. A gazetteer includes words and chunks of words that are well-known named entities.

NER is essentially a sequence labelling task for which, for obvious reasons, the most widely used ANNs are variants of recurrent Neural Networks (RNNs), such as LSTM networks and CNNs. Some popular choices for the decoder, which is the tagging layer that produces a sequence of tags representing the Named Entity Class of the text, are the softmax function (with a Multilayer Perceptron) and CRF [33]. In one of the first proposed uses of Deep Neural Networks for various NLP tasks, including NER [34], a CNN-based architecture was used over a sentence. After that, a number of researchers have proposed further improvements, such as a bidirectional LSTM Neural Network [35] and using additional bidirectional LSTMs instead of character-level features [36]. One of the most notable variations proposed is the use of CRF at the tagging layer.

In recent years, research on domain-specific Named Entity Recognition (NER) has made significant strides, particularly with the integration of advanced deep learning techniques. For instance, a study [37] explored the application of metric learning to improve NER in life sciences, highlighting how knowledge transfer between domains can enhance model performance while reducing mislabeling risks. Another approach introduced fine-grained multimodal NER, for leveraging textual and visual information to achieve superior entity classification, particularly in complex documents [38]. Furthermore, the emergence of pre-trained models like BioBERT, tailored for biomedical texts, proves that fine-tuning of relevant datasets is able to effectively solve the problem of domain-specific NER [39]. These advancements underscore the importance of specialized NER systems that can navigate the intricacies of specific domains, providing valuable tools for real-world applications in healthcare, finance, and other sectors

Although researchers have proposed deep learning models for NER in some Indian languages [40, 41] and created gazetteers for Indian languages [42], models and datasets for English-language text in the Indian domain are very few, which is the primary motivation behind this work. In the context of Indian elections, the application of NER has gained traction due to the unique characteristics of electoral data, including a diverse array of geopolitical entities. Recent studies have explored various methodologies for NER in election-related texts, focusing on specific challenges such as the identification of constituency names and political organizations. For instance, a hybrid approach to machine learning with rule-based systems has shown promise in recognizing entities from regional languages, emphasizing the need for tailored solutions in multilingual settings. While several models have been proposed for NER in Indian languages, there remains a significant gap in research focusing on comprehensive NER systems that effectively integrate deep learning techniques with domain-specific knowledge. Another approach to improve NER in the domain of Indian Elections is to develop a framework for generating a domain-specific corpus that enables NER models to classify named entities into domain-specific categories [43].

This chapter aims to show that the problem of domain-specific NER can be solved by using a robust deep learning model for extracting geopolitical entities from Indian election data. By incorporating a custom gazetteer that lists relevant geographical and political entities, the proposed approach enhances the models accuracy and applicability to real-world election scenarios. Through this work, we not only contribute to the growing body of knowledge in NER but also provide valuable insights into the intricacies of Indian election data, highlighting the importance of advanced NER systems in facilitating informed decision-making and analysis in the electoral domain.

## METHODOLOGY

The task of classifying geopolitical entities was carried out in three phases. The first phase consisted of building an NER model and categorization of text from the Indian Election Domain into five NER types, *i.e.*, Geo-political, Organization, Cardinal, Date, and Person. In the second phase, a gazetteer for geo-political entities was created, and in the third phase, gazetteer features were integrated into the model to increase the accuracy of recognizing geo-political entities.

## Phase I – Initial Model Building Testing

In this work, Embedding from Language Models (ELMo) was used for distributed word representations, and Bi-directional LSTM was used as an encoder with Softmax activation function for the decoder. The model was trained on the CoNLL–2003 dataset.

The ELMo model, introduced by some authors [44], was utilized for word embeddings due to its ability to capture both the semantic meaning of words and their contextual nuances, for example, in terms of its connections with other words (*e.g.*, polysemy). Consider the two sentences "He has a sharp tongue" and "The knife has a sharp blade". The term "sharp" in the two sentences carries diametrically opposed meanings. ElMo model is able to capture this difference, whereas the earlier models were unable to do so. In effect, the embedding generated using ELMo, illustrated in Fig. (**1**), is a function of the complete sentence and has been proven to increase the performance of NER systems.

ELMo starts with building the non-contextual word representations using a CNN, which it feeds into two stacked LSTMs. Convolutional Neural Networks (CNNs), initially developed for image processing, have found applications in various natural language processing (NLP) tasks. They are particularly effective at capturing local patterns from the character sequences of individual input tokens. This process begins by mapping each character within a token to its corresponding character vector. The embedding matrix is then used to apply filters of various sizes to capture essential properties of nearby inputs. A max-pooling technique is used in the final phase of a CNN, to derive a single representative feature from all feature maps. Each word is then represented by concatenating the output characteristics, which retain the local information. To produce contextual embedding, this is then fed to the stacked LSTMs - one LSTM reads the sentence in the forward direction to produce an embedding based on the left context of the current word, and the other in the backward direction to produce an embedding based on the right context of the current word. Both these networks are trained separately based on the language model. The forward LSTM is trained on a forward language model given by Equation (1)

$$p(w_1, w_2, ....w_n) = \prod_{i=1}^{n} p(w_i \mid w_1, w_2, ...., w_{i-1}) \quad \textbf{(1)}$$

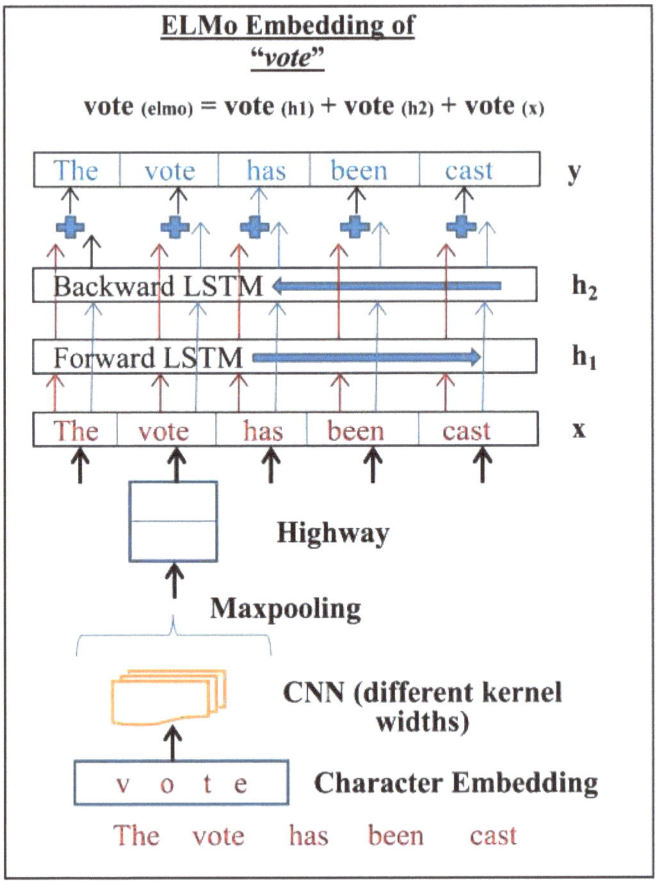


**Fig. (1).** ELMo embedding.

Where $w_1$, $w_2$, ….., $w_n$ are the sequence of words in a sentence, and the probability of the sentence is expressed as in equation (1), indicating that the i[th] word of the sentence depends upon its left context. The backward LSTM is trained on a backward language model, which takes into account that the probability of a word *w* in a sentence also depends upon the words that come after *w* as expressed by Equation (2)

$$p(w_1, w_2, \ldots, w_n) = \prod_{i=1}^{n} p(w_i \mid w_{i+1}, w_{i+2}, \ldots, w_n) \tag{2}$$

Thereafter, the forward and backward LSTMs are combined by jointly maximizing the log likelihood in both directions.

The final embedding is generated by calculating a weighted average of all the contextual and non-contextual word embeddings. The ELMo embedding $e_i$ for the $i^{th}$ word is thus given by the following equation (3).

$$e_i = \gamma c h_i^{char} + \gamma \sum_{j=0}^{L} f_j h_{i,j}^{for} + \sum_{j=0}^{L} b_j h_{i,k}^{back} \quad \textbf{(3)}$$

where $\gamma$, $f_j$ and $b_j$ are trainable parameters, and L is the number of layers.

The model was applied to Election Commission Manuals, which provide detailed information about various election functionaries. These manuals encompass guidelines on election management practices and insights from previous elections. Additionally, the Election Commission of India (ECI) offers several handbooks and guidebooks that cover election management procedures, case studies, political party dynamics, and processes within the Commission. The manuals used to test the model include:

- Manual of Model Code of Conduct: This manual by the ECI aims to educate individuals about the Model Code of Conduct, statutory instructions, relevant provisions, and selected court case details. An example is illustrated in Fig. (**2**).
- Manual on Electronic Voting Machine and VVPAT: This 4th edition manual by the ECI has been updated to reflect the universal implementation of VVPATs alongside EVMs. It provides an overview of the genesis and evolution of electronic voting.
- Manual on Polling Stations (2016): This manual outlines the ECIs procedures and guidelines related to polling station arrangements.
- Manual on Regulatory Audit (2016): It standardizes the application of audit policies and procedures nationwide, as specified by the ECI.
- Manual on Vulnerability Mapping (2016): This manual serves as a key component to ensure free and fair participation of voters in the electoral process.

These documents were in PDF format and were converted to text files and pre-processed as shown in Fig. (**3**). Text pre-processing is very crucial to transform raw data into useful information. The collected documents, which included headers, footers, and other non-relevant textual elements, were first preprocessed to transform the raw data into a more structured form. This preprocessing involved:

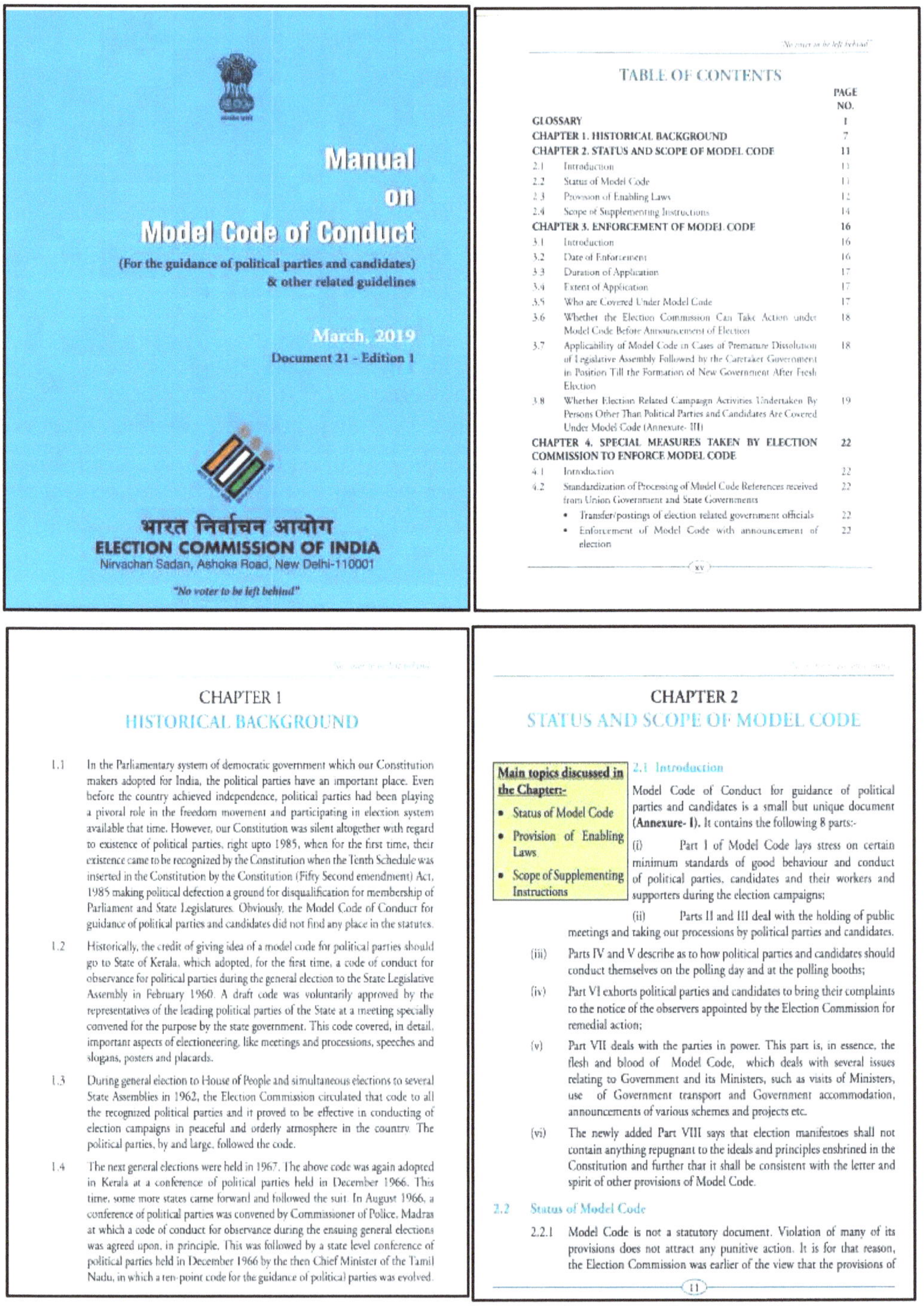

Manual on Model Code of Conduct

(For the guidance of political parties and candidates) & other related guidelines

March, 2019

Document 21 - Edition 1

भारत निर्वाचन आयोग

ELECTION COMMISSION OF INDIA

Nirvachan Sadan, Ashoka Road, New Delhi-110001

"No voter to be left behind"

"No voter to be left behind"

TABLE OF CONTENTS



xv

CHAPTER 1

HISTORICAL BACKGROUND

1.1 In the Parliamentary system of democratic government which our Constitution makers adopted for India, the political parties have an important place. Even before the country achieved independence, political parties had been playing a pivotal role in the freedom movement and participating in election system available that time. However, our Constitution was silent altogether with regard to existence of political parties, right upto 1985, when for the first time, their existence came to be recognized by the Constitution when the Tenth Schedule was inserted in the Constitution by the Constitution (Fifty Second amendment) Act, 1985 making political defection a ground for disqualification for membership of Parliament and State Legislatures. Obviously, the Model Code of Conduct for guidance of political parties and candidates did not find any place in the statutes.

1.2 Historically, the credit of giving idea of a model code for political parties should go to State of Kerala, which adopted, for the first time, a code of conduct for observance for political parties during the general election to the State Legislative Assembly in February 1960. A draft code was voluntarily approved by the representatives of the leading political parties of the State at a meeting specially convened for the purpose by the state government. This code covered, in detail, important aspects of electioneering, like meetings and processions, speeches and slogans, posters and placards.

1.3 During general election to House of People and simultaneous elections to several State Assemblies in 1962, the Election Commission circulated that code to all the recognized political parties and it proved to be effective in conducting of election campaigns in peaceful and orderly atmosphere in the country. The political parties, by and large, followed the code.

1.4 The next general elections were held in 1967. The above code was again adopted in Kerala at a conference of political parties held in December 1966. This time, some more states came forward and followed the suit. In August 1966, a conference of political parties was convened by Commissioner of Police, Madras at which a code of conduct for observance during the ensuing general elections was agreed upon, in principle. This was followed by a state level conference of political parties held in December 1966 by the then Chief Minister of the Tamil Nadu, in which a ten-point code for the guidance of political parties was evolved.

CHAPTER 2

STATUS AND SCOPE OF MODEL CODE

**Main topics discussed in the Chapter:-**

- Status of Model Code
- Provision of Enabling Laws
- Scope of Supplementing Instructions

2.1 Introduction

Model Code of Conduct for guidance of political parties and candidates is a small but unique document (**Annexure- I**). It contains the following 8 parts:-

(i) Part I of Model Code lays stress on certain minimum standards of good behaviour and conduct of political parties, candidates and their workers and supporters during the election campaigns;

(ii) Parts II and III deal with the holding of public meetings and taking out processions by political parties and candidates.

(iii) Parts IV and V describe as to how political parties and candidates should conduct themselves on the polling day and at the polling booths;

(iv) Part VI exhorts political parties and candidates to bring their complaints to the notice of the observers appointed by the Election Commission for remedial action;

(v) Part VII deals with the parties in power. This part is, in essence, the flesh and blood of Model Code, which deals with several issues relating to Government and its Ministers, such as visits of Ministers, use of Government transport and Government accommodation, announcements of various schemes and projects etc.

(vi) The newly added Part VIII says that election manifestoes shall not contain anything repugnant to the ideals and principles enshrined in the Constitution and further that it shall be consistent with the letter and spirit of other provisions of Model Code.

2.2 Status of Model Code

2.2.1 Model Code is not a statutory document. Violation of many of its provisions does not attract any punitive action. It is for that reason, the Election Commission was earlier of the view that the provisions of

11

**Fig. (2).** A sample document.

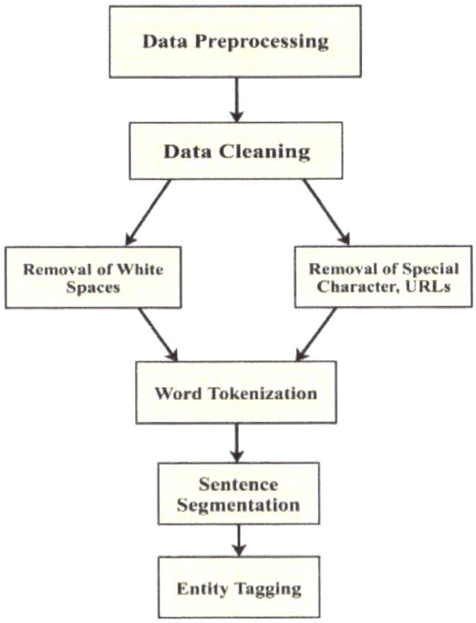


**Fig. (3).** Pre-processing of input text.

- Removing special characters, extra whitespace, and irrelevant content like URLs.
- Tokenizing the text into individual words or phrases for easier manipulation.
- Filtering unnecessary elements such as footnotes, page numbers, and tables that could interfere with the entity recognition task.

After pre-processing, the text was tagged using the model. The initial results obtained were not satisfactory. Some anomalies are shown in Fig. (**4**). After observation and analysis of incorrectly identified geopolitical entities, two major issues were identified, which are

- Some GPEs were incorrectly tagged (*e.g.*, a state tagged as ORG) and
- Some GPE entities are not recognized at all.

Fig. (**4**) shows a screenshot of the results obtained. Table (**1**) shows the statistics of incorrectly tagged GPEs from one manual, from which it can be observed that more than half of the GPEs were not tagged correctly, emphasizing the need to improve the results.

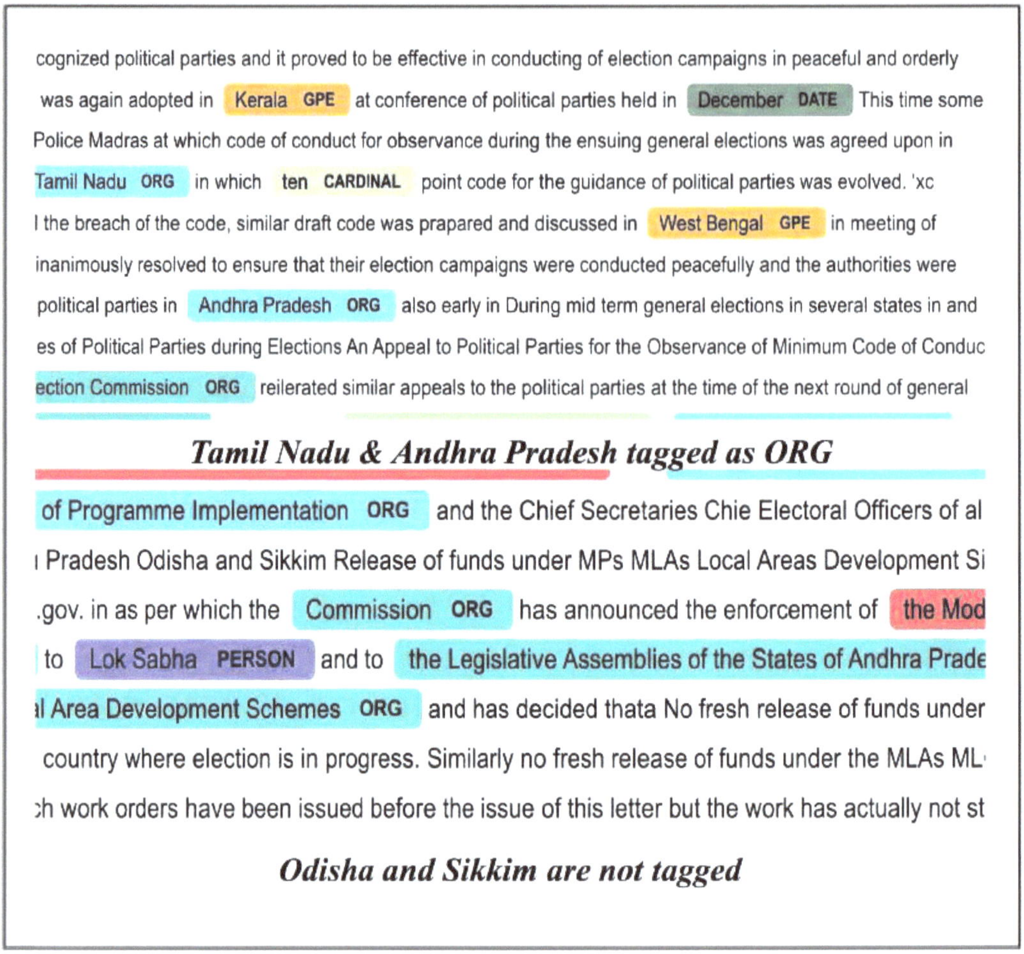


**Fig. (4).** Incorrectly tagged GPEs.

**Table 1. Statistics of incorrectly tagged GPEs from one EC manual.**

| No of Actual GPEs | No of Correctly Tagged GPEs | No of incorrectly Tagged GPEs | No of untagged GPEs |
|---|---|---|---|
| 297 | 143 | 134 | 20 |

## Phase II - Gazetteer Generation

In this work, the major focus was on increasing the accuracy of tagging geopolitical entities. To produce more accurate results, a gazetteer for geopolitical entities was created and incorporated into the model, as the use of gazetteers has been shown to increase NER accuracy (Magnolini *et al.*, 2019). A gazetteer is a compilation of entities belonging to a specific category. To enhance the input sentence embeddings, information regarding the presence or absence of a word or phrase in the gazetteer was integrated. Then, a gazetteer for geo-political entities (GPE) was created. The features from the gazetteer were added to the word embedding while tagging to generate the final tagged output. The methodology is illustrated in Fig. (**5**).

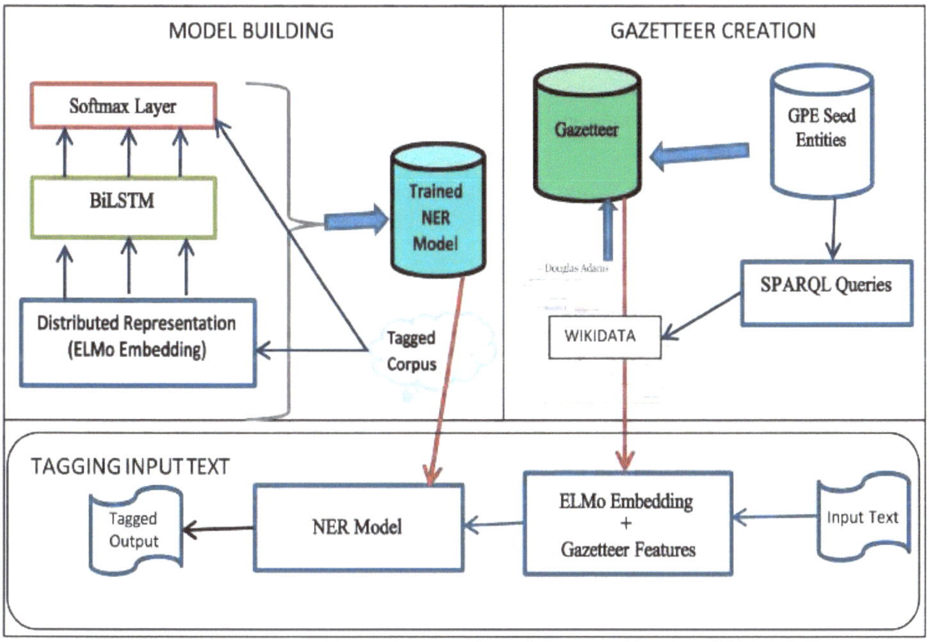


**Fig. (5).** Methodology.

For gazetteer generation consisting of GPEs, initially a seed list containing the names of states, districts, Lok Sabha (the lower house of the Indian Parliament) or Parliamentary constituencies (PCs), and Vidhan Sabha (The State Legislative Assembly) or Assembly constituencies (ACs) was downloaded from the Election Commission website.

It contained 36 states and union territories, 674 districts, 543 Lok Sabha constituencies, and 4129 Vidhan Sabha constituencies. This list was enhanced using SPARQL queries on Wikidata to retrieve aliases of the entries in the seed list (*e.g.*, UP may be used in texts instead of Uttar Pradesh).

Wikidata is a vast knowledge graph that undergoes collaborative editing, containing information sourced from and utilized by various Wikimedia projects. Each entry is labelled with a unique identifier (*e.g.*, Q1498 for Uttar Pradesh), as shown in Fig. (**6**), along with other information, such as a short description and aliases for the entry. Also, duplicate entries for districts were removed (*e.g.*, there is a district named 'Aurangabad' in Bihar as well as Maharashtra). This process resulted in a gazetteer containing 5405 entries, as shown in Table (**2**).

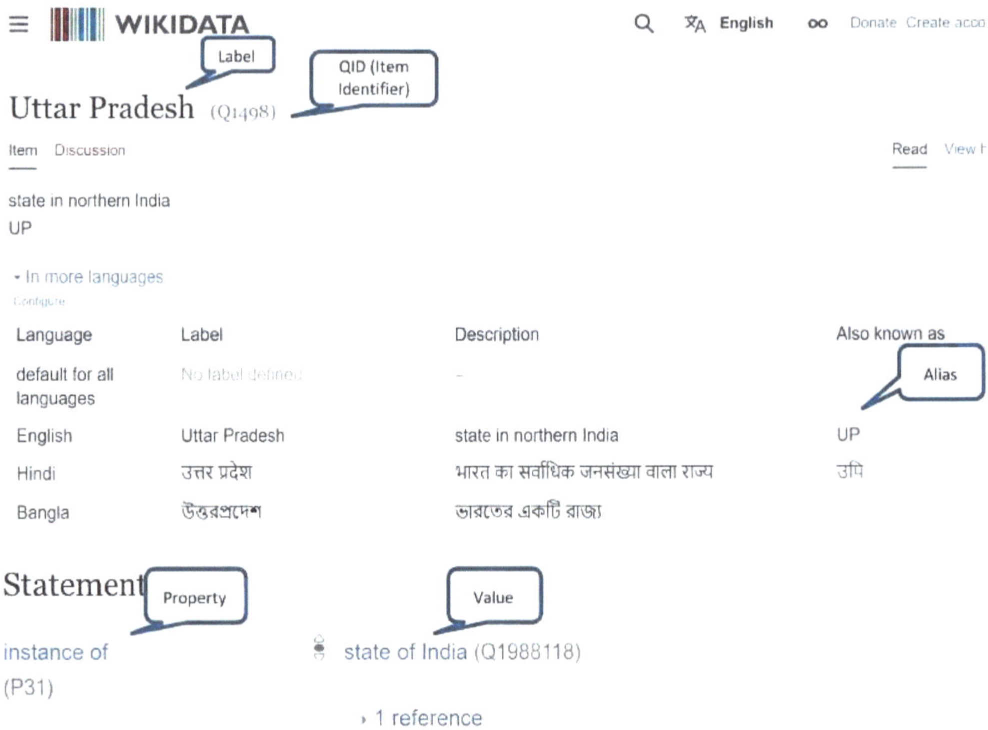


**Fig. (6).** Snapshot of wikidata.

**Table 2. GPE Gazetteer details.**

| Type | No of Unigrams | No of Bigrams | No of Trigrams | No of 4-grams | No of 5-grams | Total |
|---|---|---|---|---|---|---|
| States | 47 | 12 | 5 | 3 | 0 | 67 |
| Districts | 570 | 76 | 17 | 5 | 0 | 668 |
| PCs | 485 | 50 | 5 | 2 | 0 | 542 |
| ACs | 3581 | 499 | 46 | 2 | 0 | 4128 |
| **Total** | 4683 | 637 | 73 | 12 | 0 | 5405 |

## Phase III - Incorporating Gazetteer Features

The approach employed in this work involves generating one-hot vectors for each word in a sentence as gazetteer features. These vectors indicate whether a word or phrase is present in the gazetteer. This results in a sparse encoding, ggg, of length nnn, where each element ϵ{0,1}\in \{0,1\}ϵ{0,1}, and nnn represents the total number of entries in the gazetteer. 1 to 4-grams from the input sentences were matched with the longest geopolitical entries in the gazetteer, since, as evident from Table **2**, the gazetteer contains at most 4-gram entries. If a match is found at the $i^{th}$ entry, the $i^{th}$ element is set as 1, while all remaining elements are 0. Although the matching input phrase is clearly a GPE entity, this information is not passed to the BiLSTM. The reason is that the phrase may be part of another type of entity. For example, "Uttar Pradesh Assembly" is an ORG entity, and the model should not classify Uttar Pradesh in this phrase as a GPE entity. Instead, the gazetteer feature g is concatenated with the ELMo embedding of each token in the input sentence. The process of recognizing named entities after incorporating gazetteer features is illustrated in Fig. (**7**).

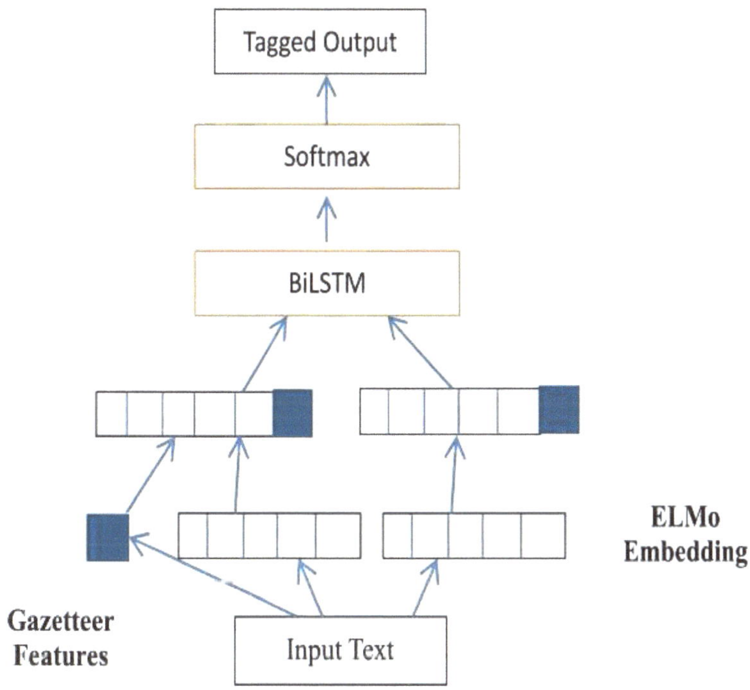


**Fig. (7).** Incorporating *Gazetteer* features.

## RESULTS

To assess the effectiveness of the proposed methodology, test textual data was sourced from various Election Commission-related platforms, including ECI Manuals, Wikipedia, the Official Website of the Election Commission of India (ECI), and Specialized Election Websites.

Five text documents were generated using the above-mentioned data sources, with each document consisting of approximately 8,000 to 10,000 words. All GPEs were identified manually in the documents by three domain experts separately. The domain experts also classified the actual GPEs into states, districts, PCs, and ACs. A phrase/ word was accepted as GPE of the classified type only if at least two of the experts >gave the same classification. The statistics of these documents are presented in Table (**3**).

**Table 3. Statistics of manually identified GPEs.**

| Document No | No of States | No of Districts | No of PCs | No of ACs | Total No of GPEs |
|---|---|---|---|---|---|
| 1 | 142 | 93 | 56 | 26 | 317 |
| 2 | 87 | 79 | 48 | 21 | 235 |
| 3 | 262 | 45 | 40 | 34 | 381 |
| 4 | 152 | 77 | 42 | 26 | 297 |
| 5 | 94 | 51 | 42 | 12 | 199 |
| **Total** | **737** | **345** | **228** | **119** | **1429** |

The NER model illustrated in Fig. (**5**) was trained using three standard datasets, namely, CoNNL-2003 [45], OntoNotes [46], and WikiGold [47]. These datasets were chosen because they are most closely related to the domain. Table (**4**) gives an overview of these datasets. The LOC entity type in these datasets was treated as the GPE tag.

**Table 4. Dataset statistics.**

| Dataset | Domain of Text | No of Tags | No of Sentences | No of Tokens | No of Entities |
|---|---|---|---|---|---|
| CoNLL03 | Reuters news | 4 | 22.1k | 301.4k | 35.1k |
| OntoNotes | Magazine, news, web, etc. | 18 | 103.8k | 2067k | 161.8k |
| WikiGold | Wikipedia | 4 | 1.7k | 39k | 3.6k |

An exact match approach was used for the evaluation of the proposed methodology of this work. An exact match means that a GPE is considered accurately labeled when the system correctly identifies an entity within a document, including the accurate type, start, and end points. NER models trained on the three datasets were employed to extract named entities from ten test documents. Additionally, the proposed gazetteer-based approach was applied to the same set of documents to extract geopolitical entities (GPEs). The results obtained were manually compared against the actual entities listed in Table **4**, with the outcomes presented in Table **5**. Standard metrics for evaluating

NER—precision, recall, and F1-score [10]—were calculated using the quantities of True Positives (TP), False Positives (FP), and False Negatives (FN) derived from the confusion matrix. An occurrence of an FP entity happens when an NER system identifies an entity that is not actually an entity. An occurrence FN is one when an entity is not recognized as an entity by an NER system, although it is one. An occurrence of a TP entity happens when an NER system identifies an actual entity as an entity. Table (**5**) shows the results of tagging and the confusion matrix.

**Table 5. Tagging results.**

| **Datas set** | **Type of GPE** | **Without Gazetteers** | | | | **With Gazetteers** | | | |
|---|---|---|---|---|---|---|---|---|---|
| | | **No. of Entities Correctly Tagged as GPE (TP)** | **No. of Entities Incorrectly Tagged as GPE (FP)** | **No. of Incorrectly Tagged GPEs (FN)** | **No. of Untagged GPE Entities (FN)** | **No. of Entities Correctly Tagged as GPE (TP)** | **No. of Entities Incorrectly Tagged as GPE (FP)** | **No. of Incorrectly Tagged GPEs (FN)** | **No. of Untagged GPE Entities (FN)** |
| CoNLL03 | States | 382 | 23 | 332 | 23 | 436 | 19 | 296 | 5 |
| | Districts | 212 | | 92 | 41 | 262 | | 76 | 7 |
| | PCs | 112 | | 70 | 46 | 164 | | 61 | 3 |
| | ACs | 66 | | 38 | 15 | 98 | | 18 | 3 |
| | **Tota l** | **772** | | **532** | **125** | **960** | | **451** | **18** |
| Onto Notes | States | 358 | 30 | 353 | 26 | 412 | 21 | 317 | 8 |
| | Districts | 198 | | 105 | 42 | 262 | | 77 | 6 |
| | PCs | 103 | | 74 | 51 | 152 | | 74 | 2 |
| | ACs | 67 | | 39 | 13 | 90 | | 25 | 4 |
| | **Tota l** | **726** | | **571** | **132** | **916** | | **493** | **20** |
| WikiGold | States | 369 | 32 | 345 | 23 | 412 | 32 | 318 | 7 |
| | Districts | 208 | | 98 | 39 | 262 | | 76 | 7 |
| | PCs | 104 | | 76 | 48 | 153 | | 71 | 4 |
| | ACs | 63 | | 41 | 15 | 97 | | 20 | 2 |
| | **Tota l** | **744** | | **560** | **125** | **924** | | **485** | **20** |

Subsequently, standard metrics such as precision, recall, and F1-score were calculated to evaluate and compare performance. Precision, as computed in equation (4), measures the proportion of the NER systems outputs that are correctly identified. Recall, as shown in equation (5), quantifies the proportion of total entities that the NER system correctly recognizes. The F1-score, the harmonic mean of precision and recall, is computed as shown in equation (6), combining both metrics into a single performance measure.

$$P = \text{Number of TPs} / (\text{Number of TPs} + \text{Number of FPs}) \quad (4)$$

$$R = \text{Number of TPs} / (\text{Number of TPs} + \text{Number of FNs}) \quad (5)$$

$$\text{F1-score} = (2 \times P \times R) / (P + R) \quad (6)$$

The precision, recall, and F1-score results are presented in Table (**6**).

**Table 6. Performance evaluation.**

| Dataset (with/ without Gazetteer) | Precision | Recall | F1-score |
|---|---|---|---|
| CoNLL03 [48] | 0.9711 | 0.5402 | 0.6942 |
| OntoNotes [49] | 0.9603 | 0.5080 | 0.6645 |
| WikiGold [50] | 0.9588 | 0.5206 | 0.6748 |
| CoNLL04 + Gazetteer [51] | 0.9806 | 0.6718 | 0.7973 |
| OntoNotes + Gazetteer [52] | 0.9776 | 0.6410 | 0.7743 |
| WikiGold + Gazetteer [53] | 0.9665 | 0.6466 | 0.7748 |

It can be seen from Table **6** that while the model trained on the dataset demonstrates proficient entity extraction, evident from high precision values, it exhibits low confidence, occasionally misclassifying the entity as a different type, which is evident from low recall values. This is often observed in domain-specific named entity extraction. When the gazetteer is included with the model, the misclassification or absence of classification of entities decreases, leading to a rise in the F1-score.

Fig. (**8**) illustrates the performance with and without the gazetteer. It can be seen that the inclusion of gazetteer features in the NER model results in significant improvement in the F1-score in all three standard datasets. An improved F1-score in Named Entity Recognition (NER) indicates that the models performance in identifying and classifying named entities has become better. It indicates that the model is becoming more effective at correctly recognizing entities because it is able to recognize entities missed by the initial model (without gazetteer features), thus minimizing false negatives, which increases the recall value of the model. A higher F1-score indicates that the proposed NER model strikes a better balance between precision and recall, leading to enhanced overall performance in extracting named entities from the text.

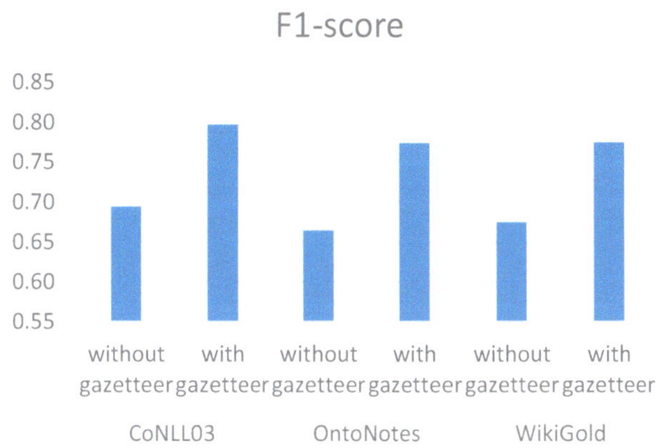


**Fig. (8).** F1-scores with and without gazetteer.

## CONCLUSION

In conclusion, this chapter highlights the effectiveness of combining deep learning techniques with a custom-built gazetteer for Named Entity Recognition (NER) in the context of Indian election data. By leveraging ELMo embeddings for word representation and BiLSTM networks for sequence encoding, the model demonstrated significant accuracy in extracting and classifying geopolitical entities such as states, districts, and constituencies. The integration of the gazetteer enhanced the models performance by incorporating domain-specific knowledge, as reflected in improved precision, recall, and F1 Scores across various datasets. Overall, this work contributes valuable insights into the application of NER in the Indian election domain, offering tools that can facilitate deeper analysis and more informed decision-making in electoral processes. In this chapter, the sparse encoding is $g \in N^{n X k}$, where k is the number of entity types in the gazetteer. This approach, however, may not work for nominal entities or noun phrases describing an entity such as "assembly constituency". For dealing with such entities, an ANN may be trained on gazetteers, and the output of such a classifier can be used as gazetteer features. While the approach yielded promising results, it is essential to recognize its limitations. Gazetteers depend on pre-defined lists of named entities and may fail to capture newly emerging entities or those not included in the gazetteers. Additionally, the accuracy of the system is highly influenced by the quality and comprehensiveness of the gazetteers utilized. Future work could explore techniques to automatically update and expand the gazetteers to enhance the systems performance.

In summary, this chapter demonstrates the effectiveness of using gazetteers for named entity extraction from Indian election-related texts. The results indicate that gazetteer-based approaches can serve as a valuable tool for extracting named entities in domains where datasets may be unavailable. This approach can enhance tasks such as information retrieval, sentiment analysis, and trend analysis within the specific domain context.

## REFERENCES

[1] D. Jurafsky, and J. H. Martin, *Speech and Language Processing: An Introduction to Natural Language Processing, Computational Linguistics, and Speech Recognition* 3rd. Stanford University, 2026.

[2] B. Babych, and A. Hartley, "Improving Machine Translation Quality with Automatic Named Entity Recognition", In: *Proceedings of the 10th Conference of the European Chapter of the Association for Computational Linguistics (EACL 2003)*, Budapest, Hungary, 2003, pp. 139-146. [http://dx.doi.org/10.3115/1609822.1609823]

[3] D. Mollá, M. van Zaanen, and D. Smith, "Named Entity Recognition for Question Answering", In: *Proceedings of the Australasian Language Technology Workshop (ALTW 2006)*, Sydney, Australia, 2006, pp. 51-58.

[4] D. M. Bikel, S. Miller, R. Schwartz, and R. Weischedel, "Nymble: A High-Performance Learning Name-finder", In: *Proceedings of the Fifth Conference on Applied Natural Language Processing (ANLP)*, Washington, DC, USA, 1997, pp. 194-201.

[5] J.P.C. Chiu, and E. Nichols, "Named Entity Recognition with Bidirectional LSTM-CNNs", *Trans. Assoc. Comput. Linguist.*, vol. 4, pp. 357-370, 2016. [http://dx.doi.org/10.1162/tacl_a_00104]

[6] C. Wen, T. Chen, X. Jia, and J. Zhu, "Medical named entity recognition from un-labelled medical records based on pre-trained language models and domain dictionary", *Data Intell.*, vol. 3, no. 3, pp. 402-417, 2021. [http://dx.doi.org/10.1162/dint_a_00105]

[7] T. Repke, and R. Krestel, "Extraction and Representation of Financial Entities from Text", In: *Data Science for Economics and Finance,* S. Consoli, D. Reforgiato Recupero, M. Saisana, Eds., Springer: Cham, Switzerland, 2021, pp. 69-92. [http://dx.doi.org/10.1007/978-3-030-66891-4_11]

[8] D. Nadeau, and S. Sekine, "A survey of named entity recognition and classification", *Lingvist. Investiga.*, vol. 30, no. 1, pp. 3-26, 2007. [http://dx.doi.org/10.1075/li.30.1.03nad]

[9] V. Yadav, and S. Bethard, "A survey on recent advances in named entity recognition from deep learning models", *Proc. COLING 2018 – 27th Int. Conf. on Computational Linguistics,* pp. 2145-2158, 2018.

[10] J. Li, A. Sun, J. Han, and C. Li, "A Survey on Deep Learning for Named Entity Recognition", *IEEE Trans. Knowl. Data Eng.*, vol. 34, no. 1, pp. 50-70, 2022. [http://dx.doi.org/10.1109/TKDE.2020.2981314]

[11] A. Ranjan, and M. Ravinder, "Deep learning based image deblurring: A comparative survey", *Proc. 2022 4th Int. Conf. on Advances in Computing, Communication Control and Networking (ICAC3N),* pp. 996-1002, 2022. [http://dx.doi.org/10.1109/ICAC3N56670.2022.10074406]

[12] A. Mansouri, L.S. Affendey, and A. Mamat, "Named Entity Recognition Approaches", *J. Comput. Sci.,* vol. 8, no. 2, pp. 221-225, 2008.

[13] R. Collobert, "Natural language processing (almost) from scratch", *J. Mach. Learn. Res.,* vol. 12, pp. 2493-2537, 2011.

[14] Y.C. Wu, T.K. Fan, Y.S. Lee, and S.J. Yen, "Extracting named entities using support vector machines", *Lect. Notes Comput. Sci.,* vol. 3886, pp. 91-103, 2006.

[http://dx.doi.org/10.1007/11683568_8]

[15] F. Peng, and A. McCallum, "Information extraction from research papers using conditional random fields", *Inf. Process. Manage.,* vol. 42, no. 4, pp. 963-979, 2006. [http://dx.doi.org/10.1016/j.ipm.2005.09.002]

[16] W. Liao, and S. Veeramachaneni, "A simple semi-supervised algorithm for named entity recognition", *Proc. HLT-NAACL.* Boulder, USA, 2009, pp. 58–65. [http://dx.doi.org/10.3115/1621829.1621837]

[17] G. Wang, J.C. Ye, K. Mueller, and J.A. Fessler, "Image reconstruction is a new frontier of machine learning", *IEEE Trans. Med. Imaging,* vol. 37, no. 6, pp. 1289-1296, 2018. [http://dx.doi.org/10.1109/TMI.2018.2833635] [PMID: 29870359]

[18] S. Gorla, L.B.M. Neti, and A. Malapati, "Enhancing the performance of Telugu named entity recognition using gazetteer features", *Information (Basel),* vol. 11, no. 2, p. 82, 2020. [http://dx.doi.org/10.3390/info11020082]

[19] A. Goyal, V. Gupta, and M. Kumar, "Recent Named Entity Recognition and Classification techniques: A systematic review", *Comput. Sci. Rev.,* vol. 29, pp. 21-43, 2018. [http://dx.doi.org/10.1016/j.cosrev.2018.06.001]

[20] A. Ranjan, and M. Ravinder, "ROBDD-TrOCRBERTa: a novel robust-optimized blurred document text deblurring and completion with DCGAN-TrOCR and DistilRoBERTa", *Int. J. Inf. Technol.,* vol. 16, no. 7, pp. 4611-4619, 2024. [http://dx.doi.org/10.1007/s41870-024-02073-9]

[21] Z. Huang, W. Xu, and K. Yu, "Bidirectional LSTM-CRF models for sequence tagging", *arXiv preprint arXiv:1508.01991,* 2015.

[22] R. Jiang, R. E. Banchs, and H. Li, "Evaluating and Combining Name Entity Recognition Systems", In: *Proceedings of the Sixth Named Entity Workshop (NEWS 2016).* Association for Computational Linguistics: Berlin, Germany, 2016, pp. 21-27. [http://dx.doi.org/10.18653/v1/W16-2703]

[23] V Keselj, "Speech and language processing (second edition) by Daniel Jurafsky and James H. Martin", *Computational Linguistics,* vol. 35, no. 3, 2009. [http://dx.doi.org/10.1162/coli.b09-001]

[24] Y. LeCun, Y. Bengio, and G. Hinton, "Deep learning", *Nature,* vol. 521, no. 7553, pp. 436-444, 2015. [http://dx.doi.org/10.1038/nature14539] [PMID: 26017442]

[25] I Goodfellow, Y Bengio, and A Courville, *Deep Learning* MIT Press: Cambridge, MA, USA, 2016.

[26] Y. Shen, H. Yun, Z. C. Lipton, Y. Kronrod, and A. Anandkumar, "Deep Active Learning for Named Entity Recognition", In: *Proceedings of the 6th International Conference on Learning Representations (ICLR)*, Vancouver, BC, Canada, 2018.

[27] H. Liu, Q. Wang, P. Karisani, and H. Ji, "Named Entity Recognition Under Domain Shift via Metric Learning for Life Sciences", In: *Proceedings of the 2024 Conference of the North American Chapter of the Association for Computational Linguistics: Human Language Technologies (Volume 1: Long Papers).* Association for Computational Linguistics: Mexico City, Mexico, 2024, pp. 1-21. [http://dx.doi.org/10.18653/v1/2024.naacl-long.1]

[28] S. Magnolini, V. Piccioni, V. Balaraman, M. Guerini, and B. Magnini, "How to use gazetteers for entity recognition with neural models", *Proc. IJCAI 2019 - 5th Workshop on Semantic Deep Learning (SemDeep).* Macau, China, 2019, pp. 40–49.

[29] K. Nastou, M. Koutrouli, S. Pyysalo, and L.J. Jensen, "Improving dictionary-based named entity recognition with deep learning", *Bioinformatics,* vol. 40, suppl. Suppl. 2, pp. ii45-ii52, 2024. [http://dx.doi.org/10.1093/bioinformatics/btae402] [PMID: 39230709]

[30] A.K. Sangaiah, Ed., *Deep Learning and Parallel Computing Environment for Bioengineering*

*Systems.*. 1st ed. Cambridge, MA, USA: Academic Press (Elsevier), 2019.

[31] Y. Bi, B. Xue, and M. Zhang, *Genetic Programming for Image Classification: An Automated Approach to Feature Learning.* Springer Nature, 2021. [http://dx.doi.org/10.1007/978-3-030-65927-1]

[32] G. Park, H.G. Lee, and H. Kim, "Named entity recognition model based on neural networks using parts of speech probability and Gazetteer features", *Adv. Sci. Lett.,* vol. 23, no. 10, pp. 9530-9533, 2017. [http://dx.doi.org/10.1166/asl.2017.9740]

[33] G. Lample, M. Ott, A. Conneau, L. Denoyer, and M. A. Ranzato, "Phrase-Based and Neural Unsupervised Machine Translation", In: *Proceedings of the 2018 Conference on Empirical Methods in Natural Language Processing (EMNLP)*, Brussels, Belgium, 2018, pp. 5039-5049. [http://dx.doi.org/10.18653/v1/D18-1549]

[34] P. Patil, A. Ranade, M. Sabane, O. Litake, and R. Joshi, "L3Cube-MahaNER: A Marathi named entity recognition dataset and BERT models", In: *Proceedings of the 6th Workshop on Indian Language Data: Resources and Evaluation (WILDRE-6)*, Marseille, France, 2022, pp. 31-36.

[35] C. Häger, and H.D. Pfister, "Physics-based deep learning for fiber-optic communication systems", *IEEE J. Sel. Areas Comm.,* vol. 39, no. 1, pp. 280-294, 2021. [http://dx.doi.org/10.1109/JSAC.2020.3036950]

[36] S. Pradhan, A. Moschitti, N. Xue, H. T. Ng, A. Björkelund, O. Uryupina, Y. Zhang, and Z. Zhong, "Towards Robust Linguistic Analysis using OntoNotes", In: *Proceedings of the Seventeenth Conference on Computational Natural Language Learning (CoNLL 2013)*, Sofia, Bulgaria, 2013, pp. 143-152.

[37] R. Sharma, S. Morwal, and B. Agarwal, "Named entity recognition using neural language model and CRF for Hindi language", *Comput. Speech Lang.,* vol. 74, p. 101356, 2022. [http://dx.doi.org/10.1016/j.csl.2022.101356]

[38] S. Shukla, G. Ansari, A. Jaiswal, K. Gupta, P. Agarwal, and V. N. Shukla, "Framework for Generation of Annotated Corpus for Recognition & Categorization of Geo-Political Entities from Indian Election Domain", In: *Proceedings of the 2023 6th International Conference on Contemporary Computing and Informatics (IC3I)*, Gautam Buddha Nagar, India, 2023, pp. 633-638. [http://dx.doi.org/10.1109/IC3I59117.2023.10397648]

[39] Y. Wang, and C. Jiang, "Fine-grained multimodal named entity recognition with heterogeneous image-text similarity graphs", *Int. J. Mach. Learn. Cybern.*. Vol. 16, 2401–2415. 2025. [http://dx.doi.org/10.1007/s13042-024-02398-8]

[40] F. Mehryary, K. Nastou, T. Ohta, L.J. Jensen, and S. Pyysalo, "STRING-ing together protein complexes: corpus and methods for extracting physical protein interactions from the biomedical literature", *Bioinformatics,* vol. 40, no. 9, p. btae552, 2024. [http://dx.doi.org/10.1093/bioinformatics/btae552] [PMID: 39276156]

[41] A. Goyal, V. Gupta, and M. Kumar, "A deep learning-based bilingual Hindi and Punjabi named entity recognition system using enhanced word embeddings", *Knowl. Base. Syst.,* vol. 234, p. 107601, 2021. [http://dx.doi.org/10.1016/j.knosys.2021.107601]

[42] E.F. Tjong Kim Sang, and F. de Meulder, "Introduction to the CoNLL-2003 Shared Task: Language-Independent Named Entity Recognition", *Proc. 7th Conf. on Natural Language Learning at HLT-NAACL 2003.* Edmonton, Canada. vol 4, pp. 142–147. [http://dx.doi.org/10.3115/1119176.1119195]

[43] S. Gorla, S.S. Tangeda, L.B.M. Neti, and A. Malapati, "Telugu named entity recognition using bert", *Int. J. Data Sci. Anal.,* vol. 14, no. 2, pp. 127-140, 2022. [http://dx.doi.org/10.1007/s41060-021-00305-w]

[44] A.K. Shukla, "Analyzing the importance of Hindi literature and language to Indian society",

*Neuroquantology,* vol. 20, no. 21, p. 67, 2022.

[45] R. Salama, F. Al-Turjman, S. Bhatla, and S.P. Yadav, "Social engineering attack types and prevention techniques—A survey", *Proc. 2023 Int. Conf. on Comput. Intell., Commun. Technol. and Netw. (CICTN),* pp. 817-820, 2023.Ghaziabad, India [http://dx.doi.org/10.1109/CICTN57981.2023.10140957]

[46] R. Salama, F. Al-Turjman, P. Chaudhary, and S.P. Yadav, "Benefits of Internet of Things (IoT) applications in healthcare—An overview", *Proc. 2023 Int. Conf. on Comput. Intell., Commun. Technol. and Netw. (CICTN),* pp. 778-784, 2023.Ghaziabad, India [http://dx.doi.org/10.1109/CICTN57981.2023.10141452]

[47] S. Pradhan, "Towards robust linguistic analysis using OntoNotes", *Proc. 17th Conf. on Computational Natural Language Learning,* pp. 143-152, 2013.

[48] A.D. Mishra, and Y.B. Singh, "Big data analytics for security and privacy challenges", *Proc. Int. Conf. on Comput., Commun. and Autom. (ICCCA),* pp. 50-53, 2016. [http://dx.doi.org/10.1109/CCAA.2016.7813688]

[49] S. Rücker, and A. Akbik, "CleanCoNLL: A Nearly Noise-Free Named Entity Recognition Dataset", *arXiv preprint arXiv:2310.16225,* 2023. [http://dx.doi.org/10.18653/v1/2023.emnlp-main.533]

[50] SS Pradhan, and N Xue, "OntoNotes: The 90% solution", *Proceedings of the Human Language Technologies: The 2009 Annual Conference of the North American Chapter of the ACL, Companion Volume: Tutorial Abstracts,* pp. 11-12, 2009. [http://dx.doi.org/10.3115/1620950.1620956]

[51] D. Šuba, M. Šuppa, J. Kubík, E. Hamerlik, and M. Takáč, ""WikiGoldSK: Annotated dataset, baselines and few-shot learning experiments for slovak named entity recognition"", *arXiv preprint arXiv:2304.04026,* 2023. [http://dx.doi.org/10.18653/v1/2023.bsnlp-1.16]

[52] J. Kleb, and R. Volz, "Ontology based entity disambiguation with natural language patterns", *Proc. 2009 Fourth Int. Conf. on Digital Information Management,* IEEE., pp. 1-8, 2009. [http://dx.doi.org/10.1109/ICDIM.2009.5356769]

[53] C. H. Song, D. Lawrie, T. Finin, and J. Mayfield, "Gazetteer Generation for Neural Named Entity Recognition", In: *Proceedings of the 33rd International Florida Artificial Intelligence Research Society Conference (FLAIRS-33)*, North Miami Beach, FL, USA, 2020.

# CHAPTER 5

# An Efficient Remote Patient Monitoring: The Convergence of Blockchain and Artificial Intelligence

**Inderpreet Kaur[1,*], Mohammad Mudassir[2], Sanjay Kumar[3]** and **Kirti Seth[4]**

[1] *Department of Computer Science and Engineering, The Sharda School of Engineering and Technology, Sharda University, Greater Noida, Uttar Pradesh, India*

[2] *Support Engineer, Algorand Foundation, New York, USA*

[3] *Department of Computer Science and Engineering, Galgotias College of Engineering and Technology, Greater Noida, Uttar Pradesh, India*

[4] *School of Computer and Information Engineering, Inha University, Tashkent, Uzbekistan*

**Abstract:** With a notable trend towards remote patient monitoring (RPM), propelled by technological progress and the increasing demand for accessible, efficient healthcare solutions, the medical care landscape has undergone substantial changes. Blockchain and artificial intelligence (AI) are the core of this transformation, which collectively redefine RPM systems. This study investigated the combination of blockchain and AI, offering an innovative approach to improve patient care, data protection, and operational effectiveness. Blockchain technology ensures data integrity and privacy through a decentralized, immutable ledger, fostering transparency, secure information transfer, and seamless interoperability among health care platforms. AI algorithms deliver sophisticated analytics and predictive capabilities, enabling the real-time detection of health irregularities and tailored interventions. AI-powered RPM systems promote proactive healthcare, decrease hospital readmissions, and enhance patient outcomes by continuously tracking vital signs, medication compliance, and behavioral patterns. The merging of blockchain and AI has established a robust ecosystem that optimizes healthcare processes, diminishes administrative tasks, and reduces operational expenses. This integration encourages data-driven decision-making and preventive healthcare, laying the groundwork for a sustainable, patient-focused healthcare system. In summary, the integration of blockchain and AI into RPM represents a revolutionary advancement, addressing the evolving healthcare needs of the digital era and heralding a new era of innovation and accessibility in care provision.

**Keywords:** Blockchain technology, Healthcare evolution, Interoperability, Remote patient monitoring.

* **Corresponding author Inderpreet Kaur:** Department of Computer Science and Engineering, The Sharda School of Engineering and Technology, Sharda University, Greater Noida, Uttar Pradesh, India;
E-mail: Inderpreet.kaur@sharda.ac.in

**Ravinder M., Arti Ranjan, Youddha Beer Singh (Eds.)**

# INTRODUCTION

## Background and Literature Survey

From General-Purpose Blockchains to Decentralized Applications (DApps), the development of blockchain technology has opened the door to innovative and safe digital ecosystems. A blockchain functions as a distributed digital ledger that keeps track of transactions across several computers, guaranteeing the data's immutability.

This concept was first introduced in 2008 by an individual or group known as Satoshi Nakamoto, with its initial implementation in 2009 as a key part and requirement of Bitcoin transactions [1]. The following image (Fig. **1**) depicts the process of executing a transaction within a blockchain.

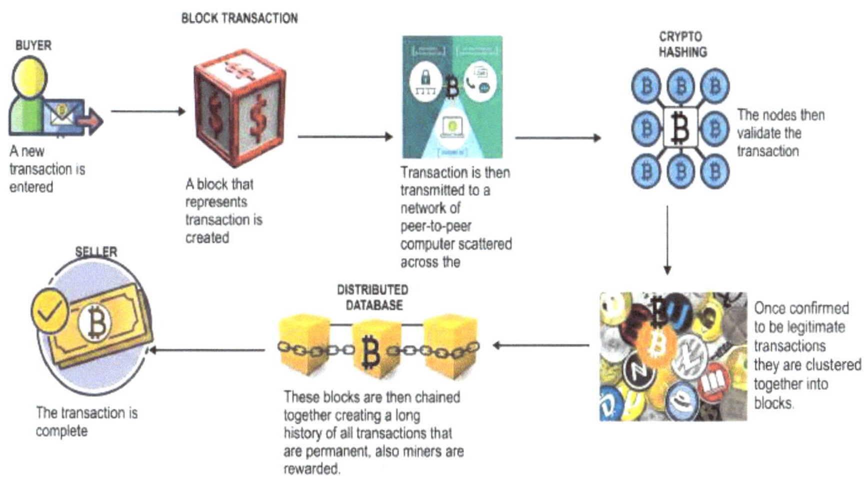


**Fig. (1).** Blockchain execution.

The healthcare industry has been transformed by blockchain technology, which offers a secure, decentralized, and transparent method for managing medical information. The following is an elaborate explanation of how blockchain functions in healthcare. (Fig. **2**) shows the flowchart for Blockchain in Healthcare, which illustrates the steps employed in the RPM. Protecting health information presents significant challenges.

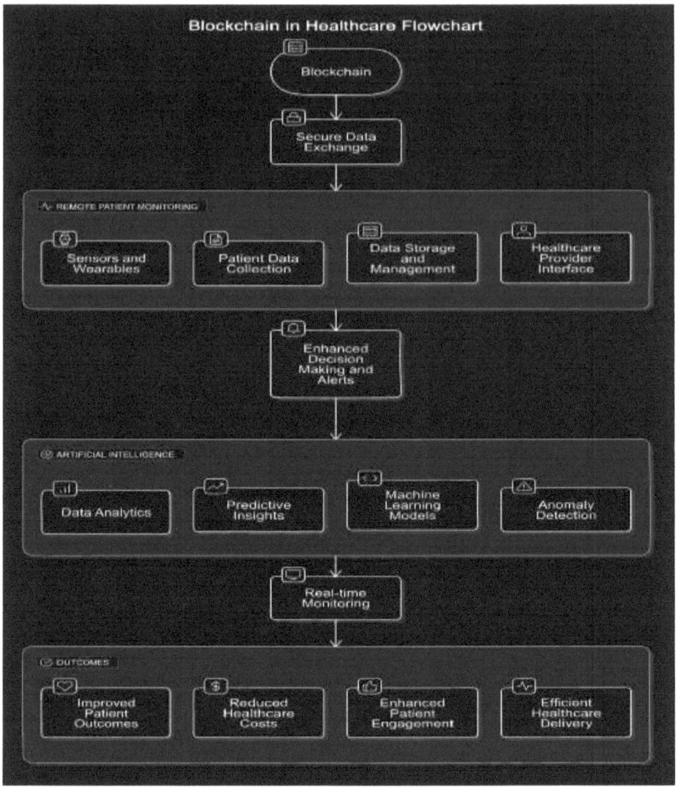


**Fig. (2).** Flowchart for Blockchain in healthcare.

In a study [2], the author has examined the incorporation of Blockchain and AI in telemedicine, highlighting their advantages and implementation hurdles. In a study [3], Taherdoost explored the fusion of blockchain and artificial intelligence technologies, concentrating on their joint applications. This Applied Sciences publication investigated the potential benefits and obstacles of combining these technologies. The research [4] offers valuable perspectives on automated systems that could be applicable for understanding AI and automation implementation in various fields, including healthcare. The authors [5] proposed a three-layered framework designed to enhance Medicare interoperability through intelligent, thoughtful, and strategic API-driven integration. In a study [6], the author delved into the convergence of big data and machine learning in healthcare, providing a comprehensive analysis of how these technologies are revolutionizing healthcare practices and decision-making processes. Another study [7] authors examined the effect of big data on organizational decision quality, stressing the significance of data quality and diagnosticity. Their research investigated whether high-quality data can enhance firm decision–making. In a study [8], the authors propose a secure electronic health record (EHR) system based on an attribute-based cryptosystem and blockchain technology to ensure confidentiality, authentication, and integrity of medical data, while supporting fine-grained access control. The research [9 - 11] investigates how blockchain and AI work together in healthcare systems, with blockchain providing secure data handling and AI offering predictive analysis and automation, creating a combined effect that addresses various healthcare issues. A framework proposed [12] employs blockchain to securely collect and store patient data from remote monitoring devices, aiming to boost data protection, safeguard patient confidentiality, and enable instant health tracking and response. Another study [13] examines how these technologies can resolve current limitations in telehealth services, such as data security, patient involvement, and system compatibility, providing an in-depth analysis of practical uses and future research areas. The work by some authors [14] focuses on using blockchain to protect sensitive patient information and maintain healthcare transaction integrity, discussing the technical aspects of implementing blockchain in healthcare systems and its benefits. In a study [15], the researchers evaluated potential blockchain applications in various e-healthcare areas, including patient data management, clinical trials, and health information exchange.

### *Patient Information Processing*

Data Acquisition: Medical information, including health records, care histories, and test outcomes, is gathered from diverse sources, such as medical centers, healthcare facilities, testing laboratories, and personal health devices.

Security Measures: Collected information is encrypted to safeguard patient confidentiality and ensure the protection of sensitive data.

### *Blockchain Infrastructure*

Distributed Record-Keeping: Encrypted patient information was incorporated into the distributed database. This database is overseen by a network of computer systems that confirms and logs data exchanges.

Agreement Protocol: Data give-and-take is verified through a consensus mechanism (such as Proof of Work or Proof of Stake). These kinds of protocols ensure an agreement that is network-wide, on the legitimacy of each exchange before its inclusion in the blockchain.

### *Information Verification and Block Generation*

Exchange Authentication: Network participants verify data exchanges by confirming the genuineness of the information and their adherence to predetermined standards.

Block Assembly: Upon verification, the exchange is combined with other confirmed exchanges to form a block.

Cryptographic Linking: Each block incorporates the cryptographic digital signature of the preceding block and establishes a sequence of interconnected blocks (a blockchain). This signature guarantees the consistency and inalterability of the blockchain.

### *Data Preservation and Administration*

Permanent Records: The newly formed block is appended to the blockchain, creating an unalterable record of the exchange. This means that, once recorded, the information cannot be modified or erased.

Shared Database: The Blockchain acts as a shared database and is stored across multiple computer systems. This decentralized approach ensures data redundancy and enhances security.

### *Blockchain Interface for Healthcare Providers*

Developing an effective blockchain interface for healthcare providers requires creating a user-friendly platform that enables seamless interaction with blockchain networks. This interface should incorporate various functionalities, including access to patient information, record modifications, authorization management, and additional features [16, 17]. The key components include a dashboard, patient record retrieval, data input and modification capabilities, permission controls, and audit and compliance tools. This interface aims to facilitate efficient patient data management, ensure regulatory compliance, and enhance patient care through a secure and accessible platform. The healthcare industry can create a safe, open, and effective system for handling and using patient data by implementing blockchain technology [18]. This will ultimately improve patient outcomes and streamline healthcare operations. The flowchart is shown in Fig. (**2**).

## REMOTE PATIENT MONITORING (RPM): AN OVERVIEW

The field of Remote Patient Monitoring (RPM) has seen considerable progress, spurred by technological innovations and a growing need for more effective healthcare delivery methods [19 - 21]. This technology allows medical professionals to track patients' vital signs, symptoms, and health markers in real-time, enabling swift detection of health irregularities or changes in condition. RPM facilitates early detection, enabling prompt medical intervention and modification of treatment strategies, thereby reducing complications and hospital stays [20]. Through continuous home monitoring of their health markers, those with chronic terrible conditions, including diabetes, high blood pressure, and various heart diseases can benefit from RPM. By providing regular feedback and support from healthcare teams, RPM encourages adherence to prescribed medications and lifestyle changes, leading to better management of chronic conditions. This approach is especially advantageous for older adults who may have complex health needs requiring frequent monitoring. RPM supports aging in place by providing continuous medical supervision without the need for repeated clinic visits. The field of RPM has recently experienced several advancements [21 - 23].

- **Wearable Technology Integration Wearable Smart Devices**: RPM has been transformed by the increasing use of wearable technology with sensors to track vital signs, including blood pressure, heart rate, and physical activity [24].
- **Ongoing Data Collection:** Outside conventional medical settings, wearable devices provide continuous monitoring of patients' health parameters, giving medical personnel access to real-time information. Growth of New Technology in Telemedicine and Telehealth: The COVID-19 pandemic has accelerated the adoption of RPM and telehealth, leading to expanded payment guidelines and government support [25].
- **Smartphone Apps:** Incorporating RPM features into mobile telehealth applications enables patients to remotely monitor their health and interact with healthcare providers.
- **Predictive Analysis:** AI methods analyze vast datasets generated by RPM to forecast health outcomes, identify anomalies, and tailor new treatment strategies.
- **Preemptive Care:** Early intervention and proactive healthcare management are made possible by ML models' ability to identify trends and patterns in patient data. Remote Monitoring of Chronic Health Conditions: RPM has expanded to encompass remote monitoring of chronic conditions like heart disease, diabetes, and high blood pressure.
- **Enhanced Results:** Improved quality of life, better patient outcomes, and fewer hospital admissions are all facilitated by ongoing monitoring and prompt intervention through RPM. Patient Independence and Participation Tools for Self-Care: By providing people with access to their medical records and encouraging proactive involvement in health care, RPM empowers patients.
- **Improved Dialogue:** Improved communication between patients and providers through RPM platforms improves patient satisfaction and care coordination.

## PATIENT-FOCUSED HEALTHCARE SYSTEMS

Establishing a sustainable healthcare system is essential. To ensure long-term effectiveness, accessibility, and quality in health services, this system leverages cutting-edge technologies and creative strategies [26, 27].

A key component of creating such a system is combining blockchain technology and artificial intelligence (AI) with remote patient monitoring (RPM). (Fig. **3**) shows the smart healthcare model. The following is a thorough analysis of how various technologies can be integrated to create a healthcare system that is more effective, transparent, and long-lasting [28, 29].

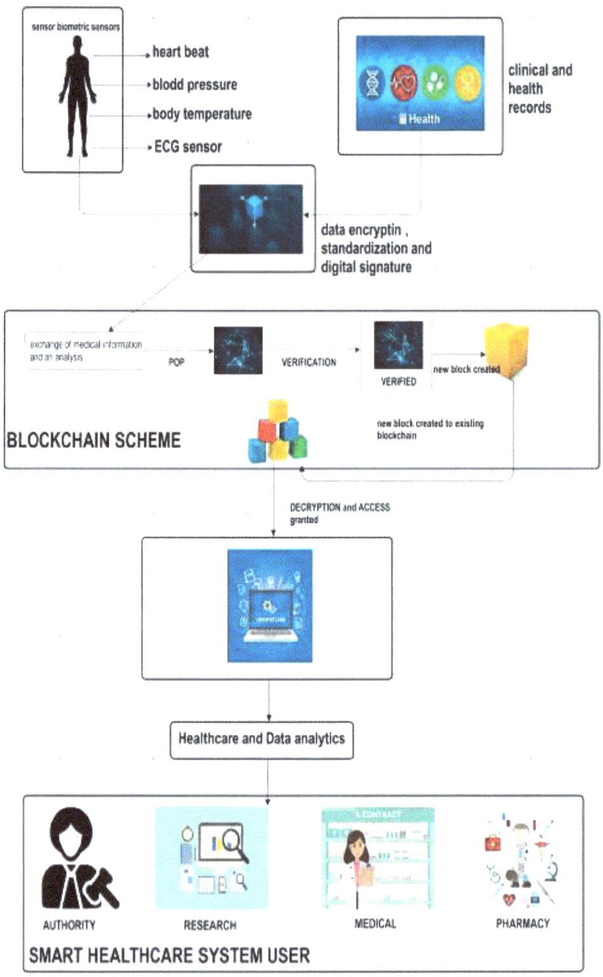


**Fig. (3).** Smart healthcare model.

### Data Management and Integration

AI has the potential to analyze large-scale healthcare datasets, identify trends, predict outcomes, and provide insights for personalized medical treatment. Machine learning algorithms can process electronic health records, medical imagery, and genetic data. The use of blockchain technology ensures the security, confidentiality, and integrity of healthcare information by creating a distributed, tamper-resistant database that logs and authenticates all data exchanges among participants. This method improves data precision and reduces the likelihood of fraudulent activities [30 - 32].

### Patient-Centric Care

Artificial intelligence facilitates the personalization of medical treatments, tailoring them to each patient's unique health history, genetic makeup, and lifestyle factors. This personalized approach has the potential to improve treatment outcomes and reduce unwanted side effects [33]. Additionally, the integration of blockchain networks into healthcare allows patients to take control of their health records, providing access to medical professionals when needed. This feature enhances the continuity of care and ensures a complete and accurate medical history is maintained.

### Operational Efficiency

Artificial intelligence has the potential to predict patient admissions, streamline workforce distribution, and improve the management of hospital resources. These functions contribute to shorter wait times, alleviate overcrowding, and increase overall operational efficiency. In parallel, blockchain technology can track the medical supply chain from start to finish, ensuring the genuineness of medications, minimizing the presence of counterfeit goods, and enhancing visibility throughout the supply process [34].

### Regulatory Compliance and Reporting

Artificial intelligence can monitor adherence to healthcare regulations, spot potential issues, and generate reports. This helps medical institutions avoid fines and improve patient safety measures. Meanwhile, blockchain technology creates and maintains an immutable record of all compliance-related actions and exchanges, making audits easier, safer, increasing transparency, and ensuring regulatory requirements are met. The inclusion of artificial intelligence and blockchain technologies can establish a more streamlined, open, and long-lasting healthcare framework, ultimately resulting in better patient outcomes and lower healthcare costs [35].

## Cooperation and Information Sharing

For AI and blockchain technologies to be used effectively for Remote Patient Monitoring (RPM), interoperability and data exchange are essential. Standard protocols ensure that different systems and hardware devices can communicate and share data easily. Here are some of the standard protocols and frameworks commonly used:

### *i. FHID (Fast Healthcare Interoperability Databases)*

Developed by HL7, FHID is a standard for exchanging important healthcare information electronically. It uses a set of resources and application interfaces to facilitate interoperability between different healthcare systems. In RPM, FHIR can be used to standardize the data exchanged between RPM devices, EHRs, and other healthcare systems, ensuring consistent data representation and communication [36].

### *ii. HL7 (Health Level Seven Protocol)*

HL7 provides a set of international rules for the transfer of diagnostic and administrative data between software applications used by various healthcare providers. In the HL7 standards, including HL7 v2 and HL7 v3, patient monitoring data can be structured and exchanged across different platforms [37].

### *iii. DICOTM (Digital Imaging and Communications in Telemedicine):*

DICOTM is a set of rules for handling, storing, printing, and transmitting information in medical imaging. In RPM, DICOM ensures that medical imaging data from RPM devices can be shared and accessed consistently and accurately by healthcare providers [38 - 40].

### *iv. IHE (Integrating the Healthcare Enterprise)*

IHE is an initiative that explores the coordinated use of established standards, such as HL7, DICOM, and others, to address specific clinical needs. IHE profiles can help ensure that different systems involved in RPM can work together effectively by providing guidelines for interoperability.

### *v. IEEE 11073*

IEEE 11073 is a family of standards for health informatics that facilitates interoperability of medical devices and systems. In RPM, these standards are particularly useful for ensuring that data from various medical devices used in RPM can be consistently communicated and understood by different systems.

### *vi. SMART on FHIR*

A collection of open specifications called SMART (Substitutable Medical Applications and Reusable Technologies) on FHIR is used to interface apps with portals, EHRs, and other health IT systems. The utility and usability of patient data are improved by RPM SMART on FHIR, which makes it possible to integrate AI applications with RPM systems and EHRs.

### *vii. Blockchain Platforms*

- **Hyperledger Fabric**

An open-source blockchain framework developed by The Linux Foundation, which was designed for enterprise use. In RPM Hyperledger Fabric, it can be used to create a permissioned blockchain network for secure and verifiable data exchange in RPM [41, 42].

- **Ethereum**

A decentralized platform that runs different conditions using smart contracts. In RPM, Ethereum can be used for creating smart contracts that automate and secure the exchange of RPM data.

### *viii. OMOP (Observational Medical Outcomes Partnership):*

OMOP provides a common data model (CDM) for standardizing the format and content of health data. In RPM, OMOP can be used to ensure that data from RPM systems are standardized, facilitating easier data analysis and AI integration [43, 44].

Implementing these protocols involves several steps:

- **Data Standardization:**
- Ensure all data collected from RPM devices follows a standardized format, such as FHIR resources or IEEE 11073 standards.
- **API Integration:**
- Use APIs, such as those provided by FHIR, to enable seamless data exchange between RPM devices, EHRs, and other healthcare systems.
- **Smart Contracts:**
- Implement conditions using smart contracts on blockchain architecture like Ethereum or Hyperledger to automate data sharing and ensure data integrity.
- **Security and Privacy:**
- Apply blockchain's encryption and authorization features to save patient data and comply with rules and regulations like GDPR and HIPAA.

- **Testing and Validation:**
- Conduct interoperability testing to ensure that all systems and devices can communicate effectively and that data is accurately exchanged and interpreted.
- By leveraging these standards and protocols, RPM systems can achieve high levels of interoperability and data exchange efficiency, thereby improving patient results, enhancing data security and privacy, and minimizing healthcare costs.

## CHALLENGES AND SOLUTIONS IN IMPLEMENTING RPM

Protecting patient data is critical, and RPM systems must comply with stringent regulations like HIPAA. They should implement robust encryption methods, ensure secure data transmission, and adhere to regulatory standards. Regularly update security protocols and conduct audits. Integrating RPM technology with existing Electronic Health Records (EHR) and hospital systems can be complex. Standardized APIs and interoperable systems to facilitate seamless integration should be used. Collaboration with EHR vendors can also streamline the process. Ensuring patients consistently use RPM devices and engage with the technology can be difficult. User-friendly devices and interfaces, training and support, and the use of motivational techniques such as reminders and gamification to enhance engagement should be included. Technical malfunctions and the reliability of RPM devices can impact the quality of monitoring. Choose high-quality, layered resilience devices, and establish a support system for troubleshooting. To guarantee optimum operation, perform routine maintenance and updates on the devices. High costs of RPM technology and unclear reimbursement policies can be barriers to implementation, so advocate for clearer reimbursement guidelines and make clear the cost-effectiveness of RPM in improving patient outcomes. Explore funding options and partnerships to offset initial costs. Cultural resistance and behavioral factors can hinder RPM adoption, so engagement with patients and communities to understand their concerns and provide culturally sensitive education and support should be included. The benefits of RPM to build trust and acceptance should be highlighted. Implementing RPM involves addressing several technical, logistical, and cultural challenges. By adopting comprehensive solutions, healthcare providers can overcome these barriers and successfully integrate RPM into their care delivery models, ultimately enhancing patient outcomes and efficiency in healthcare management.

## FUTURE TRENDS IN RPM, BLOCKCHAIN, AND AI

Remote patient monitoring (RPM) methods are evolving very rapidly, leveraging advancements in AI and blockchain to enhance healthcare delivery. Here are some key future trends in RPM that integrate these technologies:

### Advanced AI Personalization and Analytics

- **Analytics for Prediction:** AI algorithms will increasingly and rapidly use predictive analytics to identify unseen health problems before they become critical. By analyzing real-time data from portable devices and sensors, AI can forecast exacerbations of chronic conditions or predict acute events.
- **Personalized Health Insights:** AI will provide more personalized health recommendations based on individual health data, lifestyle, and genetic information. This enables tailored interventions and proactive care.

### Improved Interoperability and Data Integration

- **Unified Health Records:** Fusion of AI and blockchain will work together to integrate data from various sources (wearables, EHRs, mobile apps) into a unified patient record. Blockchain will ensure the integrity and security of this data, while AI will facilitate its analysis and interpretation.
- **Seamless Data Sharing:** Blockchain will enable secure, seamless sharing of health data across platforms and healthcare stakeholders, improving interoperability and care coordination.

### Decentralized Health Platforms

- **Blockchain-Based Health Platforms:** Decentralized platforms will allow patients to control, manage, and share their health records privately. Blockchain will manage authorization permissions and ensure data privacy, while AI will analyze data for actionable insights.
- **Smart Contracts for RPM:** Smart contracts will automate various aspects of remote monitoring, such as triggering alerts for specific health metrics or managing billing for RPM services based on predefined conditions.

### Improved Patient Engagement and Compliance

- **Instant Feedback:** AI will provide instant feedback to patients based on their health data, encouraging adherence to treatment plans and lifestyle changes. For example, if AI detects a trend indicating poor medication adherence, it can prompt the patient with reminders or educational content.
- **Blockchain-Based Incentives:** Blockchain can facilitate reward systems for patients who adhere to their treatment plans or achieve health milestones. This could be implemented through tokens or digital rewards.

### Enhanced Security and Privacy

- **Immutable Records:** Blockchain will provide immutable records of patient data, keeping its integrity and protecting it from unauthorized modifications or breaches. This will be crucial for maintaining trust in remote monitoring systems.
- **Secure Data Transactions:** AI algorithms will make sure that data transactions on the blockchain network are secure and are in compliance with regulations like HIPAA and GDPR.

### AI-Driven Remote Diagnostics and Decision Support

- **Remote Diagnostics:** AI-powered tools will assist in diagnosing conditions remotely by analyzing data from sensors and wearables. This can minimize the need for in-person visits and enable earlier intervention.
- **Decision Support Systems:** AI will provide decision support to healthcare providers by analyzing remote monitoring data and suggesting potential diagnoses or treatment adjustments.

### Integration with Telemedicine

- **Seamless Telemedicine Integration:** AI and blockchain will facilitate the integration of remote monitoring data with telemedicine platforms, allowing for more comprehensive virtual consultations and follow-ups.
- **Enhanced Virtual Consultations:** Real-time data from RPM systems will provide clinicians with up-to-date patient information during virtual consultations, improving the quality of care.

### Predictive and Preventive Care

- **Early Warning Systems:** AI will develop sophisticated early warning systems for detecting potential health issues based on patterns in remote monitoring data. This can enable timely interventions and preventive care.
- **Personalized Preventive Plans:** AI will use remote monitoring data to create personalized preventive care plans that target specific health risks and optimize wellness strategies.

### Automated and Efficient Workflow

- **AI-Driven Automation:** AI will automate routine tasks related to data analysis, reporting, and patient communication, streamlining workflows and reducing administrative burdens for healthcare providers.

- **Blockchain for Streamlined Billing:** It will automate and streamline billing processes for remote monitoring services, ensuring accurate, transparent transactions.

**International Exchange of Health Data**

- **Cross-Border Data Sharing:** Blockchain will enable the safe and effective sharing of health data across borders, promoting international cooperation and research in the management of global health concerns.
- **Global Health Networks:** AI will analyze global health data and records to identify the latest trends and patterns, contributing to better pandemic management and global health initiatives.

The involvement of AI and blockchain in remote patient record keeping and management will lead to a more efficient, secure, and patient-centric healthcare system. By leveraging these technologies, future RPM solutions will offer advanced analytics, improved data integration, enhanced security, and personalized care, ultimately leading to better health outcomes and more effective management of chronic conditions.

- Successful implementations of blockchain with AI in RPM
- Lessons learned from real-world examples
- Potential for scalability and wider adoption

## NEED FOR BLOCKCHAIN AND AI TOGETHERNESS

Blockchain technology and artificial intelligence (AI) have several potential synergistic advantages that can greatly improve a variety of businesses, including IoT, supply chain management (SCM), healthcare, and finance. (Fig. **4**) highlights three key aspects of healthcare: Role in Healthcare, Electronic Health Records (EHR), and AI Security, each emphasizing critical concerns such as privacy, protection, record management, and security controls. In modern healthcare, integrating Blockchain and AI is essential to effectively address these challenges. Privacy and protection of patient data are crucial, and Blockchain ensures secure, decentralized, and tamper-proof storage, while AI enhances security through intelligent monitoring and threat detection. In EHR management, where both total and current health records need secure access, Blockchain provides transparency and immutability, preventing unauthorized alterations, while AI extracts insights and automates diagnostic processes. Furthermore, as AI systems become integral to healthcare, their security must be tightly controlled to prevent data breaches and adversarial attacks. Blockchain can enhance AI security by creating verifiable and auditable decision-making processes, ensuring AI remains unbiased and tamper-resistant. The synergy between Blockchain and AI is crucial in building a trustworthy, efficient, and intelligent healthcare ecosystem, ensuring secure data exchange, privacy protection, and transparent healthcare advancements. Here are some reasons why combining blockchain technology and AI can be very beneficial:

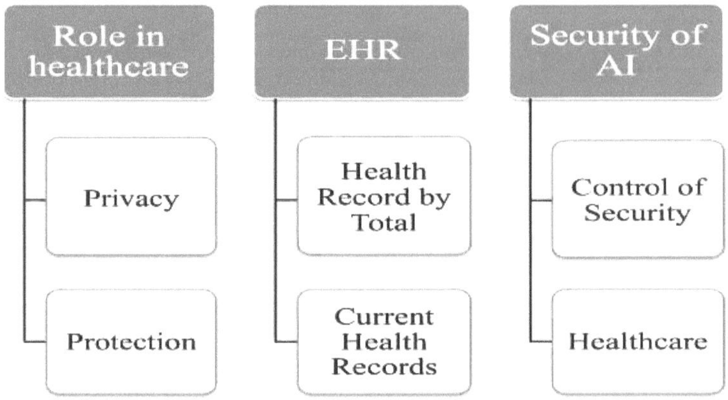


**Fig. (4).** Healthcare applications of fusioned blockchain and AI [4].

## Enhanced Data Integrity and Security

- **Immutable Records:** In telemedicine applications, electronic healthcare, and remote patient monitoring systems, blockchain can safeguard information exchange, ensuring that patient data is kept securely and accurately, and sent securely between medical personnel and devices.
- **Safe Data Sharing**: Blockchain's encryption algorithms ensure that information exchanged between AI systems and other parties remains secure, shielding critical and sensitive data from manipulation or unauthorized access.

## Improved Data Quality and Trustworthiness

- **Trusted Data Sources:** Blockchain technology ensures that AI algorithms operate on reliable, accurate data by validating and verifying the data's source. In sectors like healthcare and finance, where data quality is critical and cannot be compromised, this is particularly vital.
- **Transparent Audits:** Blockchain’s clear, auditable nature enables tracking of data values and changes, enhancing trust in the data used by AI models.

### Simplified Data Administration

- **Effective Data Integration**: Blockchain can combine data from multiple sources into a single, consistent dataset that AI can analyze to build more thorough, precise models.

### Enhanced Privacy and Compliance

- **Controlled Access:** Smart contracts on the blockchain ensure that only authorized people can access the patient records.
- **Regulatory Compliance:** Blockchain can provide data protection using regulations (*e.g.*, GDPR, HIPAA)

### Automation and Efficiency

- **Smart Contracts:** By interacting with blockchain smart contracts, artificial intelligence (AI) can automate and execute transactions or other procedures according to predefined criteria, minimizing human error and intervention.
- **Streamlined Operations:** By automating repetitive operations like data verification, contract execution, and compliance reporting, artificial intelligence (AI) and blockchain networks can optimize a number of corporate processes.

### Superior Decision-Making and Understanding

- **Data-Driven Insights:** Artificial intelligence can use blockchain network data to make predictions that drive decision-making. For example, Artificial intelligence algorithms can analyze financial transactions to detect patterns and predict market trends.
- **Real-Time Analysis:** Real-time blockchain data analysis is enabled by the integration, which provides timely insights and enables quicker decision-making.

### Fraud Detection and Prevention

- Immutable Records: By providing a verifiable history of transactions and data alterations, blockchain's immutable records help detect and prevent fraud.
- Anomalies Detection Powered by AI: AI can analyze blockchain data for anomalies, improving the ability to identify fraudulent activity and defend against threats.

### Increased Flexibility and Scalability

- **Scalable Solutions:** The decentralized architecture of blockchain enables scalable solutions that enable AI models to operate efficiently across distributed networks.
- **Flexible Integration:** The fusion of AI and blockchain provides easy ways for the integration of various technologies and systems, useful for changing demands and specifications

### Creative Use Cases

- **Decentralized AI Models:** Blockchain can support distributed AI algorithms, enabling collaboration and innovation.
- **Tokenization:** Blockchain can make it easier to create and manage digital assets, or tokens, that can be used with AI for a variety of purposes, such as rewarding data collaboration or granting access to AI-driven services.

### Collaborative Environments

- **Shared Data Ecosystems:** Blockchain enables the development of integrated ecosystems in which various stakeholders can safely access and contribute to shared data. AI can evaluate this aggregate data and produce insights that benefit all parties involved.
- **Interoperability:** For seamless data transfer, fusion of blockchain and AI can be used. It provides good interoperability and seamless data exchange.

## APPLICATIONS IN THE REAL WORLD AND CASE STUDIES

1. Medical records storage and Management: Electronic health records (EHRs) can be safely stored, used, and managed with blockchain technology, guaranteeing data privacy, confidentiality, and ease of access for all parties involved, including patients and healthcare providers.
2. Drug Traceability and Supply Chain: Blockchain promotes transparency and lowers the possibility of counterfeit medications by facilitating tracking of the whole pharmaceutical chain from medicine making to delivery, from production to distribution to merchants. Data can be safely stored on a blockchain to guarantee traceability, transparency, and to guard against data alteration or tampering.
3. Patient Consent Management: Blockchain improves privacy and control over patients' personal health data by allowing people to grant and manage consent for data sharing with stakeholders.
4. Telehealth and Remote Patient Monitoring: In telemedicine applications and remote patient monitoring systems, blockchain can safeguard information

exchange, guaranteeing that patient medical information is securely and accurately sent between medical personnel and devices.

## CONCLUSION

The fusion of blockchain and AI within Remote Patient Monitoring (RPM) is revolutionizing healthcare by creating secure, efficient, and patient-centered systems. This synergy allows for revolutionary improvements in disease management, preventive care, and patient involvement by fusing blockchain's strong data integrity and transparency with artificial intelligence's sophisticated analytical powers. Together, they pave the way for a future where healthcare is more connected, reliable, and responsive, unlocking new potential across diverse domains and setting a new standard for innovative health solutions.

## REFERENCES

[1] S Nakamoto, "Bitcoin: A peer-to-peer electronic cash system", *Bitcoin.org,* 2009. [Online].

[2] H. Taherdoost, "Blockchain technology and artificial intelligence together: A critical review on applications", *Appl. Sci. (Basel),* vol. 12, no. 24, p. 12948, 2022. [http://dx.doi.org/10.3390/app122412948]

[3] R. Salama, F. Al-Turjman, S. Bhatla, and S.P. Yadav, "Social engineering attack types and prevention techniques: A survey", *Proc. Int. Conf. Comput. Intell., Commun. Technol. Netw. (CICTN),* pp. 817-820, 2023.Ghaziabad, India [http://dx.doi.org/10.1109/CICTN57981.2023.10140957]

[4] M. Ghasemaghaei, and G. Calic, "Can big data improve firm decision quality? The role of data quality and data diagnosticity", *Decis. Support Syst.,* vol. 120, pp. 38-49, 2019. [http://dx.doi.org/10.1016/j.dss.2019.03.008]

[5] R. Salama, F. Al-Turjman, P. Chaudhary, and S.P. Yadav, "Benefits of Internet of Things (IoT) applications in healthcare: An overview", *Proc. Int. Conf. Comput. Intell., Commun. Technol. Netw. (CICTN),* pp. 778-784, 2023. [http://dx.doi.org/10.1109/CICTN57981.2023.10141452]

[6] M.Y. Jabarulla, and H.N. Lee, "A blockchain and artificial intelligence-based, patient-centric healthcare system for combating the COVID-19 pandemic: Opportunities and applications", *Healthcare (Basel),* vol. 9, no. 8, p. 1019, 2021. [http://dx.doi.org/10.3390/healthcare9081019] [PMID: 34442156]

[7] H. Wang, and Y. Song, "Secure cloud-based EHR system using attribute-based cryptosystem and blockchain", *J. Med. Syst.,* vol. 42, no. 8, p. 152, 2018. [http://dx.doi.org/10.1007/s10916-018-0994-6] [PMID: 29974270]

[8] S. Sai, V. Chamola, K.K.R. Choo, B. Sikdar, and J.J.P.C. Rodrigues, "Confluence of blockchain and artificial intelligence technologies for secure and scalable healthcare solutions: A review", *IEEE Internet Things J.,* vol. 10, no. 7, pp. 5873-5897, 2023. [http://dx.doi.org/10.1109/JIOT.2022.3232793]

[9] J. Hathaliya, P. Sharma, S. Tanwar, and R. Gupta, "Blockchain-based remote patient monitoring in healthcare 4.0", *Proc. IEEE Int. Conf. Adv. Comput. (IACC),* pp. 87-91, 2019. [http://dx.doi.org/10.1109/IACC48062.2019.8971593]

[10] H. Bansal, D. Gupta, and D. Anand, Blockchain and artificial intelligence in telemedicine and remote patient monitoring in *Handbook on Augmenting Telehealth Services*, 2024, pp. 279–294.

[11] R. Kaur, Mishra, M. Narwaria, and S. Saxena, "Opportunities and applications of blockchain for empowering tele-healthcare.*Advancements in Bio-Medical Image Processing and Authentication in Telemedicine.* IGI Global, 2023, pp. 111-126.
[http://dx.doi.org/10.4018/978-1-6684-6957-6.ch007]

[12] S.S. Rohini, and P. Sujatha, "Secure transaction approach in healthcare using blockchain", *Proc. Int. Conf. Emerging Trends Eng. Technol. (ICETET-SIP),* pp. 1-5, 2022.

[13] A.K. Deshmukh, Tyagi, H. Hansora, and S. C. Menon, "Applications of distributed ledger (blockchain) technology in e-healthcare. In: *Internet of Medical Things (IoMT) and Telemedicine Frameworks and Applications.* IGI Global, 2023, pp. 248-261.

[14] L.M. Udechukwu, O.M. Olaniyi, E.A. Oluyinka, O.O. Olateju, and R.O. Olasege, "Blockchain-enabled secure credentialing and access management for remote healthcare providers and patients across fragmented digital health platforms", *Asian J. Res. Comput. Sci.,* vol. 18, no. 11, pp. 18-31, 2025.
[http://dx.doi.org/10.9734/ajrcos/2025/v18i11776]

[15] H.S. Kazmi, "Trusted remote patient monitoring using blockchain-based smart contracts", *Proc. BWCCA,* pp. 765-776, 2020.
[http://dx.doi.org/10.1007/978-3-030-33506-9_70]

[16] A.D. Dwivedi, G. Srivastava, S. Dhar, and R. Singh, "A decentralized privacy-preserving healthcare blockchain for IoT", *Sensors (Basel),* vol. 19, no. 2, p. 326, 2019.
[http://dx.doi.org/10.3390/s19020326] [PMID: 30650612]

[17] K.N. Griggs, O. Ossipova, C.P. Kohlios, A.N. Baccarini, E.A. Howson, and T. Hayajneh, "Healthcare blockchain system using smart contracts for secure automated remote patient monitoring", *J. Med. Syst.,* vol. 42, no. 7, p. 130, 2018.
[http://dx.doi.org/10.1007/s10916-018-0982-x] [PMID: 29876661]

[18] A. Zhang, and X. Lin, "Towards secure and privacy-preserving data sharing in e-health systems via consortium blockchain", *J. Med. Syst.,* vol. 42, no. 8, p. 140, 2018.
[http://dx.doi.org/10.1007/s10916-018-0995-5] [PMID: 29956061]

[19] S.H. Han, J.H. Kim, W.S. Song, and G.Y. Gim, "An empirical analysis on medical information sharing model based on blockchain", *Int. J. Adv. Comput. Res.,* vol. 9, no. 40, pp. 20-27, 2019.

[20] A.T. Pãnescu, and V. Manta, "Smart contracts for research data rights management over the Ethereum blockchain network", *Sci. Technol. Libr.,* vol. 37, no. 3, pp. 235-245, 2018.
[http://dx.doi.org/10.1080/0194262X.2018.1474838]

[21] S. Wu, and J. Du, "Electronic medical record security sharing model based on blockchain", *Proc. Int. Conf. Cryptography, Security Privacy,* pp. 13-17, 2019.
[http://dx.doi.org/10.1145/3309074.3309079]

[22] K. Košťál, P. Helebrandt, M. Belluš, M. Ries, and I. Kotuliak, "Management and monitoring of IoT devices using blockchain", *Sensors (Basel),* vol. 19, no. 4, p. 856, 2019.
[http://dx.doi.org/10.3390/s19040856] [PMID: 30791392]

[23] H. Tian, J. He, and Y. Ding, "Medical data management on blockchain with privacy", *J. Med. Syst.,* vol. 43, no. 2, p. 26, 2019.
[http://dx.doi.org/10.1007/s10916-018-1144-x] [PMID: 30603816]

[24] S. Rahmadika, and K.H. Rhee, "Blockchain technology for providing an architecture model of decentralized personal health information", *Int. J. Eng. Bus. Manag.,* vol. 10, p. 1847979018790589, 2018.
[http://dx.doi.org/10.1177/1847979018790589]

[25] M. Awais, *"Energy efficient routing with void hole alleviation in underwater wireless sensor networks",* M.S. thesis, Dept. Elect. Comput. Eng., COMSATS Univ. Islamabad, Pakistan, 2019.

[26] A. Mateen, *"Towards energy efficient routing in blockchain-based underwater WSNs"*, M.S. thesis, Dept. Elect. Comput. Eng., COMSATS Univ. Islamabad, Pakistan, 2019.

[27] M. Naz, N. Javaid, and S. Iqbal, *"Research-based data rights management using blockchain over ethereum network"*, M.S. thesis, COMSATS Univ., Pakistan, 2019.

[28] A. Ranjan, and M. Ravinder, "ROBDD-TrOCRBERTa: a novel robust-optimized blurred document text deblurring and completion with DCGAN-TrOCR and DistilRoBERTa", *Int. J. Inf. Technol.*, vol. 16, no. 7, pp. 4611-4619, 2024. [http://dx.doi.org/10.1007/s41870-024-02073-9]

[29] H. S. Z. Kazmi, N. Javaid, and M. Imran, *"Towards energy efficiency and trustfulness in complex networks using data science techniques and blockchain"*, M.S. thesis, COMSATS Univ., Pakistan, 2019.

[30] M. Zahid, N. Javaid, and M. B. Rasheed, *"Balancing electricity demand and supply in smart grids using blockchain"*, M.S. thesis, COMSATS Univ., Pakistan, 2019.

[31] Z. Noshad, N. Javaid, and M. Imran, *"Analyzing and securing data using data science and blockchain in smart networks"*, M.S. thesis, COMSATS Univ., Pakistan, 2019.

[32] A. Ali, N. Javaid, and S. Iqbal, *"An incentive mechanism for secure service provisioning for lightweight clients"*, M.S. thesis, COMSATS Univ., Pakistan, 2019.

[33] A Ranjan, and S. M. Azeemuddin, "Image denoising using convolutional neural network", In: *Proc. ICAC3N*, , 2022, pp. 2315-2319. [http://dx.doi.org/10.1109/ICAC3N56670.2022.10074437]

[34] O. Samuel, "A blockchain model for fair data sharing in deregulated smart grids", *Proc. IEEE GLOBECOM.* (GLOBECOM), Waikoloa, HI, USA, 2019, pp. 1-7. [http://dx.doi.org/10.1109/GLOBECOM38437.2019.9013372]

[35] M. Rehman, N. Javaid, M. Awais, M. Imran, and N. Naseer, "Cloud based secure service providing for IoTs using blockchain", *Proc. IEEE Global Commun. Conf. (GLOBECOM),* pp. 1-7, 2019. [http://dx.doi.org/10.1109/GLOBECOM38437.2019.9013413]

[36] G. Srivastava, A. D. Dwivedi, and R. Singh, "Automated remote patient monitoring: Data sharing and privacy using blockchain", *arXiv.* preprint arXiv:1811.03417, 2018.

[37] S. Angraal, H.M. Krumholz, and W.L. Schulz, "Blockchain Technology", *Circ. Cardiovasc. Qual. Outcomes,* vol. 10, no. 9, p. e003800, 2017. [http://dx.doi.org/10.1161/CIRCOUTCOMES.117.003800] [PMID: 28912202]

[38] Y.B. Singh, A.D. Mishra, and P. Nand, "Use of machine learning in image analysis and processing", *Proc. ICACCCN,* pp. 117-120, 2018. [http://dx.doi.org/10.1109/ICACCCN.2018.8748338]

[39] G. Irving, and J. Holden, " How blockchain timestamped protocols could improve the trustworthiness of medical science", *F1000Res.,* vol. 6, p. 805, 2017.

[40] M. Mettler, "Blockchain technology in healthcare: The revolution starts here", *Proc. IEEE Healthcom,* pp. 1-3, 2016. [http://dx.doi.org/10.1109/HealthCom.2016.7749510]

[41] P. B. Nichol, "Blockchain applications for healthcare", *CIO,* 2016. Available from: https://www.cio.com/article/240485/blockchain-applications-for-healthcare.html

[42] G. Prisco, "The Blockchain for Healthcare: Gem Launches Gem Health Network with Philips Blockchain Lab", *Bitcoin Magazine,* p. 26, 2016.

[43] Y Sompolinsky, and A Zohar, "Phantom, GhostDAG: Two scalable blockDAG protocols", *IACR Cryptology ePrint Archive,* vol. 2018, p. 104, 2018.

[44] P Taylor, "Applying blockchain technology to medicine traceability", *Securing Industry,* 2016.

# CHAPTER 6

# Handwritten English Character and Digit Recognition using Deep Learning Techniques (CNN and SVM)

**Shradhanwita Mukherjee**[1,*] and **Sumanta Kuila**[1]

[1] *Department of Computer Science and Engineering, Haldia Institute of Technology, Haldia, West Bengal, India*

**Abstract:** Recognizing patterns in handwritten characters is challenging because each individual has a unique writing style. Nonetheless, this recognition field holds great promise across applications such as historical document digitization and accessibility enhancements for individuals with low vision. As a result, researchers highly prefer the Handwritten Character Recognition (HCR) field. Recently, using deep learning algorithms, the overall performance of HCR models has greatly improved. Our chapter proposes a CNN-SVM hybrid model for handwritten English character and digit recognition on the MNIST dataset. The major features of both classifiers are combined in this model. In our model, handwritten characters and numbers are automatically processed by the CNN's receptive fields to extract the most identifiable features. After extracting the feature, the data is classified using Support Vector Machines (SVMs) to determine the recognized alphabet or number.

**Keywords:** Convolutional neural networks, Handwritten character recognition, Hybrid model, MNIST dataset, Optical character recognition, Support vector machine.

## INTRODUCTION

HCR converts handwriting into data that can be studied further. HCR is one of the key machine learning topics being researched today. However, it remains one of the most difficult problems because each person's handwriting varies greatly and is inconsistent, making it extremely challenging to identify handwritten characters. Moreover, there may be a lot of noise in the scanned handwritten character image input. Despite these difficulties, identifying handwriting patterns can be helpful in many fields, such as historical document digitization, signature

* **Corresponding author Shradhanwita Mukherjee:** Department of Computer Science and Engineering, Haldia Institute of Technology, Haldia, West Bengal, India; E-mail: shradhanwita.r@gmail.com

**Ravinder M., Arti Ranjan, Youddha Beer Singh (Eds.)**

verification, and processing blank cheques. Therefore, researchers highly prefer the HCR field, which has been the subject of extensive research over the past few years. However, conventional methods had some drawbacks that prevented them from being more dependable. Common problems in scanned handwritten character recognition include similarity in handwriting, distorted shapes, or varying thicknesses. These problems increase

the uncertainty in the input data. Recent research has shown that deep learning algorithms work very accurately for the OCR process. By using deep learning methods, we can overcome these shortcomings, and extracting features becomes easier and more efficient [1].

There are two steps involved in identifying the characters. The handwritten characters are first scanned, and then the key elements of the supplied data are extracted using feature extraction. Subsequently, the characters are categorized according to the way the attributes extracted in Step 1 are categorized. A branch of machine learning called neural networks (NNs) is modeled after how the human brain functions. Neurons lay the foundation of the neural network by processing information and using cues from the biological neural network. Weights for inputs, biases, and connections make up the main components of a neural network. In a neural network (NN), every node is referred to as a perceptron [2]

In 1980, CNNs were first implemented, inspired by the architecture of the human brain. Because we have seen so many images of things as humans, we can identify stuff we have seen before, even as young children. Similar to one another, CNNs use the MLP architecture to analyze visual pictures as a kind of deep neural network. This suggests that every neuron within the layer is interconnected. The present study employs Convolutional Neural Networks (CNNs) to extract features from scanned handwriting inputs, achieving high character recognition accuracy. CNNs' ability to recognize patterns in photos makes them popular in the field of image categorization. CNNs, or feed-forward neural networks, operate on multiple layers. CNNs are more accurate at feature extraction and classification than other algorithms because they are composed of artificial neurons with the same capacity for optimization and learning as real neurons.

It requires very little preprocessing of input data and treats every pixel in an image as a feature during image classification. However, advancements in GPU and computational technology have made these tasks far more efficient [3, 4]. Fig. (**1**) represents the basic working principle of a Convolutional Neural Network.

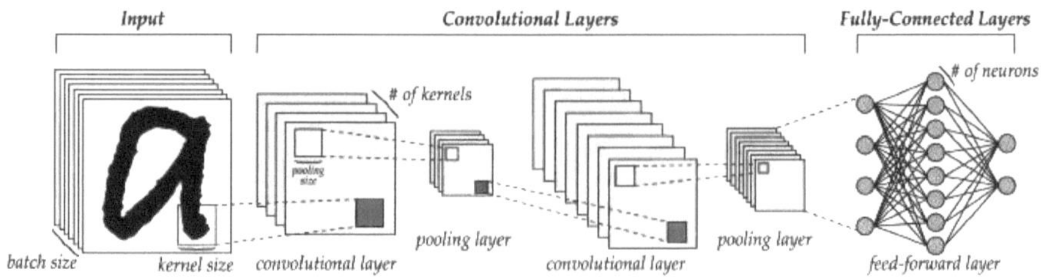


**Fig. (1).** Basic working principle of convolutional neural network [5].

Having the biggest margin makes a hyperplane optimal. Comparing kernel SVM and training time, linear SVM uses less memory and is more efficient. In order to classify data, linear SVM operates in the original spatial dimension. But sometimes linear SVM works better than kernel SVM, for example, when classifying documents or handling big datasets. We reduced computing time in our investigation by using a linear SVM as the final classifier. The handwritten character recognition (HCR) system was built using the suggested approach in our study. OCR research in computer science includes the recognition of handwritten characters.

## RELATED WORK

Many studies are being conducted in response to the widespread use of HCR in the present day. So, the model could be both far more dependable and efficient. S. Khan *et al.* [6] applied symbol identification to handwritten digits for machine learning classification. The character recognition system uses features such as temporal, statistical, and structural. A fuzzy model was used to implement the recognition system. Y. Boulid *et al.* [7] developed a model where, in the process, the character images are pre-processed, and the image components are categorized using different classification methods. N. Ahmad *et al.* [8] suggested OCR to extract specific highlights from an input image, which arranges its content to classify defined characters, such as letters and numbers. A recognition model that can identify both uppercase and lowercase letters, as well as handwritten characters in English, was presented there.

M. Askari *et al.* [9] represented the method for an image character that was a special implementation of Arabic character recognition. Here, comparisons were conducted using the Random Forest Classifier, K-Nearest Neighbors, and SVM. F. Sarvaramini *et al.* [10] implemented Convolutional Neural Networks to achieve promising results. High accuracy was obtained in the feature extraction and classification. M. A.A. Bhuiyan *et al.* [11]used a multi-resolution approach with their model. R. Tavoli *et al.* [12] addressed the recognition of handwritten Arabic characters. Here, image recognition uses a mean vector for an unknown pattern vector. K. S. Younis *et al.* [13], implemented learning rules using an ANN, which increases recognition accuracy. The product of generated recognition scores with Euclidean distances is used to implement the classification process.

Using distortion-tolerant template-matching approaches and a small amount of data, Toru [14] addresses the challenge of improving k-NN classification. It takes a long time to use the k-NN classification approach. A recognition model for identifying English handwritten characters, including letters, capital and lowercase letters, was proposed by Nasien [15]. An image character was represented using the Freeman chain coding (FCC) approach. A character image's boundaries are provided *via* a chain code representation, where the codes indicate the direction of the subsequent pixel. The FCC approach employs an 8-neighborhood, beginning with the directions 1 through 8. The features vector was constructed using the FCC, which was generated using a randomized process. The chain code that was transformed to 64 features serves as the feature criterion for entering the categorization. For the classification stage, support vector machines (SVMs) were selected. The experiment uses data from NIST databases.

Olarik [16] explored handwritten character recognition by leveraging local gradient feature descriptors, including the histogram of oriented gradients and the scale-invariant feature transform keypoint descriptor. The feature vectors of the handwritten images were extracted using these descriptors, and the images were then classified using machine learning methods. Specifically, support vector machines (SVMs) and k-nearest neighbors (KNN) were employed as classifiers.

The study evaluated these methods on three different language scripts—Thai, Bangla, and Latin—comprising handwritten characters and digits. Results indicated that local gradient feature descriptors significantly outperformed those based solely on raw pixel intensity values. Remarkably high accuracy levels were achieved across the Latin character and digit datasets, the Bangla digit dataset, and the Thai handwritten datasets when combining the proposed feature descriptors with the SVM classifier.

Mubarok [17] suggested using hierarchical graph matching to recognize handwritten characters. The underlying skeletal structure of handwritten characters was used to convert them into graphs. The extracted graph's edges were divided into distinct shapes, and the line-simplification approach was used to extract vertices from each edge. The graph's matching process was carried out hierarchically using subgraph isomorphism principles. Using a validated CEDAR dataset, the suggested method's performance was assessed, and it achieved a 93.40% recognition rate.

By comparing the manually computed values with those obtained using the suggested technique, Bautista [18] examined the precision and accuracy of the system. Solving equations and measuring accuracy was the final step. A database containing the distinct characteristics that correspond to each character was also built. Lei [19] described the current status of research on handwritten character recognition and feature selection challenges.

Using CNN and sample set expansion, Xuchen Song *et al.* [20] have also presented a method for recognizing Chinese handwritten characters. In order to train the network and improve accuracy, CNN, a deep learning approach, needs a lot of data. However, acquiring a sizable collection of high-quality Chinese characters is challenging. To extend the dataset without sacrificing its quality, the author proposed several strategies for dataset expansion. The accuracy of this approach was 94.7%.

A technique for enhancing the classification accuracy of handwritten Bangla compound characters was put forth by Akm Ashiquzzaman *et al.* [21]. This study proposed a technique that uses a greedy layer-wise training methodology with a Deep Convolutional Neural Network (DCNN). The two primary issues are vanishing gradient and overfitting. Dropout and Exponential Linear Unit (ELU) are used to address them, respectively. The accuracy of the suggested approach is 93.68%. In literature [22], the paper emphasizes the synergy between image processing, OCR, and NLP in overcoming the limitations of blurred image text extraction, particularly within the IoV ecosystem. It showcases the potential for integrating federated learning to enhance scalability and privacy in real-world deployments. LI Pengchao *et al.* [23] proposed a technique to decrease misclassification and increase recognition accuracy. Although character recognition has already achieved an accuracy of 0.95, occasional misclassifications still occur. A CNN with confidence estimation is recommended in this approach. The softmax function is applied to the CNN's last layers to determine confidence. This confidence is then compared to a predetermined threshold to accomplish error rejection. The mistake rate dropped to less than 2%.

CNN has experimented with a number of models to increase the recognition accuracy of deep learning techniques. The author emphasizes the synergy between image processing, OCR, and NLP in overcoming the limitations of text extraction, particularly within the IoV ecosystem [24]. It showcases the potential for integrating federated learning to enhance scalability and privacy in real-world deployments. The cascade technique is used to teach the network. Pre-training, relaxing weight initialization, and fine-tuning are all part of cascading training. At last, 96% accuracy is attained by the relaxation neural network. In a study put out by Ravinder M *et al.* [25], a radical extraction method is used to identify and categorize unusual Chinese handwritten characters. Characters are mostly characterized by radicals. It also extracts global features. The classification at the character level is finished, and a Radical Extraction Network is constructed. The technique yields an accuracy of 96.2%.

## TERMINOLOGIES USED IN TEXT EXTRACTION

### Optical Character Recognition (OCR)

When text is not available in an easily navigable digital format, it is very beneficial. OCR technology is applied in many areas, including data entry, text extraction from pictures, and document scanning. To recognize characters and words within an image, OCR software uses a range of techniques, including feature extraction, character recognition, image preprocessing, and post-processing to improve accuracy. The software recognizes text characters and converts them to digital form by analyzing their shapes, patterns, and other features. One of the many applications of OCR technology is the scanning and digitization of documents to produce editable digital text from printed materials [26]. Fig. (**2**) represents the basic handwritten character recognition (HCR) system. Text extraction from images involves removing text from pictures, like screenshots, scanned documents, and photos. Forms, invoices, and other structured documents can have their text extracted to automate data entry processes [27]. Handwriting recognition is the process of converting handwritten text into digital text. It is helpful for preserving historical documents and for digital note-taking.

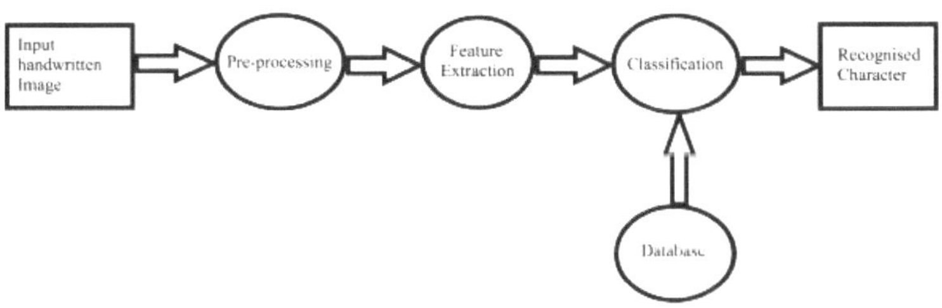


**Fig. (2).** A basic handwritten character recognition (HCR) system [26].

### Image Pre-processing

Creating an accurate handwritten character and digit recognition system requires effective image preprocessing. The preprocessing pipeline in this case consists of Gray Scaling, Binarization, Inversion, and Normalization. Every stage is essential to improving the consistency and quality of the input data.

### *Gray Scaling*

Grayscale image conversion is the first step in preparing color images. By reducing the three-color channels (RGB) to a single intensity channel, this transformation efficiently reduces computational complexity while simplifying the data. By reducing color information to a minimum, gray scaling helps ensure the model focuses on important aspects of character shape and structure rather than unimportant information for recognition tasks.

### *Binarization*

The thresholding technique sets pixel values below a threshold to black (0) and those over a threshold to white (1). By increasing the contrast between the foreground handwritten characters and the background, this procedure makes the characters easier for the model to recognize and interpret.

### *Inversion*

To invert the binary pictures, this step is performed. This involves flipping the color scheme such that the characters are white on a black background. This inversion aligns with the preferred input format of many neural network architectures, thereby improving feature extraction and recognition performance.

### *Normalization*

Pixel values are normalized to fall inside a predetermined range, usually [0, 1]. This is crucial for stabilizing and speeding up training by ensuring the neural network receives consistent input, leading to faster convergence and improved model accuracy.

## Dimensionality Reduction using LDA

Using a lower-dimensional space where the separation between classes is maximized, LDA projects the data. LDA alleviates the dimensionality curse by focusing on the most discriminative features, thereby improving computational efficiency and classifier performance. To handle high-dimensional data and ensure the most pertinent information is retained for the recognition task, this step is essential.

### Feature Extraction

Here, feature extraction involves locating and separating important visual structures and patterns—such as edges, textures, and shapes—from an image to enable a model to classify or recognize information more precisely and effectively.

Convolutional layers are the first step in the process; they apply multiple filters to the input image to extract important features, such as edges, textures, and patterns. Next, to reduce dimensionality and incorporate translation invariance, pooling layers, usually *via* max pooling, downsample these feature maps. This ensures that the network concentrates on the most prominent characteristics, independent of their position. The high-level features that the convolutional and pooling layers extracted are merged in the fully connected layers, which make up the last stage. By establishing connections between neurons in the preceding layer, these layers enable the network to acquire intricate, nonlinear representations and perform precise classifications. CNNs can effectively extract and use both low-level and high-level features by combining these layers, making them very useful for applications such as digit and handwritten character recognition. By using a multi-layered architecture, CNNs can accurately recognize and classify a wide range of inputs and capture the fine details required for accurate recognition.

### Classification

The process of classifying an input involves determining which category or class it belongs to, depending on its features. This is the process of teaching a machine learning model to identify patterns in labeled data so it can correctly classify new, unseen inputs. In a high-dimensional space, they operate by determining the best hyperplane to segregate data points belonging to various classes maximally. SVMs are adaptable and broadly applicable to a variety of classification problems because they can effectively perform non-linear classification using kernel functions.

## PROPOSED WORK

The MNIST dataset for digits and the Kaggle dataset for alphabets are two different datasets used. Several procedures are included in preprocessing to enhance the input data's quality, including Gray Scaling, Binarization, Inversion, Normalization, and Linear Discriminant Analysis (LDA) for dimensionality reduction. The aim is high character and digit recognition accuracy using an improved deep learning strategy. Fig. (**3**) represents the Model diagram.

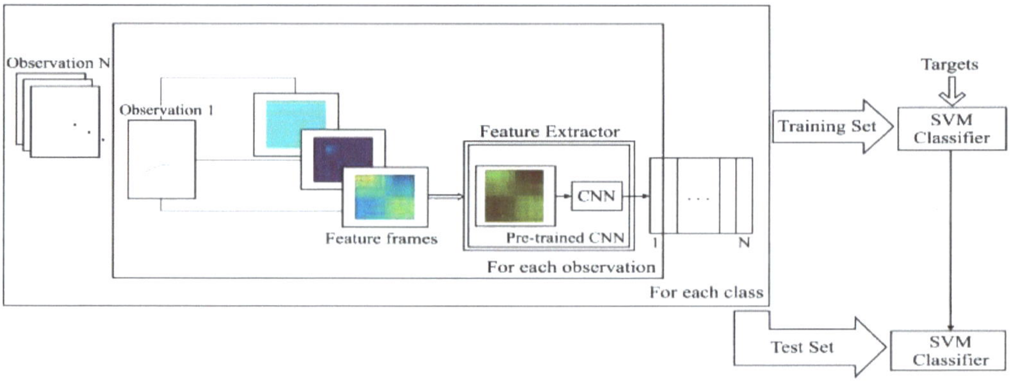


**Fig. (3).** Model diagram [26].

## Description of the Dataset

### *MNIST Dataset*

It includes 10,000 testing images of handwritten numbers (0–9) and 60,000 training images. Every image is a 28 x 28-pixel picture.

### *The Kaggle Dataset*

Includes a huge assortment of handwritten English alphabet characters (A–Z).

The size and format of images vary; thus, preprocessing is required to ensure uniformity.

## Steps in Preprocessing

### *Gray Scaling*

To focus on important elements and minimize computing complexity, convert all photos to grayscale.

### *Binarization*

Utilize a threshold to transform grayscale pictures into binary ones, thereby improving the contrast between the character's foreground and background.

### *Inversion*

To conform to the CNN model's format, flip the binary pictures so that the characters are white on a black background.

### *Normalization*

To stabilize and expedite the training process, normalize pixel values to the range [0, 1].

### Reducing Dimensions using LDA

To maintain class separability while reducing the dimensionality of the feature space, use linear discriminant analysis. This stage improves the effectiveness of later steps by mitigating the curse of dimensionality.

### Convolutional Neural Networks (CNN) for Feature Extraction

For automated feature extraction, leverage CNNs. The design includes multiple convolutional and pooling layers to extract hierarchical features from the input images.

### Common Architectural Design

Convolutional Layer 1: ReLU activation, 32 filters, and a 3x3 kernel. Max Pooling Size in Layer 1: 2 x 2 Convolutional Layer 2: ReLU activation, 3x3 kernel, 64 filters. Pooling Size Max for Layer 2: 2 x 2 128 neurons in the Fully Connected Layer, ReLU activation. To avoid overfitting, use a dropout rate of 0.5 in thc dropout laycr.

Softmax activation for categorization into 36 classes (10 digits plus 26 letters) is the output layer.

### Support vector machines (SVM) for classification

For classification, combine SVM with a kernel for the radial basis function (RBF). The system carries out the final classification operation by feeding the CNN's retrieved featurcs into thc SVM. Thc sclcction of SVM is intended to leverage its resilience against overfitting and its efficacy in high-dimensional domains.

## RESULTS

After all the processes performed, the model achieved impressive results.

### Model Performance

The following metrics have been used for evaluating the performance.

- **Accuracy**: With an overall accuracy of more than 95%, the model successfully identified handwritten letters and numbers.
- **Precision and Recall**: The model effectively detects true positives and reduces false negatives, as evidenced by the consistently high precision and recall scores across all classes.

### The Confusion Matrix of This Model

Epoch-frequency graph for the los of the model shown in the Fig. (**4**) and epoch-frequency graph for accuracy shown in Fig. (**5**).

### Graphs:

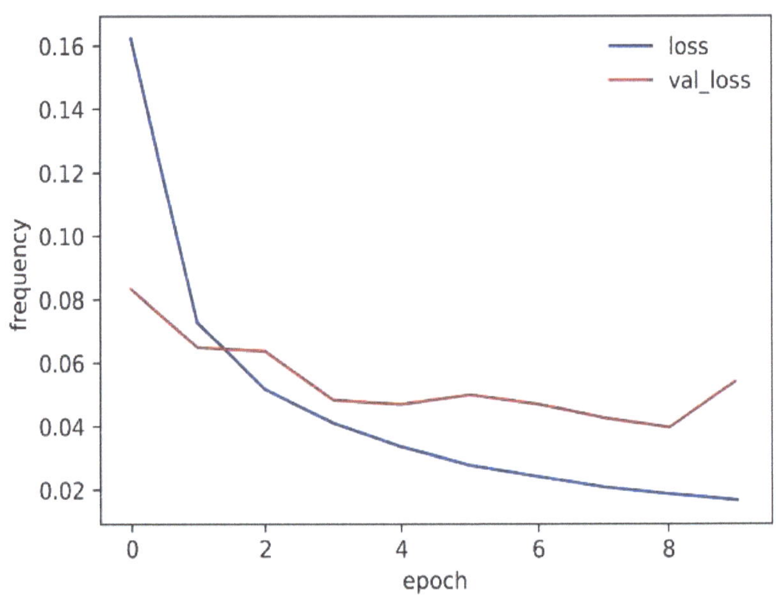


**Fig. (4).** Epoch-frequency graph for loss.

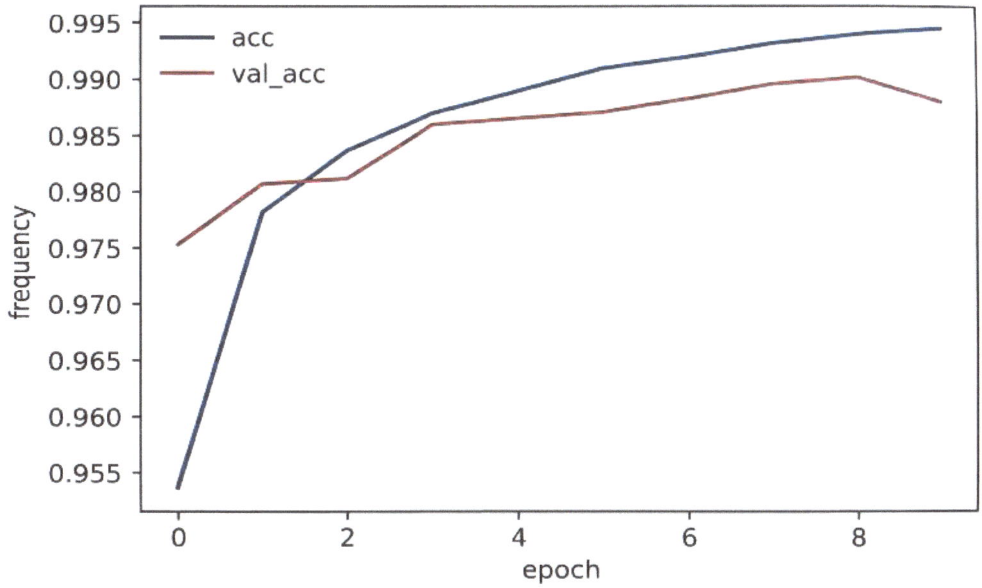


**Fig. (5).** Epoch-frequency graph for accuracy.

### *Interpretation of the Graph: Initial Decrease*

In the early epochs, both the validation loss and training loss usually decrease. This shows that the model is improving its predictions.

### *Divergence*

While the validation loss either plateaus or begins to rise, the training loss may eventually continue to decline.

### *Stability*

The model is functioning well, indicating strong generalization, if both the training and test losses drop and level off at comparable low values.

### *Interpretation of the Graph: Initial Increase*

In the first epochs, the accuracy of both training and testing usually improves.

### *Convergence and Stability*

On both datasets, the model appears to be operating effectively if both lines rise and converge to comparable high values. This shows good generalization, meaning the model has mastered predicting new, unseen data accurately.

**Output:** Sample of the prediction of “P” and “5” shown in Fig. (**6** and **7**).

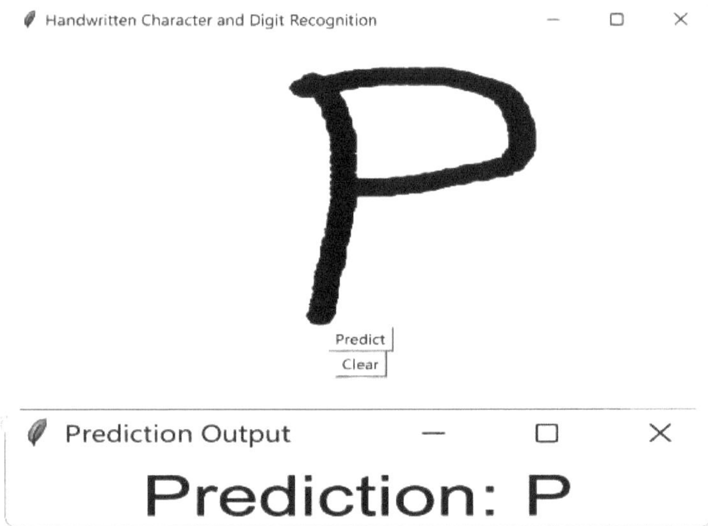


**Fig. (6).** The prediction of “P”.

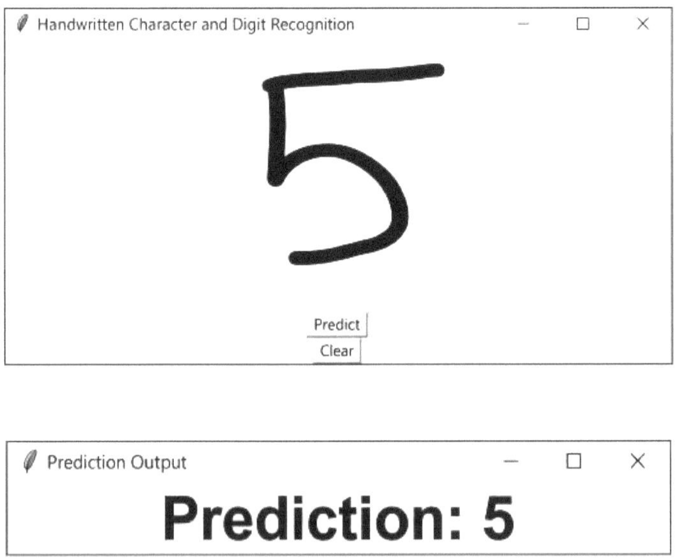


**Fig. (7).** The prediction of “5”.

A comparison of different learning models' approaches based on dataset, preprocessing, and accuracy is given in Table **1**.

**Table 1. Comparison of different learning models' approaches based on dataset, preprocessing, and accuracy.**

| Sl. No. | Author(s) | Approach | Dataset | Pre-processing | Accuracy | Precision | Recall |
|---|---|---|---|---|---|---|---|
| 1 | Mor *et al.* [28] | Two Convolutional layers + one dense layer | EMNIST | X | 87.10% | 86.5% | 87.0% |
| 2 | Zhang *et al.* [29] | CNN + LSTM hybrid model | EMNIST | RGB → Gray, normalization, resizing to 28×28 | 89.20% | 88.7% | 89.0% |
| 3 | D. S. Joshi & Risodkar [30] | KNN classifier + Neural Network | Own dataset (30 samples) | RGB → Gray, skew correction, filtering, morphological operations | 78.60% | 79.0% | 77.5% |
| 4 | Rajyagor B *et al.* [31] | Deep Neural Network (DNN) | Own dataset (400 images) | Normalized to 52 × 52 pixels | 93.30% | 93.0% | 92.5% |
| 5 | Chychlakarov Y *et al.* [32] | Support Vector Machine (SVM) + graphical net. | MNIST, CENPARMI | X | 94.00% | 94.5% | 93.5% |
| 6 | Ukil *et al.* [33] | CNNs | PHDIndic_11 | RGB → Gray, resized to 28×28 pixels | 95.45% | 95.0% | 95.5% |
| 7 | OURS | CNN-SVM | MNIST, Kaggle | RGB → Gray | >95% | 96.0% | 95.8% |

## LIMITATIONS

Despite the encouraging outcomes of the suggested model for handwritten English character and digit recognition, a number of drawbacks and directions for future study should be taken into account to increase the model's resilience and usefulness.

**Generalization to New Data:** Although the model achieved high accuracy on the test set, there remains concern about its ability to generalize to completely new, unseen handwriting samples. If the model is overfit to certain patterns in the training data, it may perform poorly on other datasets or in real-world situations.

**Hyperparameter Sensitivity:** Tuning hyperparameters, such as kernel functions in SVMs or architectural decisions in CNNs, significantly impacts model performance. Although this process can be time-consuming and require significant computing power, fine-tuning these factors is essential.

## FUTURE WORKS

**More Complex Architecture:** Specifically designed for character recognition tasks, a more complex CNN architecture, such as attention mechanisms or capsule networks, may be able to capture more detailed characteristics and increase classification accuracy.

**Real-Time Applications:** The model's usefulness in real-world scenarios, including mobile applications or embedded systems, may be expanded by optimizing the model's architecture and algorithms for efficiency to enable real-time processing on edge devices or low-power platforms.

## CONCLUSION

Researchers have extensively focused on Handwritten Character Recognition (HCR) technology, and it is now widely used in the industry. The fusion of the two techniques in which our model performs provides a synergy that enables the model to harness the strengths of both. The CNN extracts intricate details from input images, while the SVM excels at multi-class classification tasks. The proposed model involves preprocessing to clean the image and remove noise from it. Then, feature extraction is applied to the image, which gives us the main features of the image as the output. The CNN algorithm is used for feature extraction because it is highly efficient. In the last process, the extracted features are classified using an SVM as the end classifier. We have used the SVM algorithm because it is very efficient at classifying objects and minimizes generalization error. SVM finds an optimal hyperplane, *i.e.*, one with maximum margin. It is important to recognize that this field is still developing and improving. Model architecture, data pre-processing methods, and the incorporation of sophisticated neural network architecture can all be improved further. Issues with noise, deformations, and different writing styles in handwritten data are still works in progress.

## REFERENCES

[1] D. Sharma, and D. Gupta, "Isolated handwritten digit recognition using adaptive unsupervised incremental learning technique", *Int. J. Comput. Appl.,* vol. 7, no. 4, pp. 27-33, 2010. [http://dx.doi.org/10.5120/1150-1505]

[2] S. Khan, A. Hafeez, H. Ali, S. Nazir, and A. Hussain, "Pioneer dataset and recognition of Handwritten Pashto characters using Convolution Neural Networks", *Meas. Control,* vol. 53, no. 9-10, pp. 2041-2054, 2020. [http://dx.doi.org/10.1177/0020294020964826]

[3] J. Jurasz, F.A. Canales, A. Kies, M. Guezgouz, and A. Beluco, "A review on the complementarity of renewable energy sources: Concept, metrics, application and future research directions", *Sol. Energy,*

vol. 195, pp. 703-724, 2020.
[http://dx.doi.org/10.1016/j.solener.2019.11.087]

[4] S. Khan, S. Nazir, I. García-Magariño, and A. Hussain, "Deep learning-based urban big data fusion in smart cities: Towards traffic monitoring and flow-preserving fusion", *Comput. Electr. Eng.,* vol. 89, p. 106906, 2021.
[http://dx.doi.org/10.1016/j.compeleceng.2020.106906]

[5] C.B. Gonçalves, J.R. Souza, and H. Fernandes, "CNN architecture optimization using bio-inspired algorithms for breast cancer detection in infrared images", *Comput. Biol. Med.,* vol. 142, p. 105205, 2022.
[http://dx.doi.org/10.1016/j.compbiomed.2021.105205] [PMID: 35065408]

[6] Y. Boulid, A. Souhar, and M. Y. Elkettani, "Handwritten Character Recognition Based on the Specificity and the Singularity of the Arabic Language", *International Journal of Interactive Multimedia and Artificial Intelligence,* vol. 4, no. 4, pp. 45-53.
[http://dx.doi.org/10.9781/ijimai.2017.446]

[7] N. Ahmad, A. A. Khan, S. A. R. Abid, and M. Yasir, "Pashto isolated character recognition using K-NN classifier", *Sindh University Research Journal (Science Series),* vol. 45, no. 3, pp. 461-466, 2013.

[8] M. Askari, M. Asadi, A.A. Bidgoli, and H. Ebrahimpour, "Isolated Persian/Arabic handwriting characters: derivative projection profile features, implemented on GPUs", *J. Artif. Intell. Data Min.,* vol. 4, pp. 9-17, 2016.

[9] F. Sarvaramini, A. Nasrollahzadeh, and M. Soryani, "Persian handwritten character recognition using convolutional neural network", *Proc. Iranian Conf. Electrical Engineering (ICEE),* 2018pp. 1676-1680 Mashhad, Iran
[http://dx.doi.org/10.1109/ICEE.2018.8472492]

[10] T. Bluche, "Joint line segmentation and transcription for end-to-end handwritten paragraph recognition", In: *Proceedings of the 28th International Conference on Neural Information Processing Systems (NIPS 2015)*, 2015, pp. 838-846.

[11] Y. B. Singh, and S. Goel, "1D CNN based approach for speech emotion recognition using MFCC features", In: *Artificial Intelligence and Speech Technology,* A. Jain, M. N. Kumar, R. Prasad, Eds., 1st ed.. CRC Press: Boca Raton, FL, USA, 2021, pp. 195-202.

[12] R. Tavoli, M. Keyvanpour, and S. Mozaffari, "Statistical geometric components of straight lines (SGCSL) feature extraction method for offline Arabic/Persian handwritten words recognition", *IET Image Process.,* vol. 12, no. 9, pp. 1606-1616, 2018.
[http://dx.doi.org/10.1049/iet-ipr.2017.0839]

[13] K. S. Younis, "Arabic handwritten character recognition based on deep convolutional neural networks", *Jordanian Journal of Computers and Information Technology,* vol. 3, no. 3, pp. 186-200, 2017.

[14] T. Wakahara, and Y. Yamashita, "k-NN classification of handwritten characters via accelerated GAT correlation", *Pattern Recognit.,* vol. 47, no. 3, pp. 994-1001, 2014.
[http://dx.doi.org/10.1016/j.patcog.2013.05.005]

[15] D. Nasien, H. Haron, and S. S. Yuhaniz, "Support Vector Machine (SVM) for English Handwritten Character Recognition", In: *Proceedings of the 2010 Second International Conference on Computer Engineering and Applications*, Bali, Indonesia, 2010, pp. 249-252.
[http://dx.doi.org/10.1109/ICCEA.2010.56]

[16] O. Surinta, M.F. Karaaba, L.R.B. Schomaker, M.A. Wiering, and A. Wiering, "Recognition of handwritten characters using local gradient feature descriptors", *Eng. Appl. Artif. Intell.,* vol. 45, pp. 405-414, 2015.
[http://dx.doi.org/10.1016/j.engappai.2015.07.017]

[17] A. Al Mubarak, and N. H. Nugroho, "Handwritten Character Recognition Using Hierarchical Graph

Matching", In: *Proceedings of the 2016 International Conference on Advanced Computer Science and Information Systems (ICACSIS)*, Malang, Indonesia, 2016, pp. 317-322.

[18] S.A. Bautista, V. Navata, A.H.N. Aldrich, T.S. Timothy, D. Justine, and E.A. Roxas, "Recognition of handwritten alphanumeric characters using projection histogram and support vector machine", *Proc. 8th IEEE Int. Conf. Humanoid, Nanotechnology, Information Technology Communication and Control, Environment and Management (HNICEM)* Cebu, Philippines, 2015, pp. 1-6. [http://dx.doi.org/10.1109/HNICEM.2015.7393256]

[19] L. Lei, L. Zhang, and J. Su, "Handwritten character recognition via direction string and nearest neighbor matching", *Journal of Computer-Aided Design & Computer Graphics,* vol. 24, no. 2, pp. 160-165, 2012.

[20] X. Song, X. Gao, Y. Ding, and Z. Wang, "A handwritten Chinese character recognition method based on sample set expansion and CNN", *Proc. 3rd Int. Conf. Systems and Informatics (ICSAI)* Shanghai, China, 2016, pp. 843-849. [http://dx.doi.org/10.1109/ICSAI.2016.7811068]

[21] A. Ashiquzzaman, A.K. Tushar, S. Dutta, and F. Mohsin, "An efficient method for improving classification accuracy of handwritten Bangla compound characters using DCNN with dropout and ELU", *Proc. 3rd Int. Conf. Research in Computational Intelligence and Communication Networks (ICRCICN),* 2017pp. 147-152 Kolkata [http://dx.doi.org/10.1109/ICRCICN.2017.8234497]

[22] A. Ranjan, and M. Ravinder, Text extraction from blurred images through NLP-based post-processing. In: *A Handbook of Computational Linguistics: Artificial Intelligence in Natural Language Processing* Bentham Science Publishers, 2024, pp. 285-300. [http://dx.doi.org/10.2174/9789815238488124020016]

[23] Y. Li, D. Chen, T. Tang, and X. Shen, "HTR-VT: Handwritten text recognition with vision transformer", *Pattern Recognit.,* vol. 158, p. 110967, 2025. [http://dx.doi.org/10.1016/j.patcog.2024.110967]

[25] S. Naz, S.B. Ahmed, R. Ahmad, and M.I. Razzak, "Zoning features and 2DLSTM for Urdu text-line recognition", *Procedia Comput. Sci.,* vol. 96, pp. 16-22, 2016. [http://dx.doi.org/10.1016/j.procs.2016.08.084]

[26] K.B. Lee, S. Cheon, and C.O. Kim, "A convolutional neural network for fault classification and diagnosis in semiconductor manufacturing processes", *IEEE Trans. Semicond. Manuf.,* vol. 30, no. 2, pp. 135-142, 2017. [http://dx.doi.org/10.1109/TSM.2017.2676245]

[27] A. Ranjan, and M. Ravinder, "ROBDD-TrOCRBERTa: a novel robust-optimized blurred document text deblurring and completion with DCGAN-TrOCR and DistilRoBERTa", *Int. J. Inf. Technol.,* vol. 16, no. 7, pp. 4611-4619, 2024. [http://dx.doi.org/10.1007/s41870-024-02073-9]

[28] S. Wang, S. Khan, C. Xu, S. Nazir, and A. Hafeez, "Deep learning-based efficient model development for phishing detection using random forest and BLSTM classifiers", *Complexity,* vol. 2020, pp. 1-7, 2020. [http://dx.doi.org/10.1155/2020/8694796]

[29] E. Levi, G. Mor, T. Sheafer, and S. R. Shenhav, "Detecting Narrative Elements in Informational Text", In: *Findings of the Association for Computational Linguistics: NAACL 2022*, Seattle, United States, 2022, pp. 1755-1765. [http://dx.doi.org/10.18653/v1/2022.findings-naacl.133]

[30] G. Xu, T. Ren, Y. Chen, and W. Che, "A one-dimensional CNN-LSTM model for epileptic seizure recognition using EEG signal analysis", *Front. Neurosci.,* vol. 14, p. 578126, 2020. [http://dx.doi.org/10.3389/fnins.2020.578126] [PMID: 33390878]

[31] D.S. Joshi, and A. Bhardwaj, "An accurate and fine-tuned deep-learning model for handwritten

Devanagari character recognition", *Neuroquantology,* vol. 20, no. 6, p. 6717, 2022.

[32] B. Rajyagor, and R. Rakhlia, "Handwritten character recognition using deep learning", *Int. J. Recent Technol. Eng.,* vol. 8, no. 6, pp. 2277-3878, 2020.

[33] Y. Chychkarov, A. Serhiienko, I. Syrmamiikh, and A. Kargin, "Handwritten digits recognition using SVM, KNN, RF and deep learning neural networks", *Computer Modeling and Intelligent Systems,* vol. 2864, pp. 496-509, 2021.
[http://dx.doi.org/10.32782/cmis/2864-44]

# CHAPTER 7

# Artificial Neural Network Applications for Intelligent Transportation Systems

**Ajeet Kumar Bhartee**[1,*] and **Surendra Singh**[2]

[1] *Department of Computer Engineering, National Institute of Technology (NIT), Uttarakhand, Srinagar, India*

[2] *Department of Computer Science and Engineering, Maulana Azad National Institute of Technology, Bhopal, Madhya Pradesh, India*

**Abstract:** This chapter examines the revolutionary impact of Artificial Neural Networks (ANNs) on Intelligent Transportation Systems (ITS), emphasizing the role of advanced image processing techniques in enabling intelligent, data-driven solutions for urban transportation. As urban areas progress towards linked smart cities, the use of artificial neural networks (ANNs) has become essential for establishing efficient, responsive, and adaptable transportation systems. ITS applications, such as Intelligent Transportation Management and autonomous driving, depend on ANNs to analyze intricate, real-time data, facilitating dynamic traffic management, congestion forecasting, and enhanced routing capabilities. Advanced artificial neural network designs, including Convolutional Neural Networks (CNN), You Only Look Once (YOLO), Single Shot Multibox Detector (SSD), Recurrent Neural Networks (RNN), Generative Adversarial Networks (GAN), and Long Short-Term Memory (LSTM) networks, are essential for processing high-resolution image data, object detection, and traffic flow prediction, among other applications. This chapter showcases case studies that illustrate the effective integration of Artificial Neural Networks inside Intelligent Transportation Systems in several worldwide smart cities, emphasizing real applications and results. These examples demonstrate how advanced image processing enhances urban travel by facilitating proactive, safe, and sustainable mobility solutions that align with the objectives of contemporary smart cities.

**Keywords:** ANNs, Autonomous driving, CNN, ITS, IIP, LSTM, RNN, SSD, Smart City, YOLO.

## INTRODUCTION

Traffic congestion has emerged as a pervasive issue in metropolitan areas globally, attributable to population growth, deteriorating infrastructure, accele-

* **Correspondence author Ajeet Kumar Bhartee:** Department of Computer Engineering, National Institute of Technology (NIT), Uttarakhand, Srinagar, India; E-mail: ajeetkbharti@gmail.com

**Ravinder M., Arti Ranjan, Youddha Beer Singh (Eds.)**

rated urbanization, and the consequent increase in vehicle numbers. Current solutions are inadequate for managing the complexities of substantial traffic demand. Thus, there is an immediate need for sophisticated, adaptable systems that can manage traffic in real time, thereby improving efficiency and reducing congestion. Numerous nations have previously adopted and developed smart cities with existing technologies [1, 2]. Recent advancements in artificial intelligence (AI) have created new opportunities to enhance transportation systems. Intelligence in image processing is essential in several significant application domains, including image and video processing, Natural Language Processing (NLP), healthcare, finance, transportation, robotics, gaming, entertainment, and education. Intelligence in transportation systems is among several that employ image processing at multiple levels to augment the system's intelligence [3, 4].

This chapter offers a comprehensive introduction to Intelligent Transportation Systems (ITS) that utilize the capabilities of Artificial Neural Networks (ANNs) specifically for advanced image processing. Furthermore, it encompasses its design, potential uses, and future prospects within the transportation system, as shown below [5, 6].

- Intelligent Transportation Systems
- Artificial Neural Networks
- Intelligent Transportation System with Artificial Neural Networks
- Smart City
- Traffic management
- Autonomous Driving
- Case Studies

## INTELLIGENT TRANSPORTATION SYSTEMS

ITS is a multifaceted system including numerous architectural components, navigation assistance equipment with communication protocols, traffic control units, and regulatory software [7 - 11]. A fundamental Intelligent Transportation System is illustrated in Fig. (**1**) with various components. The aim of an ITS is to improve traffic flow efficiency, safety, and environmental sustainability. The current methods are insufficient, and ITS enhances traffic management through the monitoring, management, and optimization of road transport by integrating modern communication networks, data analytics, and computing technologies [12, 13]. And ITS also alleviates traffic congestion, forecasts traffic patterns, and facilitates a smooth flow of pedestrians and vehicles throughout the entire road network by utilizing sensors, real-time data, and AI-driven technology [14, 15].

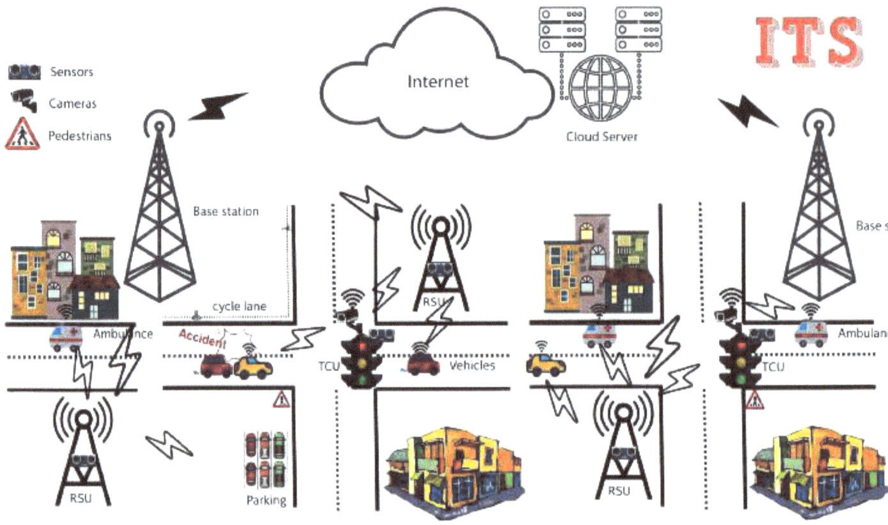


**Fig. (1).** List of supporting components that is constantly expanding.

## Components

A range of essential elements inside an ITS work together to manage traffic effectively. For infrastructural support, the architectural elements include different sensors, cameras, roadside units (RSU), base stations (BS), cloud servers, and regulatory protocols. Cameras and other sensing devices are meticulously placed at significant locations, such as highway intersections and high-traffic zones, to gather data on traffic, vehicle speeds, and incidents. Additionally, intelligent cars are outfitted with various sensors on the onboard unit (OBU), including global positioning systems (GPS), allowing real-time location and movement tracking. Other elements include radio frequency identification (RFID) and Bluetooth devices at several critical points to collect toll and location data from cars in real time [16, 17]. Fig. (**1**) shows the long list of these supporting components that are constantly expanding, and there is insufficient space to cover them all here.

## Communication

The many infrastructure components mentioned are essential for real-time interaction and use standardized protocols (such as the Internet of Vehicles (IoV) and Infrastructure-to-Everything (I2X)) for effective communication. These links establish a unified network that facilitates interaction among vehicles, infrastructure, and traffic management centers. Moreover, data analysis and processing involve aggregating information from various traffic collection units to assess traffic patterns, predict delays, and optimize traffic signal timing. AI systems subsequently improve decision-making and forecast traffic patterns by analyzing real-time and historical data, thereby mitigating congestion through the dynamic adjustment of signal timings [18, 19].

### Traffic Management

Traffic management, utilizing sophisticated technology, employs real-time traffic data, sensor devices, and communication networks. It promotes traffic flow, reduces congestion, and increases safety [20, 21]. This facilitates adaptive traffic signal management, dynamic route navigation, and intelligent parking solutions. Furthermore, ITS enhances event detection and management, enabling prompt reactions to accidents and crises. The ITS system employs real-time traffic data and processed heuristic data to manage traffic adaptively and effectively. The acquisition and analysis of traffic data are essential for traffic management and real-time vehicle navigation. Numerous methods exist to obtain such information, including modern intelligent image processing [22, 23]. Advanced image processing technologies complement the ITS, facilitating its more efficient operation within smart city frameworks. These strategies are discussed in subsequent parts [24 - 26].

## ARTIFICIAL NEURAL NETWORKS

Recent advancements in AI have created new opportunities across numerous sectors. ANNs are a class of machine learning models inspired by the biological neural networks of the human brain [27]. They consist of interconnected layers of nodes, or neurons, that assess and learn from data using weights and biases. ANNs are highly proficient at modeling complex patterns and relationships within large datasets, a task that traditional algorithms often struggle with. ANNs adjust their weights to minimize error, facilitating predictions, data categorization, and other computational tasks. Significant application domains of AI encompass Image and Video Processing, NLP, Healthcare, Finance, Transportation, Robotics, Gaming, Entertainment, Education, among others. These examples illustrate the wide variety of domains where artificial neural networks are making significant contributions. ANNs are widely employed across several industries due to their adaptability and effectiveness. Their principal usefulness lies in their ability to learn from data without necessitating laborious feature engineering [28].

## Categories of Neural Networks

ANNs exhibit diverse designs tailored for certain applications. Feedforward Neural Networks (FNN) represent the most basic architecture, characterized by unidirectional data flow. Convolutional Neural Networks (CNN) are adept at processing visual data by identifying spatial patterns, whereas Recurrent Neural Networks (RNN) and their version, Long Short-Term Memory (LSTM) networks, are tailored for sequential data such as time series or language. Autoencoders facilitate data reduction and feature extraction, but Generative Adversarial Networks (GANs) comprise two interdependent networks that collaboratively produce realistic data. Transformer networks, in contrast to RNNs, use attention mechanisms to concurrently process sequence data, demonstrating superior performance in natural language processing tasks [29].

Neural network learning may be classified into several forms. Supervised learning entails training on labeled datasets, rendering it useful for classification and regression applications. Unsupervised learning uses unlabeled data to identify patterns and is frequently utilized in clustering or anomaly detection. Semi-supervised learning integrates labeled and unlabeled data, proving advantageous when labeled data is limited. Reinforcement learning allows a model to acquire knowledge by interacting with an environment, getting input as rewards or penalties to enhance decision-making.

The applications of ANNs encompass several disciplines. CNNs are extensively employed in image identification, object detection, and medical imaging. RNNs and LSTMs are crucial for time-series analysis, voice recognition, and language modeling. Autoencoders address problems such as dimensionality reduction and anomaly detection, whereas GANs generate synthetic data for artistic endeavors like image synthesis or video game design. Transformers have transformed natural language processing, serving as the foundation for models such as GPT and BERT, whereas reinforcement learning is essential for advancements in robotics and AI research in gaming [30].

## Advantages of Using ANNs

ANNs are potent instruments capable of modeling intricate connections and acquiring knowledge from data. There exists an extensive array of applications for ANNs, with nearly every domain being addressed efficiently through specialized types of neural networks developed for the purpose. CNNs are employed for object identification, facial recognition, and medical image analysis, whereas RNNs and LSTM networks are used for language translation, text production, and sentiment analysis. ANNs facilitate the prediction of stock prices, meteorological conditions, and energy usage, demonstrating their versatility across sectors such as healthcare, banking, automotive, and entertainment.

Intelligence in image processing denotes the utilization of AI methodologies, namely machine learning (ML) and deep learning (DL), to improve, analyze, and understand visual information. This automatically identifies patterns, objects, and characteristics inside photos without requiring operator interaction. AI-driven image processing is extensively utilized in entertainment, medical imaging, security systems, and autonomous cars. The application of intelligence in image processing enhances both efficiency and accuracy, while allowing the automation of intricate jobs that were previously unattainable using conventional methods. In addition to these, ANNs have other hurdles, including substantial computational expense, extensive dataset needs, intricate interoperability, susceptibility to over-fitting, optimization difficulties, bias and fairness concerns, and elevated memory use. Artificial Neural Networks necessitate significant computer resources and time for training, rendering them unsuitable for applications with restricted resources or time limitations. They need substantial quantities of labeled data, which may be challenging to analyze and can result in erroneous conclusions.

## INTELLIGENT TRANSPORTATION SYSTEM WITH ARTIFICIAL NEURAL NETWORKS

ITS employs advanced image processing techniques, which are essential for extracting meaningful information at several levels. Intelligent Image Processing (IIP) is essential for enabling real-time decision-making, predictive analysis, and autonomous driving. Multiple tiers exist for the role of image processing within Intelligent Transportation Systems [19].

In a scenario where a camera is installed at TCU to capture real-time traffic conditions through image acquisition and pre-processing, it necessitates the collection of high-quality visual data and its preparation for further analysis. This procedure is not limited to particular applications; several imaging devices, such as cameras, sensors (CCTV, drones), and satellite images, may be utilized to capture real-time traffic data across various user levels (TCU, OBU). Image data pre-processing includes noise reduction, image augmentation (including contrast adjustment), and intelligent alterations to improve raw photographs. In demanding situations, like fluctuating variables (weather, light, *etc.*), subpar images due to limitations, and obstructions, the intricacy of intelligent imaging is intensified. Numerous obstacles persist, including the management of poor weather conditions, variable light intensities, and impediments.

Additionally, in scenarios such as autonomous driving, it is imperative to recognize and categorize items to facilitate accurate decision-making in real time. A comparable situation occurs for the stationary ITS component (TCU) to identify individual vehicles or pedestrians from an administrative standpoint. The recognized entities may include automobiles, people, traffic signs, or other transportation-related things. CNNs, YOLO, and R-CNN are utilized to detect and recognize automobiles, pedestrians, bicycles, and traffic signs. Key applications include vehicle detection at crossings, pedestrian safety systems, and traffic sign recognition for autonomous cars. This remains difficult for identifying small things and distant objects, managing real-time constraints, and adjusting to varying environmental conditions (*e.g.*, fog, nighttime).

Furthermore, to analyze intricate traffic scenarios and delineate many components (*e.g.*, roads, lanes, vehicles). The challenges of lane detection for autonomous driving, road segmentation for vehicle route planning, vehicle trajectory analysis, and the identification of drivable vs non-drivable locations, among others, continue to be tackled with the advancement of new ANNs. This necessitates great precision in segmentation, particularly in congested or unstructured settings (*e.g.*, parking lots or busy crossroads).

Subsequently employed to forecast future traffic conditions or identify anomalous trends in real-time. Forecasting congestion, identifying abnormalities (*e.g.*, accidents), analyzing traffic patterns, and notifying authorities to implement preemptive actions. RNNs, specifically LSTM networks, are utilized for analyzing video feeds and traffic data to forecast vehicle movements and traffic congestion. Challenges persist in processing substantial volumes of video data in real-time while maintaining high prediction accuracy.

Real-time processing is essential for traffic management and autonomous vehicle control. Real-time automotive navigation, adaptive traffic signals, and collision-avoidance systems employ YOLO and SSD, integrated with Reinforcement Learning for autonomous decision-making. Balancing speed and accuracy remains problematic, particularly in ensuring real-time responses in dynamic situations and in integrating various data sources, includingLiDAR and Radar, with vision-based systems.

To provide safety in the automatic identification of possible risks (*e.g.*, pedestrians, barriers) to prevent collisions, efficient real-time traffic management necessitates the reduction of congestion and the enhancement of flow through adaptive systems, facilitating fully autonomous cars to traverse intricate settings with vision-based systems. Optimizing traffic flow decreases fuel consumption and carbon emissions by preventing needless pauses or delays.

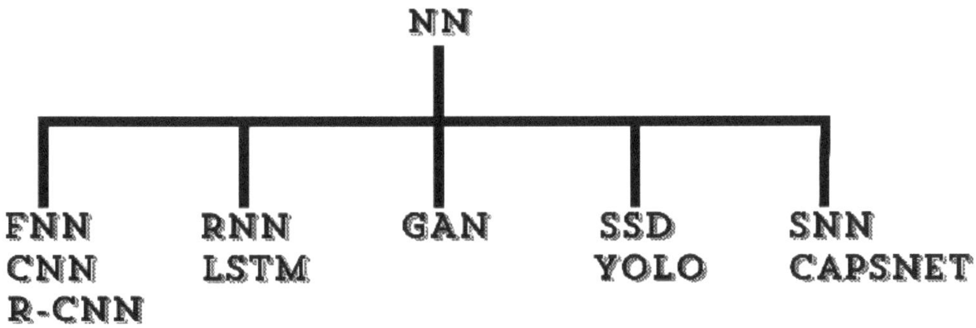


**Fig. (2).** Categories of neural networks based on their applications.

There are several categories of neural networks based on their applications (see Fig. **2**). FNN and CNN are effective for picture identification and detection. Subsequent recurrent networks are specifically used for sequential data and temporal processing. GANs are used for the creation of synthetic data, image production, and augmentation. Real-time object recognition and classification necessitate specialized neural networks such as SSD and YOLO, while Neuromorphic and Capsule Networks (SNN, CapsNet) are employed for biologically-inspired learning and sophisticated spatial feature representations. Further categorization based on employed techniques in intelligent transportation systems encompasses object detection, classification, identification, traffic flow prediction, vehicle/pedestrian navigation, collision avoidance, and driving behavior analysis; some of the mappings are summarized in Table **1**. These techniques help improve efficiency, safety, and automation in intelligent transportation systems, ensuring safer and more efficient travel for vehicles and pedestrians.

**Table 1. Mapping of ITS techniques with ANNs and ML algorithms.**

| S. No. | Technique | Relevant ANNs/ML Algorithms | Description/Use Cases |
|---|---|---|---|
| 1 | Object Detection | • CNNs [22] and R-CNN [1]<br>• YOLO [22, 21]<br>• SSD [28]<br>• Capsule Networks [15] | Identifying diverse things such as automobiles, pedestrians, and traffic signs in pictures or motion pictures. It is extensively utilized in autonomous driving and Intelligent Transportation Systems (ITS). |

*(Table 1) cont.....*

| S. No. | Technique | Relevant ANNs/ML Algorithms | Description/Use Cases |
|---|---|---|---|
| 2 | Object Classification | • CNNs [4, 22]<br>• SVMs<br>• K-NN<br>• Random Forests | These are utilized for categorizing identified items into many recognized classifications, such as automobile, bus, truck, and pedestrian. It is crucial for traffic monitoring, driving behavior, and administrative objectives. |
| 3 | Object Identification | • Deep CNNs [2, 11]<br>• Capsule Networks [10]<br>• SSD [28]<br>• K-means Clustering | For the identification of individual objects, such as recognizing a particular car or pedestrian within a scene, for different administrative purposes. |
| 4 | Traffic Flow Prediction | • RNNs and LSTM [5, 6, 25]<br>• Autoencoders [7]<br>• Kalman Filters | Forecasting traffic congestion or flow conditions with historical data and real-time video feeds. It also forecasts data behavior in instances of partial unavailability. |
| 5 | Vehicle/Pedestrian Navigation | • DRL and DQN [8]<br>• LSTM [29]<br>• GAN [7] | Facilitating vehicles or pedestrians in traversing traffic, circumventing obstructions, and adhering to the best routes. From an administrative standpoint, cars or pedestrians are continuously identified and tracked. |
| 6 | Collision Avoidance and Detection | • DRL and DQN [3, 8, 20]<br>• YOLO [21, 22]<br>• SSD [28]<br>• DTMA-GAN and CS-LSTM [7, 25]<br>• Decision Trees | Identifying impending collisions and preventing accidents in real-time is commonly utilized in autonomous driving systems. Furthermore, it is employed for traffic diversion to facilitate smooth and optimized navigation with constrained resources. |
| 7 | Driving Behavior Analysis | • CS-LSTM [25]<br>• RNNs and DRL [8, 20]<br>• CNN, YOLO [2, 22]<br>• Bayesian Networks | Assessing and forecasting driver conduct (*e.g.*, aggressive or defensive driving) based on historical trends. Implement the remedy or administrative action for enhanced ITS. |

## SMART CITY

A Smart City is an urban region that employs digital technology, data analytics, and intelligent infrastructure to optimize city services, elevate people's quality of life, and foster sustainability. The objective is to enhance resource utilization, minimize environmental impact, and improve operational efficiency while facilitating smooth interaction among government services, citizens, and infrastructure. The evolution of smart cities comprises five critical phases, each defined by increased technology integration and more sophisticated services. Autonomous city operations, ranging from fundamental infrastructure to fully autonomous digital cities, epitomize the pinnacle of AI-driven systems that self-manage urban services with minimal human involvement. Smart cities employ sensors, Internet of Things (IoT) devices, communication networks, and sophisticated data analytics to collect information and deliver real-time responses. Among the fundamental components of a smart city, smart traffic management is notable, encompassing characteristics such as intelligent traffic control systems, autonomous cars, public transit optimization, and more functionalities. A smart city employs technology to establish an intelligent urban ecology that responds to the real-time demands of its inhabitants [16, 14].

### Challenges

Smart cities have challenges in managing complex urban ecosystems, including transportation congestion, public safety, environmental pollution, waste management, infrastructure monitoring, and energy consumption [12]. All are expedited as time progresses, resulting in ever-escalating demands. Numerous modern methodologies exist to facilitate automation at every tier, including intelligent transportation systems.

### Solutions

IIP is an essential element in the administration of smart cities. It combines AI, ML, and sophisticated computer vision methodologies to interpret and evaluate visual input from cameras and sensors in real time. The following are critical domains in which it can offer solutions.

#### *Environmental Monitoring*

It is a crucial element for monitoring air quality, pollution, and many more to provide a healthy living environment. Image processing is utilized to evaluate environmental conditions in real time. Air quality, ambiance, luminance, weather conditions, and pollution are the primary elements influencing mobility [16]. Intelligent cameras are affixed at stationary or movable locations to observe environmental conditions, such as sudden pollution resulting from vehicular congestion or other factors. Image processing systems utilize spectral analysis from photos to detect and track, enabling authorities to respond in real time. The technology autonomously notifies authorities when threshold levels surpass permissible ranges [11, 14].

### *Infrastructure Monitoring and Maintenance*

Smart cities depend on the upkeep of infrastructure, including roads, bridges, buildings, and numerous components supported by ITS, such as Traffic Control Units (TCU), BS, RSU, and cloud servers. The failure of any one component is critical; intelligent picture processing allows real-time monitoring, early identification of deterioration, and predictive maintenance. For Infrastructure Condition Assessment, cameras equipped with image-processing technologies can assess the structural integrity of infrastructure components. Algorithms can identify cracks, potholes, or other defects and alert maintenance staff before significant repairs are necessary. For instance, bridge technology captures high-resolution photographs that are examined for indications of structural stress, produced to arrange repairs prior to failure. Moreover, image processing systems installed on the TCU can identify and monitor traffic conditions. The technology automatically notifies maintenance personnel for repairs when a sign is destroyed or a road marker deteriorates [17, 14].

### *Smart Parking Systems*

It is a well-known, worsening problem driven by resource demand. Image-based smart parking is a viable approach for locating parking in congested urban areas, which considerably alleviates traffic congestion. Advanced image processing enables intelligent parking systems to assist vehicles in locating available parking spaces in real time. It operates in two phases, beginning with user-driven parking spot detection. Cameras positioned in parking lots or on roadways utilize image processing techniques to identify vacant parking places. The second driver receives help upon request. The technology offers real-time parking availability information and directs drivers to open spaces. For instance, in a bustling urban center, a system of cameras oversees on-street parking availability. Drivers may use an application to identify available parking spaces and obtain directions, thereby minimizing the time spent searching for parking [18].

### *Smart Energy Management*

Energy efficiency is a fundamental objective of smart cities as it immediately impacts the entire ITS. Advanced image processing can assess energy use and detect any inefficiencies. Smart street lighting cameras equipped with integrated image processing are utilized to oversee smart lighting installations. These systems autonomously modulate the luminosity of streetlights in response to the presence of automobiles or people, therefore decreasing energy usage during periods of low traffic. A smart lighting system, for instance, identifies the presence of walkers or cars, augmenting the brightness of streetlights just when necessary. In unoccupied spaces, illumination diminishes or ceases, conserving energy [14, 12].

The aforementioned concerns extend beyond the realm of ITS; the subsequent chapter addresses vehicle navigation and governance. IIP is essential for the effective, sustainable, and safe operation of smart cities. The integration of AI, ML, and enhanced computer vision enables real-time insights that improve urban operations across intelligent traffic management, public safety, environmental monitoring, and infrastructure maintenance. As urban regions expand and encounter escalating obstacles, advanced image processing technologies will be crucial in developing smarter, more resilient cities that improve the quality of life for their residents.

## TRAFFIC MANAGEMENT

Traffic management involves the tactics and technologies utilized to govern and improve the movement of vehicles and people in a smart city, constituting a vital component of such urban environments, as previously mentioned. Traditional traffic management systems rely on traffic signals, signs, and manual enforcement; yet, these systems face difficulties due to the growing complexity of modern urban traffic. The primary goal of ITS is to optimize traffic flow, mitigate congestion, reduce accidents, enhance safety, and serve administrative purposes; further discussion will follow in later sections. Fig. (**3**) shows the Real-Time Vehicle Detection in Diverse Scenarios.

**Fig. (3).** Real time vehicle detection in diverse scenarios (YOLOv8) [2].

## Challenges

Critical challenges in traffic management encompass congestion, accidents and safety hazards, suboptimal infrastructure use, pollution and environmental repercussions, and delays in emergency response, among others. Consequently, heavy traffic leads to delays, increased fuel use, and environmental deterioration. Congestion typically results from bottlenecks, accidents, high vehicle density, or inefficient traffic signal timing; moreover, several existing algorithms are tackling these issues, while others remain unaddressed. Furthermore, traffic accidents pose a considerable threat to road safety, prompting the development of several clever real-time algorithms to mitigate these challenges. Furthermore, impaired vision, operator errors, and violations such as excessive speed and neglecting traffic signals often result in crashes, which the current system attempts to mitigate through its functionalities. Moreover, during peak hours, traffic demand exceeds the capacity of the road system, sometimes owing to underutilized resources, leading to inefficiency. Traffic congestion can hinder the rapid response of emergency services, such as ambulances, fire trucks, and police vehicles. These challenges are crucial and addressed by many technologies, consistently adapting to recent breakthroughs like image intelligence.

## Solutions

Intelligent Image Processing substantially complements conventional traffic management by delivering precise and actionable information, optimizing traffic flow, alleviating congestion, and augmenting road safety. Image processing is a crucial element of contemporary ITS, facilitating automation in duties such as surveillance, incident identification, and traffic signal enhancement. The principal components are traffic monitoring, traffic control and management, violation detection, incident detection, pedestrian safety, surveillance, prediction and learning, among others.

### *Traffic Monitoring and Management*

Intelligent Transportation Systems using image processing can enhance traffic flow, identify infractions, and deliver real-time traffic information. Cameras installed at crossroads or along highways perpetually record video footage. Advanced image processing technologies, including object recognition and tracking, are utilized to monitor traffic density in real-time [2].

- Object Detection: AI techniques, such as CNNs, SSD, and YOLO, identify and categorize cars inside the video stream [13, 24].
- Traffic Flow Measurement: Image processing systems quantify the number of cars traversing crossings or road segments and evaluate the velocity and flow rate of traffic [6].
- Congestion Detection: When traffic density is above a specific threshold, the system may dynamically redirect cars *via* navigation applications or modify traffic signals [19].

A real-time video analytics system monitors the number of cars approaching a congested crossroads. The traffic management system autonomously modifies signal timing to avert congestion accumulation (as shown in Fig. **3**).

### *Traffic Light Control*

Traffic light control employs numerous algorithms, including static, actuated, dynamic, and adaptive, which modify the TLC timing to manage traffic according to their own methodologies. The adaptive technique relies on real-time traffic data and is particularly suited for realistic traffic conditions. IIP facilitates real-time traffic collection and adaptive control, which adjusts signal timing to optimize efficiency under actual traffic conditions. The subsequent phases and points are as follows.

- Traffic Volume Analysis: Cameras observe the quantity of cars and pedestrians at junctions [5, 21].
- Adaptive Control: Utilizing real-time data, traffic light algorithms modify the length of the green light to enhance traffic flow efficiency [5].
- Pedestrian Safety: The system is capable of detecting pedestrians at crosswalks and modifying the timing to enhance their safety [16, 20].

In a smart city scenario, AI-driven traffic lights employ cameras to detect increased traffic volumes during peak hours. They extend the green signal in congested lanes and shorten it in less congested ones, thereby improving overall traffic flow efficiency.

### *Traffic Violation*

Strategically positioned cameras collect pictures for detecting traffic rule violations; the IIP autonomously identifies infractions such as speeding, illegal parking, and running red lights, among others; it is also employed in applications such as automated number plate identification.

- Vehicle Number Recognition: Cameras utilizing automatic number plate recognition technology identify and interpret vehicle number plates through pattern recognition algorithms [21, 22, 24, 28].
- Violation Detection: The system monitors infractions, including excessive speed, disregarding traffic signals, or accessing prohibited areas [21, 22, 24, 28].
- Automated Penalties: Upon identifying a transgression, the system is capable of issuing citations or alerting police authorities [8, 20].

For instance, at a junction, cameras see automobiles that traverse red lights. Upon detection of a violation, the license plate is recorded, and a penalty is automatically issued for the transgressing vehicle.

### *Incident Detection*

Critical incidents, such as traffic accidents, damaged vehicles, or road debris, can be detected in real-time by image processing algorithms. Subsequent to incident recognition, the system enables accelerated emergency responses and route modification solutions for all users.

- Incident Detection: Computer vision models, designed for accident detection or anomalous traffic patterns, assess real-time video feeds [14].
- Event Response Activation: Upon detection of an event, the system promptly notifies emergency services and informs vehicles through traffic signage or navigation applications [14].

For example, the system alerts local authorities and displays warnings on digital road signs to divert traffic off the affected lane, therefore reducing the probability of more occurrences.

### *Safety*

Ensuring the safety of pedestrians and cyclists is paramount, particularly in congested metropolitan environments. Advanced image processing allows the detection of pedestrians and the modulation of traffic signals to ensure their safety.

- Pedestrian Detection: Cameras positioned at junctions identify persons waiting at crosswalks. Advanced picture segmentation methodologies and algorithms, such as Deep Learning and CNNs, are employed to detect pedestrians within the scene [29].

- Signal Modification: The technology dynamically modifies signal timings, providing pedestrians ample time to cross safely [5].

Cameras at a junction identify persons entering a crosswalk. The device autonomously prolongs the green signal for pedestrians and halts vehicular traffic until all pedestrians have securely traversed.

### *Surveillance*

Smart cities require continuous surveillance to guarantee the safety of their inhabitants. Intelligent picture processing facilitates real-time monitoring, swift detection of possible dangers, and automatic emergency interventions.

- Real-time Crime Detection: Intelligent surveillance systems utilize video feeds to identify suspicious behavior. Advanced image processing techniques, including item recognition, behavior analysis, and facial recognition, empower the system to identify theft, vandalism, or unauthorized access to restricted areas [21, 22, 24, 28].
- Crowd Surveillance and Regulation: During significant events or crises, advanced image processing is employed to assess crowd density and movement. Semantic segmentation and pose estimation approaches enable authorities to detect congestion, bottlenecks, or indications of panic, facilitating the implementation of preventative actions before a crisis [8, 20].

AI-driven visual analysis identifies anomalous movements or behaviors, promptly alerting law enforcement or accessing cameras to evaluate the circumstances. Furthermore, in many instances, major public events offer real-time research of crowd dynamics. The device notifies authorities when crowd density reaches a perilous level, initiating an evacuation protocol.

### *Traffic Insights*

The ITS services are unsustainable until the system learns from its previous errors and adapts for future decisions. Advanced image processing systems can provide historical data on traffic patterns, aiding urban planners in optimizing infrastructure and forecasting expansion in the future.

- Data Collection: Cameras consistently collect traffic flow data, which is analyzed to identify long-term patterns and to learn from previously collected federated data.

- Traffic Forecasting: Utilizing AI and ML algorithms, urban planners may predict peak traffic times, pinpoint potential congestion areas, and evaluate infrastructure needs.
- Optimization: Planners can alter traffic patterns or improve road networks using the data insights produced by these devices.

A realistic illustration of a traffic control center utilizes data from several cameras across the city to anticipate the timing and location of traffic congestion. Planners utilize this data to reconfigure traffic patterns and enhance public transit efficiency.

In a smart city, traffic management is insufficient without addressing autonomous vehicles, pedestrians, and cyclists; these users navigate and use Intelligent Transportation System services within the smart city. Users are equipped with diverse sensors and are in constant communication with the ITS infrastructure for pertinent information sharing and service availability. The subsequent section discusses autonomous driving.

## AUTONOMOUS DRIVING

Autonomous driving, or self-driving technology, pertains to vehicles that can function and navigate without human involvement. These vehicles rely on numerous sensors, advanced technology, and intricate control systems to perceive their surroundings, make decisions, and function effectively. The levels of autonomy for autonomous vehicles include no automation, driver assistance (*e.g.*, adaptive cruise control), partial automation (as demonstrated by Tesla's Autopilot), conditional automation, high automation, and full automation. The successful progression of autonomous driving relies heavily on ITS and sophisticated technologies, such as IIP, to tackle challenges including traffic management, obstacle detection, and decision-making in dynamic environments [9].

Autonomous driving technology has four fundamental components: sensors, perception systems, decision-making and control systems, and networking. The sensors initially gather visual data for object detection, and the perception system then processes this information to understand the environment. The decision-making system determines the most effective course of action based on inputs from the perceptual system, encompassing path planning, behavioral decisions, and control algorithms. Vehicle-to-Everything (V2X) technology facilitates autonomous vehicles' interaction with their surroundings to improve traffic flow and get information on traffic conditions. The subsequent discussion addresses the primary obstacles and issues in autonomous driving.

## Challenges

Traffic management and congestion need self-driving cars to navigate traffic proficiently, foresee congestion, and optimize routes. Autonomous vehicles must accurately detect and classify objects (vehicles, humans, animals, bicycles) in their environment.

Misidentification or delayed processing might lead to accidents. The significance of sensors for environmental understanding becomes evident as vehicles navigate complex environments, including various weather conditions (rain, fog, snow) that may impede sensor data collection, such as camera vision or LiDAR performance. Furthermore, autonomous vehicles need efficient vehicle-to-vehicle (V2V) and vehicle-to-infrastructure (V2I) communication to convey information on traffic conditions, road hazards, and optimal driving speeds. Insufficient coordination led to traffic inefficiencies or accidents. Real-time decisions on lane changes, deceleration, or stopping are crucial for autonomous cars. This requires swift, accurate awareness of the environment and reaction to dynamic situations, such as sudden lane changes by other drivers. Autonomous vehicles have challenges, including the legal framework (establishing culpability in accidents), safety regulations, and ethical considerations (*e.g.*, prioritization in unavoidable collision situations). Emerging ITS seeks to mitigate the aforementioned problems and challenges through the utilization of modern technology. Image Processing is one such technology that offers promising answers, as outlined below.

## Solutions

The resolution of intelligent image processing is crucial for autonomous vehicles, since it analyzes real-time visual data from cameras, LiDAR, and radar. Additionally, object detection and classification, scene understanding, management of adverse weather conditions, lane detection, and detection of depth information are also included. A couple of them are detailed below.

1. Object Detection and Classification: Deep learning architectures, including CNNs, YOLO, and SSD, are employed to identify and categorize things such as pedestrians, automobiles, and barriers in real-time. Image processing systems detect objects and forecast their trajectories, enabling autonomous vehicles to execute instantaneous judgment. Utilizing YOLO [21, 22], R-CNN [1], SSD [28], and similar algorithms for real-time pedestrian recognition to prevent accidents by forecasting their trajectory and modifying the vehicle's course appropriately [9].

2. Image Segmentation and Scene Understanding: Fully Convolutional Networks (FCNs) and U-Net architectures execute image segmentation to delineate distinct areas within an image (*e.g.*, road, sidewalk, buildings). This enables the vehicle to comprehend its surroundings, distinguishing navigable zones from impediments [29]. For example, segregating road lanes from the adjacent environment in a highway enables the vehicle to remain inside its assigned lane.
3. Management of Adverse Weather Conditions: Image augmentation methodologies, such as GANs [7], augment image quality in low-visibility environments (rain, fog, snow). These networks augment camera feeds or LiDAR outputs, facilitating the safe operation of autonomous cars in difficult settings. GANs are used to improve visibility in foggy environments, enabling the vehicle to identify and manoeuvre around obstacles despite adverse weather [14, 22].
4. 3D Object Detection and Depth Estimation: Vehicles may generate three-dimensional representations of their surroundings using LiDAR and stereo cameras. Neural networks analyze this data to evaluate depth and detect objects at varying distances, hence improving safety in real-time navigation. For example, using LiDAR data to create a three-dimensional representation of the surroundings and detect nearby cars or obstacles, irrespective of their visibility to the camera [22].
5. Real-time Lane Detection: Image processing algorithms identify lane markers and road limits, even when they are faint or partially concealed. This guarantees that vehicles stay in the appropriate lane. For instance, Employing CNN-based lane identification models to recognize obscured or provisional lane markers during road construction [3, 30].

The list is comprehensive, and it is impractical to address all items here; just a selection is handled. Autonomous driving has significant challenges; nevertheless, ITS offers answers by enabling real-time communication between cars and infrastructure, advanced traffic management, and predictive traffic modeling. IIP enhances the vehicle's ability to see and react to its environment, even under difficult conditions, through the use of deep learning models for object detection, scene segmentation, and 3D mapping. The integration of ITS with advanced image processing enhances the safety, efficiency, and reliability of autonomous driving systems. The next section examines several case studies and real-world implementations.

## CASE STUDIES

The use of ANNs in ITS represents both a theoretical progression and shown efficacy in practical applications, yielding concrete advantages in traffic management, autonomous driving, and smart city infrastructure. This section emphasizes case studies and practical applications of ANN-based systems that have notably influenced transportation systems.

## A Smart City

An innovative Intelligent Transportation System (ITS) has been partially implemented in New York City to enhance traffic flow and urban mobility through real-time data processing and analysis [14]. Similar deployments of ITS have occurred in various cities worldwide, including San Francisco, Boston, Chicago, London, Barcelona, Amsterdam, Berlin, Copenhagen, Paris, Stockholm, Singapore, Seoul, Tokyo, and Melbourne [27]. New York City employs CNNs and image processing methods on video captured from more than 12,000 traffic cameras situated at critical junctions and congested zones. This technology recognizes congestion, detects events, and automatically changes traffic signals to enhance traffic flow and minimize emissions. The system utilizes historical data and employs predictive algorithms, including RNN and LSTM models, to forecast peak traffic times and implement modifications prior to congestion occurring [23]. The Intelligent Transportation Systems (ITS) of these cities deploy AI-based image processing for smart city traffic management, showcasing the ability to improve passenger experience and reduce traffic-related environmental impacts.

## Implemented ITS

Singapore's Land Transport Authority (LTA) has utilized ITS with a sophisticated data analytics platform employing LSTM networks and image processing to oversee real-time traffic and forecast congestion trends [14]. Traffic camera video streams are analyzed using image recognition models that evaluate traffic density, identify cars, and detect abnormalities such as traffic incidents [2]. The data is analyzed to generate real-time heat maps that highlight high-traffic zones and offer insights for adaptive traffic management [18]. By integrating image processing with LSTM predictive models, the system anticipates probable congestion areas, allowing traffic control centers to implement proactive actions such as modifying traffic light patterns, providing notifications to vehicles, and recommending alternate routes. Singapore's strategy demonstrates how ITS, utilizing AI-driven image processing, may mitigate congestion and enhance traffic safety in densely populated metropolitan areas.

### Autonomous Driving

Waymo, a prominent enterprise in autonomous driving technology, utilizes sophisticated image processing and deep learning algorithms to attain precise navigation and object recognition [14]. A comprehensive list of several manufacturers is actively contributing to autonomous driving vehicles, including Tesla (Full Self-Driving), Argo AI, Aurora Innovation, Pony.ai, Cruise, and others. These vehicles are outfitted with a variety of sensors, such as high-resolution cameras, LiDAR, and radar, which provide substantial amounts of real-time data for neural networks like YOLO and SSD to analyze. These models enable autonomous cars to identify objects, including people, automobiles, and bicycles, at elevated speeds and with remarkable accuracy. The technology employs CNNs and RNNs to assess the spatial and temporal dimensions of traffic, allowing cars to react adeptly to evolving urban settings [18]. Waymo has developed an advanced autonomous driving platform through continuous data training and testing, adept at navigating complex urban settings, notably demonstrated in Phoenix, Arizona, where it has been operational and delivering safe and efficient services to the public; other companies have made similar contributions as well [23, 27].

These case studies highlight the transformational influence of ANNs on practical ITS. ANNs provide enhanced, secure, and efficient transportation solutions, ranging from predictive traffic management to autonomous vehicle training and real-time accident detection. As these technologies advance, their implementation in cities globally is anticipated to increase, further propelling the evolution of interconnected, adaptable, and sustainable transportation networks worldwide

## CONCLUSION

The use of ANNs in ITS signifies a notable progress in achieving efficient, adaptable, and robust urban transportation solutions. Utilizing several ANN designs, including CNN, RNN, and novel models such as GAN and CapsNet, ITS can address the complex data requirements of smart cities. These neural networks enable computers to analyze real-time traffic data, forecast congestion, optimize vehicle routing, and improve autonomous driving capabilities. Applications like YOLO and SSD offer rapid and precise object identification, essential for real-time decision-making in autonomous driving, whilst models like LSTM are proficient in predicting traffic patterns, facilitating dynamic urban traffic management. Advanced networks such as CapsNet and SNN offer energy-efficient processing and enhanced interoperability, crucial for sustaining resilient ITS infrastructure against resource limitations. These developments are together altering transport networks, advancing them towards the ideal of safe, sustainable, and linked smart cities.

The use of ANNs in ITS is ushering in a new epoch of mobility defined by intelligent, responsive, and adaptive systems. This chapter underscores that, despite considerable advancements, continuous research and development are essential to fully exploit the capabilities of ANNs. Future advancements in neural network topologies, along with enhanced data integration from many sources, will further augment ITS capabilities, ultimately transforming urban mobility and improving quality of life in smart cities globally.

## REFERENCES

[1] T. Bai, J. Luo, S. Zhou, Y. Lu, and Y. Wang, "Vehicle-Type Recognition Method for Images Based on Improved Faster R-CNN Model", In: *Sensors* vol. 24. , 2024, no. 8, p. 2650. [http://dx.doi.org/10.3390/s24082650]

[2] M. Bakirci, "Utilizing YOLOv8 for enhanced traffic monitoring in intelligent transportation systems (ITS) applications", *Digital Signal Processing,* vol. 152, p. 104594, 2024. [http://dx.doi.org/10.1016/j.dsp.2024.104594]

[3] F. A. Barrios, A. Biswas, and A. Emadi, "Deep Learning-Based Motion Prediction Leveraging Autonomous Driving Datasets: State-of-the-Art", *IEEE Access,* vol. 12, pp. 93318-93332, 2024. [http://dx.doi.org/10.1109/ACCESS.2024.3423809]

[4] W. Chen, Q. Sun, J. Wang, J. J. Dong, and C. Xu, "A Novel Model Based on AdaBoost and Deep CNN for Vehicle Classification", *IEEE Access,* vol. 6, pp. 60445-60455, 2018. [http://dx.doi.org/10.1109/ACCESS.2018.2875525]

[5] G. Comert, Z. Khan, M. Rahman, and M. Chowdhury, "Grey models for short-term queue length predictions for adaptive traffic signal control", *Expert Syst. Appl.,* vol. 185, p. 115618, 2021. [http://dx.doi.org/10.1016/j.eswa.2021.115618]

[6] S.P. Yadav, and D.P. Mahato, *Distributed Artificial Intelligence: A Modern Approach.* CRC Press, 2020. [http://dx.doi.org/10.1201/9781003038467]

[7] M. A. Jan, M. Adil, B. Brik, S. Harous, and S. Abbas, "Making sense of big data in intelligent transportation systems: Current trends, challenges and future directions", *ACM Computing Surveys,* vol. 57, no. 8, pp. 1-43, 2025.

[8] B. Ben Elallid, N. Benamar, M. Bagaa, and Y. Hadjadj-Aoul, "Enhancing Autonomous Driving Navigation Using Soft Actor-Critic", In: *Future Internet* vol. 16. , 2024, no. 7, p. 238. [http://dx.doi.org/10.3390/fi16070238]

[9] H. Garg, A.K. Bhartee, A. Rai, M. Kumar, and A. Dhakrey, "A Review of Object Detection Algorithms for Autonomous Vehicles: Trends and Developments", In: *Proc. 5th Int. Conf. on Advances in Computing, Communication Control and Networking (ICAC3N)*, 2023, pp. 1173-1181. [http://dx.doi.org/10.1109/ICAC3N60023.2023.10541773]

[10] M. H. Ha, and O. T. C. Chen, "Deep Neural Networks Using Capsule Networks and Skeleton-Based Attentions for Action Recognition", *IEEE Access,* vol. 9, pp. 6164-6178, 2021. [http://dx.doi.org/10.1109/ACCESS.2020.3048741]

[11] I.W.H. Ho, S.C.K. Chau, E.R. Magsino, and K. Jia, "Efficient 3D road map data exchange for intelligent vehicles in vehicular fog networks", *IEEE Trans. Vehicular Technol.,* vol. 69, no. 3, pp. 3151-3165, 2020. [http://dx.doi.org/10.1109/TVT.2019.2963346]

[12] M. Jafari, A. Kavousi-Fard, T. Chen, and M. Karimi, "A Review on Digital Twin Technology in Smart Grid, Transportation System and Smart City: Challenges and Future", *IEEE Access,* vol. 11, pp. 17471-17484, 2023.
[http://dx.doi.org/10.1109/ACCESS.2023.3241588]

[13] T. Jiang, "Application of SSD network algorithm in panoramic video image vehicle detection system", *Open Computer Science,* vol. 13, no. 1, p. 20220270, 2023.
[http://dx.doi.org/10.1515/comp-2022-0270]

[14] R. A. Khalil, "Advanced Learning Technologies for Intelligent Transportation Systems: Prospects and Challenges", *IEEE Open Journal of Vehicular Technology,* vol. 5, pp. 397-427, 2024.
[http://dx.doi.org/10.1109/OJVT.2024.3369691]

[15] K. P. M. Patrick, A. F. Adekoya, A. M. Baagyire, and E. B. Y. Edward, "Capsule Networks – A survey", *Journal of King Saud University - Computer and Information Sciences,* vol. 34, no. 1, pp. 158-171, 2022.
[http://dx.doi.org/10.1016/j.jksuci.2019.09.014]

[16] A. Muniswamy, and R. Rathi, "A Detailed Review on Enhancing the Security in Internet of Things-Based Smart City Environment Using Machine Learning Algorithms", *IEEE Access,* vol. 12, pp. 120389-120413, 2024.
[http://dx.doi.org/10.1109/ACCESS.2024.3450180]

[17] A. Paul, N. Chilamkurti, A. Daniel, and S. Rho, *Intelligent Vehicular Networks and Communications.* Elsevier, 2016.

[18] S. Rahmani, A. Baghbani, N. Bouguila, and Z. Patterson, "Graph Neural Networks for Intelligent Transportation Systems: A Survey", In: *IEEE Transactions on Intelligent Transportation Systems* vol. 24. , 2023, no. 8, pp. 8846-8885.
[http://dx.doi.org/10.1109/TITS.2023.3257759]

[19] F. Rasheed, K.-L. A. Yau, R. M. Noor, C. Wu, and Y.-C. Low, "Deep Reinforcement Learning for Traffic Signal Control: A Review", *IEEE Access,* vol. 8, pp. 208016-208044, 2020.
[http://dx.doi.org/10.1109/ACCESS.2020.3034141]

[20] G. P. Rosati Papini, A. Plebe, M. Da Lio, and R. Donà, "A Reinforcement Learning Approach for Enacting Cautious Behaviours in Autonomous Driving System: Safe Speed Choice in the Interaction With Distracted Pedestrians", In: *IEEE Transactions on Intelligent Transportation Systems* vol. 23. , 2022, no. 7, pp. 8805-8822.
[http://dx.doi.org/10.1109/TITS.2021.3086397]

[21] W. Shariff, M. S. Dilmaghani, P. Kielty, M. Moustafa, J. Lemley, and P. Corcoran, "Event Cameras in Automotive Sensing: A Review", *IEEE Access,* vol. 12, pp. 51275-51306, 2024.
[http://dx.doi.org/10.1109/ACCESS.2024.3386032]

[22] T. Sharma, A. Chehri, I. Fofana, S. Jadhav, S. Khare, B. Debaque, N. Duclos-Hindie, and D. Arya, "Deep Learning-Based Object Detection and Classification for Autonomous Vehicles in Different Weather Scenarios of Quebec", In: *IEEE Access* vol. 12. , 2024, pp. 13648-13662.
[http://dx.doi.org/10.1109/ACCESS.2024.3354076]

[23] M. Talebkhah, A. Sali, M. Gordan, S. J. Hashim, and F. Z. Rokhani, "Comprehensive Review on Development of Smart Cities Using Industry 4.0 Technologies", *IEEE Access,* vol. 11, pp. 91981-92030, 2023.
[http://dx.doi.org/10.1109/ACCESS.2023.3302262]

[24] A. Wang, H. Chen, L. Liu, K. Chen, Z. Lin, J. Han, and G. Ding, "YOLOv10: Real-Time End-to-End Object Detection", *arXiv preprint arXiv:2405.14458,* 2024.

[25] J. Wu, W. Zhang, M. Wu, G. Cui, X. Wang, and J. Gong, "Distributed Multi-Attention Generative Adversarial Network for Surrounding Vehicles Trajectories Prediction Based On Comprehensive Social Repulsion", *IEEE Access,* vol. 10, pp. 125254-125263, 2022.

[http://dx.doi.org/10.1109/ACCESS.2022.3224481]

[26] L. Wu, R. Zhang, R. Zhou, and D. Wu, "An edge computing based data detection scheme for traffic light at intersections", *Comput. Commun.,* vol. 176, pp. 91-98, 2021. [http://dx.doi.org/10.1016/j.comcom.2021.05.014]

[27] J. Yang, Y. Kwon, and D. Kim, Regional Smart City Development Focus: The South Korean National Strategic Smart City Program. *IEEE Access*, Vol. 9. 7193-7210, 2021. [http://dx.doi.org/10.1109/ACCESS.2020.3047139]

[28] T. Yang, R. Liang, and L. Huang, "Vehicle counting method based on attention mechanism SSD and state detection", *The Visual Computer,* vol. 38, no. 9, pp. 2871-2881, 2022. [http://dx.doi.org/10.1007/s00371-021-02161-y]

[29] J. Ye, X. Li, X. Zhang, Q. Zhang, and W. Chen, "Deep learning-based human activity real-time recognition for pedestrian navigation", *Sensors (Basel),* vol. 20, no. 9, p. 2574, 2020. [http://dx.doi.org/10.3390/s20092574] [PMID: 32366055]

[30] N.J. Zakaria, M.I. Shapiai, R.A. Ghani, M.N.M. Yassin, M.Z. Ibrahim, and N. Wahid, *Lane Detection in Autonomous Vehicles: A Systematic Review.. IEEE Access*, Vol. 11, 3729-3765, 2023. [http://dx.doi.org/10.1109/ACCESS.2023.3234442]

# CHAPTER 8

# Advanced Image Analysis Techniques Using Machine Learning and Transformers

**Sulaxan Jadhav**[1,*], **Harsimran Singh**[2], **M. Masilamani**[3], **Abhijeet Gajanan Chimankar**[4], **T Sivamani**[5] and **Atowar Ul Islam**[6]

[1] *Symbiosis School of Economics, Symbiosis International (Deemed University), Pune, Maharashtra, India*

[2] *Department of Electrical Engineering, Guru Kashi University, Talwandi Sabo, Punjab, India*

[3] *Department of Artificial Intelligence and Data Science, Dr. Mahalingam College of Engineering and Technology, Pollachi, Tamil Nadu, India*

[4] *Department of Computer Science, Radhai Mahavidyalaya, Chhatrapati Sambhajinagar, Maharashtra, India*

[5] *Department of Electronics and Communication Engineering, Hindusthan Institute of Technology, Coimbatore, Tamil Nadu, India*

[6] *Department of Computer Science, University of Science and Technology, Baridua, Meghalaya, India*

**Abstract:** Computer vision has witnessed remarkable progress in recent years, particularly in the domain of image analysis, which forms the foundation for numerous real-world applications. Traditional methods for image understanding often rely on handcrafted features and shallow models, which struggle to handle the complexity, high dimensionality, and unstructured nature of modern visual data. This limitation reduces their effectiveness in tasks such as medical imaging, remote sensing, and scene understanding, where accurate interpretation of intricate patterns is critical. The emergence of deep learning has fundamentally transformed this landscape, enabling models to automatically learn hierarchical representations directly from raw data and to capture complex spatial and semantic relationships. Convolutional neural networks (CNNs) have long dominated image analysis, offering strong performance in classification, detection, and segmentation tasks. However, recent advances highlight the limitations of CNNs in modeling global dependencies, motivating the exploration of alternative architectures. Transformers, originally developed for natural language processing, have demonstrated exceptional capability in capturing long-range correlations and contextual dependencies. Their application to computer vision tasks has opened new avenues for achieving state-of-the-art results across diverse benchmarks. This research investigates advanced methods for image analysis that integrate transformer architectures with machine learning, seeking to enhance model

* **Corresponding author Sulaxan Jadhav:** Symbiosis School of Economics, Symbiosis International (Deemed University), Pune, Maharashtra, India; E-mail: slxnjdhv@gmail.com

**Ravinder M., Arti Ranjan, Youddha Beer Singh (Eds.)**

accuracy, robustness, and interpretability. By leveraging the strengths of both CNNs and transformers, this study aims to address existing challenges in picture analysis and contribute to the development of more generalizable and efficient vision systems. The findings offer promising directions for future applications where precise and scalable image analysis is indispensable.

**Keywords:** Advanced image analysis techniques, Convolutional neural Network (CNNs), Machine learning, Transformers, Vision transformers (ViTs).

## INTRODUCTION

The field of image analysis has significantly evolved with the advent of machine learning (ML) and deep learning (DL) techniques [1, 2]. Traditional image processing methods have been largely replaced or augmented by sophisticated models that can learn complex patterns from vast datasets. Recently, transformers—originally developed for natural language processing—have demonstrated remarkable potential in vision tasks, pushing the boundaries of image recognition, segmentation, and enhancement. This review examines advancements in image analysis enabled by machine learning and transformers, highlighting their impact across various applications. Earlier image processing techniques relied on feature extraction and rule-based approaches. Methods such as edge detection, histogram equalization, and morphological operations were generally used for object recognition and classification. Traditional machine learning (ML) models were employed to improve classification accuracy by learning from handcrafted features. However, these approaches were often limited by their inability to generalize well across diverse datasets and complex visual patterns [3, 4].

## MACHINE LEARNING AND DEEP LEARNING APPROACHES

The introduction of deep learning (DL) revolutionized image analysis, enabling models to learn hierarchical features directly from data. CNNs became the foundation of modern image analysis, excelling in tasks such as image classification, segmentation, and object detection. Architectures like AlexNet, VGG, ResNet, and EfficientNet significantly improved performance by leveraging deep hierarchical structures. These models employ layers of convolutional filters to extract spatial features, allowing for robust feature representation. Further advancements included (GANs) and autoencoders [5], which enhanced image synthesis, super-resolution, and de-noising. GANs, in particular, facilitated high-quality image generation through adversarial training, in which a generator and a discriminator compete to improve image authenticity. Meanwhile, RNNs and LSTM networks contributed to video analysis and sequential image processing, but their limitations in handling long-range dependencies prompted the need for more advanced architectures [6, 7].

## THE RISE OF TRANSFORMERS IN IMAGE ANALYSIS

Transformers, initially designed for natural language processing (NLP), have gained major traction in computer vision due to the ability to model long-range dependencies without relying on spatial locality. Vision Transformers (ViTs) have emerged as powerful alternatives to CNNs, demonstrating competitive performance in image classification and segmentation [8]. ViTs divide images into patches and process them using self-attention mechanisms, capturing global contextual relationships more effectively than traditional CNNs. Hybrid models, such as the Convolutional Vision Transformer (CvT) and the Swin Transformer [9], combine convolutional layers with transformer-based attention mechanisms to balance computational efficiency with performance. These architectures have proven effective in various image analysis applications, including medical imaging, autonomous driving, and remote sensing. Throughout this chapter, we will investigate how convolutional neural networks (CNNs) have emerged as the cornerstone of modern image processing. When it comes to image segmentation, object recognition, and classification, computer networks (CNNs) have been shown to be quite effective [10]. In the next section, we will investigate the role that transformers play in image analysis, with a particular emphasis on their ability to capture global dependencies in images and their potential to either replace or enhance CNNs in certain applications. Additionally, we investigate new developments that combine CNNs with transformers, such as vision transformers (ViTs) and transformer-based object identification models. These developments are still being investigated. These methods take advantage of the merging of CNNs and transformers in image processing to provide better efficiency and performance. We examine the issues currently being faced in this area, as well as the future directions being pursued. These challenges include the need for more interpretable and explainable models that are resistant to adversarial attacks and scalable to large-scale image datasets. The purpose of this article is to present a complete review of sophisticated image analysis approaches that make use of machine learning and transformers, demonstrating the revolutionary influence that these techniques have had on the area of computer vision. Fig. (**1**) shows the advanced Image Analysis Techniques using machine learning and transformers, and Table **1** shows the image analysis using machine learning.

**Table 1. Image analysis techniques using machine learning.**

| TECHNIQUE | DESCRIPTION |
|---|---|
| *(CNNs)* | CNNs are great for image classification, object identification, and segmentation because they learn hierarchical representations of pictures [17]. |
| ***Transfer Learning*** | By utilising the information gained from big datasets, transfer learning allows for the fine-tuning of pre-trained models on specific image analysis tasks. |
| ***Object Detection*** | Object detection techniques identify and locate objects within images, often using methods like region-based CNNs (R-CNNs) or single-shot detectors (SSDs). |
| ***Image Segmentation*** | Medical image analysis and scene understanding are two applications that can benefit from image segmentation, which splits an image into relevant segments or areas. |
| ***Generative Adversarial Networks (GANs)*** | For GANs to produce convincing images, it is necessary to train not one but two neural networks simultaneously: one to generate images and another to assess their realism. |
| ***Image Classification*** | Classifying images is a common practice in image recognition, and it frequently makes use of deep learning models, such as convolutional neural networks (CNNs), to do so. |
| ***Feature Extraction*** | In order to facilitate picture retrieval and other machine learning operations, feature extraction methods extract useful attributes from images. |
| ***Dimensionality Reduction*** | A few dimensionality reduction techniques that may be employed to simplify picture data include principal component analysis (PCA) and t-distributed stochastic neighbour embedding (t-SNE). |
| ***Object Tracking*** | Object tracking algorithms follow objects' movement in videos or image sequences, which can be useful for surveillance or activity recognition applications [18]. |
| ***Image Enhancement*** | Denoising, colour correction, and sharpening are just a few examples of image enhancement methods that may make a picture seem better and so aid in further research [19] |

In medical image analysis, ViTs have been applied to tasks including classification, segmentation, detection, registration, synthesis, and clinical report generation. A comprehensive review by Gao *et al.* (2023) [11] highlights the versatility of transformers in these applications, emphasizing their potential to enhance diagnostic accuracy and efficiency. Similarly, a survey by Bian *et al.* (2023) [12] examines the application of transformers in histopathological image analysis, covering various topics and demonstrating the adaptability of transformer models for processing complex medical images.

Beyond medical applications, ViTs have been explored in general image classification tasks. A study by El-Nouby *et al.* (2021) [13] introduces the Cross-Covariance Image Transformer (XCiT), which operates across feature channels rather than tokens, allowing efficient processing of high-resolution images. This model combines the accuracy of conventional transformers with the scalability of convolutional architectures, achieving excellent results on multiple vision benchmarks. Furthermore, Touvron *et al*. (2021) [14] investigate the optimization of deeper transformer networks for image classification. Their work presents architectural changes that significantly improve the accuracy of deep transformers, leading to models that achieve state-of-the-art performance on ImageNet without external data.

These studies collectively underscore the transformative impact of machine learning and transformer-based models on advanced image analysis techniques, paving the way for future research and applications in various fields [15]. (Fig. **1**) shows Advanced Image Analysis Techniques using machine learning and transformers.

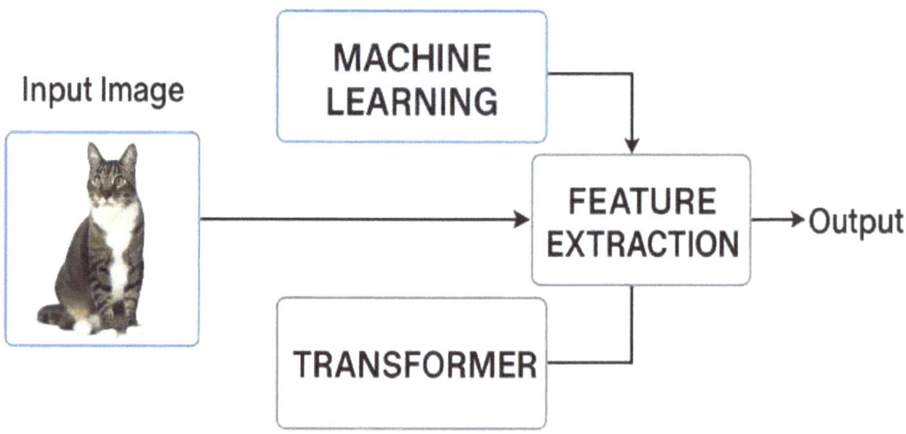


**Fig. (1).** Advanced image analysis techniques using machine learning and transformers [16].

Image analysis techniques using machine learning are given in Table **1**.

## RECOGNITION OF OBJECTS IN IMAGES, THE PROCESS OF SEGMENTATION, AND CLASSIFICATION OF IMAGES

CNNs have shown to be an essential tool in achieving state-of-the-art performance in several image processing tasks, such as picture classification, object recognition, and segmentation [20, 21]. Their function in these tasks is explained here:

***Image Classification:*** One reason CNNs are so effective in picture classification is their capacity to learn hierarchical representations of images. They are composed of many layers, including convolutional, pooling, and fully connected layers. Pooling layers decrease the spatial dimensions of the features, whereas convolutional layers employ filters to extract features from the input image [22, 23]. Following this, classification using the discovered features is performed by fully connected layers.

With regard to picture classification benchmarks such as ImageNet, CNNs have shown exceptional performance, even surpassing the level of accuracy achieved by humans in some instances. As a result of their ability to successfully learn to detect intricate patterns and objects in pictures, they are suited for a wide variety of categorization jobs.

***Object Recognition*** Object recognition is the process of identifying and categorizing items that are included in a picture. Because CNNs are able to learn hierarchical features, they are an excellent choice for this particular job [1]. CNNs can locate objects and categorize them into predefined categories because they are trained on datasets with tags [24].

CNNs are used in applications, such as autonomous driving, which recognize automobiles, pedestrians, and other things in real time. Object identification is an essential component of these kinds of systems. The accuracy and dependability of such systems have been greatly enhanced by the implementation of CNN-based object recognition systems, as shown in Table **2**.

***Segmentation*** The process of splitting an image into multiple segments or areas to simplify its representation is called image segmentation. Using CNNs has proven to be quite beneficial in semantic segmentation, where every picture pixel is assigned a class name [25].

Some CNN-based segmentation models that have achieved impressive results in medical image analysis, scene understanding, and satellite image processing include U-Net and Fully Convolutional Networks (FCNs). The production of detailed segmentation masks is accomplished by these models by using the spatial information that is gathered by convolutional layers [26].

The introduction of very effective tools for picture categorization, object recognition, and segmentation within images, as seen in Fig. (**2**) by (CNNs has completely transformed the field of image analysis. Computer vision has advanced significantly thanks to its ability to learn complex features from data; these advancements have broad practical implications [27].

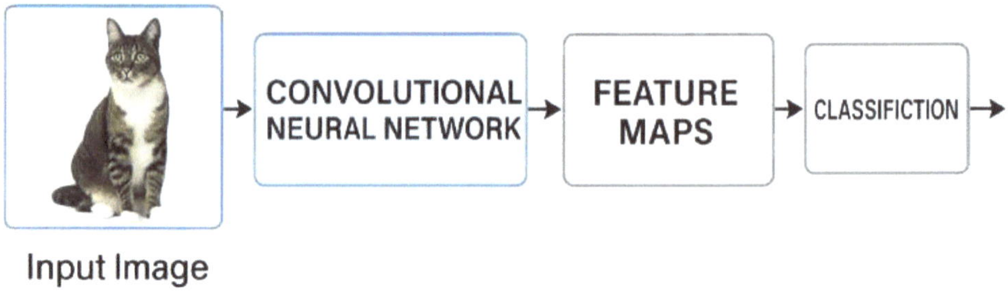


**Fig. (2).** CNNs in image analysis task [15].

**Table 2. Data analysis presenting picture categorization, object identification, and segmentation.**

| *Task* | Description | CNN Role |
|---|---|---|
| ***Image Classification*** | Classifying a complete image with a name or description. | Building hierarchical picture representations using convolutional, pooling, and completely interconnected levels enables the learning of complicated patterns and object recognition. |
| ***Object Recognition*** | Detecting and classifying objects within an image. | Localize objects and classify them into predefined categories by training on labeled datasets. |
| ***Segmentation*** | Partitioning an image into multiple segments or regions, often assigning each pixel a class label. | Leverage spatial information captured by convolutional layers to produce detailed segmentation masks [28]. |

When it comes to advanced image analysis techniques, the use of transformers and machine learning presents a number of obstacles, including the following:

When compared to typical machine learning models, transformer-based models are often criticized for their lack of interpretability. This aspect of the models is a common source of criticism. When it comes to applications that demand openness, it is particularly important to have a solid understanding of how these models arrive at their conclusions.

- ***Computational Resources:*** Hardware for Computers. Transformers need a substantial quantity of RAM and processing power due to their computational demands. This may make it difficult to deploy them in settings with limited resources or in applications that require real-time processing.
- ***Data Efficiency:*** Transformers sometimes require a large amount of labelled data for training, which is not necessarily easily available. This is particularly true in specialized areas or for specific tasks [29].

- ***Generalization:*** It is essential to make certain that models are able to generalize successfully to data that has not yet been encountered. The problem of overfitting to the training data may be difficult to solve, particularly with complex models such as transformers [30].
- ***Robustness to Adversarial Attacks:*** In the same way as other deep learning models are vulnerable to adversarial attacks, transformers are also subject to these attacks. These attacks include making modest perturbations to the input data in a well-prepared manner, which may result in inaccurate predictions.
- ***Scalability:*** One of the challenges that might arise when attempting to handle large-scale picture datasets or real-time applications is scaling transformer-based models. This is because of the complexity and resource needs of these models.
- ***Integration with Existing Systems:*** Integrating sophisticated image analysis methods into processes and systems that are already in place may be a tough endeavour. It requires careful planning and consideration of compatibility and interoperability concerns [31].
- ***Ethical and Legal concerns:*** When implementing sophisticated image analysis methods, it is imperative that ethical and legal concerns, such as data privacy, bias, and responsibility, be thoroughly addressed. This is the case with every artificial intelligence system.

To solve these problems, it is necessary to conduct continual research and development activities with the goal of enhancing the robustness, efficiency, and interpretability of sophisticated image analysis approaches that make use of transformers and machine learning.

## TRANSFORMERS' CAPACITY IN GLOBAL DEPENDENCIES' POTENTIAL TO REPLACE OR IMPROVE CNNS IN SOME APPLICATIONS

An intriguing area of study is the role of transformers in image analysis, particularly their ability to capture global dependencies in images. Although they were first developed for sequential data such as spoken language, transformers have shown the potential to capture spatial connections in photos.

- ***Capturing Global Dependencies:*** Transformers are able to capture long-range relationships over the whole picture, in contrast to Convolutional Neural Networks (CNNs), which analyze images in a hierarchical and local way rather than capturing global connections. In order for the model to focus on the parts of the image that are relevant to the prediction process, self-attention mechanisms are responsible for achieving this aim [32].

- ***Replacing or Enhancing CNNs:*** Transformers have the potential to supplant or supplement CNNs in specific applications. This is because transformers can either replace or enhance CNNs. The ability of transformers to capture global context and linkages makes them excellent for applications in which it is essential to have a comprehensive grasp of the picture. CNNs, on the other hand, are particularly good at catching local characteristics and patterns.
- ***Applications:*** Many image analysis tasks have made use of transformers, such as object detection, segmentation, and picture classification. Vision Transformers, also known as ViTs, are a particularly well-known design that exemplifies the efficiency of transformers in the context of image processing activities.
- ***Challenges:*** In spite of their promise, transformers are confronted with a number of obstacles in the field of image analysis. Scalability to high-resolution images is one of these obstacles, along with the difficulty of computation and the requirement for a large amount of training data [33]. In order to understand the complete possibilities of transformers in image processing, researchers are actively attempting to find solutions to these issues [34].
- ***Hybrid Approaches:*** The employment of transformers in combination with CNNs is one example of a hybrid technique. This strategy takes advantage of the similarities and differences between the two systems. For example, using transformers for global context and CNNs for local feature extraction may improve performance.
- ***Directions for the Future:*** Improving the efficiency and scalability of image processing models based on transformers may be the focus of future research in this area, as well as investigating novel designs and training methodologies to further improve their capabilities [35].

In general, transformers have the potential to revolutionize image analysis by offering a new method to represent global dependencies in pictures. This would be in addition to the capabilities of conventional CNN, as shown in Table **3**.

**Table 3. Table summarizing transformers' capacity to portray global dependencies in images and their potential to replace or improve CNNs in some applications.**

| *Aspect* | **Description** | **Transformers** |
|---|---|---|
| ***Global Dependency Representation*** | Transformers excel at capturing long-range dependencies in images, allowing them to understand the context of the entire image rather than just local features. | Leverage self-attention mechanisms to focus on relevant parts of the image and capture global context effectively. |

*(Table 3) cont.....*

| *Aspect* | **Description** | **Transformers** |
|---|---|---|
| ***Potential to Replace CNNs*** | In certain applications, transformers have the potential to replace CNNs, especially when understanding global context is crucial, such as in image captioning or scene understanding. | Offer a more holistic picture of images than typical CNNs, which may increase performance in applications that involve comprehending complicated visual interactions. |
| ***Potential to Improve CNNs*** | By combining local feature extraction with global context awareness, transformers can improve CNN models' robustness and accuracy. | Used in conjunction with CNNs, transformers can improve performance by providing additional context and enhancing feature representations, especially in tasks where both local and global information are important. |
| ***Computational Efficiency*** | Transformers are computationally intensive, requiring significant resources for training and inference, which can be a limiting factor in applications with strict resource constraints. | Require large-scale parallel computing resources for training due to their self-attention mechanism, making them less efficient compared to CNNs in terms of computational requirements. |
| ***Data Efficiency*** | In specialised fields or for specific tasks, transformer training requires significant volumes of tagged data, which may not be accessible. | Need extensive training data to learn meaningful representations, which can be a challenge in domains with limited annotated data or in scenarios where collecting labelled data is expensive or time-consuming. |
| ***Interpretability*** | Transformer forecasts are sometimes criticised for being harder to comprehend than CNN predictions. | Their self-attention mechanism makes it tougher to comprehend how individual visual elements affect the character's decision-making. |

## THE FUTURE OF ADVANCED IMAGE ANALYSIS TECHNIQUES USING MACHINE LEARNING AND TRANSFORMERS

A revolutionary potential exists for the future of sophisticated image analysis approaches that make use of machine learning and transformers, as shown in Fig. (3). This potential will have an influence on a variety of different fields and applications. A few important future directions and the possible impacts they might have are as follows:

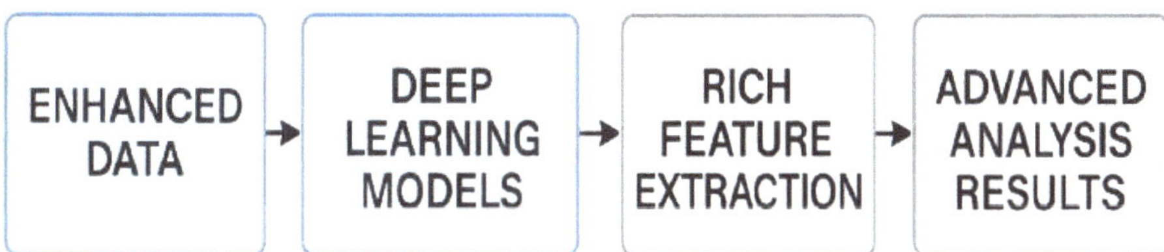


**Fig. (3).** Future of advanced image analysis techniques using machine learning [15].

- ***Improved Interpretability:*** Improving the interpretability of models will be essential in order to successfully implement them in applications that are of vital importance. Methods such as attention visualization and model explanation techniques will help people understand and trust conclusions driven by artificial intelligence.
- ***Efficient and Scalable Models:*** Models that are both efficient and scalable. The development of models that are both more efficient and scalable will make it possible for them to be deployed in settings that are resource-constrained and in real-time applications. A few examples of this include the optimization of transformers for image processing jobs and the investigation of lightweight structures.
- ***Learning Under and Outside of Supervision:*** By combining semi-supervised and self-supervised learning methods, we may train models using sparse labelled data, expanding their applicability to many other fields.
- ***Improved Generalization:*** There will be a primary emphasis placed on improving the generalization of the model to data that has not yet been encountered. Both the resilience and reliability of the model will be improved by the use of techniques such as domain adaptation and robust training against adversarial assaults.
- ***Integration with Other Technologies:*** Apps will become smarter and more immersive when image analysis approaches are combined with other emerging technologies like AR, VR, and the IoT.
- ***Ethical and Responsible Artificial Intelligence:*** It will be essential to address ethical and legal aspects, such as the reduction of bias, the protection of privacy, and transparency, in order to guarantee the responsible deployment of AI-driven image analysis systems.
- ***Personalized and Adaptive Systems:***Image analysis systems that are personalized and adaptable will improve the user experience and cater to the specific requirements of each individual, particularly in the fields of healthcare, education, and personalized services.
- ***Cross-Domain Applications:*** Investigating cross-domain applications, such as applying image analysis methods that were established for one domain (for example, medical imaging) to another domain (for example, environmental monitoring), will result in the development of novel solutions and discoveries.

These future prospects shed light on the transformational potential of sophisticated image analysis approaches that make use of machine learning and transformers. They also pave the way for revolutionary breakthroughs across a wide range of businesses and fields.

Table **4** below presents the future advanced image analysis techniques. The AI-driven image analysis is depicted in Fig. (**4**).

**Table 4. The future of advanced image analysis techniques.**

| *Aspect* | **Description** |
|---|---|
| ***Improved Interpretability*** | Enhancing the interpretability of models will be crucial for deploying them in critical applications. Techniques such as attention visualization and model explanation methods will help users understand and trust AI-driven decisions. |
| ***Efficient and Scalable Models*** | Developing more efficient and scalable models will enable their positioning in real-time applications and resource-constrained surroundings. This includes optimizing transformers for image analysis tasks and exploring lightweight architectures. |
| ***Semi-Supervised Learning*** | Leveraging semi-supervised and self-supervised learning approaches will enable training models with limited labelled data, making them more accessible for diverse applications and domains. |
| ***Improved Generalization*** | Enhancing model generalization to unseen data will be a key focus. Techniques such as domain adaptation and robust training against adversarial attacks will improve model robustness and reliability. |
| ***Integration with Other Technologies*** | Improved, more intelligent applications may be achieved by combining image analysis methods with other cutting-edge technologies like VR, IoT, and AR. |
| ***Ethical and Responsible AI*** | Addressing ethical and legal considerations, such as bias mitigation, privacy preservation, and transparency, will be critical for ensuring the responsible deployment of AI-driven image analysis systems. |
| ***Personalized and Adaptive Systems*** | Developing personalized and adaptive image analysis systems will enhance user experience and cater to individual needs, especially in healthcare, education, and personalized services. |
| ***Cross-Domain Applications*** | Exploring cross-domain applications, such as using image analysis techniques developed for one domain (*e.g.*, medical imaging) in another domain (*e.g.*, environmental monitoring), will lead to innovative solutions and discoveries. |

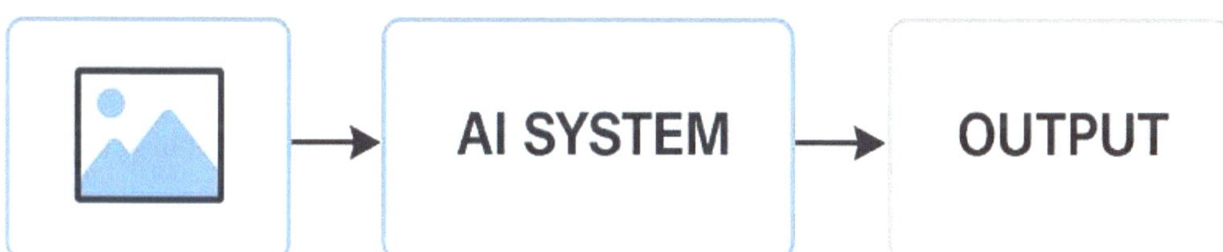


**Fig. (4).** AI-driven image analysis systems.

## CONCLUSION

To conclude, the subject of computer vision has been greatly affected by improved image analysis approaches that use transformers and machine learning.

These methods enable complicated model construction that is able to comprehend and interpret visual information. Transformers have shown potential for capturing global dependencies in images, while Convolutional Neural Networks (CNNs) have proven crucial for tasks such as object recognition, segmentation, and image classification. There is a lot of hope for these methods' future developments, which will likely concentrate on making them more efficient, scalable, and interpretable. Better and faster visual data processing is becoming possible thanks to ever-improving techniques such as object identification, image segmentation, and transfer learning. Still, there are obstacles to overcome, such as making models more interpretable, improving computational and data efficiency, and ensuring AI-driven systems are used ethically. While these obstacles remain, researchers and developers are working tirelessly to overcome them, opening the door to even more groundbreaking developments in sophisticated picture processing.

## REFERENCES

[1] M. A. Al-Asadi, and S. Tasdemir, "Medical Image Analysis Using Machine Learning Techniques: A Systematic Review", In: *Machine Learning and Deep Learning in Efficacy Improvement of Healthcare Systems,* O. P. Jena, B. Bhushan, N. Rakesh, P. N. Astya, Y. Farhaoui, Eds., CRC Press: Boca Raton, FL, USA, 2024, pp. 1-25.

[2] R. E. Soans, *"Image analysis methods for identification and segmentation of biological structures using machine learning techniques"*, Ph.D. dissertation, Dept. Elect. Comput. Eng., Drexel Univ., Philadelphia, PA, USA, 2017.

[3] A. Banerjee, S. Paul, and S. Bhattacharya, "Advanced Agricultural Systems: Identification, Crop Yields and Recommendation Using Image Processing Techniques and Machine-Learning Algorithms", In: *Machine Learning, Blockchain, and Cyber Security in Smart Environments: Application and Challenges,* S. Tanwar, S. Badotra, A. Rana, Eds., CRC Press: Boca Raton, FL, USA, 2022, pp. 81-97.

[4] A. P. Begum, and P. Selvaraj, "Multiclass Diagnosis of Alzheimer's Disease Analysis Using Machine Learning and Deep Learning Techniques", *Int. J. Image. Graph.,* vol. 24, no. 3, p. 2450031, 2024.

[5] M. Gogoi, and S.A. Begum, "Image classification using deep autoencoders", *Proc. IEEE Int. Conf. Computational Intelligence and Computing Research (ICCIC).* Coimbatore, India, 2017, pp. 1-5.

[6] A Tiwari, M Masilamani, T. S. Rao, S Zope, S. A. Deepak, and L Karthick, "Shaping the future: Emerging trends and strategic predictions in big data and AI", In: *AI and the Revival of Big Data,* M. M. T. Ayyalasomayajula, Ed., IGI Global, 2025, pp. 125-154. [http://dx.doi.org/10.4018/979-8-3693-8472-5.ch006]

[7] M. Li, Y. Jiang, Y. Zhang, and H. Zhu, "Medical image analysis using deep learning algorithms", *Front. Public Health,* vol. 11, 2023.1273253 [http://dx.doi.org/10.3389/fpubh.2023.1273253] [PMID: 38026291]

[8] O. Moutik, H. Sekkat, S. Tigani, A. Chehri, R. Saadane, T.A. Tchakoucht, and A. Paul, "Convolutional neural networks or vision transformers: Who will win the race for action recognitions in visual data?", *Sensors (Basel),* vol. 23, no. 2, p. 734, 2023. [http://dx.doi.org/10.3390/s23020734] [PMID: 36679530]

[9] Z. Liu, "Swin transformer: Hierarchical vision transformer using shifted windows", *Proc. IEEE/CVF Int. Conf. Comput. Vis. (ICCV).* Montreal, QC, Canada, 2021, pp. 9992-10002. [http://dx.doi.org/10.1109/ICCV48922.2021.00986]

[10] Q. Geng, Z. Zhou, and X. Cao, "Survey of recent progress in semantic image segmentation with CNNs", *Sci. China Inf. Sci.,* vol. 61, no. 5, 2018. [http://dx.doi.org/10.1007/s11432-017-9189-6]

[11] Y. Gao, Y. Zhou, Z. Zhang, H. Liu, and Z. Hu, "A survey on vision transformers in medical image analysis: Recent advances, challenges, and future trends", *arXiv preprint arXiv:2301.03505,* 2023.

[12] W. Bian, Z. Shao, X. Lin, S. Wang, and Q. Wang, "Transformers in histopathological image analysis: A comprehensive review", *Biomed. Eng. Online.* vol. 22, no. 1, p. 88, 2023.

[13] A.G. Wirayasa, Chimankar, N. Madhumithaa, U. Shankar, and L. Karthick, "Machine learning-based HR business intelligence with predictive maintenance integration. In: *Trends and Applications in Mechanical Engineering, Composite Materials and Smart Manufacturing.* IGI Global, 2024, pp. 381-396. [http://dx.doi.org/10.4018/979-8-3693-1966-6.ch025]

[14] H. Touvron, M. Cord, A. Sablayrolles, G. Synnaeve, and H. Jégou, "Going deeper with Image Transformers", *Proc. IEEE/CVF Int. Conf. Comput. Vis. (ICCV),* pp. 32-42, 2021. [http://dx.doi.org/10.1109/ICCV48922.2021.00010]

[15] L. Karthick, Mishra, R. Shanmugasundaram, S. Saravanan, and S. K. Trivedi, "AI-empowered smart electricity system with predictive maintenance integration. In: *Trends and Applications in Mechanical Engineering, Composite Materials and Smart Manufacturing.* IGI Global, 2024, pp. 307-320. [http://dx.doi.org/10.4018/979-8-3693-1966-6.ch020]

[16] S. Bogle, "Using Sentiment Analysis and Machine Learning Algorithms to Determine Citizens' Perceptions", In: *Machine Learning - Advanced Techniques and Emerging Applications,* H. Pirim, Ed., IntechOpen: London, UK, 2018. [http://dx.doi.org/10.5772/intechopen.72521]

[17] P. Divyashree, and P. Dwivedi, "Smart digital healthcare solutions using medical imaging and advanced AI techniques", In: *Machine Learning and Deep Learning Techniques for Medical Image Recognition,* S. B. Othman, C. Chakraborty, Eds., CRC Press: Boca Raton, FL, USA, 2023, pp. 76-89. [http://dx.doi.org/10.1201/9781003366249-5]

[18] A. Harshith Kumar, B. S. Thind, and C. C. Reddy, "Improving Reliability of Transformers based on DGA Analysis using Machine Learning Techniques", *Proc. IEEE Conf. Electr. Insul. Dielectr. Phenom. (CEIDP),* 2021pp. 151-154 [http://dx.doi.org/10.1109/CEIDP50766.2021.9705451]

[19] C. K. Jha, A. Choubey, M. H. Kolekar, and C. Chakraborty, "Automated Acute Lymphoblastic Leukemia Detection Using Blood Smear Image Analysis", In: *Machine Learning and Deep Learning Techniques for Medical Image Recognition,* S. B. Othman, C. Chakraborty, Eds., CRC Press: Boca Raton, FL, USA, 2023, pp. 64-75. [http://dx.doi.org/10.1201/9781003366249-4]

[20] P. Makam, and G. Janardhan, "Survival Analysis of Heart Failure Patients Using Advanced Machine Learning Techniques", *Proc. Int. Conf. Adv. & Global Eng. Challenges (AGEC),* 2023pp. 91-95 [http://dx.doi.org/10.1109/AGEC57922.2023.00029]

[21] V. K. Karthick, K. Keshamoni, B. P. Rani, R. J. K., and S. More, "A Comprehensive Review of Automation in Agriculture using Artificial Intelligence", *Proc. Int. Conf. Recent Innov. Smart Sustainable Technol. (ICRISST),* 2024pp. 1-5 [http://dx.doi.org/10.1109/ICRISST59181.2024.10921963]

[22] E. Romero, and F. González, "From biomedical image analysis to biomedical image understanding using machine learning", In: *Machine Learning: Concepts, Methodologies, Tools and Applications* IGI Global, 2012, pp. 1321-1345.

[23] P. Dhruv, and S. Naskar, "Image Classification Using Convolutional Neural Network (CNN) and Recurrent Neural Network (RNN): A Review", In: *Machine Learning and Information Processing,*

*Advances in Intelligent Systems and Computing,* D. Swain, P. Pattnaik, P. Gupta, Eds., vol. 1101. Springer: Singapore, 2020, pp. 367-381. [http://dx.doi.org/10.1007/978-981-15-1884-3_34]

[24] R. Salama, F. Al-Turjman, P. Chaudhary, and S.P. Yadav, "Benefits of Internet of Things (IoT) applications in healthcare – An overview", *Proc. Int. Conf. Computational Intelligence, Communication Technology and Networking (CICTN),* pp. 778-784, 2023.

[25] G. Vikram, S. S. Kadam, R. K. Mishra, M. V. Narasimha Rao, R. Prasanna Venkatesh, and L. Karthick, "Optimizing AI Through Data Mining and Statistical Tools for Enhanced Model Performance", In: *AI and the Revival of Big Data,* M. Ayyalasomayajula, Ed., IGI Global: Hershey, PA, USA, 2025, pp. 155-176. [http://dx.doi.org/10.4018/979-8-3693-8472-5.ch007]

[26] C-C. Wang, and C-H. Kuo, "Detecting dyeing machine entanglement anomalies by using time series image analysis and deep learning techniques for dyeing-finishing process", *Adv. Eng. Inform.,* vol. 55, 2023.101852 [http://dx.doi.org/10.1016/j.aei.2022.101852]

[27] K. Chauhan, "Internet of Things routing protocol with mobility awareness and energy efficiency", *Proc. Int. Conf. Advance Computing and Innovative Technologies in Engineering (ICACITE),* pp. 437-441, 2023. [http://dx.doi.org/10.1109/ICACITE57410.2023.10183117]

[28] P. Prabakaran, Integrating mechanical systems with biological inspiration: Implementing sensory gating in artificial vision. In: *Trends and Applications in Mechanical Engineering, Composite Materials and Smart Manufacturing.* IGI Global, 2024, pp. 190-202. [http://dx.doi.org/10.4018/979-8-3693-1966-6.ch012]

[29] S.S. Kadam, "Harnessing machine learning approaches for accurate energy demand forecasting in the power sector", *Proc. Int. Conf. Networking, Embedded and Wireless Systems (ICNEWS),* pp. 1-6, 2024. [http://dx.doi.org/10.1109/ICNEWS60873.2024.10731096]

[30] A.D.M. Singh, and P. Nand, "Use of machine learning in the area of image analysis and processing", *Proc. ICACCCN,* pp. 117-120, 2018. [http://dx.doi.org/10.1109/ICACCCN.2018.8748338]

[31] H. M. Kelagadi, R. K. Billady, R. Shanmugasundaram, K. R. Thilak, L. Karthick, and N. K. Patil, "An Enhanced Taxi Demand Perception System Leveraging Fusion and Automated Sensor Integration", In: *Trends and Applications in Mechanical Engineering, Composite Materials and Smart Manufacturing,* S. Padhi, Ed., IGI Global: Hershey, PA, USA, 2024, pp. 35-46. [http://dx.doi.org/10.4018/979-8-3693-1966-6.ch002]

[32] A. Arya, and A. Ranjan, "Beyond Syntax and Semantics: The Quantum Leap in Natural Language Processing", In: *A Handbook of Computational Linguistics: Artificial Intelligence in Natural Language Processing* 1st ed. Bentham Science Publishers: Sharjah, UAE, 2024, pp. 255-284.

[33] F. Sultana, A. Sufian, and P. Dutta, "Advancements in image classification using convolutional neural network", *Proc. Int. Conf. Research in Computational Intelligence and Communication Networks (ICRCICN),* pp. 122-129, 2018. [http://dx.doi.org/10.1109/ICRCICN.2018.8718718]

[34] A. Arya, A. Ranjan, and A. K. Agrawal, "Post-quantum image security: Challenges and opportunities", In: *Digital Image Security,* A. K. Singh, S. Berretti, A. Anand, A. K. Agrawal, Eds., 1st ed.. CRC Press: Boca Raton, FL, USA, 2024, pp. 165-197.

[35] J. Qin, W. Pan, X. Xiang, Y. Tan, and G. Hou, "A biological image classification method based on improved CNN", *Ecol. Inform.,* vol. 58, 2020.101093 [http://dx.doi.org/10.1016/j.ecoinf.2020.101093]

# CHAPTER 9

# Intelligent Agricultural Monitoring Framework Based on Machine Learning Techniques

**Isha Sood**[1,*], **L. Karthick**[2,*], **Ashutosh C Kakde**[3], **Punam Dattatray Gawali**[4], **Ankush Patil**[5] and **Ayushi Godiya**[1]

[1] *School of Engineering, Ajeenkya DY Patil University, Charholi Buduruk, Pune, Maharashtra, India*

[2] *Department of Mechanical Engineering, Hindusthan College of Engineering and Technology, Coimbatore, Tamil Nadu, India*

[3] *Department of Agricultural Engineering, Nehru Institute of Technology, Coimbatore, Tamil Nadu, India*

[4] *School of Humanities and Engineering Sciences, MIT Academy of Engineering, Pune, Maharashtra, India*

[5] *Department of Mathematics, Research Centre, L.V.H ASC College, Nashik & MIT Academy of Engineering, Pune, Maharashtra, India*

**Abstract:** The term smart agriculture refers to a relatively new academic discipline that makes use of technology to enhance agricultural methods in order to maximize crop output, quality, and sustainability. Using monitoring systems that apply machine learning (ML) algorithms to analyze data from field sensors, is an essential component of smart agriculture. With the data these technologies may provide, farmers would be able to make more informeddecisions about watering, fertilising, and insect control, among other crucial farming tasks. This study aims to thoroughly examine smart agriculture monitoring systems that utilise machine learning applications. Data collection, pre-processing, feature selection, model construction, model deployment, and feedback loops are among the key components of such systems. Furthermore, we examine the most popular machine learning algorithms used in smart agriculture, including neural networks, decision trees, random forests, and support vector machines. We also discuss how these algorithms are applied to forecast crop production, identify diseases, and schedule irrigation.

**Keywords:** Crop production prediction, Disease detection, Farming techniques, Irrigation scheduling, Monitoring systems, Machine Learning (ML), Smart agriculture, Support vector machines.

* **Corresponding authors Isha Sood and L. Karthick:** School of Engineering, Ajeenkya DY Patil University, Charholi Buduruk, Pune, Maharashtra, India; Department of Mechanical Engineering, Hindusthan College of Engineering and Technology, Coimbatore, Tamil Nadu, India; E mails: ishasweet1984@gmail.com, bemechkarthick@gmail.com

**Ravinder M., Arti Ranjan, Youddha Beer Singh (Eds.)**

# INTRODUCTION

Precision agriculture, or smart agriculture, is a new kind of farming that uses technology to improve farming techniques and boost output. Utilizing monitoring systems that employ machine learning (ML) algorithms to analyze data from various field sensors is an essential part of smart agriculture. To help farmers make better choices and increase productivity, these tools provide them with helpful information and suggestions. The use of ML in agricultural monitoring systems may completely alter how farmers oversee their harvests and use available resources. Machine learning algorithms may aid farmers in real-time optimization of agricultural techniques by analysing massive volumes of data to identify trends, forecast results, and make predictions. Greater sustainability, less resource usage, and higher agricultural yields are all possible outcomes of this [1].

This chapter discusses the various parts of a machine learning (ML)- based smart agricultural monitoring system. Everything from the sensors used to the data they gather will be covered in our discussion of the information-gathering process. Fig. (**1**) illustrates data-preprocessing techniques, such as cleaning and standardisation, used to prepare data for machine learning algorithms. Furthermore, we will thoroughly examine the various machine learning models used in smart agriculture, including decision trees, artificial neural networks, random forests, and support vector machines. We will go over the process of training these models using historical data and then deploying them to the monitoring system so that farmers may get real-time insights and suggestions [2]. Considering all factors, machine learning-driven smart agricultural monitoring systems have the potential to transform farming by enhancing its efficiency, cost-effectiveness, and environmental sustainability. Increased agricultural yields, reduced environmental impact, and food security for decades to come are all possible outcomes of farmers embracing this technology, as shown in Table **1**.

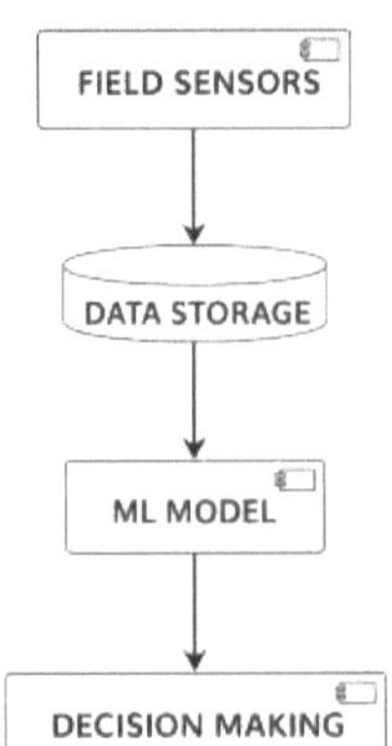


**Fig. (1).** ML in agricultural monitoring systems.

**Table 1. A smart agricultural system that makes use of machine learning might keep tabs on and analyse the data and metrics shown in this table.**

| *Metric* | *Description* | *Example Value* |
|---|---|---|
| ***Temperature*** | Measure of the temperature in the agricultural environment. | 25.6°C |
| ***Humidity*** | Measure of the humidity level in the agricultural environment. | 65% |
| ***Soil Moisture*** | Measure of the moisture content in the soil. | 35% |
| ***Light Intensity*** | Measure of the intensity of light in the agricultural environment. | 1200 lux |
| ***Crop Growth Stage*** | Classification of the current growth stage of the crops using machine learning algorithms. | Vegetative |
| ***Pest Infestation*** | Detection of pest infestation using machine learning algorithms. | Low |
| ***Disease Detection*** | Detection of diseases in crops using machine learning algorithms. | None |
| ***Irrigation Scheduling*** | Scheduling of irrigation based on soil moisture levels and weather forecasts using machine learning algorithms. | Next irrigation in 2 days |
| ***Crop Yield Prediction*** | Estimation of agricultural productivity using machine learning techniques. | 5000 kg/ha |

## ARTIFICIAL INTELLIGENCE APPLICATION IN AGRICULTURAL MONITORING TOOLS

Empirical evidence has demonstrated that the integration of machine learning (ML) into agricultural monitoring systems has yielded significant enhancements in the efficiency, output, and environmental performance of farming practices (2023). The assessment of extensive data collected from sensors and other sources by machine learning algorithms has the potential to provide farmers with valuable insights and recommendations. The following is a list of important parts of agricultural monitoring systems that make use of machine learning:

- ***Crop Yield Prediction:*** Agricultural yield prediction is the capacity of machine learning algorithms to analyse past data on weather conditions, soil quality, and crop characteristics to estimate future crop yields. Farmers canmake more informed choices about planting, harvesting, and resource allocation with this information [3].
- ***Detection of illness:*** Machine learning algorithms are able to examine photographs of crops in order to identify indications of illness or pest infestation. The practice of early detection enables farmers to take prompt action, such as the application of pesticides or the implementation of quarantine measures, in order to avoid the spread of disease and reduce the damage to their crops.

- ***Weed Identification and Management:*** Machine learning algorithms can differentiate between crops and weeds using photographs collected in the field in 2017. This allows for the identification and management of weeds. Farmers can implement tailored weed control techniques with this information, thereby reducing herbicide use and minimizing crop damage.
- ***Soil Health Monitoring:*** Machine learning algorithms are able to examine soil data, such as nutrient levels and pH, to assess the fertility and biological condition of the soil. With the use of this knowledge, farmers are able to make more educated judgments on the practices of fertilization and soil management [4].
- ***Irrigation Management:*** The application of machine learning systems in managing irrigation involves the analysis of soil moisture data obtained from sensors to enhance irrigation schedules, as seen in Fig. (**2**). Farmers may optimise both watering conservation and crop yields by ensuring that their crops receive the optimal amount of water at the targeted time [5].
- ***Crop surveillance and control:*** In the context of agricultural monitoring and management, machine learning algorithms may interpret data from drones and satellite photography to monitor the development and health of crops. This material helps farmers analyse and pinpoint ranges of concern, such as deficits in nutrients or infestations of pests, and in taking the required actions to address these issues [6].
- ***Harvest Forecasting:*** Using machine learning models, harvest forecasting can be achieved by analysing data on crop maturity and meteorological conditions to estimate harvest time and yield. Farmers can more effectively organize their harvest operations with this information.

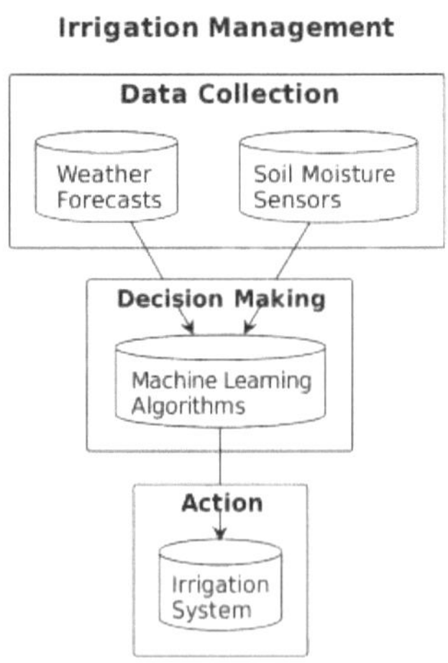


**Fig. (2).** Irrigation management.

In general, the use of machine learning in agricultural monitoring systems has the potential to change farming methods by enabling the implementation of techniques that are both more accurate and more sustainable [7]. Farming processes may be optimized, yields can be increased, and environmental impact can be reduced if farmers take advantage of the capabilities of machine learning systems, as depicted in Table **2**. Table **3** provides an overview of the parameters for crop monitoring and management.

**Table 2. Machine learning in agricultural tools for monitoring.**

| Tool | Description | Machine Learning Applications |
|---|---|---|
| ***Soil Moisture Sensors*** | Soil moisture sensors assist producers in determining when and to what extent to apply irrigation to their crops. | • Forecasting soil moisture availability using meteorological predictions and past data.<br>• Optimizing irrigation schedules for different crop types and soil conditions [8]. |
| ***Crop Health Sensors*** | Crop health monitoring sensors identify early indications of parasite problems, nutrient deficiency, and diseases. | • Identifying crop diseases and pests from sensor data and images.<br>• Recommending appropriate treatments and interventions.<br>• Monitoring crop health over time for early detection of issues [9]. |
| ***Weather Stations*** | Stations that gather data on meteorological parameters, including moisture, temperature, precipitation, and wind speed, offer excellent insights for agricultural practitioners. | • Predicting weather patterns and extreme events to help farmers plan their activities.<br>• Advising on optimal planting and harvesting times based on weather forecasts and historical data [10]. |
| ***Satellite Imagery*** | Satellites capture images of agricultural fields, providing valuable information regarding crop health, development, and external variables [4]. | • Monitoring crop growth and health from satellite images.<br>• Detecting changes in land use and vegetation cover.<br>• Assessing the impact of climate change on agricultural productivity [11]. |
| ***Drones*** | Drones equipped with cameras and sensors can acquire information and high-resolution images from agricultural fields, providing farmers with comprehensive views. | • Conducting aerial surveys to monitor crop health and growth.<br>• Identifying areas of crop stress or damage for targeted interventions.<br>• Mapping fields to optimize resource allocation and improve efficiency. |

*(Table 2) cont.....*

| Tool | Description | Machine Learning Applications |
|---|---|---|
| ***Automated Tractors*** | Tractors that are outfitted with GPS technology and devices are capable of performing planting, fertilizing, and harvesting tasks independently, thereby increasing productivity and decreasing labor expenses. | • Using GPS data to create precision maps of fields for optimized planting and harvesting.<br>• Monitoring crop health and growth during automated operations.<br>• Analyzing data to improve the efficiency and performance of automated tasks. |
| ***Irrigation Systems*** | By regulating water flow in accordance with real-time data, automated irrigation systems guarantee that crops are supplied with an optimal quantity of water at the appropriate moment. | • Forecasting irrigation needs using meteorological predictions, soil moisture levels, and crop water demands.<br>• Optimising irrigation schedules to minimise water inefficiency and enhance agricultural productivity. |

**Table 3. Providing an overview of the parameters for crop monitoring and management.**

| Metric | Description | Example Value |
|---|---|---|
| ***Crop Type*** | The type of crop being cultivated. | Wheat |
| ***Planting Date*** | Seeding date of the crop. | March 1, 2024 |
| ***Expected Harvest Date*** | The anticipated date for harvesting the crop. | June 30, 2024 |
| ***Growth Stage*** | Classification of the current growth stage of the crop | Vegetative |
| ***Soil Moisture Level*** | The amount of moisture present in the soil. | 25% |
| ***Temperature*** | The temperature of the crop's environment. | 28°C |
| ***Humidity*** | The humidity level of the crop's environment. | 70% |
| ***Light Intensity*** | The intensity of the light the crop is receiving. | 1500 lux |
| ***Pest Infestation*** | The severity of pest infestation on the crop. | Low |
| ***Disease Presence*** | Indication of any diseases affecting the crop. | None |
| ***Nutrient Levels*** | The levels of essential nutrients in the soil. | Nitrogen: 20 ppm, Phosphorus: 15 ppm, Potassium: 25 ppm |
| ***Irrigation Status*** | Whether the crop has been irrigated and when the next irrigation is scheduled. | Irrigated, Next irrigation in 2 days |
| ***Crop Health Score*** | A score indicating the overall health of the crop, calculated based on various factors. | 85 (out of 100) |

## THE DIFFERENT COMPONENTS THAT MAKE UP A SMART AGRICULTURAL MONITORING SYSTEM THAT USES MACHINE LEARNING (ML)

A machine learning (ML) smart agricultural monitoring system is made up of many critical components that collaborate with one another to gather, process, analyse, and act upon data in order to enhance farming methods, as shown in Fig. (**3**). Here are the primary components that make up such a system:

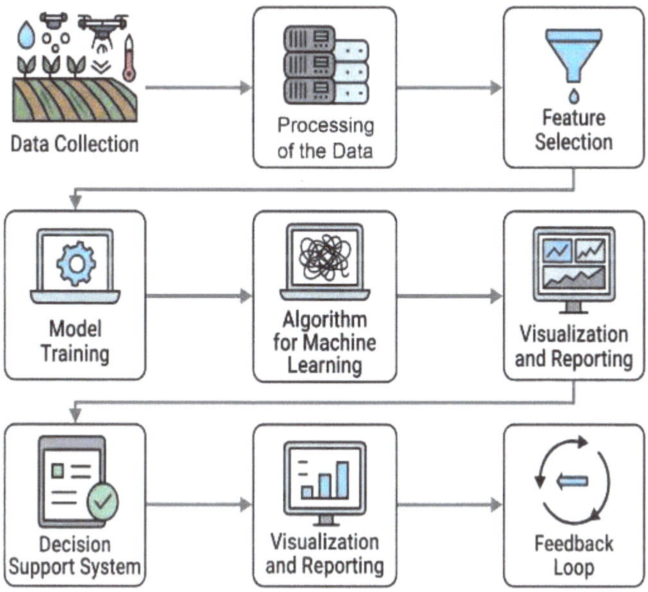


**Fig. (3).** Smart agriculture monitoring system.

***Data Collection:*** The collection of data from the agricultural field is accomplished via the use of sensors. These sensors have the capability to monitor a wide range of characteristics, including crops' health, soil moisture, temperature, and humidity, as well as ambient variables. Data gathering may also be accomplished via the use of satellites and drones, which can provide not just aerial photographs but also other useful information [12].

***Processing of the Data:*** Prior to analysis, it is essential to pre-process the obtained data to ensure its suitability. In this phase of preprocessing, the data is cleaned, noise is removed, and it is converted into a format usable by machine learning algorithms.

***Feature* Selection:** Determining which attributes are relevant to the analysis follows the conclusion of data preparation. An additional benefit of this stage is that it improves the efficiency of machine learning algorithms by reducing data dimensionality.

***Algorithms for Machine Learning:*** In-depth data analysis and intelligent conclusions are achieved through the application of ML algorithms. A lot of machine learning methods, including decision trees, random forests, support vector machines, and neural networks, are utilised in smart agriculture monitoring systems [13].

***Model Training:*** In the process of training machine learning models, historical data is used to teach the models about the patterns and correlations that exist within the data. With the aid of this training process, the models are able to provide accurate predictions and suggestions depending on newly acquired data.

***Model Deployment:*** Once the models have been trained, they are then deployed to the monitoring system. After reaching that point, they may analyse data in real-time and provide farmers with advice and recommendations.

***Feedback Loop:*** The system employs a feedback loop to continuously improve the effectiveness of the machine learning models it uses. The models are retrained to integrate new information as it is gathered, along with new data and observed results.

***Decision Support System:*** With the help of the machine learning models' insights and recommendations, the decision support system aids farmers in making crucial decisions

It is possible for this to incorporate advice for various agricultural operations such as irrigation, fertilization, insect control, and others.

***Visualization and Reporting***: The system is able to show the data and model outputs, which makes it simpler for farmers to comprehend the insights that are presented and to take action based on those insights. It is also possible to develop reports that provide a summary of the most important results and suggestions.

***Integration with Farm Management Systems:*** The intelligent agricultural monitoring system has the capability of being integrated with farm management systems, which allows for the automation of duties and organization of activities. More effective coordination and optimization of agricultural methods are made possible as a result of this connection. Table **4** depicts an integration with Farm Management Systems.

**Table 4. Integration with farm management systems.**

| | | |
|---|---|---|
| ***Data Integration*** | The farm administration system should incorporate information gathered from a variety of sources, including weather stations, sensors, drones, and satellites, in order to facilitate exhaustive analysis and decision-making. | • Provides a holistic view of farm operations<br>• Facilitates the analysis and surveillance of agricultural information in real time.<br>• Improves data accuracy and reliability |
| ***Analytics for the Future*** | Machine learning algorithms can sift through both past and present data to predict things like when to plant seeds, when pests will strike, and how much food crops will produce. | • Facilitates producers' decision-making by employing data-driven findings on data.<br>• Improves resource allocation and planning.<br>• Reduces risks and uncertainties in farming operations. |
| ***Agricultural Expertise*** | Utilising data-driven insights, precision planting, and variable rate technology (VRT) are some of the precision agricultural approaches used to maximise input efficiency and harvest yields. | • Reduces input costs and wastage.<br>• Increases crop yields and quality.<br>• Enhances environmental sustainability by minimizing chemical usage and runoff. |
| ***System for Assisting Decisions*** | Create a DSS that uses machine learning to provide farmers with advice and data they can use to run their farms more efficiently.• Helps farmers make well-informed choices quickly. | • Makes agricultural operations more efficient and productive • Makes farms more profitable and long-lasting in the long run. |
| ***Remote Monitoring*** | Data collected from field conditions and crop health is integrated into the farm management system for analysis using remote monitoring technology, such as Internet of Things (IoT) sensors and satellite imagery. | • Enables farmers to monitor their fields remotely and in real time.<br>• Allows for the prompt identification of problems like insect infestations and drought by facilitating early detection.<br>• Allows for timely intervention and decision-making to mitigate risks. |
| ***Automation and Robotics*** | Integration of automation and robotics in farm management systems to automate tasks such as planting, harvesting, and spraying, based on data-driven insights and algorithms. | • Reduces labour costs and manual labour requirements.<br>• Improves the efficiency and accuracy of farming operations.<br>• Enables round-the-clock operation and monitoring of farm activities. |

*(Table 4) cont.....*

| | | |
|---|---|---|
| ***Environmental Monitoring*** | In order to maximise the efficiency of irrigation and fertilisation, environmental monitoring technologies are used to measure and assess elements including soil moisture, temperature, and humidity. | • Improves water and resource management.<br>• Reduces environmental impact and carbon footprint.<br>• Enhances soil health and fertility. |
| ***Market Analysis*** | To aid farmers in making educated decisions on crop selection and marketing, farm management systems should incorporate tools for market research and forecasting. These tools would assist farmers in assessing market trends and pricing. | • Allows farmers to identify profitable crops and markets.<br>• Helps farmers plan their planting and harvesting schedules based on market demand.<br>• Maximizes returns on investment and improves farm profitability. |
| ***Risk Management*** | Integration of risk management tools that use machine learning to assess and mitigate risks such as crop failures, price fluctuations, and weather events, enabling farmers to make proactive decisions to minimize losses. | • Helps farmers identify and prioritize risks to their operations<br>• Enables farmers to develop risk mitigation strategies and contingency plans<br>• Improves resilience and sustainability of farming enterprises |
| ***Mobile and Cloud Solutions*** | By utilising cloud-based and mobile farm management systems that utilise machine learning for data analysis and decision-making, farmers will have access to up-to-the-minute information and tools wherever they are. | • Facilitates better communication and cooperation among agricultural stakeholders; streamlines processes to increase efficiency and production; makes it easier for farmers to run their operations remotely. |

When taken as a whole, a machine learning-based smart agricultural monitoring system incorporates data collection, preprocessing, analysis, and decision-making to optimize farming methods and increase crop output, quality, and sustainability.

The machine learning smart agricultural monitoring system is a comprehensive framework designed to optimize farming practices through advanced data collection, analysis, and decision-making. It begins with the collection of diverse environmental and crop-related data using sensors, drones, and satellites, which is then preprocessed to ensure quality and usability. Feature selection reduces the data's dimensionality by identifying relevant attributes, enhancing the efficiency of machine learning algorithms such as decision trees, neural networks, and support vector machines [14 - 16]. These algorithms are trained on historical data to uncover patterns and correlations, enabling accurate predictions and real-time analysis when deployed. A feedback loop continuously refines the models by integrating new data, improving their performance over time. Insights from the models feed into a decision support system that provides actionable recommendations for critical agricultural tasks like irrigation, fertilization, and pest control. Visualization tools present these insights in an accessible manner, while integration with farm management systems automates processes and organizes activities for better coordination. Together, these components create a robust, sustainable, and data-driven approach to modern agriculture, enhancing productivity and resource efficiency. Basically, the machine learning smart agricultural monitoring system represents a transformative approach to modern farming by seamlessly integrating data collection, analysis, and decision-making processes [17]. By leveraging advanced technologies such as sensors, drones, blockchain, and machine learning algorithms, the system ensures real-time monitoring and proactive management of agricultural operations. Its feedback-driven learning mechanisms continuously refine predictive models, while visualization and integration with farm management systems simplify decision-making and operational efficiency. This comprehensive framework not only enhances crop productivity and resource sustainability but also empowers farmers with actionable insights, paving the way for a smarter, more resilient agricultural future [18, 19].

## MACHINE LEARNING TECHNIQUES UTILISED IN INTERCONNECTED AGRICULTURE: NEURAL SYSTEMS, RANDOM FORESTS, DECISION TREES, AND ASSISTANCE VECTOR MACHINES

In smart agriculture, a number of different machine learning (ML) models are used to do data analysis and create predictions in order to increase the efficiency of agricultural techniques, as shown in Fig. (**4**). The following is a list of some of the machine learning models that are most often used [20].

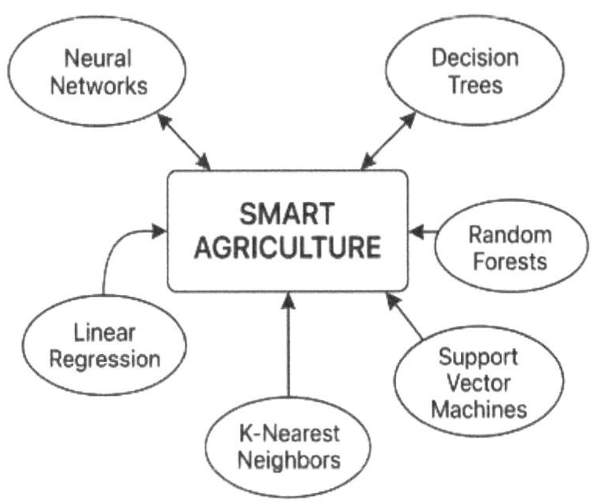


**Fig. (4).** Machine Learning (ML) algorithm design.

***Neural Networks:*** An example of a class of machine learning models is the neural network, which takes its inspiration from the organization of the human brain. Image recognition (for example, diagnosing crop diseases from photos) and time series forecasting (for example, projecting crop yields based on historical data) are two examples of the activities that are performed by these technologies in the context of smart agriculture [21].

***Decision Trees:*** Decision trees are structures that resemble trees and are used for classification applications and regression analysis. In the field of intelligent agriculture, decision trees may be used to categorize crops based on their current health status or to forecast crop output based on environmental parameters [22].

***Random Forests:*** Random forests are a kind of ensemble learning approach that uses a number of different decision trees in order to create predictions. Random forests are a useful tool in smart agriculture for a variety of tasks, including the detection of weeds, the identification of diseases, and the prediction of yields.

***Support Vector Machines (SVM):*** An example of a supervised learning model that is used for classification and regression problems is the Support Vector Machine, often known as SVM. The support vector machine (SVM) can be used in smart agriculture to classify crops based on their current health status or to forecast crop yields based on environmental parameters.

***K-Nearest Neighbours (KNN):*** The K-Nearest Neighbours (KNN) machine learning model is a straightforward and user-friendly tool that is used for classification and regression problems [23]. Knowledge-based networks (KNN) may be used in smart agriculture to categorize crops based on their current health status or to forecast crop yields based on environmental parameters.

***Linear Regression:*** On the other hand, linear regression is a straightforward machine learning model that is used for regression problems. In the field of intelligent agriculture, linear regression can be used to forecast crop yields by accounting for environmental factors such as temperature, humidity, and soil conditions.

In smart agriculture, these machine learning models are used to evaluate data gathered from sensors, drones, satellites, and other sources. The goal of this analysis is to give farmers important insights and suggestions that maximize the effectiveness of their agricultural techniques [24 - 27].

## CONCLUSION

The conclusion is that machine-learning-driven smart agricultural monitoring systems have the potential to transform farming operations by making them more productive, cost-effective, and environmentally benign. Farmers can improve their operations, increase agricultural yields, reduce their environmental impact, and ensure future generations have access to food by leveraging the power of machine learning. The use of these technologies has the potential to result in more environmentally friendly and lucrative agricultural businesses, which would be to the advantage of farmers as well as society as a whole.

## REFERENCES

[1] S. Acharya, "Plant health monitoring using nanosensor system", In: *Nanosensors for Smart Agriculture, Micro and Nano Technologies,* C. M. Hussain, S. K. Shukla, Eds., Elsevier: Amsterdam, Netherlands, 2022, pp. 479-492. [http://dx.doi.org/10.1016/B978-0-12-824554-5.00033-1]

[2] I. Ahmad, and K. Pothuganti, "Smart Field Monitoring using ToxTrac: A Cyber-Physical System Approach in Agriculture", *Proc. Int. Conf. Smart Electron. Commun. (ICOSEC),* pp. 723-727, 2020. [http://dx.doi.org/10.1109/ICOSEC49089.2020.9215282]

[3] R. Arthi, S. Nishuthan, and L. Deepak Vignesh, "Smart Agriculture System Using IoT and ML", *Proc. Int. Conf. Signal Process. Comput. Electron. Power Telecommun. (IConSCEPT),* pp. 1-6, 2023. [http://dx.doi.org/10.1109/IConSCEPT57958.2023.10170555]

[4] M. Christopher, A. Sivakumar, A. S. M. Murrugavel, and S. Priyatharsini, "A study on smart agriculture monitoring system using different IoT applications", *Proc. Int. Conf. Comput. Intell. Knowl. Econ. (ICCIKE),* pp. 129-133, 2019.

[5] T. Humoud, M. Alrushoud, F. Almutairi, W. Almutairi, F. Almarri, and H. Kanj, "Smart Agriculture Monitoring and Controlling System using Multi-agents model", *Proc. 2023 5th Int. Conf. Bio-eng. Smart Technol. (BioSMART),* pp. 1-4, 2023. [http://dx.doi.org/10.1109/BioSMART58455.2023.10162030]

[6] A. Ranjan and R. M, "Deep learning based image deblurring: A comparative survey", *Proc. 4th Int. Conf. Advances in Computing, Communication Control and Networking (ICAC3N),* pp. 996-1002, 2022.Greater Noida, India [http://dx.doi.org/10.1109/ICAC3N56670.2022.10074406]

[7] A. Jain, "Smart agriculture monitoring system using IoT", *Int. J. Res. Appl. Sci. Eng. Technol.,* vol. 8, no. 7, pp. 366-372, 2020.

[8] P. Kuruba, and V. Madhusudhan, "Smart growth monitoring system in agriculture using IoT", *J. Adv. Res. Dyn. Control Syst.,* vol. 11, no. 12-SPECIAL ISSUE, pp. 620-630, 2019. [http://dx.doi.org/10.5373/JARDCS/V11SP12/20193258]

[9] O. Elijah, T.A. Rahman, I. Orikumhi, C.Y. Leow, and M.H.D.N. Hindia, "An overview of Internet of Things (IoT) and data analytics in agriculture: Benefits and challenges", *IEEE Internet Things J.,* vol. 5, no. 5, pp. 3758-3773, 2018. [http://dx.doi.org/10.1109/JIOT.2018.2844296]

[10] W. Li, T. Logenthiran, V.T. Phan, and W.L. Woo, "A novel smart energy theft system (SETS) for IoT-based smart home", *IEEE Internet Things J.,* vol. 6, no. 3, pp. 5531-5539, 2019. [http://dx.doi.org/10.1109/JIOT.2019.2903281]

[11] D. Shin, K. Yun, J. Kim, P.V. Astillo, J.N. Kim, and I. You, "A security protocol for route optimization in DMM-based smart home IoT networks", *IEEE Access,* vol. 7, pp. 142531-142550, 2019.
[http://dx.doi.org/10.1109/ACCESS.2019.2943929]

[12] J. An, F. Le Gall, J. Kim, J. Yun, J. Hwang, M. Bauer, M. Zhao, and J. Song, "Le Gall, J. Kim, J. Yun, J. Hwang, M. Bauer, M. Zhao, and J. Song, "Toward global IoT-enabled smart cities interworking using adaptive semantic adapter,"", *IEEE Internet Things J.,* vol. 6, no. 3, pp. 5753-5765, 2019.
[http://dx.doi.org/10.1109/JIOT.2019.2905275]

[13] H. Khan, M.S. Hossain, and G. Muhammad, "AI-driven smart agriculture monitoring systems: A comprehensive review", *IEEE Access,* vol. 12, pp. 112345-112360, 2024.

[14] M. Ammad, M.A. Shah, S.U. Islam, C. Maple, A.A. Alaulamie, J.J.P.C. Rodrigues, S. Mussadiq, and U. Tariq, "Shah, S. U. Islam, C. Maple, A. A. Alaulamie, J. J. P. C. Rodrigues, S. Mussadiq, and U. Tariq, "A novel fog-based multi-level energy-efficient framework for IoT-enabled smart environments,"", *IEEE Access,* vol. 8, pp. 150010-150026, 2020.
[http://dx.doi.org/10.1109/ACCESS.2020.3010157]

[15] S.P. Yadav, S. Zaidi, C.D.S. Nascimento, V.H.C. de Albuquerque, and S.S. Chauhan, "Analysis and design of automatically generating for GPS-based moving object tracking system", *Proc. IEEE AISC,* pp. 1-5, 2023.
[http://dx.doi.org/10.1109/AISC56616.2023.10085180]

[16] S. Zhang, Y. Li, and X. Wang, "Edge-AI based intelligent transportation and vehicle safety systems", *IEEE Trans. Intell. Transp. Syst.,* vol. 25, no. 2, pp. 1456-1468, 2024.

[17] F. Kiani, A. Seyyedabbasi, S. Nematzadeh, F. Candan, T. Çevik, F.A. Anka, G. Randazzo, S. Lanza, and A. Muzirafuti, "Adaptive metaheuristic-based methods for autonomous robot path planning: Sustainable agricultural applications", *Appl. Sci. (Basel),* vol. 12, no. 3, p. 943, 2022.
[http://dx.doi.org/10.3390/app12030943]

[18] P.S. Kumar, and A. Verma, "Advanced material optimization using AI for mechanical systems", *Mater. Today Commun.,* vol. 35, 2024.105432

[19] A. Vangala, A.K. Das, N. Kumar, and M. Alazab, "Smart secure sensing for IoT-based agriculture: Blockchain perspective", *IEEE Sens. J.,* vol. 21, no. 16, pp. 17591-17607, 2021.
[http://dx.doi.org/10.1109/JSEN.2020.3012294]

[20] Y. B. Singh, and S. Goel, "1D CNN based approach for speech emotion recognition using MFCC features", In: *Artificial Intelligence and Speech Technology,* A. Jain, M. N. Kumar, R. Prasad, Eds., 1st ed.. CRC Press: Boca Raton, FL, USA, 2021, pp. 195-202.

[21] M. Patel, S. Gupta, and R. Shah, "AI-driven healthcare robotics for elderly care applications", *IEEE J. Biomed. Health Inform.,* vol. 29, no. 1, pp. 122-134, 2025.

[22] A. Singh, K. S. H., A. K. Pandey, T. G. Kumar, S. B. Rajasekaran, and S. K. Kamble, "Smart agriculture irrigation system using integrated system using IOT and ML", *Proc. 3rd Int. Conf. Advance Comput. Innov. Technol. Eng. (ICACITE),* pp. 1049-1052, 2023.

[23] Y. Chen, X. Liu, and Z. Zhao, "Bio-inspired artificial vision systems using deep learning", *IEEE Trans. Neural Netw. Learn. Syst.,* vol. 35, no. 3, pp. 1789-1802, 2024.

[24] V.G. Sharma, and N. Kumar, "Machine learning-based energy demand forecasting in smart grids", *IEEE Trans. Smart Grid,* vol. 15, no. 1, pp. 890-902, 2025.

[25] A. V. Srinivasan, N. Saritakumar, V. Amarnath, and S. Amrithaa, "Implementation of Water and Air Quality Monitoring System for Smart Agriculture using LoRa", *Sustainable Digital Technologies for Smart Cities,* 1st ed.CRC Press: Boca Raton, FL, USA, pp. 243-258, 2023.
[http://dx.doi.org/10.1201/9781003307716-3]

[26] J. Zhang, *"The smart traffic monitoring system using cement-based piezoelectric transducers",* Ph.D.

dissertation, The Hong Kong University of Science and Technology, Hong Kong, 2013.

[27] K.P. Kumar, B. Singh, K.V. Malini, A. Ranjan, S.D. Bonde, S. Rout, and A. Firos, "IoT and machine learning based effective plant disease classification and detection for agricultural applications", *IJFANS,* vol. 11, no. 8, pp. 415-423, 2022.

# CHAPTER 10

# Artificial Intelligence for Image-based Weed Identification in Agriculture

**Sapna Nigam**[1,*], **V. K. Choudhary**[2], **Akshay Dheeraj**[1], **Madhu**[1], **Rajni Jain**[3] and **Sudeep Marwaha**[1]

[1] *ICAR-Indian Agricultural Statistics Research Institute, New Delhi, Delhi, India*

[2] *ICAR-Directorate of Weed Research, Jabalpur, Madhya Pradesh, India*

[3] *ICAR-National Institute of Agricultural Economics and Policy Research, New Delhi, Delhi, India*

**Abstract:** Weeds are undesired plants that grow in places where they are not intentionally planted, competing with crops for vital resources like water, nutrients, and sunlight. The competition can significantly reduce agricultural productivity. Moreover, conventional weed control methods often have detrimental environmental effects. As a result, effective weed management strategies are crucial for mitigating infestations and preserving the productivity and sustainability of agricultural systems. These strategies encompass a range of approaches, including cultural practices, mechanical methods, chemical treatments, and biological controls. In response to the growing demand for sustainable solutions, new technologies aimed at reducing herbicide use have gained attention. One such solution is automated weed control, which offers a more precise and efficient way of targeting weeds, ultimately reducing the need for herbicides. Recent advancements in computing power, particularly the use of GPUs, have accelerated the adoption of artificial intelligence (AI) and deep learning (DL) technologies in agriculture. These AI-driven techniques have demonstrated significant promise in accurately identifying and classifying weeds from field image data. By automating weed detection, AI-based algorithms not only minimize herbicide use but also help boost crop productivity and promote sustainable agricultural practices.

**Keywords:** Artificial Intelligence, Image classification, Machine learning, Precision agriculture, Weeds identification.

## INTRODUCTION

In agriculture, effective weed control plays a role in maintaining the health of crops, ensuring sustainability, conserving natural resources, and ultimately enhancing global food security on a larger scale. Weeds in fields compete with

* **Correspondence author Sapna Nigam:** ICAR-Indian Agricultural Statistics Research Institute, New Delhi, Delhi, India; E-mail: sapna.nigam1010@gmail.com

**Ravinder M., Arti Ranjan, Youddha Beer Singh (Eds.)**

crops for resources like water, nutrients, and sunlight, resulting in significant reductions in crop yields and quality. This detrimental impact on crops not only leads to losses for farmers but also poses a threat to food production worldwide. Furthermore, the economic effects of weeds go beyond just yield losses; they also include expenses related to labor, herbicides, machinery, as well as effects on crop quality and market value [1]. Additionally, ecosystem health and biodiversity can be maintained through effective weed management practices, as traditional weed control methods like herbicide use can have consequences such as soil erosion, water pollution, and deterioration of biodiversity [2]. Moreover, the rise of herbicide-resistant weed populations has highlighted the need for integrated weed management strategies to prevent resistance development and ensure the efficacy of herbicides. As a result, these challenges can be tackled through automated weed control methods to improve productivity**, meet the growing demand for food supplies,** while reducing the risks associated with food shortages and famines.

Some authors [3] and [4] highlight the use of both traditional machine learning (ML) and deep learning (DL) techniques for this application. These approaches generally reduce the reliance on manual labor and improve crop management, especially in weed detection [5]. The key distinction between these methods lies in their complexity [6, 7]. Machine learning relies on manually designed algorithms and statistical models that allow systems to analyze data, make predictions, and recognize patterns or make decisions accordingly [8, 9]. In contrast, deep learning mimics the structure of the human brain by using multiple interconnected layers of neurons to learn autonomously. These models extract features in a hierarchical manner, with increasing complexity as the network depth grows [10, 11]. While machine learning is suitable for simpler tasks with fewer variables and lower computational demands, it is particularly suitable for applications like Internet of Things (IoT) devices [12, 13]. Our chapter aims to achieve two main objectives:

- To demonstrate how AI-based weed identification can revolutionize integrated weed management.
- To discuss the challenges, opportunities, and future directions in this area. We will explore the integration of AI with weed management to motivate experts and researchers to embrace technologies for enhanced weed control.

The steps involved in automated image-based weed identification, the challenges and limitations of AI in weed management, and development pathways will be discussed in subsequent sections. Furthermore, a few existing case studies in the literature for weed identification are also highlighted to showcase real-world applications for sustainable agriculture.

## THE NEED FOR AUTOMATED WEED IDENTIFICATION

Automated weed identification has become an invaluable asset to modern agriculture for several key reasons. First and foremost, automated methods offer greater efficiency and precision compared to manual solutions, providing faster and more accurate management strategies of unwanted vegetation. Automated weed identification contributes to cost reductions by decreasing labor hours and herbicide costs, and to environmental sustainability by enabling targeted herbicide application that minimizes chemical use while simultaneously mitigating environmental impact. Remarkably, it enables prompt intervention by providing real-time data on weed presence and distribution; farmers can then take swift action to manage infestations. Automated systems' scalability makes them ideal for efficiently covering large agricultural areas efficiently particularly useful in large-scale farming operations. Overall, using AI and computer vision technologies for weed identification increases crop yields while simultaneously decreasing environmental impacts and improving economic sustainability of agriculture operations [14]

Successful weed management maximizes crop yields by decreasing competition for essential resources, increasing economic viability of farming operations by minimizing losses and production costs, protecting ecosystems from disruption by controlling weed growth that disrupt ecosystems, leading to pollution; diversifying control tactics helps manage herbicide resistance for greater effectiveness; sustainable agriculture practices prioritize efficient resource usage while increasing ecological resilience - thus making weed control integral for long-term productivity and environmental wellbeing.

### Challenges with traditional methods

- Labour-intensive: Traditional methods for weed identification rely heavily on manual labor that requires significant manpower, taking significant time and manpower resources to complete.
- Subjectivity: Identification by human observers may result in subjective judgment and inaccurate identifications, causing inconsistent outcomes.
- Expertise Requirement: Identifying weeds accurately often requires specific botanical knowledge and training; this restricts who can effectively perform this task.

- Time Constraints: Due to manual identification's long process timeframes and potential delays associated with intervention measures, infestations often progress unchecked further and cause greater crop damage than originally hoped for.
- Cost: Weed identification can be costly for large agricultural operations that rely heavily on manual identification processes.
- Inefficiency of Large-Scale Farming Operations: Traditional methods may not be appropriate for large-scale farming operations where vast fields make manual weed identification time-consuming and inconvenient.
- Limited Coverage: Manual identification methods may only cover specific portions of fields, potentially leading to underestimation or overlooking of certain weed infestations in certain locations.
- Seasonal Variability: The composition and abundance of weed species fluctuate seasonally, making consistent management strategies difficult to implement throughout the year.

## Role of AI in addressing these challenges

Artificial Intelligence (AI) plays an integral part in meeting the challenges associated with traditional methods for weed identification and will continue to transform our approaches in many areas of weed management. Artificial Intelligence can streamline weed identification processes, drastically decreasing manual labour dependency while simultaneously increasing overall efficiency. AI-powered systems can deliver more accurate and consistent weed identification results compared to human observers, thus minimizing errors and inconsistencies [15, 16]. AI also facilitates scalability for weed identification efforts, making it possible to cover large agricultural areas efficiently. Real-time detection capabilities offered by AI-powered systems enable rapid intervention measures to be taken quickly in response to potential weed infestations, mitigating their damage in real-time. AI technologies require initial investments; however, due to long-term cost savings from reduced labour and herbicide usage costs associated with AI-based weed identification, they often become cost-effective options for farmers. AI-powered systems can also be customized to be user-friendly, eliminating the need for expert botanical knowledge while making weed identification accessible to a wider range of users [17]. AI algorithms can also be trained to recognize various weed species and adjust to seasonal fluctuations for consistent identification and management throughout the year. As AI technology develops further, its integration into agriculture could revolutionize weed identification practices for enhanced efficiency, accuracy, and sustainability.

## METHODOLOGY FOR IMAGE-BASED WEED IDENTIFICATION

AI-powered weed identification involves several stages from data acquisition to model validation - each essential in creating accurate and reliable identification systems. Fig. (**1**) graphically represents these stages involved with AI-based weed detection systems.

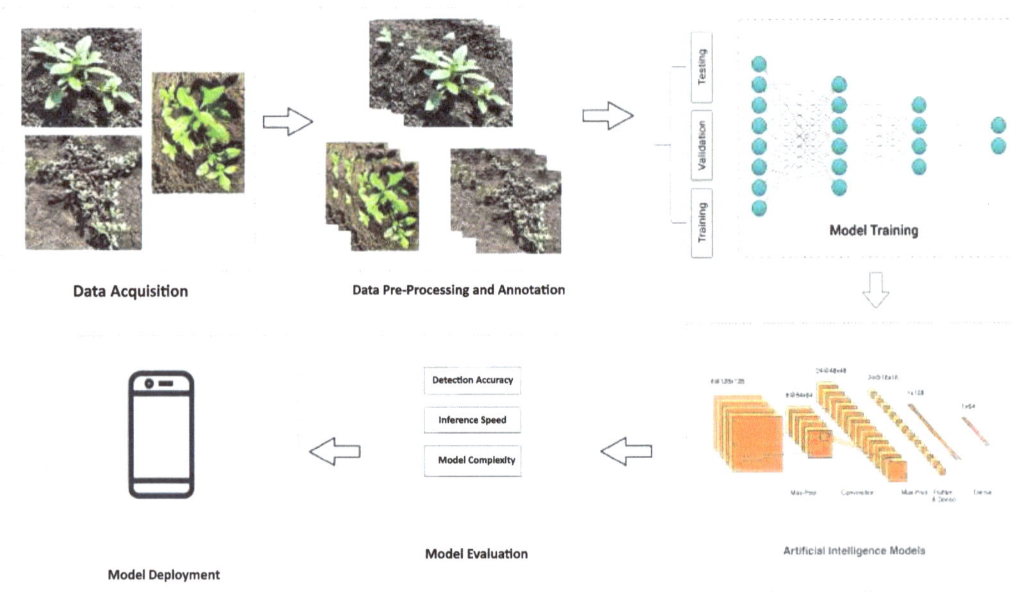


**Fig. (1).** Overall steps involved in artificial intelligence-based weed identification.

a. Data Acquisition: In this step, an initial collection of images captures different weed species, growth stages, and environmental conditions for use as training data for an AI model to recognize variability present in real-world agricultural settings. Images captured with ground cameras, drones, or satellite imagery should provide adequate representation.
b. Data Pre-processing: Once images have been collected, they go through pre-processing to increase quality and standardize format across their collection. This may involve tasks like resizing, cropping, and altering lighting conditions to maintain consistency across datasets. Pre-processing plays an essential part in optimizing AI model training performance.
c. Annotation: Next, images in the dataset must be annotated with data about where and when weeds appear in an image, typically using bounding boxes or pixel segmentation techniques to accurately label all instances. Accurate annotation is key in training an AI model to detect weeds amongst other objects within images and differentiate them accordingly.

d. Model Training: Once an annotated dataset is available, an AI model is trained using machine learning techniques such as convolutional neural networks (CNNs). Through training sessions, the model learns to recognize patterns and features associated with various weed species based on annotated images; its parameters can then be tweaked incrementally to minimize prediction errors and enhance performance.
e. Model Evaluation: Once training is complete, a separate validation dataset that the AI model has never seen before must be utilized to evaluate the performance. Model evaluation helps ensure that its performance generalizes to unseen data while still functioning reliably in real-world situations.
f. Model Deployment: After successful evaluation, an AI model is deployed for use in agricultural fields for weed identification purposes, depending on its intended application, such as real-time identification via devices like drones or smartphones, or integration into existing agricultural machinery or software platforms.
g. Model Monitoring and Updates: Regular performance reviews on an AI model's performance are necessary to detect any drift or degradation over time, while updates or retraining might also be needed in response to changes in species composition, environmental conditions, or any other factor influencing identification accuracy.

## OVERVIEW OF MACHINE LEARNING ALGORITHMS USED IN WEED IDENTIFICATION

Machine learning algorithms play an integral part in weed identification, providing automated classification based on features extracted from images. A range of machine learning techniques have been applied in these tasks; SVMs, Random Forests, CNNs, DCNNs, and transfer learning have each had unique benefits in automated classification of agricultural fields for weeds, as shown below.

a. **Support Vector Machines (SVM):** SVM is a supervised learning model commonly used for classification tasks. It operates by identifying the optimal hyperplane that effectively separates different classes within a given feature space. In weed identification, SVMs have been applied by utilizing features such as color, texture, and shape extracted from images to classify them into groups corresponding to specific weed species.
b. **Random Forest:** It is an ensemble learning method that utilizes multiple decision trees in concert to predict outcomes. Each tree in the forest is trained on random subsets of training data before making its classification decision based on features extracted from images. Random Forest has been successfully

applied to classify weed species using image features extracted with Random Forest techniques.

c. **Convolutional Neural Networks (CNNs):** CNNs are deep learning architectures specifically developed for visual data processing. CNNs consist of several layers of convolutional operations followed by fully connected layers for classification. CNNs have shown extraordinary performance when used for weed identification tasks, reaching state-of-the-art results both for crop weed discrimination and species classification tasks.
d. **Deep Convolutional Neural Networks (DCNNs):** They are the deep learning architectures that extend CNNs with additional layers and parameters, showing superior performance when applied to weed identification tasks by automatically learning hierarchical features from raw image data [18, 19]. DCNNs have also been successfully used for species classification, density estimation, and crop-weed segmentation in agricultural fields.
e. **Transfer Learning (TL):** Transfer learning is a sophisticated machine learning approach where a pre-trained model designed for one task is adapted for another with minimal training data. In weed identification, this technique has been effectively utilized by leveraging pre-trained convolutional neural network (CNN) models trained on large image datasets. These models are fine-tuned with weed-specific data, thereby enhancing their generalization and robustness and ultimately improving the accuracy of weed identification.

## CHALLENGES AND LIMITATIONS IN WEED DETECTION

AI-powered weed identification offers enormous promise to transform agriculture practices; however, several challenges discussed below must first be addressed to meet its full potential:

a. Weeds show significant variation in their appearance, from species, growth stages, leaf shapes and colours. This creates challenges for AI models developed using limited datasets, as it is difficult to identify a new weed species or stages that they have yet to encounter.
b. Field images captured can differ considerably in quality depending on factors like lighting conditions, weather, camera angle, and any occlusions present in them. Variations in image quality can compromise AI models trained on these images, leading to reduced accuracy and reliability when it comes to weed identification.
c. Generating large image datasets for AI training models can be time-consuming and laborious, requiring expertise to annotate images correctly while potentially creating subjective biases that hinder training AI models effectively. Furthermore, the availability of annotated data for rare or

uncommon weed species might limit AI model training sessions.

d. Models developed may not work across different environmental conditions and geographical regions, depending on factors such as soil types, climate, cropping systems, or management practices that vary among farms or fields, leading to reduced accuracy and reliability for AI-based weed identification systems in real-world settings.
e. Real-time deployment of AI-based weed identification systems can present technical constraints related to processing speed, memory requirements, and power consumption. Achieving real-time performance on edge devices like drones or agricultural machinery may necessitate optimizing AI algorithms as well as hardware acceleration techniques for optimal real-time performance.

## EXISTING CASE STUDIES

As reported in the literature, a few studies summarized in Table **1** illustrate the broad range of AI applications for weed detection across various crops, including the models or algorithms used and their corresponding accuracies.

**Table 1. Summary of the existing studies for AI-driven weed identification.**

| References | Crop | Weeds | Model/Algorithms | Accuracy (%) |
|---|---|---|---|---|
| Santos *et al.*, (2017) [20] | Soybean | Broadleaf and grass weeds | ConvNets | 99% |
| Peteinatos *et al.*, (2020) [21] | Maize, Sunflower, Potato | 9 weed classes | VGG16, ResNet–50, and Xception | Between 77% and 98% |
| Zhuang *et al.*, (2021) [22] | Wheat | Broadleaf weed seedlings | AlexNet, DenseNet, ResNet, and VGGNet | Precision 97% |
| Liu *et al.*, (2021) [23] | Strawberry | Spotted spurge, Shepherd's purse | VGG16, AlexNet, GoogleNet | 97% |
| de Camargo *et al.*, (2021) [24] | Winter Wheat | *Matricaria chamomilla* L., *Papaver rhoeas* L., *etc.* | ResNet-18 model | 94% |
| Subeesh *et al.*, (2022) [25] | Bell Peppers | Weeds | Alexnet, GoogLeNet, InceptionV3, Xception | 94.5 to 97.7% |
| Razfar *et al.*, (2022) [26] | Soybean | Broadleaf and grass weeds | MobileNetV2, ResNet50 | 97.7% |
| Sunil *et al.*, (2022) [27] | Black bean, canola, corn, flax, soybean, and sugar beets | Horseweed, kochia, ragweed, and water hemp | VGG16, SVM | 90.11% |

*(Table 1) cont.....*

| References | Crop | Weeds | Model/Algorithms | Accuracy (%) |
|---|---|---|---|---|
| Chen *et al.*, (2022) [28] | Cotton | 15 weed classes | 27 SOTA ResNet101 | F1 Score 99.1% |
| Wang *et al.*, (2022) [29] | - | 25 different weed species. | YOLOv3, YOLOv5, and Faster R-CNN | 91.8%, 92.4%, and 92.15% |
| Guo *et al.*, (2023) [30] | Maize | Black-grass, Charlock, Mayweed, others | AlexNet, VGG16, MobileNetV3 | 97% |
| Daşkın *et al.*, (2024) [31] | Maize | - | VGG16, InceptionV3 | Accuracy 80-90% |
| Mckay *et al.*, (2024) [32] | Canola | Non-canola plants | ResNet-18, ResNet-34, and VGG-16 | Avg precision 0.84 |

The studies emphasize real-life applications of AI-based weed identification systems, thereby giving farmers and stakeholders in the agricultural industry practical means to solve problems. When AI approaches are used, selective weed control methods are enhanced, thus reducing herbicide application rates, increasing yields, and saving costs. By utilizing AI-based technologies, farmers can optimize their weed management practices for resource efficiency gains and environmental impact reduction, which contributes to sustainable food production as well as food security. These studies cover a multitude of crops, among them: soybean, wheat, maize, sunflower, Potato, Winter wheat, strawberry, Bell pepper, cotton, black bean, canola, corn, flax, sugar beet. This variety shows that an AI-based approach can be used in different types of farming. The species talked about include both broadleaf and grass weeds and others which have been mentioned in some studies, like *Matricaria chamomilla L., Papaver rhoeas L.,* black-grass, charlock, mayweed, *etc*. Numerous crops or species indicated the significance of managing weeds within various cropping systems.

## IMPLEMENTATION OF AI-BASED WEED IDENTIFICATION SYSTEMS

### Dataset Descriptions

Data provided from a variety of datasets, including publicly available datasets, greenhouse data, UAV images, and proprietary datasets collected by researchers, were employed by these studies.

The selection of a dataset significantly impacts the diversity and quality of the training data, thereby affecting the effectiveness of AI models. Some frequently used models in the field are VGG16, ResNet, XceptionNet, AlexNet, DenseNet,

MobileNet, SVM, YOLOv3, YOLOv5, and Faster R-CNN. These models are advanced structures in the fields of deep learning and computer vision. They can extract significant features from photos, enabling precise weed categorization. The stated accuracies range from 90% to 99%, with rates reaching 97%. The performance metrics presented here demonstrate the efficacy of AI-based methods for accurately detecting and classifying weeds. Their high accuracies show their resilience and reliability - providing confidence for the practical application of these models for weed management purposes.

## Model Implementation

In order to ensure effectiveness, reliability, and integration into farming, it is important to consider several practical issues before introducing AI-powered systems for weed identification in agricultural environments. AI models must be able to support large fields, such as those found in agriculture, while remaining resistant to changes in lighting conditions, weather patterns, or weed species composition. AI systems are robust enough to identify weeds regardless of circumstances or user interface issues. This user-friendly technology interface simplifies the technology for its users, while also helping stakeholders maximize their returns from technology investment. Costs associated with implementation, such as hardware acquisition and software maintenance, must be balanced against potential benefits in terms of improved weed management efficiency and crop yield, including hardware requirements, data collection, annotation processes, and integration with existing agricultural practices. These requirements must be satisfied when using AI-powered weeding systems in agriculture, as mentioned below:

### Hardware Requirements:

- Sensing Equipment: Drones, tractors, or other farm machinery often include high-resolution cameras or multispectral sensors designed for sensing equipment that capture images of agricultural fields.
- Computational Resources: For real-time applications on devices or in the field requiring AI algorithms to run effectively and seamlessly, sufficient computer power must be available to run them efficiently. Depending upon connectivity and latency needs, on-device or cloud processing solutions may be used.
- Power Sources: When deployed in the field, reliable power supplies such as batteries or solar panels must be available to maintain the proper functioning of sensing equipment and computing devices.

**Data Collection and Annotation:**

- Diverse and Representative Datasets: To train powerful AI models, an array of diverse and representative datasets covering crop species, weed species, growth stages, and environmental conditions must be assembled.
- Annotated Data: Manual annotation of images to label instances of weed growth can be time-consuming but essential in supervised learning approaches, so automation or semi-automated annotation tools may facilitate this process.
- Quality Control: To prevent AI models from biases or errors that might reduce their performance, annotated data should undergo quality control checks before being included in an AI program.

**Integration with Existing Agricultural Practices:**

- Compatibility: AI-powered weed identification systems should be compatible with existing farming tools, software, and machinery used by farmers.
- Seamless Integration: This can include seamlessly incorporating AI recommendations with precision agriculture technologies like GPS-guided tractors or variable rate applicators to facilitate targeted weed control actions based on AI recommendations.
- Training and Support: For successful integration into daily farming operations, training and support of users, such as farmers and agronomists of these systems, must take place.

## CASE STUDIES OF WEED IDENTIFICATION

### Rice Weed Identification

In a case study [33], the authors explored the use of convolutional neural networks (CNNs) combined with advanced deep learning techniques to develop an effective system for weed detection and classification in rice fields. The authors further fine-tuned the layers of the model to optimize performance. The dataset contains images of two common weed species—Motha and Barnyard grass—as well as healthy rice plants. These weed species are particularly problematic in rice cultivation because they compete aggressively. The dataset images were collected during the peak weed growth period from June to October 2023, capturing realistic field conditions that rice farmers face. This dataset was essential in training and validating the deep learning models for accurate weed detection in a real-world agricultural setting. The proposed model, ResNet50-CBAM, demonstrated remarkable performance in distinguishing between weeds, achieving high accuracies. The model demonstrated strong generalization to unseen data, indicating robustness in weed detection. These results highlight the effectiveness of deep learning techniques, particularly CNNs with transfer learning and attention mechanisms, in enhancing precision agriculture. This combination of techniques ensures that farmers can rely on automated systems for timely and accurate weed management, which is crucial for optimizing crop productivity and reducing the overuse of herbicides.

The results shown in this chapter show the performance of different deep learning models on the rice weed dataset, demonstrating the impact of the attention mechanism (CBAM) on model performance. The base InceptionV3 model achieved a training accuracy of 90.45% and a test accuracy of 90.13%. While these results are respectable, they highlight that the model has limitations in handling complex weed identification tasks in real-world agricultural conditions. InceptionV3 + CBAM: Adding CBAM to InceptionV3 improved both the training and testing accuracies. The training accuracy increased to 92.93%, and the testing accuracy rose to 91.67%. The attention mechanism enabled the model to focus more effectively on key regions of the image, thereby enhancing its ability to distinguish weeds from crops. ResNet50: This model achieved higher performance than InceptionV3, with a training accuracy of 93.62% and a testing accuracy of 93.81%. ResNet50 is a deeper network that allows for more complex feature learning, making it better suited for weed identification tasks. ResNet50-CBAM (Proposed Model): The model proposed by the authors, which combined ResNet50 with CBAM, outperformed all other models. It achieved a training accuracy of 96.44% and a testing accuracy of 97.75%. The ResNet50-CBAM (Proposed model) clearly outperforms the other models, suggesting that the attention mechanism is critical for improving weed classification accuracy. The results emphasize the importance of leveraging advanced deep learning techniques like CNNs combined with attention mechanisms for weed detection in precision agriculture. Such models not only increase accuracy but also reduce the need for manual labor, making weed management more efficient and easier to deploy on mobile and portable devices. This opens up possibilities for real-time, on-site weed identification, further enhancing agricultural productivity.

## Wheat Weed Identification

In this case study, the authors propose an attention-based network, XceptionNet, a lightweight deep learning model designed specifically for weed detection in wheat crops. The network is enhanced by integrating attention layers into the final layers of XceptionNet, a popular deep learning model. Attention mechanisms enable the model to focus on the most relevant features of an image, thereby improving its ability to distinguish between weeds and crops. By fine-tuning the last layers of

XceptionNet and adding the attention layers, the authors optimize the model for better weed classification performance [34].

The results of the proposed model were impressive, with training and testing accuracies of 99.92% and 97.86%, respectively. These high accuracies indicate that the model is highly effective in detecting wheat weeds, achieving near-perfect results during training and maintaining strong performance on unseen test data. One of the key strengths of the proposed model is its lightweight nature, which makes it computationally efficient. This is particularly important when deploying the model in real-time applications, such as mobile or portable devices with limited computational resources. The authors argue that their model is suitable for use in embedded systems designed for on-field weed management, where real-time decision-making is crucial for minimizing crop loss and optimizing herbicide application.

Table **2** compares the performance of InceptionResNetV2, DenseNet121, and XceptionNet—in identifying wheat weeds. All models achieved high training accuracies, but they differed in their generalization ability to new, unseen data.

**Table 2. Model performance on wheat weed identification.**

| Model | Training Accuracy | Training Loss | Validation Accuracy | Validation Loss | Testing Accuracy |
|---|---|---|---|---|---|
| InceptionResNetV2 | 98.49 | 0.062 | 95.18 | 0.320 | 94.46 |
| DenseNet121 | 99.78 | 0.007 | 97.14 | 0.107 | 97.68 |
| XceptionNet | 99.92 | 0.004 | 97.32 | 0.097 | 97.86 |

The InceptionResNetV2 model achieved a high training accuracy of 98.49%. However, it experienced a noticeable drop in both validation accuracy (95.18%) and test accuracy (94.46%). DenseNet121 also performed well in accuracy, indicating that it generalizes well to new data and makes it a reliable choice for applications where high accuracy on unseen data is required. However, XceptionNet performed the best overall, achieving the highest training accuracy of 99.92%. It also achieved excellent results on the validation (97.32%) and test datasets (97.86%), making it the most accurate model across generalization and overall performance. The minimal drop in accuracy between training, validation, and testing sets indicates that XceptionNet is well-regularized and effectively generalizes to unseen data. While all three models showed some degree of overfitting, DenseNet121 and XceptionNet outperformed InceptionResNetV2 in terms of test accuracy. Among the three, XceptionNet proved to be the most robust and reliable model for wheat weed identification and its performance makes it suitable for real-time scenarios in weed management, particularly when computational efficiency and high accuracy are both essential.

## CONCLUSION

AI has the potential to shape the future of weed management, propelling agriculture towards more environmentally friendly, efficient, and productive outcomes. By increasing weed detection precision, reducing costs, and promoting sustainable practices, AI technologies contribute not only to the profitability and productivity of farmers but also to the global goal of ensuring food security for an ever-growing population. As AI continues to advance, its integration into agricultural practices will further solidify its role in transforming agriculture into a more sustainable and resilient sector, ready to meet future challenges. The integration of Artificial Intelligence (AI) into agricultural practices, particularly in weed management, represents a transformative advancement in the way farming challenges are addressed. As demonstrated in the case studies discussed, AI-driven approaches equipped with attention mechanisms have shown remarkable success in automating the identification and classification of weeds in agricultural fields. The aforementioned case studies underscore the capability of AI to provide precise, real-time insights into weed presence and distribution, thereby offering farmers more effective tools for managing weed infestations. AI-based weed identification technologies can revolutionize agriculture by enabling more efficient and targeted weed control methods. By automating the process of weed detection, these AI systems reduce reliance on traditional, labor-intensive weed management techniques, which can be costly and environmentally harmful. The use of AI not only improves crop management but also optimizes resource utilization, ensuring that water, nutrients, and herbicides are applied more effectively. By increasing the efficiency of weed detection and reducing the need for herbicides and manual labor, these tools lower the overall costs of weed management. This cost reduction, combined with increased productivity and healthier crop yields, helps enhance the profitability and sustainability of farming operations. AI-powered weed identification systems also contribute to the broader goals of global food security by ensuring that crops are protected from the adverse effects of weed competition, thereby securing higher yields and more stable food production.

## REFERENCES

[1] D. Chen, Y. Lu, Z. Li, and S. Young, "Performance evaluation of deep transfer learning on multi-class identification of common weed species in cotton production systems", *Comput. Electron. Agric.*, vol. 198, p. 107091, 2022. [http://dx.doi.org/10.1016/j.compag.2022.107091]

[2] E.S.M. El-Kenawy, N. Khodadadi, S. Mirjalili, T. Makarovskikh, M. Abotaleb, F.K. Karim, H.K.

Alkahtani, A.A. Abdelhamid, M.M. Eid, T. Horiuchi, A. Ibrahim, and D.S. Khafaga, "Metaheuristic Optimization for Improving Weed Detection in Wheat Images Captured by Drones", *Mathematics,* vol. 10, no. 23, p. 4421, 2022.
[http://dx.doi.org/10.3390/math10234421]

[3] A.S.M.M. Hasan, F. Sohel, D. Diepeveen, H. Laga, and M.G.K. Jones, "A survey of deep learning techniques for weed detection from images", *Comput. Electron. Agric.,* vol. 184, p. 106067, 2021.
[http://dx.doi.org/10.1016/j.compag.2021.106067]

[4] A.H. Al-Badri, N.A. Ismail, K. Al-Dulaimi, G.A. Salman, A.R. Khan, A. Al-Sabaawi, and M.S.H. Salam, "Classification of weed using machine learning techniques: a review—challenges, current and future potential techniques", *J. Plant Dis. Prot.,* vol. 129, no. 4, pp. 745-768, 2022.
[http://dx.doi.org/10.1007/s41348-022-00612-9]

[5] M. Vasileiou, L.S. Kyrgiakos, C. Kleisiari, G. Kleftodimos, G. Vlontzos, H. Belhouchette, and P.M. Pardalos, "Transforming weed management in sustainable agriculture with artificial intelligence: A systematic literature review towards weed identification and deep learning", *Crop Prot.,* vol. 176, p. 106522, 2024.
[http://dx.doi.org/10.1016/j.cropro.2023.106522]

[6] B. Shah, and H. Bhavsar, "Time complexity in deep learning models", *Procedia Comput. Sci.,* vol. 215, pp. 202-210, 2022.
[http://dx.doi.org/10.1016/j.procs.2022.12.023]

[7] F.M. Siemers, C. Feldmann, and J. Bajorath, "Minimal data requirements for accurate compound activity prediction using machine learning methods of different complexity", *Cell Rep. Phys. Sci.,* vol. 3, no. 11, p. 101113, 2022.
[http://dx.doi.org/10.1016/j.xcrp.2022.101113]

[8] M. Moshawrab, M. Adda, A. Bouzouane, H. Ibrahim, and A. Raad, "Reviewing federated machine learning and its use in diseases prediction", *Sensors (Basel),* vol. 23, no. 4, p. 2112, 2023.
[http://dx.doi.org/10.3390/s23042112] [PMID: 36850717]

[9] V.K. Pandey, S. Srivastava, K.K. Dash, R. Singh, S.A. Mukarram, B. Kovács, and E. Harsányi, "Machine Learning algorithms and fundamentals as Emerging Safety Tools in Preservation of fruits and vegetables: a review", *Processes (Basel),* vol. 11, no. 6, p. 1720, 2023.
[http://dx.doi.org/10.3390/pr11061720]

[10] A. Banan, A. Nasiri, and A. Taheri-Garavand, "Deep learning-based appearance features extraction for automated carp species identification", *Aquacult. Eng.,* vol. 89, p. 102053, 2020.
[http://dx.doi.org/10.1016/j.aquaeng.2020.102053]

[11] I.S. Samanta, S. Panda, P.K. Rout, M. Bajaj, M. Piecha, V. Blazek, and L. Prokop, "A comprehensive review of deep-learning applications to power quality analysis", *Energies,* vol. 16, no. 11, p. 4406, 2023.
[http://dx.doi.org/10.3390/en16114406]

[12] K. Phasinam, and T. Kassanuk, "Machine learning and internet of things (IoT) for real-time image classification in smart agriculture", *ECS Trans.,* vol. 107, no. 1, pp. 3305-3311, 2022.
[http://dx.doi.org/10.1149/10701.3305ecst]

[13] K. Phasinam, T. Kassanuk, and M. Shabaz, "Applicability of internet of things in smart farming", *J. Food Qual.,* vol. 2022, pp. 1-7, 2022.
[http://dx.doi.org/10.1155/2022/7692922]

[14] S.P. Yadav, S. Zaidi, C.D.S. Nascimento, V.H.C. de Albuquerque, and S.S. Chauhan, "Analysis and Design of automatically generating for GPS Based Moving Object Tracking System", *Proc. 2023 Int. Conf. on Artificial Intelligence and Smart Communication (AISC),* pp. 1-5, 2023.Greater Noida, India.
[http://dx.doi.org/10.1109/AISC56616.2023.10085180]

[15] K. Purohit, S. Vats, R. Saklani, V. Kukreja, V. Sharma and S. P. Yadav, "Improvement in K-Means Clustering for Information Retrieval", *Proc. 2023 4th Int. Conf. on Electronics and Sustainable*

*Communication Systems (ICESC),* pp. 1239-1245, 2023.Coimbatore, India. [http://dx.doi.org/10.1109/ICESC57686.2023.10193031]

[16] U. Shafi, R. Mumtaz, Z. Shafaq, S.M.H. Zaidi, M.O. Kaifi, Z. Mahmood, and S.A.R. Zaidi, "Wheat rust disease detection techniques: a technical perspective", *J. Plant Dis. Prot.,* vol. 129, no. 3, pp. 489-504, 2022.
[http://dx.doi.org/10.1007/s41348-022-00575-x]

[17] X. Bai, X. Wang, X. Liu, Q. Liu, J. Song, N. Sebe, and B. Kim, "Explainable deep learning for efficient and robust pattern recognition: A survey of recent developments", *Pattern Recognit.,* vol. 120, p. 108102, 2021.
[http://dx.doi.org/10.1016/j.patcog.2021.108102]

[18] M.A. Haque, S. Marwaha, C.K. Deb, S. Nigam, A. Arora, K.S. Hooda, P.L. Soujanya, S.K. Aggarwal, B. Lall, M. Kumar, S. Islam, M. Panwar, P. Kumar, and R.C. Agrawal, "Deep learning-based approach for identification of diseases of maize crop", *Sci. Rep.,* vol. 12, no. 1, p. 6334, 2022.
[http://dx.doi.org/10.1038/s41598-022-10140-z] [PMID: 35428845]

[19] U. Barman, R.D. Choudhury, D. Sahu, and G.G. Barman, "Comparison of convolution neural networks for smartphone image based real time classification of citrus leaf disease", *Comput. Electron. Agric.,* vol. 177, p. 105661, 2020.
[http://dx.doi.org/10.1016/j.compag.2020.105661]

[20] A. dos Santos Ferreira, D. Matte Freitas, G. Gonçalves da Silva, H. Pistori, and M. Theophilo Folhes, "Weed detection in soybean crops using ConvNets", *Comput. Electron. Agric.,* vol. 143, pp. 314-324, 2017.
[http://dx.doi.org/10.1016/j.compag.2017.10.027]

[21] G.G. Peteinatos, P. Reichel, J. Karouta, D. Andújar, and R. Gerhards, "Weed identification in maize, sunflower, and potatoes with the aid of convolutional neural networks", *Remote Sens. (Basel),* vol. 12, no. 24, p. 4185, 2020.
[http://dx.doi.org/10.3390/rs12244185]

[22] J. Zhuang, X. Li, M. Bagavathiannan, X. Jin, J. Yang, W. Meng, T. Li, L. Li, Y. Wang, Y. Chen, and J. Yu, "Evaluation of different deep convolutional neural networks for detection of broadleaf weed seedlings in wheat", *Pest Manag. Sci.,* vol. 78, no. 2, pp. 521-529, 2022.
[http://dx.doi.org/10.1002/ps.6656] [PMID: 34561954]

[23] Y. B. Singh, and S. Goel, "1D CNN based approach for speech emotion recognition using MFCC features", In: *Artificial Intelligence and Speech Technology,* A. Jain, M. N. Kumar, R. Prasad, Eds., 1st ed.. CRC Press: Boca Raton, FL, USA, 2021, pp. 195-202.

[24] T. de Camargo, M. Schirrmann, N. Landwehr, K.H. Dammer, and M. Pflanz, "Optimized deep learning model as a basis for fast UAV mapping of weed species in winter wheat crops", *Remote Sens. (Basel),* vol. 13, no. 9, p. 1704, 2021.
[http://dx.doi.org/10.3390/rs13091704]

[25] A. Subeesh, S. Bhole, K. Singh, N.S. Chandel, Y.A. Rajwade, K.V.R. Rao, S.P. Kumar, and D. Jat, "Deep convolutional neural network models for weed detection in polyhouse grown bell peppers", *Artificial Intelligence in Agriculture,* vol. 6, pp. 47-54, 2022.
[http://dx.doi.org/10.1016/j.aiia.2022.01.002]

[26] N. Razfar, J. True, R. Bassiouny, V. Venkatesh, and R. Kashef, "Weed detection in soybean crops using custom lightweight deep learning models", *J. Agric. Food Res.,* vol. 8, p. 100308, 2022.
[http://dx.doi.org/10.1016/j.jafr.2022.100308]

[27] G.C. Sunil, Y. Zhang, K. Howatt, L.G. Schumacher, and X. Sun, "Multi-species weed and crop classification comparison using five different deep learning network architectures", *J. ASABE.* vol. 67, no. 1, pp. 111–123, 2024.

[28] K. Zou, Q. Liao, F. Zhang, X. Che, and C. Zhang, "A segmentation network for smart weed management in wheat fields", *Comput. Electron. Agric.,* vol. 202, p. 107303, 2022.

[http://dx.doi.org/10.1016/j.compag.2022.107303]

[29] P. Wang, Y. Tang, F. Luo, L. Wang, C. Li, Q. Niu, and H. Li, "Weed25: A deep learning dataset for weed identification", *Front. Plant Sci.,* vol. 13, p. 1053329, 2022. [http://dx.doi.org/10.3389/fpls.2022.1053329] [PMID: 36531369]

[30] X. Guo, Y. Ge, F. Liu, and J. Yang, "Identification of maize and wheat seedlings and weeds based on deep learning", *Front. Earth Sci. (Lausanne),* vol. 11, p. 1146558, 2023. [http://dx.doi.org/10.3389/feart.2023.1146558]

[31] Z.D. Daşkın, M.S. Alam, and M.U. Khan, "Ensemble transfer learning using MaizeSet: A dataset for weed and maize crop recognition at different growth stages", *Crop Prot.,* vol. 184, p. 106849, 2024. [http://dx.doi.org/10.1016/j.cropro.2024.106849]

[32] M. Mckay, M.F. Danilevicz, M.B. Ashworth, R.L. Rocha, S.R. Upadhyaya, M. Bennamoun, and D. Edwards, "Focus on the Crop Not the Weed: Canola Identification for Precision Weed Management Using Deep Learning", *Remote Sens. (Basel),* vol. 16, no. 11, p. 2041, 2024. [http://dx.doi.org/10.3390/rs16112041]

[33] R. Alfred, J.H. Obit, C.P.Y. Chin, H. Haviluddin, and Y. Lim, "Towards paddy rice smart farming: a review on big data, machine learning, and rice production tasks", *IEEE Access,* vol. 9, pp. 50358-50380, 2021. [http://dx.doi.org/10.1109/ACCESS.2021.3069449]

[34] K.P. Kumar, B. Singh, K.V. Malini, A. Ranjan, S.D. Bonde, S. Rout, and A. Firos, "Iot and machine learning based effective plant disease classification and detection for agricultural applications", *IJFANS Int. J. Food Nutr. Sci.,* vol. 11, no. 8, pp. 415-423, 2022.

# CHAPTER 11

# A Machine Learning-based Approach for Smart Agriculture Monitoring and Decision Support

**Ankit Jain**[1,*], **Anita Shukla**[2] and **Imran Ullah Khan**[3]

[1] *Department of Electronics and Communication Engineering, Pranveer Singh Institute of Technology, Kanpur, Uttar Pradesh, India*

[2] *Department of Basic Sciences and Humanities, Pranveer Singh Institute of Technology, Kanpur, Uttar Pradesh, India*

[3] *Department of Electronics and Communication Engineering, Integral University, Lucknow, Uttar Pradesh, India*

**Abstract:** The field of machine learning is expanding and has a wide range of potential uses in agriculture. Machine learning is used to forecast pests and illnesses, decrease water usage, and increase crop yields, which is a topic of investigation for farmers and agricultural experts. Machine learning is capable of improving resource efficacy along with food production sustainability for farmers in the future. Numerous factors either directly or indirectly affect crop growth. Among these are the climate parameters. We can boost productivity by employing machine learning to monitor and regulate these parameters. In addition, there is a need for technological solutions to address a number of issues, including fire alerts, maintaining humidity levels and appropriate temperatures, and meeting the needs of sophisticated plants while monitoring unauthorized entry into agricultural areas. The significance of an appropriate and satisfactory supply of power cannot be understated. By using a NodeMCU Wi-Fi module, the technology offers a practical and effective solution to the issues identified in the Indian farming system. Various sensors such as those for temperature, fire, light, PIR, humidity, and soil moisture, have been utilized to monitor and regulate a variety of technological issues. Using IOT and machine learning, the projected system uses a Wi-Fi module to display real-time data that can be watched online from any location in the world. The farmer is automatically notified by this module about the need for water, site temperature, moisture and humidity, light, fire warning, and unwelcome occupancy or encroachment. Using the machine learning principle, an experiment was conducted with varying soil and plant levels. It was established that the sensor exhibited sufficient sensitivity to yield consistent results under varying water level situations for diverse combinations of plants and soil.

**Keywords:** Automatic farming, Blynk server, Humidity sensor, Machine learning, Node MCU, PIR sensor, Soil moisture sensor.

* **Corresponding author Ankit Jain:** Department of Electronics and Communication Engineering, Pranveer Singh Institute of Technology, Kanpur, Uttar Pradesh, India; E-mail: ankit2483jain@gmail.com

**Ravinder M., Arti Ranjan, Youddha Beer Singh (Eds.)**

## INTRODUCTION

In many regions of Southern India, the agricultural legacy of India extends even further, dating back to the Indus Valley Civilization [1]. India is currently the second-largest producer of agricultural products worldwide. Despite the country's overall economic growth, the contribution of agriculture to India's GDP continues to decline. However, in terms of population, agriculture is India's largest economic segment and plays a major role in the nation's overall socioeconomic structure. With $38 billion in agricultural exports in 2013, India ranked seventh globally and sixth globally in terms of net exports [2]. Most agricultural exports are sent to emerging or developing countries. India exports agricultural, horticultural, and processed food items to about 120 countries; the majority of these destinations include the SAARC countries, the Middle East, Southeast Asia, the European Union, and the United States [3, 4].

Some important industries in our country still haven't fully embraced or utilized automation, even though everything in our society can be controlled and operated automatically. These include the agricultural sector. The process of automated farming involves monitoring and modifying the climate variables that have an impact on plant growth and the final result, either directly or indirectly.

India's problems with groundwater overexploitation would unavoidably get worse and spread if corrective action is not taken before the problem is intractable or not worth solving. Technology is needed to address other farming problems, such as monitoring unauthorized entry into agricultural fields and maintaining proper temperature, humidity, and light levels for sophisticated plants. However, the most important element for agriculture is a regular and sufficient electricity supply. Farmers, who ensure the availability of power because their task cannot begin without it, have also faced challenges due to a very erratic power source that frequently experiences power disruptions, in addition to decreased efficiency. Using IOT technology, this system can display real-time data that is accessible or viewed online from any location in the world. The internet was accessed with the Node MCU WiFi module. Applications in agriculture are made much simpler and more efficient by machine learning.

Complex problems are usually solved by machine learning algorithms, while human skill becomes inadequate. In agriculture, one can employ machine learning to predict soil properties like moisture content and organic carbon content, as well as to identify weeds and diseases in crops, detect species, and estimate crop production [5]. By employing several functions on the input and increasing the model's complexity, deep learning improves on traditional machine learning. Using network architecture, this allows for hierarchical data representation through several layers of abstraction. The ability of the Deep Learning model to identify novel objects, such as anomalies, instead of only a predetermined collection of objects, is a crucial component. The program finds items that are unknown, far away, and poorly obscured by taking advantage of the homogeneous characteristics of an agricultural field [6].

This hardware effectively and efficiently addresses the highlighted issue with the Indian farming system. The solution that is being given is inexpensive, safe for the environment, and electronically operated, which will improve farmer satisfaction with the Indian agricultural system.

## RELATED WORK

In the modern era, innovation and the adoption of new technology are often used to satisfy human needs. This has led to the development of the Internet of Things (IoT) [7, 8]. A network of machines, sensors, software, devices, and people connected via the Internet to exchange data, communicate, and interact is referred to as the "Internet of Things" (IoT) [9]. The goal of IoT is to create a seamless connection between the digital and physical realms. Smart homes [10, 11], smart cities [12, 13], smart energy [14, 15], autonomous automobiles [16, 17], smart agriculture [18, 19], campus management [20, 21], healthcare [22, 23], and logistics [24, 25] are just a few of the areas in which IoT has been applied recently. The number of IoT applications has been illustrated by Shafique *et al.* [26]. Information about automatic water supply to fields is detailed by Satya Prasanth Yalla *et al.* [27]. Modules and soil moisture sensors are included in the automation of the system, and sunlight is used as the preferred renewable energy source for power generation. E. Pradeep *et al.* developed a PV-powered farmer pump [28], considering components such as the power source, AC, DC, GSM technology, inverter frequency, well, waterline in the well, and submersible pump. Researchers demonstrate a state-of-the-art technique utilizing a GSM module. Jia Uddin *et al.* proposed a variable-rate autonomous microcontroller-based irrigation system [29].

All power needed to run the system comes from solar energy. Sensors are placed on the paddy field. The farmer receives continual readings of the water level from these sensors. The solar tracking system design maximizes solar energy capture and subsequently converts it into electrical energy for the irrigation system. The power was investigated by Binoy Seal *et al.* in [30]. Ishwar Kumar *et al.* proposa solar-powered vehicle trailer in conjunction with an autonomous water flow management system based on moisture sensors in [31]. It is a recommended solution to the energy issues that Indian farmers are currently facing. Nilesh R. Patel *et al.* [32] list several monitoring and regulating methods developed to increase crop yield. Illness is one of the primary reasons for yield reduction, and a tracking mechanism has been developed to forecast when diseases may begin to spread. Different environmental conditions on the farm are detected by a sensor module, and the sensor data is displayed on an LCD by the CPU.

Irrigation, as described by Shiraz Pasha B.R. *et al.* [33], refers to the application of water to land or soil with the aim of supporting crop growth, preserving landscapes, and preventing soil degradation in arid areas or during dry spells. Basava Sidramappa Dhanne *et al.* [34] investigated automatic irrigation systems that use modules and soil moisture sensors, powered primarily by sunlight as a renewable energy source. M. Chetan Dwarkani *et al.* [35] developed a system to obtain real-time data, minimize water loss during irrigation, and shorten fieldwork duration. Nikesh Gondchawar *et al.* [36] proposed technology to read and analyze systems that allow farmers to monitor soil quality and crop growth. These systems help manage irrigation, temperature, humidity, and other environmental factors. Microcontrollers and agricultural parameter sensors can be readily interfaced, and using the Internet of Things (IoT), it is possible to regulate growth conditions and optimize yield.

To improve reliability and usability for farmers, Sriram Rakshith K *et al.* [37] focus on strategies and programs that advance farming through technological knowledge and innovation. Machine learning algorithms are used to recommend the most suitable crops based on soil conditions, weather, and market trends. Factors considered include pH, nitrogen content, phosphate-potassium (NPK) levels, temperature, precipitation, and humidity. After extensive research, Artificial Neural Networks were identified as the most appropriate method for this purpose. S.R. Rajeshwari K *et al.* [38] also emphasize machine learning techniques for predicting the most profitable crops. Their work uses an Android system that integrates weather station reports and soil quality data to provide real-time crop analysis, allowing farmers to select the most profitable planting times.

The primary goal of Abhishek L. *et al.* [39] is to increase the efficiency of the agricultural sector. The Internet of Things (IoT) is a major technological development that can benefit agriculture by enhancing productivity. By combining IoT and machine learning, crop production efficiency can be improved. Several meteorological factors are considered to predict the best crops using supervised learning techniques such as decision trees, classifiers, and regression models. S.R. Rajeshwari *et al.* [40] describe various methods to enhance agriculture through technology, highlighting the use of machine learning algorithms to predict agricultural outputs based on soil pH, nitrogen, phosphate-potassium levels, temperature, precipitation, and humidity. Their research concludes that Support Vector Machines (SVM) are highly effective for this purpose.

Nevavuori P *et al.* [41] focus on applying multi-temporal UAV data combined with spatio-temporal deep learning models to predict crop yields, emphasizing the role of remote sensing and machine learning in improving prediction accuracy and agricultural management. Abhishek L. *et al.* [42] investigate automation in agriculture using IoT and machine learning, examining various sensors and models to monitor and optimize crop growth and resource use. Elavarasan D *et al.* [43] present a reinforced random forest model that integrates agrarian parameters for enhanced crop yield prediction, demonstrating improved accuracy by combining environmental and soil data. Rezk N.G. *et al.* [44] developed an IoT-based smart farming system using machine learning algorithms to monitor and manage agricultural parameters in real time, improving productivity and sustainability. Rizg A *et al.* [45] provide a comprehensive survey of deep learning applications in agriculture, analyzing the use of convolutional neural networks (CNN) and other models. The survey highlights contributions, challenges, and potential for increased accuracy and efficiency in agricultural monitoring and management.

## SMART FARMING SYSTEM

"Smart agriculture" can be defined as a broad range of methods in that the Internet of Things (IoT) is being used in farming and other agricultural domains. Various elements like sensors, wireless networks, cloud services, and data analytics are already changing the farming and agricultural sectors.

Anything that increases agricultural and animal productivity through more exacting and regulated farming methods might be considered under this category. The utilization of IOT and other instruments, including sensors, control systems, robots, autonomous vehicles, automated hardware, variable rate technologies, and more, is crucial to this farm management strategy. The following are the main benefits:

- Higher productivity.
- Reduced expenses for production.
- Efficiency in operations.
- Intelligent and real-time cost control.

By boosting sales or cutting expenses, these items can maximize your profits while having less of an adverse effect on the environment. As a result, farmers and ranchers may collect valuable data thanks to IoT agriculture apps. Both small and large landowners need to recognize the potential of the Internet of Things market for agriculture and use smart technologies to increase the sustainability and competitiveness of their businesses. Given the population's rapid increase, demand can be successfully met if ranchers and small farmers effectively utilize agricultural IoT, *etc.*

## ROLE OF MACHINE LEARNING (ML) IN AGRICULTURE SYSTEMS

These days, ML is a popular technology that has applications in the contemporary agriculture sector. Healthier seeds are produced thanks to the application of ML in agriculture. The techniques used in machine learning agriculture come from the process of learning. For these techniques to complete a given task, they must learn via experience. The data in the ML are derived from a collection of cases. A collection of characteristics defines an individual example. Variables or features are the names given to these collections of attributes. Binary, numeric, or ordinal representations are possible for a feature. The performance metric is used to calculate machine learning's performance. With time, as the ML model acquires experience, its performance gets better. Several mathematical and statistical models are used in agriculture for the assessment of machine learning algorithms and ML models. After learning is finished, the model can be applied to test, classify, and make assumptions about data. This is attained following the acquisition of training process experience.

## CHARACTERISTICS OF THE SUGGESTED SYSTEM

The suggested system is enhanced with multiple features aimed at improving usability and making it more farmer-friendly. Utilizing the NodeMCU Wi-Fi module, it now maintains an internet connection, allowing real-time data to be accessed globally through IoT technology. These enhancements enable efficient monitoring and management of agricultural operations, enhancing productivity and convenience for farmers.

- **Automatic Water Pump Activation**

When the soil moisture level falls below a predetermined threshold, this feature makes sure the water pump is activated automatically. This automation prevents under-watering, ensuring crops receive the necessary amount of water. Real-time soil moisture data is accessed globally via the Internet of Things (IoT), allowing growers to monitor and adjust irrigation schedules remotely.

- **Automatic Artificial Lighting System**

For crops requiring specific light conditions, an automatic lighting system is incorporated. When natural light levels fall under the predetermined threshold, the system activates artificial lights to maintain optimal light conditions for crop growth. This feature uses IoT to provide real-time light-intensity data accessible from anywhere in the world, ensuring that crops receive adequate light even in low-light conditions.

- **Automatic Humidity Control**

A water spreading jet motor that is part of the system is automatically activated when the humidity level crosses a predetermined threshold. By keeping the surrounding air at ideal humidity levels, this function keeps the crops from drying out. Real-time online monitoring of the humidity levels enables remote adjustments and monitoring.

- **Automatic Temperature Control**

To protect advanced crops from heat stress, the system includes a fan that automatically turns on when the temperature exceeds a certain limit. This feature helps maintain optimal temperature conditions for crop growth. Temperature data is updated in real time and can be accessed online, allowing farmers to monitor and control temperature remotely.

- **Alarm System for Emergencies**

In case of emergencies such as unwanted occupancy or fire, the system is equipped with a buzzer that alerts the farmer by beeping. Additionally, updates regarding these alarming situations are sent over the internet, ensuring that the farmer is promptly informed and can take immediate action to mitigate any potential damage.

- **Solar Power Backup**

A solar panel built into the system offers a dependable power supply in the event of a power loss. This feature makes sure that even in major power supply outages, the system continues to work normally and that all automatic procedures will continue to function.

- **Online Real-Time Display System**

All sensor data and the corresponding actions taken by the microcontroller are displayed in real-time on an online platform. This comprehensive display allows farmers to monitor various environmental parameters and the system's actions, providing a clear overview of the field conditions and the system's responses.

- **Remote Control via Internet**

The system includes relays that can be operated manually or automatically through switches available on an internet-accessible control panel. This feature allows farmers to control various functions of the system remotely, providing flexibility and ease of management from any location in the world. These features collectively enhance the system's functionality and make it highly farmer-friendly by providing automated solutions and real-time data access, resulting in farming methods that are more efficient and sustainable.

## ALGORITHM AND IMPLEMENTATION

We suggest employing control engineering in the model's design to address stated matter and incorporate other beneficial functionalities. The entire suggested system's hardware is developed using a step-by-step technique. The fundamental objective is to build a general system that can receive input from external devices (sensors) and modify it to produce an intended output. Fig. **1** shows the circuit diagram of the proposed model. Sensors, modules, and electronics used in making the hardware design for the current system include the following:

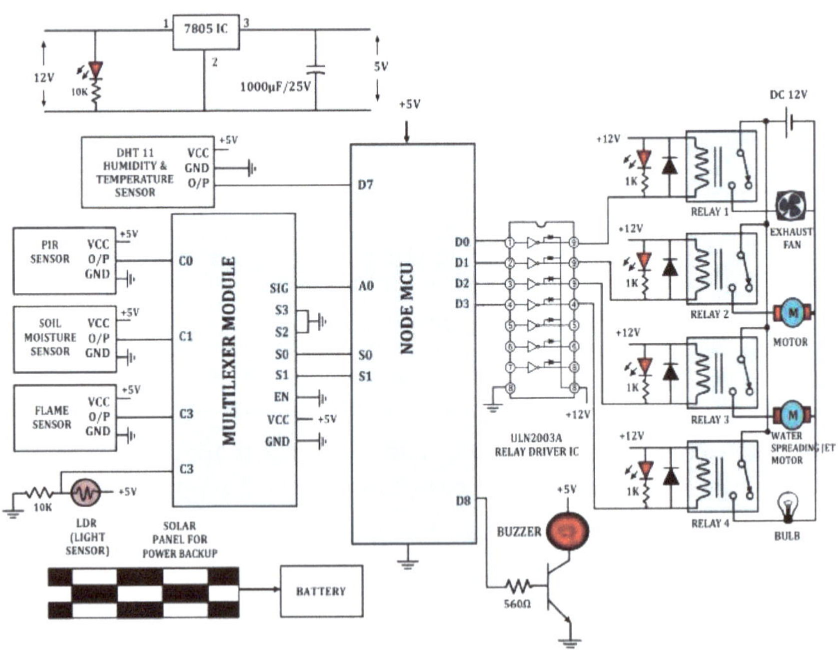


**Fig. (1).** Circuit diagram of the proposed model.

- DHT11 Temperature and Humidity sensor
- Multiplexer module
- ESP 8266 node MCU Wi-Fi module
- LDR (Light Dependent Register) sensor
- Flame sensor
- Soil moisture sensor
- Buzzer
- PIR sensor
- Relay section

## Node MCU ESP8266 Pin Out

The Node MCU ESP8266 Wi-fi Module, which has an open-source firmware based on Lua, is a development board designed especially for Internet of Things (IoT) applications, as shown in Fig. (**2**). The Node MCU ESP8266-based boards now need the ESP8266 package to be installed in the Arduino IDE, even though they originally came with the LUA scripting language for programming.

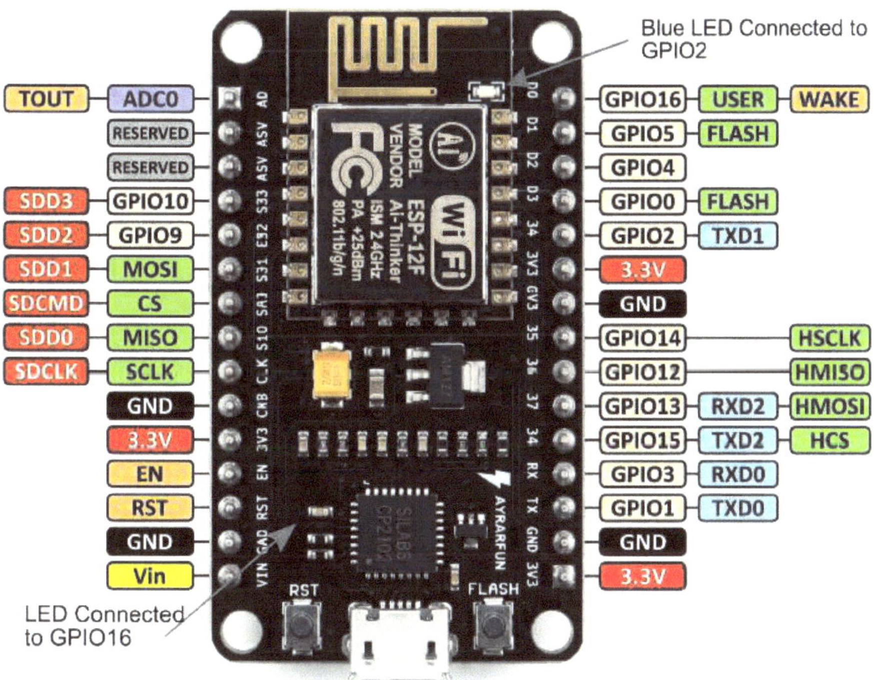


**Fig. (2).** Pin mapping of Node MCU.

## Main Sensors/Components

**Main sensors/components related to the proposed system are described below.**

| | |
|---|---|
| <br><br>(Fig **3a**) DHT11 sensor | The DHT11 digital temperature and humidity sensor, a composite sensor, generates a precisely calibrated digital signal for measuring temperature and humidity (Fig. **3a**). |
| 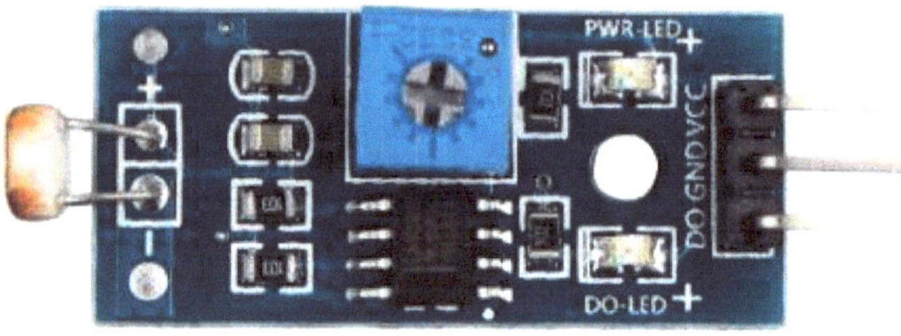<br><br>(Fig. **3b**) LDR module | A light-sensitive resistor used in the LDR, changes resistance in response to light. Resistance values, which vary in magnitude by several orders of magnitude, drop as light levels rise (Fig. **3b**). |
| 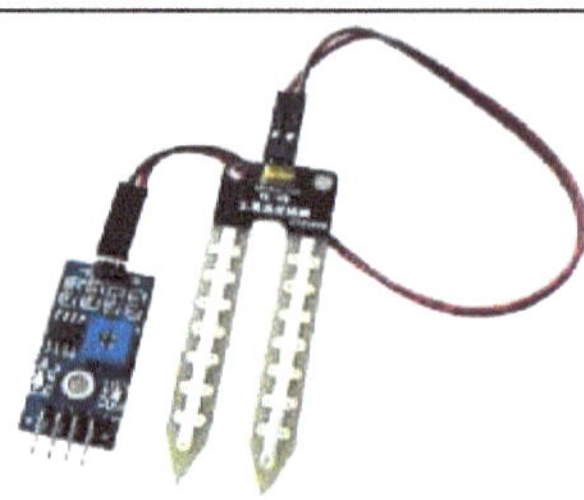<br>(Fig. **3c**) Soil moisture sensor | To measure the moisture level, this sensor utilizes two probes to pass an electrical current through the soil and assess its resistance. As illustrated in (Fig. **3c**), wet soil conducts electricity more efficiently due to lower resistance, whereas dry soil exhibits higher resistance, making conduction less effective. |
| <br>(Fig. **3d**) Pressure sensor | When an object is in its field of view, an electrical device known as a passive infrared sensor (PIR sensor) picks up the infrared (IR) light it emits. Usually, PIR-based motion detectors employ them. Autonomous lighting systems and security alarms commonly use PIR sensors (Fig. **3d**). |

*(Table) cont.....*

| | |
|---|---|
|  (Fig. **3e**) Rain sensor | Because of this, flame alarms use this sensor module. This sensor detects flames from the light source at wavelengths ranging from 760 to 1100 nm. This sensor is susceptible to damage from high temperatures. This makes it possible to position the sensor at a particular separation from the flame. At a distance of 100 cm and a 600-degree detecting angle, the flame can be found. The output of this sensor can be either digital or analog (Fig. **3e**). |
|  (Fig. **3F**) Buzzer | A piezoelectric, electromechanical, or mechanical buzzer or beeper is an example of an auditory signalling device. Timer functions, alarm clock functions, and user input confirmation are common uses for buzzers and beepers (Fig. **3f**). |
|   (Fig. **3g**) ULN 2003A relay driver IC | Linking low-level circuits with several peripheral power loads is the main application for ULN. The driver makes use of the ULN2003A driver IC. To control typical loads exceeding 230V concurrently at a rough duty cycle, many drivers can be activated based on the input sensor data (Fig. **3g**). |
|  (Fig. **3h**) Relay | One circuit can switch a second circuit that is entirely independent by using a relay. The only link between the two circuits in the relay is the mechanical and magnetic one. An armature that is mechanically attached to a moving contact is drawn by the magnetic field created when a current flows through the coil. (Fig. **3h**). |

*(Table) cont.....*

| | |
|---|---|
|  (Fig. **3i**) Solar panel PV cell | A solar cell, also known as a photovoltaic (PV) cell, converts light into an electric current by use of the photovoltaic effect. The amount of direct current (DC) electricity produced by solar cells fluctuates according to the sun's brightness. Multiple solar cells are connected within modules. An array of interconnected modules is connected to an inverter, which produces power at the desired voltage and, in the case of AC, the desired frequency/phase. A solar cell can produce 1.5 W of power. Individual cells that are joined to one another make up a solar panel, which can provide 3 to 110W of power. Panels are usually designed to deliver power at 12V (Fig. **3i**). |

## DISPLAY PANEL AND ALGORITHM DEVELOPMENT OVER IOT

To operate a hardware system, based on IOT and a Node MCU Module, a program is created in the Arduino IDE. Flow chart and related sensor systems, which served as the foundation for the program's development, are displayed in Fig. (**4**).

Fig. (**5**) shows the display panel developed here, under io.adafruit.com. This may be viewed online from anywhere around the world thanks to IOT technology. Furthermore, a gauge version of the real-time monitoring system is offered. This particular setup involves the monitoring of six sensors: the temperature, humidity, fire, motion (PIR), light, and soil moisture sensors. This display system may operate relays manually or automatically. Relay initiates automatically when any sensor reading exceeds the threshold value. We can even manually operate the relay if we so choose.

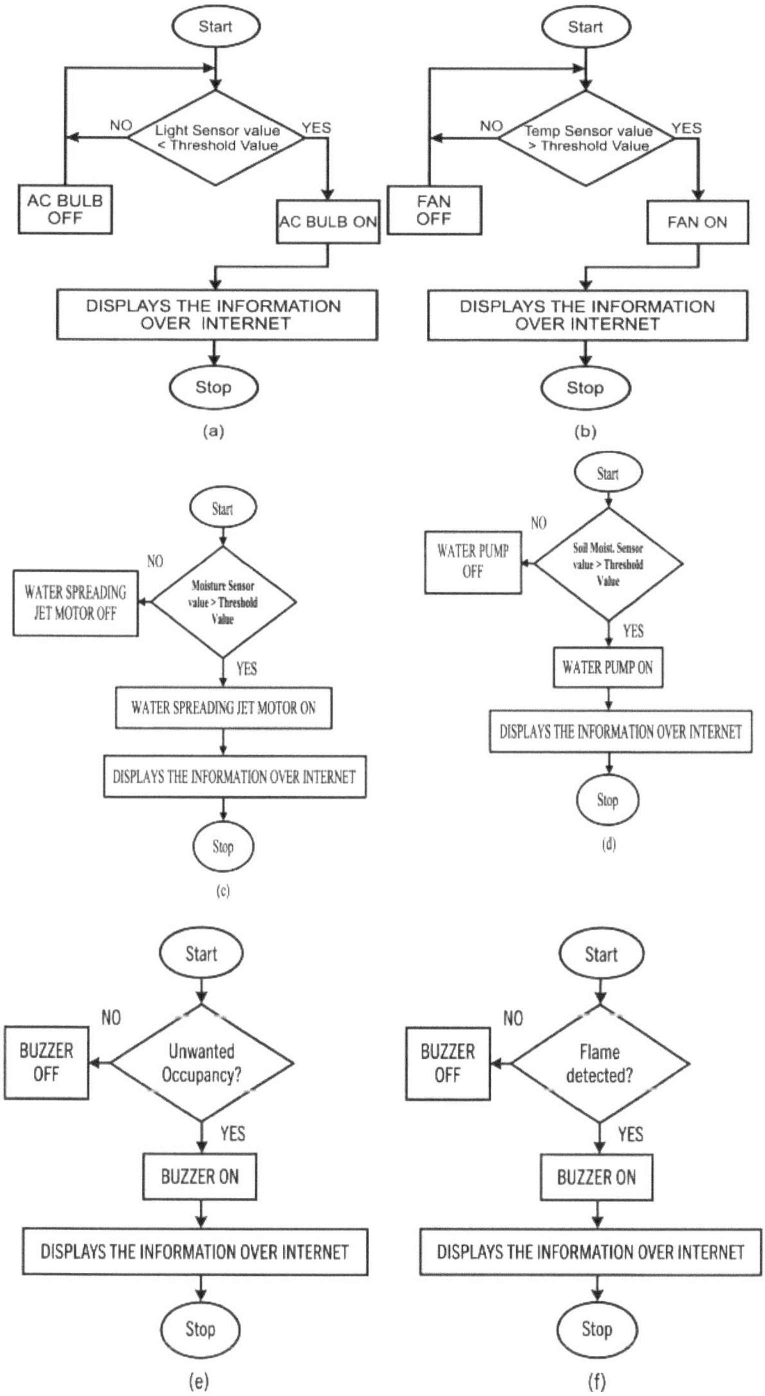


**Fig. (4).** Flow charts of the systems.

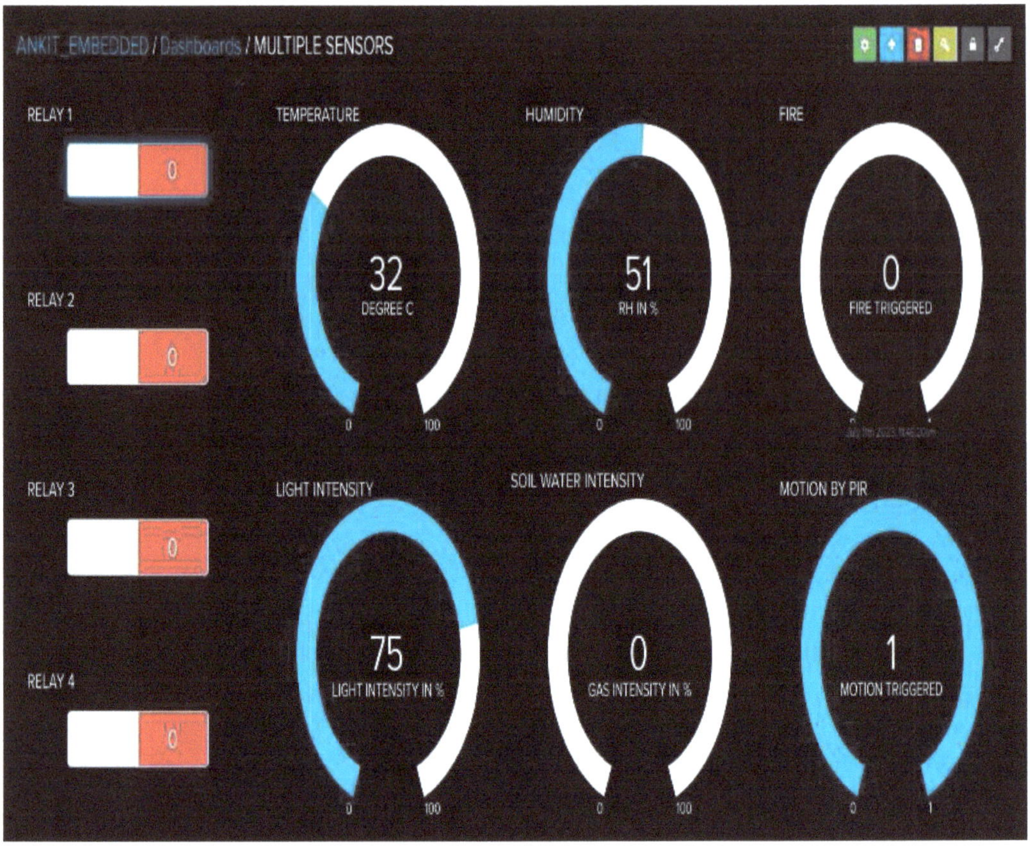


**Fig. (5).** IOT based control panel.

## Implementation of PCB and Circuit

The PCB used in this system is seen from top and bottom in Fig. (**6a**) and (**6b**). This PCB was made using Dip Trace. The original PCB is shown in Fig. (**7**).

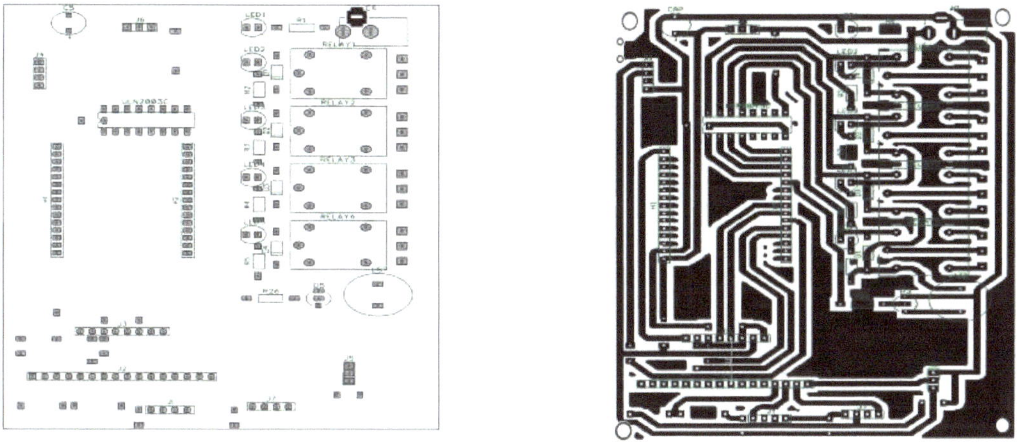

**(a) Top view** **(b) Bottom view**

**Fig. (6).** Dip trace used to prepare PCB.

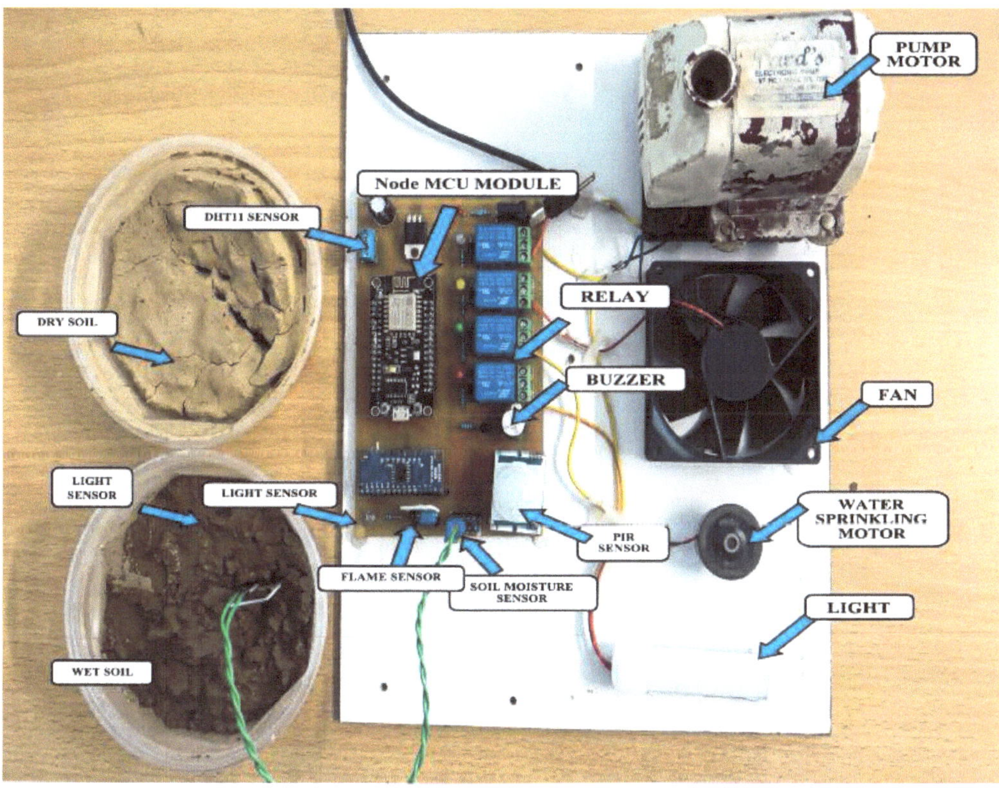


**Fig. (7).** Original hardware implementation picture.

## Implementation of Soil Moisture Sensor

Focusing on soil water retention becomes crucial because irrigation is a farming necessity with the largest role to play. In this instance, a soil moisture sensor has been used. In order to achieve successful deployment, several trials involving soil moisture sensors were required.

Three distinct plant combinations, designated A, B, and C in the experiment set, were chosen, as shown in Fig. (**8**).

**Fig. (8).** Three various plant and soil combinations A, B, and C.

Three distinct water levels low, normal, and excess were applied to Plant A, which was planted in the first type of soil. The sensor has enough intelligence to determine the water level during the experiment. Info was transmitted over controller and shown on an IOT display screen, and the appropriate actions were also taken, such as

i. The water pump would automatically turn “ON” till it reached the necessary level, as indicated in Fig. (**9**), if the water level fell below the predetermined limit.
ii. The water level would stay in passive mode, depicted in Fig. (**10**), if it reached the predetermined limit (average water).

iii. The water pump would automatically turn "OFF" if the water level exceeded the predetermined limit (excess water), as shown in Fig. (**11**).

**Fig. (9).** Combination A of soil and plants (no water).

**Fig. (10).** Combination B: soil and plants (average water).

**Fig. (11).** Combination C: soil and plants (excess water).

We employed combination B, the second plant and soil combination depicted in Fig. (**12**), to test the sensor's compatibility with other soil and plant combinations.

**Fig. (12).** Soil and Plant Combination B.

Findings were consistent with combination A. As illustrated in Fig. (**13**), the third and final combination of soil and plant, or C, was utilized to corroborate the outcomes of A and B.

**Fig. (13).** Soil and Plant Combinations C.

It was determined by repeating the results obtained with combinations A and B that the sensor was sensitive enough to yield identical results under varying water level situations and with diverse combinations of plants and soils.

The other sensors were also checked, and they were found to function as expected.

## RESULTS AND ANALYSIS

We have created a system that offers an environmentally responsible and electronic solution to issues pertaining to the Indian farming sector. The system's cost study demonstrates how inexpensive its implementation is. Farmers will see fewer issues as a result, particularly with irrigation systems.

Using this approach, we get a number of attractive results. These are:

### Solution to the Water Problem

The water pump that comes with the suggested model starts up automatically when the soil needs moisture.

### Solution to Unwanted Occupancy

An automatic buzzer system that alerts farmers to any unwelcome access or occupancy in the region where they enter their land is one way to combat the problem of unwanted occupation and vandalism of crops.

### Solution to Humidity Level Maintenance

To maintain humidity levels, an automated water-distributing jet motor is employed. It activates automatically when the humidity exceeds a predefined threshold, ensuring optimal moisture levels are maintained without manual intervention.

### Solution to Temperature Maintenance

In order to address the issue of temperature maintenance for advanced crops, fans are used. The fan is automatically activated when the temperature rises.

### Solution to Electricity Supply

Even in the case of a power loss, the system can continue to operate thanks to its solar panel and battery for continuous power backup.

### Solution to Light Arrangement for Sophisticated Plants

The autonomous artificial lighting system is used to meet the light requirements of advanced crops. It turns on when the amount of light falls below a predetermined threshold for crops.

### Solution to Communication Problem

A real-time internet-based monitoring module, which can be accessed from anywhere in the globe, is employed in the system to automatically notify farmers regarding temperature, humidity, moisture, light, fire, and unauthorized occupation. This allows the farmer to stay informed about a variety of field conditions.

## Performance Comparison

Performance comparison given on the technology, components used, and uniqueness of the proposed system is given in Table **1**. The uniqueness of the proposed system is also mentioned.

**Table 1. Performance comparisons based on the special components, technology used, and features of the system.**

<table>
<tr><th>Sr. No.</th><th>Research Paper</th><th>Special Components</th><th>Technology</th><th>Features</th><th>Uniqueness in Proposed System</th></tr>
<tr><td>1.</td><td>Dhanne BS et al. (2014) [36]</td><td>Solar Panels, ARM Processor</td><td>Solar Power, ARM</td><td>Solar Powered Irrigation</td><td rowspan="10">• Automatic Water Pump Activation<br>When soil moisture is low, it automatically turns on the water pump, with real-time data accessible globally via IoT.<br>• Automatic Artificial Lighting System<br>Activates artificial lights for crops when natural light is insufficient, with real-time light intensity data accessible online.<br>• Automatic Humidity Control<br>Automatically activates water spreading jet motor to maintain optimal humidity levels, with real-time monitoring online.<br>• Automatic Temperature Control<br>Turns on a fan when the temperature exceeds a certain limit, with real-time temperature data accessible via the internet.<br>• Alarm System for Emergencies<br>Alerts with a buzzer and internet updates in case of unwelcome occupancy or fire.<br>• Solar Power Backup<br>Uses a solar panel to power the system during power outages.<br>• Online Real-Time Display System<br>Displays all sensor data and microcontroller actions in real-time on an online platform.<br>• Remote Control via Internet<br>Allows manual or automatic operation of relays through an internet-accessible control panel.</td></tr>
<tr><td>2.</td><td>M Chetan Dwarkani et al. (2015) [37]</td><td>Various Sensors (Temperature, Humidity, Soil Moisture)</td><td>Sensors, Automation</td><td>Automated Agricultural Tasks</td></tr>
<tr><td>3.</td><td>Nikesh et al. (2016) [38]</td><td>IoT Devices, Sensors</td><td>IoT</td><td>Smart Agricultural Monitoring</td></tr>
<tr><td>4.</td><td>Sriram Rakshith K et al. (2019) [39]</td><td>Machine Learning Algorithms</td><td>Machine Learning</td><td>Crop Prediction</td></tr>
<tr><td>5.</td><td>S.R. Rajeshwari et al. (2019) [40]</td><td>Machine Learning Algorithms</td><td>Machine Learning</td><td>Farming Prediction</td></tr>
<tr><td>6.</td><td>Nevavuori P et al. (2020) [41]</td><td>UAVs, Deep Learning Models</td><td>UAV, Deep Learning</td><td>Multi-temporal Crop Yield Prediction</td></tr>
<tr><td>7.</td><td>Abhishek L, et al. (2021) [42]</td><td>IoT Devices, Machine Learning Models</td><td>IoT, Machine Learning</td><td>Automation in Agriculture</td></tr>
<tr><td>8.</td><td>Elavarasan D, et al. (2021) [43]</td><td>Random Forest Algorithm</td><td>Random Forest, Machine Learning</td><td>Enhanced Crop Yield Prediction</td></tr>
<tr><td>9.</td><td>Rezk NG et al. (2021) [44]</td><td>IoT Devices, Machine Learning Algorithms</td><td>IoT, Machine Learning</td><td>Efficient Smart Farming</td></tr>
<tr><td>10.</td><td>Rizg A et al. (2022) [45]</td><td>Deep Learning Algorithms</td><td>Deep Learning</td><td>Survey on Smart Agriculture</td></tr>
</table>

## CONCLUSION

Using this approach, we get a number of satisfactory results. This project proposes an IoT-based smart agriculture architecture in conjunction with a hybrid machine learning approach that addresses various technical issues, such as water management, undesired occupancy, temperature control, humidity level maintenance, electricity supply, lighting for sophisticated plants, fire alarm, and field condition updates for farmers. Utilizing a Wi-Fi module based on the Internet of Things (IoT), this system automatically alerts farmers to temperature, humidity, wetness, light, unwanted occupancy, and fire hazards by displaying real-time data from around the globe. Either manual or internet-based control of the relay is possible.

A complete solution created to improve farming techniques' sustainability and efficiency is the smart agriculture monitoring system. By integrating advanced technologies like IoT, machine learning, and automated control systems, this system offers several farmer-friendly features. The automatic water pump activation ensures optimal irrigation, while the artificial lighting system and humidity control maintain ideal growing conditions for crops. Temperature control mechanisms protect crops from heat stress, and the alarm system promptly alerts farmers to emergencies like unwelcome occupancy or fire. The inclusion of a solar power backup ensures uninterrupted operation, and the online real-time display system provides a holistic view of field conditions and system actions. Additionally, it is able to control the system remotely via the internet, which adds a layer of convenience and flexibility. All things considered, this smart farm monitoring system is a big step in the direction of modernizing agriculture, making it more efficient, sustainable, and accessible to farmers worldwide.

## LIMITATION

- **Limited Sensor Types:** While the current system is equipped with various sensors for monitoring soil moisture, temperature, humidity, and light, it lacks some specialized sensors that could enhance its functionality, such as gas sensors for detecting harmful gases.
- **Dependency on Internet Connectivity:** For remote control and real-time data access, the system is highly dependent on dependable internet connectivity.
- In regions with poor internet infrastructure, this could pose a challenge.
- **Initial Setup and Maintenance Costs:** The installation and maintenance of the system, including the solar panel, sensors, and microcontroller, might incur high costs, which could be a barrier for small-scale farmers.
- **Limited Battery Life:** The solar-powered backup may have limitations in battery life and efficiency, especially during prolonged cloudy or rainy periods, affecting the system's reliability.

## FUTURE SCOPE

- **Implementation of Inverter:** Since the system includes a solar panel, it can charge batteries and offer a DC supply, which the microcontroller can use as a backup power source in the event of a power outage. An inverter can be added to the system to convert DC to AC, making it easier to operate AC appliances like water pumps and automatic lighting systems.
- **Implementation of Gas Sensor:** Adding a gas sensor to the system could enhance its functionality by detecting harmful gases and protecting crops from fire-related harm.
- **Integration with Machine Learning Models:** Further integration with advanced machine learning models could improve predictive capabilities for crop diseases, pest infestations, and optimal watering schedules based on historical data and environmental conditions.
- **Expansion of Sensor Network**: Expanding the network of sensors to include more parameters, such as soil pH, nutrient levels, and atmospheric pressure, could provide a more comprehensive monitoring system for better crop management.
- **Enhanced User Interface:** Evolving a more user-friendly interface for the online real-time display system could progress accessibility and ease of use for farmers, including mobile app support for better on-the-go monitoring and control.
- **Automated Data Analysis:** Implementing automated data analysis and reporting features could help farmers make informed decisions without needing to manually interpret raw data, thus enhancing the system's practicality and usability.

## REFERENCES

[1] S Jain, A Shukla, I. U. Khan, and R Singh, "Applications of Internet of Things (IoT) technologies for agriculture", In: *Advanced IoT Technologies and Applications in the Industry 4.0 Digital Economy*, 2024, p. 173.

[2] G Abegunrin, A Jadhav, A Jauhar, and A Nagpal, "India: Agriculture data country profile", *Gates Open Research,* vol. 9, no. 8, p. 8, 2025.

[3] K. P. Kumar, B Singh, K. V. Malini, A Ranjan, S. D. Bonde, S Rout, and A Firos, "IoT and machine learning based effective plant disease classification and detection for agricultural applications", *IJFANS Int. J. Food Nutr. Sci.,* vol. 11, no. 8, pp. 415-423, 2022.

[4] W Yalla, B Bamesh, and A Ramesh, "Autonomous solar powered irrigation system", *Int. J. Eng. Res. Appl.,* vol. 3, no. 1, pp. 60-65, 2013.

[5] P Bharatkumar, P Khatun, C Kumar, and A. K. Yadav, "Role of agriculture processing in export growth of agricultural products", *J. Curr. Res. Food Sci.,* vol. 4, no. 1, pp. 49-56, 2023. [http://dx.doi.org/10.22271/foodsci.2023.v4.i1a.91]

[6] A. Kamilaris, and F. X. Prenafeta-Boldú, "Deep learning in agriculture: A survey", *Comput. Electron. Agric.,* vol. 147, pp. 70-90, 2018.

[7] Q. V. Khanh, N. V. Hoai, L. D. Manh, A. N. Le, and G Jeon, "Wireless communication technologies for IoT in 5G: Vision, applications, and challenges", *Wireless Commun. Mob. Comput.*, vol. 2022, p. 12.
[http://dx.doi.org/10.1155/2022/3229294]

[8] S Sinche, D Raposo, N Armando, A Rodrigues, F Boavida, V Pereira, and J. S. Silva, "A survey of IoT management protocols and frameworks", *IEEE Communications Surveys & Tutorials,* vol. 22, no. 2, pp. 1168-1190, 2020.
[http://dx.doi.org/10.1109/COMST.2019.2943087]

[9] O Elijah, T. A. Rahman, I Orikumhi, C. Y. Leow, and M. H. D. N. Hindia, "An overview of Internet of Things (IoT) and data analytics in agriculture: Benefits and challenges", *IEEE Internet of Things Journal,* vol. 5, no. 5, pp. 3758-3773, 2018.
[http://dx.doi.org/10.1109/JIOT.2018.2844296]

[10] W Li, T Logenthiran, V. T. Phan, and W. L. Woo, "A novel smart energy theft system (SETS) for IoT-based smart home", *IEEE Internet of Things Journal,* vol. 6, no. 3, pp. 5531-5539, 2019.
[http://dx.doi.org/10.1109/JIOT.2019.2903281]

[11] D Shin, K Yun, J Kim, P. V. Astillo, J. N. Kim, and I You, "A security protocol for route optimization in DMM-based smart home IoT networks", *IEEE Access,* vol. 7, pp. 142531-142550, 2019.
[http://dx.doi.org/10.1109/ACCESS.2019.2943929]

[12] J An, F Le Gall, J Kim, J Yun, J Hwang, M Bauer, M Zhao, and J Song, "Toward global IoT-enabled smart cities interworking using adaptive semantic adapter", *IEEE Internet of Things Journal,* vol. 6, no. 3, pp. 5753-5765, 2019.
[http://dx.doi.org/10.1109/JIOT.2019.2905275]

[13] F Cirillo, D Gomez, L Diez, I. E. Maestro, T. B. J. Gilbert, and R Akhavan, "Smart city IoT services creation through large-scale collaboration", *IEEE Internet of Things Journal,* vol. 7, no. 6, pp. 5267-5275, 2020.
[http://dx.doi.org/10.1109/JIOT.2020.2978770]

[14] M. A. Uddin, M. A. Shah, S. U. Islam, C Maple, A. A. Alaulamie, J. J. P. C. Rodrigues, S Mussadiq, and U Tariq, "A novel fog-based multi-level energy-efficient framework for IoT-enabled smart environments", *IEEE Access,* vol. 8, pp. 150010-150026, 2020.
[http://dx.doi.org/10.1109/ACCESS.2020.3010157]

[15] C. K. Metallidou, K. E. Psannis, and E. A. Egyptiadou, "Energy efficiency in smart buildings: IoT approaches", *IEEE Access,* vol. 8, pp. 63679-63699, 2020.
[http://dx.doi.org/10.1109/ACCESS.2020.2984461]

[16] V. K. Quy, V. H. Nam, D. M. Linh, N. T. Ban, and N. D. Han, "Communication solutions for vehicle ad-hoc network in smart cities environment: A comprehensive survey", *Wireless Personal Communications,* vol. 122, no. 3, pp. 2791-2815, 2022.
[http://dx.doi.org/10.1007/s11277-021-09030-w]

[17] F Kiani, A Seyyedabbasi, S Nematzadeh, F Candan, T Çevik, F. A. Anka, G Randazzo, S Lanza, and A Muzirafuti, "Adaptive metaheuristic-based methods for autonomous robot path planning: Sustainable agricultural applications", *Applied Sciences,* vol. 12, no. 3, p. 943, 2022.
[http://dx.doi.org/10.3390/app12030943]

[18] K. S. Patle, R Saini, A Kumar, and V. S. Palaparthy, "Field evaluation of smart sensor system for plant disease prediction using LSTM network", *IEEE Sensors Journal,* vol. 22, no. 4, pp. 3715-3725, 2022.
[http://dx.doi.org/10.1109/JSEN.2021.3139988]

[19] A Vangala, A. K. Das, N Kumar, and M Alazab, "Smart secure sensing for IoT-based agriculture: Blockchain perspective", *IEEE Sensors Journal,* vol. 21, no. 16, pp. 17591-17607, 2021.
[http://dx.doi.org/10.1109/JSEN.2020.3012294]

[20] B Citoni, F Fioranelli, M. A. Imran, and Q. H. Abbasi, "Internet of Things and LoRaWAN-enabled

future smart farming", *IEEE Internet of Things Magazine,* vol. 2, no. 4, pp. 14-19, 2019. [http://dx.doi.org/10.1109/IOTM.0001.1900043]

[21] A Kumar, R Mishra, H. P. Gupta, and T Dutta, "Smart sensing for agriculture: Applications, advancements, and challenges", *IEEE Consumer Electronics Magazine,* vol. 10, no. 4, pp. 51-56, 2021.
[http://dx.doi.org/10.1109/MCE.2021.3049623]

[22] Y. C. Chang, and Y. H. Lai, "Campus edge computing network based on IoT street lighting nodes", *IEEE Systems Journal,* vol. 14, no. 1, pp. 164-171, 2020.
[http://dx.doi.org/10.1109/JSYST.2018.2873430]

[23] T Sutjarittham, H Gharakheili, S. S. Kanhere, and V Sivaraman, "Experiences with IoT and AI in a smart campus for optimizing classroom usage", *IEEE Internet of Things Journal,* vol. 6, no. 5, pp. 7595-7607, 2019.
[http://dx.doi.org/10.1109/JIOT.2019.2902410]

[24] S Rani, S. H. Ahmed, and S. C. Shah, "Smart health: A novel paradigm to control the chikungunya virus", *IEEE Internet of Things Journal,* vol. 6, no. 2, pp. 1306-1311, 2019.
[http://dx.doi.org/10.1109/JIOT.2018.2802898]

[25] Y. B. Singh, and S. Goel, "1D CNN based approach for speech emotion recognition using MFCC features", In: *Artificial Intelligence and Speech Technology,* A. Jain, M. N. Kumar, R. Prasad, Eds., 1st ed.. CRC Press: Boca Raton, FL, USA, 2021, pp. 195-202.

[26] M Humayun, N. Z. Jhanjhi, B Hamid, and G Ahmed, "Emerging smart logistics and transportation using IoT and blockchain", *IEEE Internet of Things Magazine,* vol. 3, no. 2, pp. 58-62, 2020.
[http://dx.doi.org/10.1109/IOTM.0001.1900097]

[27] Y Song, F. R. Yu, L Zhou, X Yang, and Z He, "Applications of the Internet of Things (IoT) in smart logistics: A comprehensive survey", *IEEE Internet of Things Journal,* vol. 8, no. 6, pp. 4250-4274, 2021.
[http://dx.doi.org/10.1109/JIOT.2020.3034385]

[28] K Shafique, B. A. Khawaja, F Sabir, S Qazi, and M Mustaqim, "Internet of Things (IoT) for next-generation smart systems: A review", *IEEE Access,* vol. 8, pp. 23022-23040, 2020.
[http://dx.doi.org/10.1109/ACCESS.2020.2970118]

[29] W Yalla, B Ramesh, and A Ramesh, "Autonomous solar powered irrigation system", *Int. J. Eng. Res. Appl.,* vol. 3, no. 1, pp. 60-65, 2013.

[30] E Pradeep, R Ganeshmurthy, K Sekar, and E Arun, "Automation of PV farmer pump", In: *Proc. Int. Conf. Sustainable Energy and Intelligent System*, 2011, pp. 163-166.

[31] J Uddin, S. M. T. Reja, Q Newaz, T Islam, and J. M. Kim, "Automated irrigation system using solar power", In: *Proc. Int. Conf. Electrical and Computer Engineering*, 2012, pp. 228-232.

[32] O Seal, A Shirke, S Shewale, A Sirsikar, and P Hankare, "Solar based automatic irrigation system", *Int. J. Res. Advent Technol.,* vol. 2, pp. 186-189, 2014.

[33] M Kumar, J Vij, L. V. Patel, M Sharma, and D Haldar, "Solar powered auto irrigation system", *Int. J. Eng. Res. Manag. Technol.,* vol. 1, pp. 61-66, 2014.

[34] N. R. Patel, R. B. Lanjewar, S. S. Mathurkar, and A. A. Bhandekar, "Microcontroller based drip irrigation system using smart sensor", *Proc. Annu. IEEE India Conf. (INDICON),* pp. 1-5, 2013.

[35] B. D. Kumar, P. Srivastava, R. Agrawal, and V. Tiwari, "Microcontroller based automatic plant irrigation system", *Int. Res. J. Eng. Technol.,* vol. 4, no. 5, pp. 1436-1439, 2017.

[36] B. S. Dhanne, S Kedare, S. S. Dhanne, and B. S. Dhanne, "Modern solar power irrigation system using ARM", *Int. J. Res. Eng. Technol.,* vol. 3, no. 3, pp. 20-25, 2014.
[http://dx.doi.org/10.15623/ijret.2014.0315005]

[37] C. Dwarkani M, G. Ram R, S. Jagannathan, and R. Priyatharshini, "Smart farming system using

sensors for agricultural task automation", *Proc. IEEE Technol. Innov. ICT Agric. Rural Develop. (TIAR),* pp. 49-53, 2015.

[38] N Gondchawar, and R. S. Kawitkar, "IoT based smart agriculture", *Int. J. Adv. Res. Comput. Commun. Eng.,* vol. 5, no. 6, 2016.

[39] R. K. Sriram, D. G. Deepak, M Rajesh, K. S. Sudharshan, S Vasanth, and N. Harish Kumar, "A survey on crop prediction using machine learning approach", *Int. J. Res. Appl. Sci. Eng. Technol.,* vol. 7, no. 4, 2019.

[40] S. R. Rajeshwari, P Khunteta, S Kumar, A. R. Singh, and V Pandey, "Smart farming prediction using machine learning", *Int. J. Innov. Technol. Explor. Eng.,* vol. 8, no. 7, 2019.

[41] P Nevavuori, N Narra, P Linna, and T Lipping, "Crop yield prediction using multitemporal UAV data", *Remote Sensing,* vol. 12, no. 23, p. 4000, 2020. [http://dx.doi.org/10.3390/rs12234000]

[42] L Abhishek, and B. Rishi Barath, "Automation in agriculture using IoT and machine learning", *Int. J. Innov. Technol. Explor. Eng.,* vol. 8, no. 8, 2019.

[43] R Salama, F Al-Turjman, S Bhatla, and S. P. Yadav, "Social engineering attack types and prevention techniques—A survey", In: *Proc. CICTN*, 2023, pp. 817-820.

[44] R. Nabha, A. Laouiti, and A. E. Samhat, "Internet of Things-based healthcare systems: An overview of privacy-preserving mechanisms", *Appl. Sci.,* vol. 15, no. 7, p. 3629, 2025.

[45] M Altalak, M. Ammad Uddin, A Alajmi, and A Rizg, "Smart agriculture applications using deep learning technologies: A survey", *Applied Sciences,* vol. 12, no. 12, p. 5919, 2022. [http://dx.doi.org/10.3390/app12125919]

# CHAPTER 12

# The Indispensable Contribution of Satellite Imagery to Disaster Management: Insights and Perspectives

**Shivam Shukla**[1], **Mayank Dixit**[1,*], **Prateek Kumar Yadav**[1], **Anshul Khanna**[2] and **Vipul Kumar Mishra**[3]

[1] *Department of Computer Science and Engineering, Galgotias College of Engineering & Technology, Greater Noida, Uttar Pradesh, India*

[2] *Department of Computer Science and Engineering, JIMS Engineering Management Technical Campus (JEMTEC), Greater Noida, Uttar Pradesh, India*

[3] *Department of Artificial Intelligence and Data Science, Gati Shakti Viswavidyalaya, Vadodara, Gujarat, India*

**Abstract:** Natural disasters happen often and are becoming stronger. It is important to react quickly and effectively. Remote sensing technologies help officials quickly assess the damage, detect changes in the area, find important areas that need help, and plan for rescue. Also, the early detection of natural disasters plays a vital role in predicting future disasters so that the communities and officials are ready to act ahead of time. This research work explores the indispensable role of remote sensing satellite images in the areas of disaster management. The study covers a range of disasters, including earthquakes, floods, forest fires, volcanic eruptions, tsunamis, tornadoes, and cloud bursts. A significant number of relevant scholarly articles published in 2023 were identified for each disaster, and more than 1000 research papers were found by combining all the disasters' keyword searches. Of which, more than 125 papers were found to be more relevant and have been studied. The study conducts a thorough literature review to identify the importance and contributions of remote sensing imagery. The work discussed some of the popular algorithms which are predominantly used across these studies, including Convolution Neural Networks (CNN), Random Forest, Support Vector Machine (SVM), U-Net-based methodologies, and many more. The study also highlights the challenges that still persist in these areas. The work is useful for future researchers to understand the importance of satellite imagery during disasters and the key challenges persisting in this area.

**Keywords:** Challenges, Disaster, Remote sensing, Satellite images, Survey.

[*] **Corresponding author Mayank Dixit:** Department of Computer Science and Engineering, Galgotias College of Engineering & Technology, Greater Noida, Uttar Pradesh, India; E-mail: mayankdixit@galgotiacollege.edu

**Ravinder M., Arti Ranjan, Youddha Beer Singh (Eds.)**

# INTRODUCTION

## Remote Sensing

Remote sensing is a technology that is used to gather information about features (objects) like buildings, water bodies, land, vegetation, *etc*., from space with the help of satellites. It collects the data through the sensors, which can have multiple spectral bands. These inputs from the sensors are typically analyzed well by experts to know about the surface of Earth and its features without direct physical contact. There are mainly two types of remote sensing, active and passive [1]. Active remote sensing has its own radiance that sends signals and measures what reflects back to the sensor. In contrast, passive remote sensing measures reflected sunlight. There are different ways of remote sensing. One of the most popular is capturing images.

There are different types of remote sensing images which are used for extracting unique features of the Earth. One example has been shown in Fig. (**1**). Optical remote sensing uses sensors for visible, near-infrared, and short-wave infrared to create images of the Earth's surface by capturing sunlight reflected from objects on the ground. Different materials absorb and reflect light in different ways and at different wavelengths. Infrared remote sensing uses special sensors to detect infrared light reflected from the Earth. The middle-wave infrared (MWIR) and long-wave infrared (LWIR) fall under the thermal infrared region. These radiations come from warm objects like the Earth's surface. The temperature of land and water bodies can also be measured by this method. Thermal infrared remote sensing is useful for detecting forest fires. Multispectral remote sensing entails taking pictures in more than one spectral band at multiple wavelengths throughout the electromagnetic spectrum. These wavelengths may be separated through filters or detected using devices that might be sensitive to precise wavelengths, including light beyond what the human eye can see, such as infrared and ultraviolet. This method aids in gathering additional data that the human eye's red, green, and blue receptors are unable to detect. LiDAR (Light Detection and Ranging) is a remote sensing technology that examines the Earth's surface by emitting brief bursts of laser energy and collects information about nearby surroundings, as well as the distances. Then, 3D models and maps of the objects and the surrounding areas are made using this.

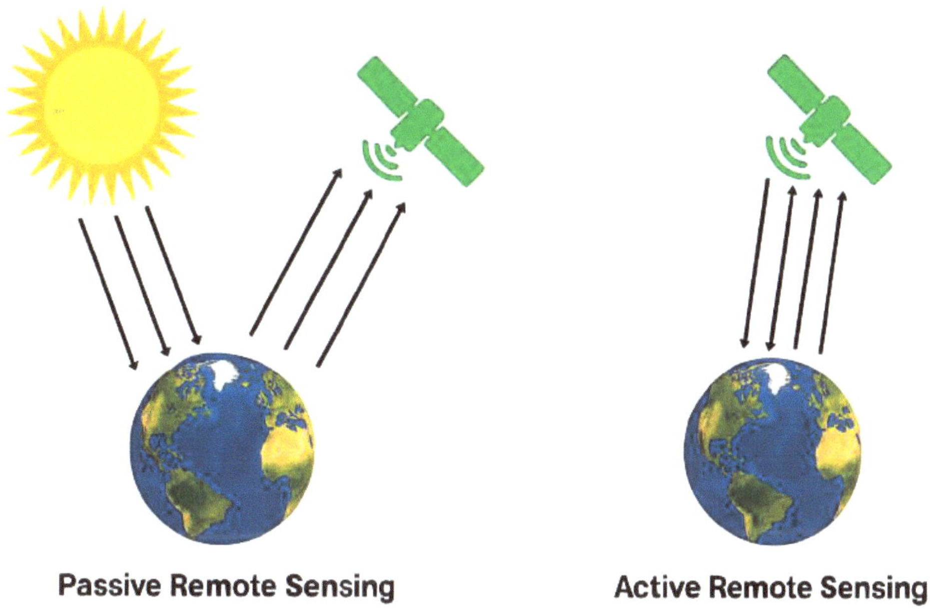


**Fig. (1).** Types of remote sensing [1].

Remote sensing images are characterized by:

1. The ability to discriminate among electromagnetic spectrum wavelengths is known as spectral resolution. The increased spectral resolution provides more precise information regarding surface properties.
2. Temporal resolution is the rate at which pictures are taken in a certain spot. It enables the monitoring of changes over time, including dynamic events and seasonal variations.
3. The ability to discriminate between minute variations in radiation intensity is known as radiometric resolution. Sufficient radiometric resolution improves the capacity to distinguish minute changes in surface characteristics.
4. Radiometric Resolution: The capacity to discriminate between minute variations in radiation dose. Sufficient radiometric resolution improves the capacity to distinguish minute changes in surface characteristics.
5. Geometric resolution is the degree of accuracy with which the spatial connections between objects in a picture are portrayed. Essential for precise mapping, geo-referencing, and spatial analysis.

These characteristics describe the properties of data obtained through remote sensing, regardless of whether it's active or passive. The data collected through remote sensing can be analyzed and processed to generate maps, monitor changes over time, and extract valuable information for decision-making processes in various fields. This data-driven approach enables the utilization of the limited resources optimally. By integrating Rapid Damage Assessment, Early Warning Systems, and Resource Allocation, remote sensing emerges as a powerful and efficient asset in the realm of disaster management.

## DATASETS FOR DISASTER MONITORING

The availability of data lies in the central part when preparing a machine or deep learning-based model. In the domain of disaster monitoring, the availability of remote sensing temporal data pre- and post-disaster is an important component, without which the analysis of post-disaster damage cannot be estimated. This section provides details on some widely used datasets in the field of disaster monitoring.

1. **SpaceNet 8**

   The SpaceNet 8 [2] dataset from GeoSpatial Imagery and Earth Observation Data Satellites can be used to extract features like building and road networks in flood disasters. It can detect over 32,000 buildings & 1300 km roads with a span of 850 km$^2$. It can be used in machine learning tasks such as multiclass segmentation and binary classification. Models evaluated on this dataset include U-Net variants, ResNet34, Siamese CNN, *etc*. Building damage can be extensive due to the flood, and thus the use of SpaceNet 8 is proposed to estimate building and road damage. The evaluation metrics for this dataset can be Intersection over Union (IoU) and Average Path Length Similarity for predicting the damage of buildings due to flood and road networks, respectively.

2. **Creating xBD**

   The xBD [3] is the largest dataset to date for the building assessment, which is from GeoSpatial Imagery and Earth Observation Data Satellites. It can be used to assess the damage to buildings due to a disaster. It contains more than 850k polygons with over 22k images. It is used for multiclass classification. The models that have been evaluated on this dataset are ResNet50 and a shallow CNN. The evaluation metrics for this dataset can be weighted F1 scores for predictingbuilding damage due to a disaster. This dataset provides both pre- and post-event satellite imagery.

3. **Next Day Wildfire Spread**

Next Day Wildfire Spread [4] dataset from GeoSpatial Imagery, Earth Observation Data Satellites, and official data from research institutes is used for the machine learning task such as image segmentation task that helps in predicting the spread of wildfire. It contains more than 18k image samples with the previous fire mask at time 't' and the fire mask at time 't+1' day. This dataset is accumulated using Google Earth Engine. The model evaluated on this dataset is a convolutional autoencoder, and the evaluation metrics include Area Under the Curve (AUC), Recall, and Precision. Unlike other datasets, it combines 2D fire regions to provide a versatile machine-learning dataset that is helpful in disaster response to wildfires.

4. **RescueNet**

RescueNet [5] dataset from Earth Observation Data and GeoSpatial Imagery (UAV) is used for assessing the damage caused by the hurricanes. The dataset contains over 4k image samples and is used for the machine learning task of semantic segmentation. The model evaluated on this dataset is the Attention U-Net, and the evaluation metric used can be Mean Intersection over Union (MIU). This dataset differs from others because of its high-resolution post-disaster images with annotation of each feature, such as buildings, trees, roads, *etc*., which is necessary for post-disaster assessment.

5. **Hephaestus**

Hephaestus [6] dataset from Earth Observation Data and GeoSpatial Imagery (InSAR) can be used for the assessment of volcano disasters because of its task of semantic segmentation used for observing ground deformation. It contains more than 19k and 100k labeled and unlabeled images, respectively, from the Sentinel-1 with 44 different volcanoes. The models that have been evaluated on this dataset are SwinPL, ResNet18, ResNet18-MoCo, and the evaluation metrics can be F-Score, Precision and Recall. This dataset can be used to overcome the challenges in computer vision tasks, such as categorizing the state of volcanoes and segmentation for ground deformation due to the volcanic events.

6. **The Multimedia Satellite Task at MediaEval 2017**

This dataset from Flood Detection in Satellite Images (FDSI), Earth Observation Data, and GeoSpatial Imagery using satellite can be used for flood detection with immediate response [7]. For 462 different floods that occurred, it contains image patches for each event, accumulated using 4 bands from the Planet satellite. It is used for binary classification tasks to detect the flood, in which metrics that can be used are the PASCAL VOC Intersection over Union (IoU).

## HARNESSING REMOTE SENSING FOR EFFECTIVE DISASTER MANAGEMENT

Natural disasters are unwanted/unsolicited/unfortunate events that occur due to natural causes, such as earthquakes, floods, volcanic eruptions, tsunamis, wildfires, hurricanes, tornadoes, *etc*., or human activities or incidents involving individuals. It is the main path of devastation and severe injuries to the life support system and ecosystem. People commonly refer to these occurrences as unexpected, highly intense, unmanageable, and fatal events related to natural phenomena in the Earth's crust. Natural disasters occur in various forms, including earthquakes, landslides, floods, tornadoes, volcanic eruptions, wildfires, and tsunamis. It is a deadly threat to human life, health, and property, and it is the worst ever one in terms of life loss, collateral damage, and the extent of destruction. It could also be destructive for the environment. As mentioned by a particular organization, a few of the deadliest catastrophes include the Gujarat Earthquake (7.7 magnitude) in 2001, which caused nearly 20,000 deaths [8]. Another major incident occurred when floods affected Bihar in 2007, which the UN labeled as the biggest floods the state had experienced in its recorded history. The Kedarnath incident in 2013 claimed over 6,000 lives and affected more than 4,550 villages [9]. The Odisha cyclone in 1999 — the most powerful and intense among all tropical cyclones — caused up to 10,000 deaths and affected 1 million people [10]. This highlights how disasters can be so destructive and widespread that the affected community is unable to effectively respond.. After a disaster affects nature, governments and communities take responsibility for the entire recovery process. When studying disasters, one of the most common challenges is the lack of precise and timely information, which makes response efforts inefficient and hinders quick decision-making, making it much harder to implement focused responses. Addressing this problem requires the government to analyze the disaster either manually or through a system. Hence, systems that introduce automation for disaster monitoring are far superior, as they require much less human presence, are faster, and more precise compared to manual methods. Remote sensing satellite images play an important role in monitoring disaster impact and assessing the damage caused. Remote sensing images enable real-time and detailed data collection, allowing authorities to act quickly and assess the extent of damage without being limited by logistical or other operational issues. This capability is crucial for Rapid Damage Assessment

(RDA) and Early Warning Systems (EWS). Moreover, it helps ensure the proper allocation of resources.

1. **Rapid Damage Assessment:** In disasters such as hurricanes, earthquakes, or wildfires, time becomes the most critical factor. Remote sensing technologies, through satellite imagery, provide a quick and comprehensive observation of the damage, allowing Rapid Damage Assessment (RDA) to be performed almost instantly. There is no time to waste in acquiring this speedy assessment, which enables authorities to determine the extent of infrastructure damage, identify stressed areas, and build a rapid response.

2. **Early Warning Systems:** Remote sensing plays a significant role in Early Warning Systems (EWS), as it routinely monitors natural factors. *In situ* detection of anomalies, such as changes in forest cover, unusual weather patterns, or temperature increases, can trigger early warnings. These systems are fundamental because they indicate potential disasters and their likely impacts, allowing communities and authorities to take necessary precautions and evacuate if needed.

3. **Resource Allocation:** During the response stage, the technology aids in resource allocation by providing accurate information about population density, locations of critical facilities, and accessible routes in the affected area.

## DISASTER MITIGATION THROUGH REMOTE SENSING TECHNOLOGY

### Earthquake

The most recent studies have made major progress in developing technologies and methods to support purposes such as earthquake damage detection and assessment. A research paper illustrated how VHR optical imagery was used with a sophisticated CNN to provide a rapid and accurate assessment of surface damage intensity. By running Geoeye1 VHR images from the 2010 Haiti earthquake, this analysis shows that it can achieve high accuracy with swift performance on a GPU K80 platform, underscoring the critical need for high-quality data and quick processing in disaster relief. In addition, the research points out that the technology involved in the satellite data should be efficiently utilized. It also concludes that spatial resolution techniques should be advanced and that consistent methodologies for validating data should be adopted when fusing two or more datasets from different satellites [11].

One study has examined the resolution of space on the detection of earthquake-triggered landslide (EQL), for instance, after the Luding earthquake in 2022 in the region of Sichuan, China. Adopting a convolution neural network architecture, the researchers realized that the number of spatial resolutions a feature map has would take a toll on the overall detection capability. The paper found that higher resolutions gave better results. These give greater weight to the importance of spatial resolution in landslide detection algorithms for the precision of assessment in a post-earthquake situation [12].

Further, a new methodology was developed to estimate building damage and map landslide data using SAR technology. Such an approach was adopted after the 2021 Haiti Earthquake and Tropical Grace, using SAR data and in-situ scenes to delineate city blocks in five damaged mountains. The application highlights the potential of SAR data for rapid intra-disaster damage assessment and landslide mapping worldwide, which can serve as a source of inspiration for improving emergency response strategies [13].

Besides remote sensing devices, the analysis of satellite data by comparing them with the in-situ measurements for structural monitoring results in diverse insights indicating opportunities and gaps in this area of science. L'Aquila, the study town, which provided a comparison between satellite readings and on-site observations of the civic tower made after seismic events in 2009, showed agreement on the detection of building movement but brought up the technical limitations of on-site sensors and the necessity of constant revisits of the building to get a better and accurate characterization of building behavior. This requires proper attention to the development of mission architecture with more frequent passes and the potential to study nonlinear responses, which can be achieved with specific SAR software tailored to improve structural monitoring accuracy [14].

The association of artificial intelligence with earthquake disaster assessment (EDA) assures the accurate and fast response of disaster relief operations. The investigation of 204 research papers shows the broad applicability of deep learning models in different seismic scenarios. It also points out issues related to the training data and models, which are addressed by various recent studies. At the same time, it makes us think of new data sources like seismo-acoustic waves and multimodal deep learning approaches. The priorities of earthquake forecasting, strengthening infrastructure assets, and enhancing the Deep learning model were emphasized to provide a feasible, error-free EDA. Correspondingly, such miniature seismic networks have been closely linked, contributing to the development of earthquake damage detection and assessment approaches that will further improve disaster management strategies and support preparedness and resilience [15].

## Flood

Machine learning (ML) and remote sensing are widely used in studying and predicting floods. In a previous study, machine learning was applied as a method of analysis to identify flood-prone areas in northern Iran [16], and it was found to be more accurate and efficient than other traditional methods. The lake area was surveyed again during a second exploration conducted in March 2022. The goal of this survey was to detect changes in the area, as a major outburst was expected. During this period, the lake overflowed, exceeding its banks [17].

The next stage of the research involved the use of remote sensing to investigate its impacts. It was highlighted that flood mapping using remote sensing is more rapid than conventional mapping approaches.

In the UAE, a study highlighted a detailed method for evaluating and mapping flash flood risks in Fujairah City. The study used remote sensing and GIS-based weights. The result classified the area into distinct vulnerability zones, providing valuable insights for planning and management strategies to mitigate flash-flood effects [18]. Furthermore, a machine learning workflow called DELTA was introduced to predict floods using satellite imagery. The model was recalled because it was overwhelmed due to obstructions like vegetation and clouds. The researchers suggest merging remote sensing data with flood models and Synthetic Aperture Radar (SAR) data for more accurate flood extents [19].

## Forest Fire

In a recent paper review, various methods for early detection of forest fires were studied. These types of methods are based on optical remote sensing technology. It draws attention to the tendency of forest fires to be more intense and frequent as a result of climate change and human interference. The document focuses on the need for powerful tools to prevent and respond to forest fires. It indicates that future research should be carried out by integrating different technology sets, including satellite, drone, and ground sensor data, along with data assimilation from crowdsourcing, social sources, and weather forecasts [20].

Equally, another paper proposes an original machine learning method that is tailored to locating wildfires. This model is only based on MODIS raw data thus stochastic (probabilistic) wildfire detection correlated with various bands, including the uncertainties. It targets problems, in particular, missing MODIS data, the fact that ground-truth data is not always homogeneous, and the need to evaluate uncertainties. This model aims to support efficient wildfire management and to provide systems and data for decision-making based on probabilities [21].

Also, a modest model that uses drones has been developed and called LMDFS (Lightweight Model for Forest Fire Smoke), which isdesigned to detect forest fire smoke. This model is built on a tailor-made dataset derived from web-collected smoke data and trained on it. It implements various advanced modes to address issues such as early detection of small smoke plumes, shadowing from clouds, and real-time detection by drones. Targeted efforts to further enhance the model's efficiency and adaptability to diverse environments are part of the planned activities [22].

### Tsunami

In Indonesia, the study applied machine learning and remote sensing to identify building damage caused by the tsunami triggered by the Anak Krakatau volcano. Satellite images from Sentinel-2A and WorldView-2, taken before and after the tsunami, were used to detect changes. Machine learning with Random Forest classifiers was employed to detect and classify damage. The findings of the study contribute to strategic disaster management for areas vulnerable to tsunamis. Future research should focus on accurate feature selection, production of higher-precision maps for damage assessment, and high-resolution digital elevation models (DEMs) to improve clarity in detecting damage zones [23]. The paper addressed the evolving tsunami threats in the Qidong County of Shanghai, China, in which the Ryukyu Sea Trench became a main zone of tsunamigenic activity. Researchers integrated satellite data with the use of the Random Forest Practice to determine how land use changed and how vulnerable it was between 2013 and 2022. The research referred to the augmentation of tsunami risk in some regions, which were in correlation with the trend in urbanization and growth of population on the coast. The paper reveals the importance of creating a tsunami prevention policy and emergency readiness plans not only for the region but for other communities that are facing the same threats too. The paper suggests using more realistic, up-to-date tsunami scenarios and higher-resolution satellite imagery [24].

### Tornado

The Canadian researchers have been involved in the detection of the damaged areas of Canadian forests after tornadoes for the period between 1982 and 2020 based on the remote sensing data. They split Canada into 484 quadrants and imaged 367 of them, which was almost 75% of the country, by using satellite images from Planet. The study aims to determine the frequency of tornadoes in densely populated areas. Furthermore, they used Google Earth and Land Viewer to detect tornado occurrences and verify them. This study contributes to the knowledge of the tornado occurrence and aids in the adoption of the laboratory of preventative measures in the Canadian area.

The study discusses the potential use of soil moisture measurements to enhance the detection of tornado early-stage tracks during the Mississippi outbreak in March 2023. Tornadoes, powerful swirling winds associated with thunderstorms, pose significant risks, making accurate tracking crucial. Four methods, including weather data analysis, eyewitness reports, ground examination, and remote sensing, are employed for detection. MODIS and Sentinel-2A and 2B satellites are used to monitor vegetation and soil moisture. The research suggested that the use of the latest computer methods, together with the real-time info on the storms, will help us understand them even more [25].

As a continuation of that study in 2023, rotating and cluster connections were studied by looking into the year when such hurricane conditions and tornadoes in the clusters were specifically investigated. The researcher used the tool of Stokes' theorem to determine the speed and rotation of such clusters that can be used by forecasters and other professionals to track accurate changes in the conditions of these hurricanes. With access to weather reports and satellite data, the forecast was among the first to estimate hurricane speed and rotation from the '60s. They could also adopt the DevNet swift-lane, which enables them to quickly identify the changes in the storm patterns as well [26].

## METHODOLOGY

In this section, a few of the major methodologies used by researchers in disaster monitoring using satellite imagery are described in detail.

### CNN (Convolution Neural Network)

Convolutional Neural Networks (CNNs) have been widely used in many areas and are particularly effective for automatic feature extraction. Using CNN, even complex patterns in images can be detected with high detail and accuracy. A CNN consists of an input layer, hidden layers, and an output layer. It contains several neurons that take input features or receive data. One example of a CNN is shown in Fig. (**2**). The data can be in the form of text, audio, images, or other formats.

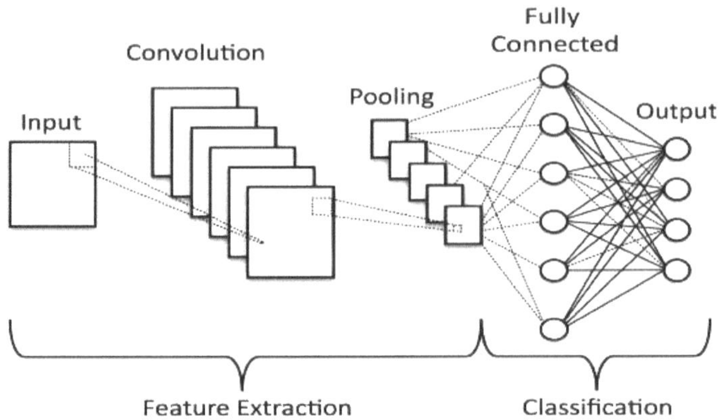


**Fig. (2).** Convolution neural network [27].

After the input layer, the CNN has multiple hidden layers. A lot of computation occurs here between neurons of different hidden layers through matrix multiplication. These computations allow the network to learn the weights between layers. Each neuron contains an activation function, which gives the network the capability to learn non-linear patterns. The number of hidden layers and the count of neurons in each layer may vary depending on the problem requirements.

The final layer of the network generates the output, such as a probability or classification. This layer uses different activation functions, such as Sigmoid or Softmax, depending on the problem requirements. The general formula is shown in Equation 1.

$$O(i, j) = \sum u \sum v I\,(i + u, j + v) \times K(u, v) \tag{1}$$

Here, the $O(i, j)$ is the output value at position $(i, j)$ in the output feature map. The $I(i{+}u, j{+}v)$ represents the pixel values in the input image at position $(i{+}u, j{+}v)$. The $K(u, v)$ represents the values of the filter at position $(u, v)$.

## Random Forest (RF)

Random Forest is a machine learning algorithm that operates by constructing several decision trees during training. One example of ***Random Forest (RF)*** is shown in Fig. (**3**). It focuses on several decision trees by calculating the average predictions of individual decision trees. This helps in increasing accuracy and preventing overfitting problems. In remote sensing satellite imagery analysis, Random Forests are often used for land cover classification, object detection, and feature extraction.

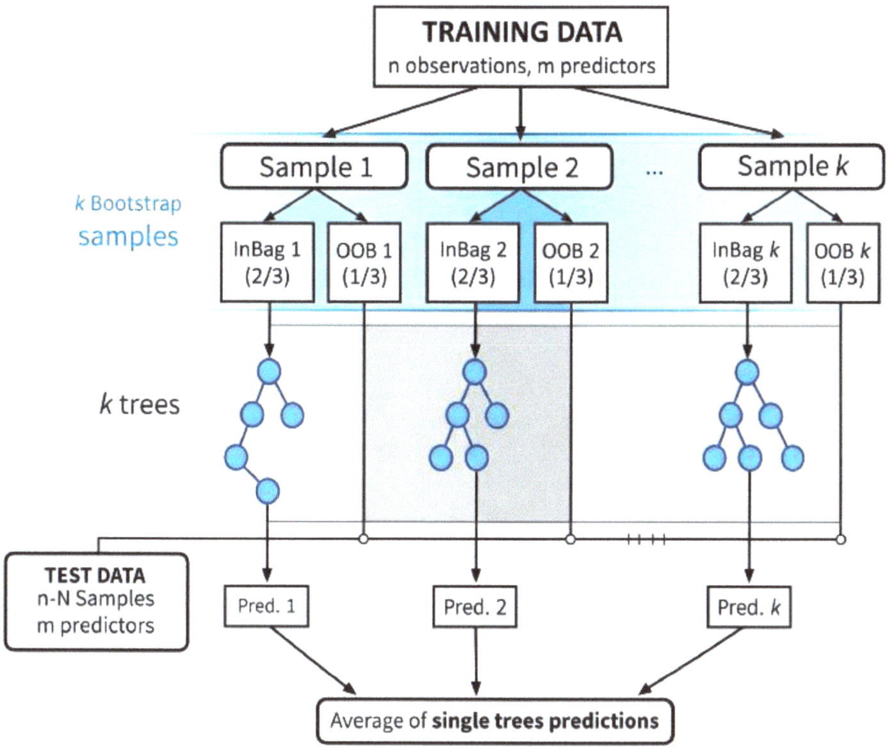


**Fig. (3).** Random forest [28]

The prediction of Random Forest is calculated by taking the average predictions of the decision trees as shown in equation 2.

$$F(x) = 1/n \sum = Ti(x) \quad \textbf{(2)}$$

Here Ti(x) represents the prediction of the i-th decision tree for a given input vector x, where i = 1, 2, 3…, n and n is the total number of trees in the Random Forest ensemble.

## Support Vector Machine (SVM)

Support Vector Machine uses a supervised machine learning approach, which is widely used for challenges including classification and regression. The application of this algorithm includes face detection, image classification, identification of handwriting, detection of spam messages, *etc*. SVM works effectively because it finds the hyperplane that separates distinct categories in input space by keeping the points with maximum separation. One example of SVM has been shown in Fig. (**4**). In the context of remote sensing, challenges like change detection, land cover classification, and segmentation of images are generally resolved by SVMs. They generalize the given sample of training data very effectively and manage the high-dimensional data as well.

The Decision Function of SVM in terms of kernelized input data is shown in equation 3.

$$f(x) = sign\ (\sum \alpha iyiK\ (x, xi) + b) \tag{3}$$

$f(x)$ is the decision function that assigns a class label to the input vector, N is the number of support vectors, and K(x, xi) is the kernel function.

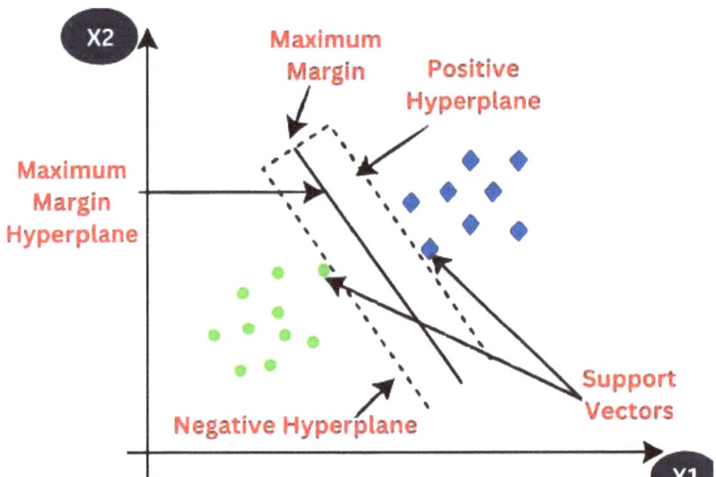


**Fig. (4).** Support vector machine [29].

## U-Net

U-Net is one of the most successful convolution-based neural networks. The architecture consists of two parts: a contracting path and an expansive path. There is an encoder part in the contracting path that has several layers of single-convolution, double convolution, or more that reduce the spatial resolution. The expansive path consists of a decoder to decode the encoded data. The contracting path is used to find relevant features, while the expansive path maintains the input's spatial resolution. The lower layer of the Unet-based network Fig. (**5**) extracts the fine details from the input image, like edges, lines, *etc*., and the upper layer of the encoder extracts a complete object. The connection between the encoder and decoder preserves the important low-level details of the image.

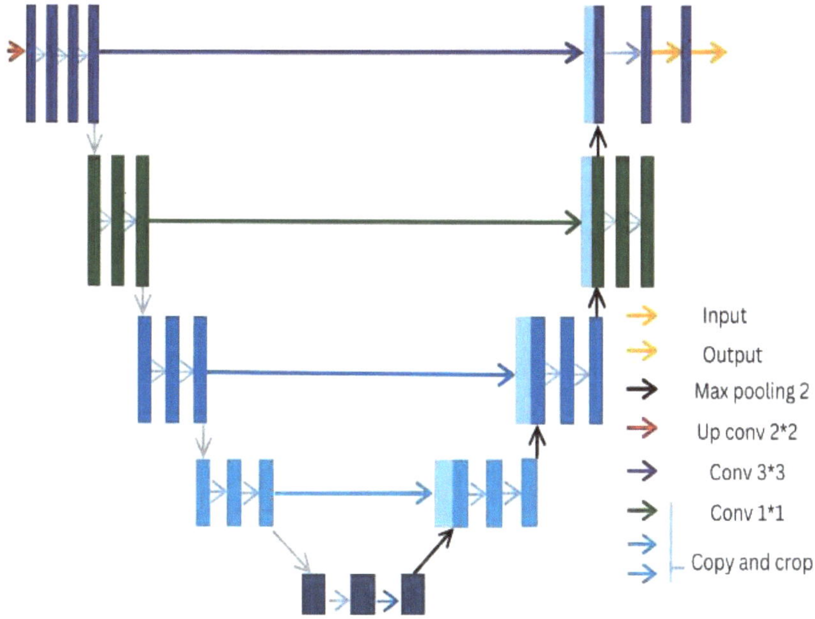


**Fig. (5).** U-Net model [30].

## Generative Adversarial Network (GANs)/Cyclic-GAN

Generative Adversarial Networks (GANs) and Cycle-GANs are deep learning models used for image generation and image-to-image translation tasks, *i.e.*, transferring the characteristics of images. GANs consist of two neural networks: a generator and a discriminator, trained adversarially to generate realistic images. In remote sensing satellite imagery analysis, different satellite sensors capture images with different characteristics like resolution, spectral bands, and noise levels. CycleGAN can be used to adapt images from one sensor to look like the images taken from another sensor, enabling the utilization of data from multiple sources for a particular task. The general structure of the Cycle GAN Model has been shown in Fig. (**6**).

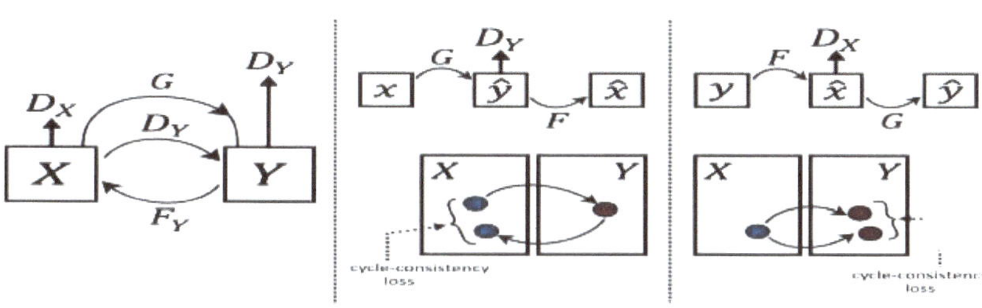


**Fig. (6).** Cycle GAN model [31].

## YOLOv5

YOLO stands for "You Only Look Once" and is an algorithm for object detection. It is efficient for real-time object detection due to its fast image processing. In remote sensing satellite imagery analysis, YOLOv5 is used to detect objects such as buildings and infrastructure. The architecture consists of three parts: Backbone, Neck, and Head Fig. (7). The Backbone extracts important features from the images using pre-trained models. The Neck improves detection accuracy by combining features from multiple layers. Objects in the image are then identified by combining these features, which is performed by the Head component. The Head also provides a confidence score associated with each detected object.

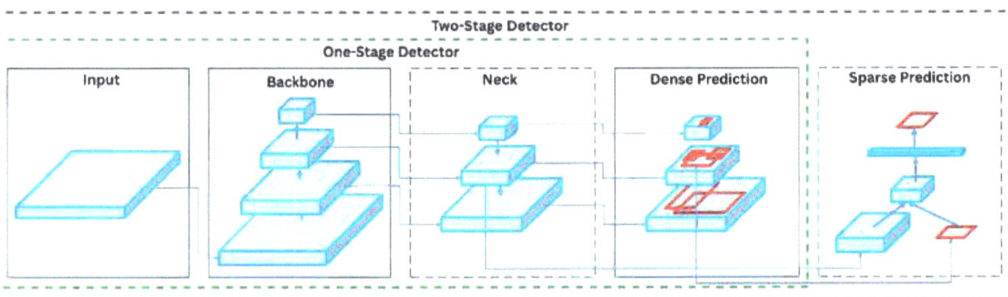


**Fig. (7).** YOLOv5 architecture [32].

## Transfer Learning

Transfer learning is an eminent technique in machine learning that involves using the knowledge gained from one problem and applying it to a different problem related to it. In the context of neural networks, transfer learning starts with a pre-trained model, such as VGG16 or ResNet. It has already learned generic features from a large dataset and applied them to another problem. The early layers retain the low-level features like edges and textures in this model.

## Optimization Strategies

Optimization strategies form a critical component in refining the feature extraction process, ensuring that Convolution Neural Networks (CNNs) are finely tuned for optimal performance. Hyper-parameter tuning is a key technique employed to systematically explore various configurations of hyperparameters, such as learning rates and batch sizes, to identify the most effective combination. Learning rate optimization is crucial for adjusting the step size during training, influencing the convergence speed and overall performance of the model. Additionally, dropout regularization is applied to prevent overfitting by randomly disabling neurons during training, promoting generalization to unseen data.

## ALGORITHM ANALYSIS FROM A DISASTER PERSPECTIVE

A thorough review was conducted using specific search keywords in Google Scholar for each disaster type. For instance, the keyword "Earthquake disaster management using remote sensing satellite images" yielded 7890 results overall, out of which 50 papers from the year 2023 were considered relevant after crawling through 20 pages sequentially. From the analysis of these research works, it is found that the algorithm that was mostly used for earthquake disasters is Convolution Neural Networks (CNN). Similarly, the keyword "Flood management remote sensing satellite images deep learning" resulted in 16700 papers. These results are first filtered based on the year 2023, and 43 relevant works are considered from the first 10 pages, which predominantly use the Random Forest (RF) algorithm as shown in Table (**1**). The study also covers other disasters such as forest fires, volcanic eruptions, tsunamis, tornadoes, and cloud bursts, each with its own set of relevant papers and predominantly used algorithms. The number of relevant papers indicates the extent of the research. It also helps to know the main algorithms used in these papers. Of 50 papers, 21 found CNN to be the most appropriate.

A variety of algorithms are utilized to mitigate the effects of disasters, both for early detection and post-disaster recovery, reflecting the complexity and unique characteristics of each disaster type.

For forest fire detection, again, Convolution Neural Network (CNN) was found to be the most widely used algorithm because of its better performance in image recognition tasks. In earthquake analysis, CNN is a preferred choice, but there are other algorithms too that are being used. The tsunami analysis field prefers the Random Forest (RF) algorithm, but also employs a range of other algorithms, including CNN, k-NN, and SVM. For flood analysis, RF is the most widely used algorithm, closely followed by CNN and U-Net-based models. The Convolution Neural Network (CNN) appears to be the most frequently used deep learning algorithm across different types of disasters, specifically in forest fire detection and management, and earthquake analysis. Even though an algorithm might be used generally, it does not mean that the usage count reflects its effectiveness or accuracy. It might be preferred because of its simplicity to implement or easier to adapt because of previous work done for that algorithm. It could be influenced by other factors as well, such as computational resources, availability of training data, specific requirements, and challenges of each disaster type. The following Table **1** presents the detailed analysis of the algorithms that have been widely used in different disaster conditions.

**Table 1. Details of the type of data and the algorithms specific to each disaster.**

| Disaster | Search string | Type (Majorly) of Data used | All Results | Relevant results from the year 2023 | Pages Crawled | Major Algorithm |
|---|---|---|---|---|---|---|
| Earthquake | Earthquake disaster management using remote sensing satellite images. | Satellite Images | 7890 | 50 | 20 | Convolution neural network (CNN) based deep learning (DL) models |
| Flood | Flood management, remote sensing satellite images, and deep learning. | Satellite Images | 16700 | 43 | 10 | Random Forest (RF) |
| Forest Fire | Forest fire disaster management using remote sensing satellite images. | Satellite Images | 7580 | 14 | 10 | Convolution neural network (CNN) |
| Volcanic Eruption | Volcano disaster management using remote sensing satellite images. | Satellite Images | 5550 | 5 | 10 | Convolution neural network (CNN) |
| Tsunami | Tsunami remote sensing satellite images, deep learning. | Satellite Images | 2450 | 8 | 10 | Random Forest (RF) |
| Tornado | Tornado remote sensing satellite images deep learning | Satellite Images | 1210 | 3 | 10 | Convolution neural network (CNN) |
| Cloud Burst | Cloudburst disaster management using remote sensing satellite images. | Satellite Images | 4130 | 5 | 10 | Deep Learning Neural Network (DLNN) |

*Data are subject to variations based on relevance and results obtained during the review

Counts of various algorithms in graphs were based on an analysis of the relevant articles published in Google Scholar in the year 2023 for that natural disaster. The conclusions that can be drawn are that Convolution Neural Networks (CNN) and its variants are widely used for the assessment of tsunamis Fig. (**8**), earthquakes Fig. (**9**), and the Random Forest algorithm in floods Fig. (**10**), forest fires Fig. (**11**), and disasters may be due to their image recognition strength. Conversely, the algorithm's dominance may be due to its ability to handle unstructured data, such as sensor readings and historical records. This does not underscore the importance of other algorithms. Additionally, the 'Others' category in the graphs encompasses a diverse range of algorithms used in disaster management.

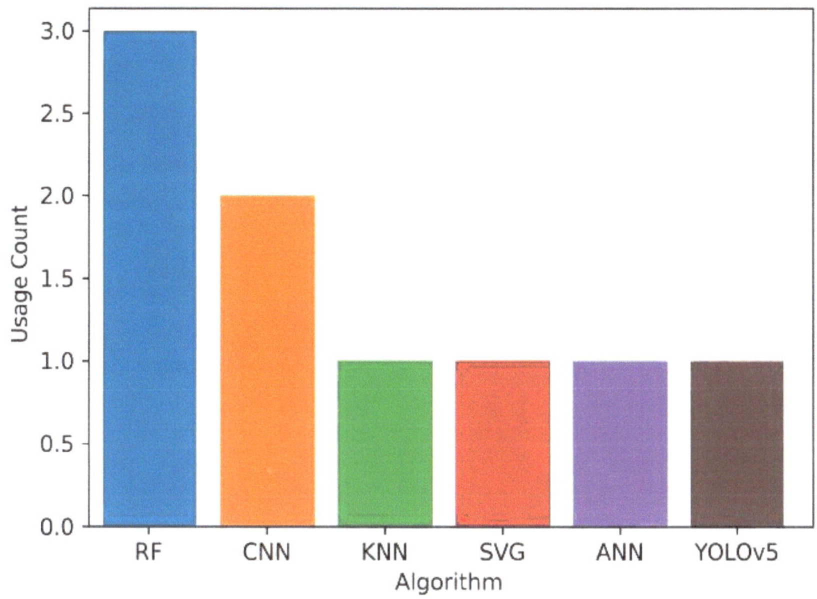


**Fig. (8).** Statistics on algorithms preferred for Tsunami analysis for the year 2023.

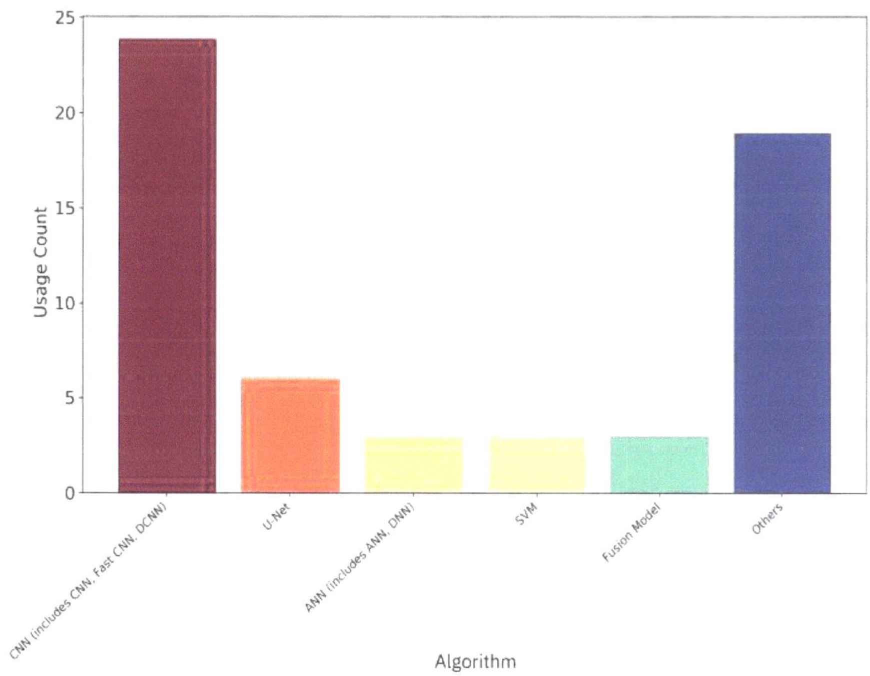


**Fig. (9).** Statistics on algorithms preferred for Earthquake analysis for the year 2023.

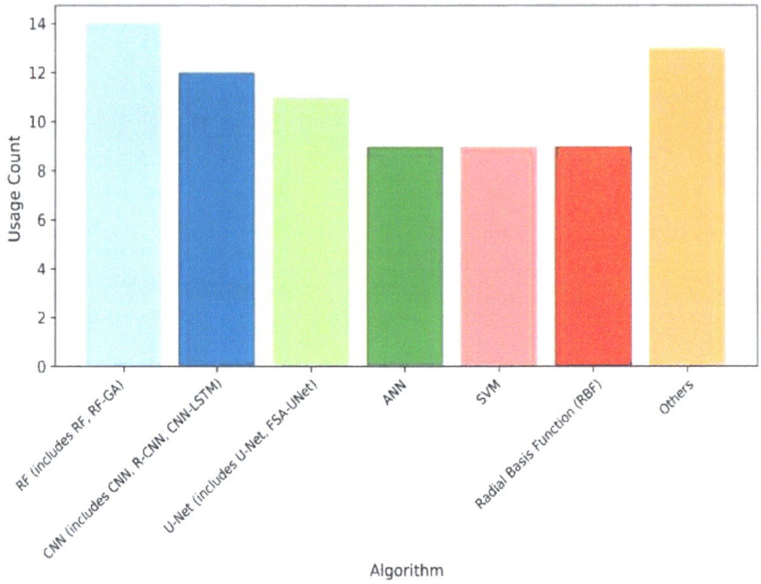


**Fig. (10).** Statistics on algorithms preferred for Flood analysis for the year 2023.

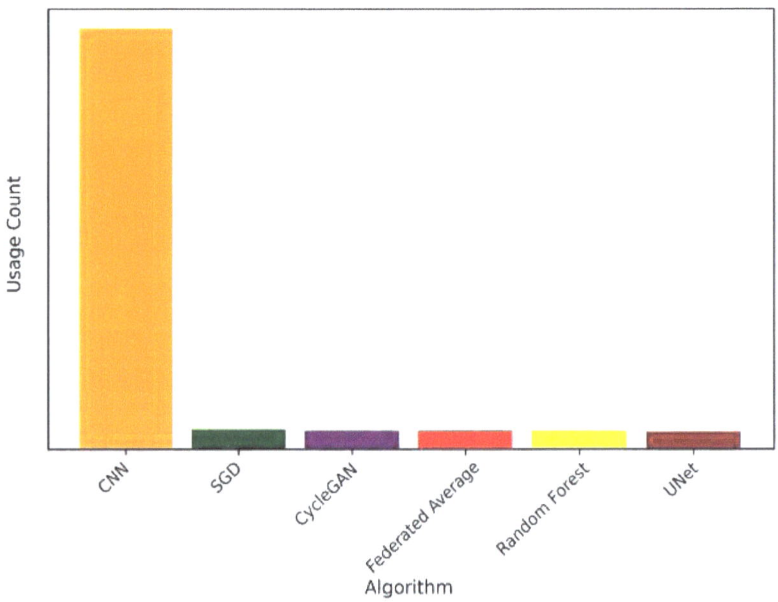


**Fig. (11).** Statistics on algorithms preferred for Forest Fire analysis for the year 2023

## CHALLENGES AND FUTURE DIRECTION

Using deep learning methods like Convolutional Neural Networks for feature extraction in the field of disaster management poses some tough challenges. First, adapting CNNs to work well with satellite images, which can be very complex, is tricky. These images show many different things, such as land, water, and buildings, and the CNNs need to be able to recognize and understand them all. Because of several features in a single image, making a CNN that can work across different types of disasters, like floods or wildfires, is a difficult task. A generalized deep learning model for all types of disaster classification and segmentation remains a persistent research problem.

Another challenge comes with transfer learning, where we use knowledge from pre-trained models to help with new tasks. The problem is that these pre-trained models might not understand satellite images well, so we need to find ways to make them work better for disaster management. Also, optimizing CNNs for disaster management means fine-tuning lots of settings, like learning rates and batch sizes. This can be hard because a balance is needed between obtaining good results without using too much computer power. Overall, making deep learning work well for disaster management means solving these challenges to get accurate and useful information from satellite images.

Efficiency and accuracy are two things that deep learning models must be capable of achieving, and thus, some of the problems that exist need to be resolved. But these are not the only challenges; there are many more challenges that are related to each disaster type. After thoroughly reviewing many articles, a few of the challenges can be described so that future work can take help from them while keeping these challenges in mind. Even after so much progress, there exists the challenges of acquiring high quality and reliable satellite data, availability of temporal and high spatial resolution free satellite data for specific areas [33, 34], uncertainty in disaster occurrences, lack of training data, cloud cover, pixel misclassification problem, efficient computing resources, detection of small-scale features, maintaining high accuracy because it decreases with decrease in resolution of image. Challenges in forest fire include smoke detection, the small size of early-stage smoke, interference from clouds, entropy estimation, uncertainty quantification in wildfire detection models, limited availability of wildfire datasets, and more.

## CONCLUSION

Remote sensing images play a vital role in mitigating the effects of disasters, both in the early detection phase and the post-analysis phase. These satellite images, available at different resolutions, are excellent sources for obtaining wide, accurate, and timely information about disasters with minimal manual effort. This work highlights the importance of satellite images for different types of disaster management by reviewing relevant papers from the year 2023. The study analyzes the algorithms used for each type of disaster monitoring or mitigation, which vary according to the specific conditions of each disaster. It also identifies the most frequently used algorithm for each disaster type. This information can be helpful for future work, where the most relevant algorithms identified here can serve as base models, along with transfer learning or other fine-tuning techniques, to develop more efficient disaster management models. More accurate models based on remote sensing satellite images would help minimize losses affecting populations, infrastructure, the economy, wildlife, and the environment. The study also investigates existing limitations and challenges, providing directions for future research.

## REFERENCES

[1] M. F. López Ornelas, *"The Mexican Water Forest: Benefits of using remote sensing techniques to assess changes in land use and land cover"*, Master's Capstone Project, University of San Francisco, 2016. Available from: https://repository.usfca.edu/capstone/371

[2] R. Hänsch, J. Arndt, D. Lunga, M. Gibb, T. Pedelose, A. Boedihardjo, D. Petrie, and T.M. Bacastow, "Spacenet 8-the detection of flooded roads and buildings", *Proceedings of the IEEE/CVF Conference on Computer Vision and Pattern Recognition,* pp. 1472-1480, 2022. [http://dx.doi.org/10.1109/CVPRW56347.2022.00153]

[3] R. Gupta, B. Goodman, N. Patel, R. Hosfelt, S. Sajeev, E. Heim, J. Doshi, K. Lucas, H. Choset, and M. Gaston, "Creating xBD: A dataset for assessing building damage from satellite imagery", *Proceedings of the IEEE/CVF Conference on Computer Vision and Pattern Recognition Workshops,* pp. 10-17, 2019.

[4] F. Huot, H. R. Lily, N. Goyal, T. Sankar, M. Ihme, and Y.-F. Chen, "Next day wildfire spread: A machine learning data set to predict wildfire spreading from remote-sensing data", *arXiv (Cornell University),* 2021.

[5] M. Rahnemoonfar, T. Chowdhury, and R. Murphy, "RescueNet: A high resolution UAV semantic segmentation dataset for natural disaster damage assessment", *Sci. Data,* vol. 10, no. 1, p. 913, 2023. [http://dx.doi.org/10.1038/s41597-023-02799-4] [PMID: 38123582]

[6] I. Nikolaos Ioannis Bountos, "Papoutsis, D. Michail, A. Karavias, P. Elias, and Isaak Parcharidis, "Hephaestus: A large scale multitask dataset towards InSAR understanding", *2022 IEEE/CVF Conference on Computer Vision and Pattern Recognition Workshops (CVPRW),* 2022. [http://dx.doi.org/10.1109/CVPRW56347.2022.00151]

[7] B. Benjamin, H. Patrick, S. Christian, S. Venkat, D. Andreas, and B. Damian (B. Bischke, P. Helber, C. Schulze, V. Srinivasan, A. Dengel, and D. Borth), "The multimedia satellite task at MediaEval 2017," in *Proc. MediaEval Workshop*, Dublin, Ireland, 2017.

[8] Encyclopaedia Britannica Editors, "Bhuj earthquake of 2001", *Encyclopaedia Britannica,* 2019. Available from: https://www.britannica.com/event/Bhuj-earthquake-of-2001

[9] "Ten years of Kedarnath tragedy: Lessons not learnt and challenges ahead", *Hindustan Times,* 2023.

[10] "Orissa super cyclone – A Synopsis", *Mausam (New Delhi),* vol. 57, no. 1, pp. 1-20, 2021.

[11] U. Bhangale, S. Durbha, A. Potnis, and R. Shinde, "Rapid Earthquake Damage Detection Using Deep Learning from VHR Remote Sensing Images", In: *IGARSS 2019 - 2019 IEEE International Geoscience and Remote Sensing Symposium*, Yokohama, Japan, 2019, pp. 2654-2657. [http://dx.doi.org/10.1109/IGARSS.2019.8898147]

[12] Y. Huang, J. Zhang, L. Zhang, Z. Ming, H. He, R. Chen, Y. Ge, and R. Liu, "How spatial resolution of remote sensing image affects earthquake triggered landslide detection: An example from 2022 Luding

earthquake, Sichuan, China", *Land (Basel),* vol. 12, no. 3, p. 681, 2023. [http://dx.doi.org/10.3390/land12030681]

[13] P. Ge, H. Gokon, and K. Meguro, "A review on synthetic aperture radar-based building damage assessment in disasters", *Remote Sens. Environ.,* vol. 240, pp. 111693-111693, 2020. [http://dx.doi.org/10.1016/j.rse.2020.111693]

[14] A. Caprino, S. Puliero, F. Lorenzoni, M. Floris, and F. da Porto, "Satellite SAR Interferometry and On-Site Traditional SHM to Monitor the Post-Earthquake Behavior of the Civic Tower in L'Aquila (Abruzzo Region, Italy)", *Remote Sens. (Basel),* vol. 15, no. 6, pp. 1587-1587, 2023. [http://dx.doi.org/10.3390/rs15061587]

[15] S.P. Yadav, and S. Yadav, "Image fusion using hybrid methods in multimodality medical images", *Med. Biol. Eng. Comput.,* vol. 58, no. 4, pp. 669-687, 2020. [http://dx.doi.org/10.1007/s11517-020-02136-6] [PMID: 31993885]

[16] S.P. Yadav, D.P. Mahato, N.T. Linh, Ed., *Distributed Artificial Intelligence: A Modern Approach.* CRC Press: Boca Raton, FL, USA, 2020. [http://dx.doi.org/10.1201/9781003038467]

[17] C. Gu, S. Li, M. Liu, K. Hu, and P. Wang, "Monitoring Glacier Lake Outburst Flood (GLOF) of Lake Merzbacher Using Dense Chinese High-Resolution Satellite Images", *Remote Sens. (Basel),* vol. 15, no. 7, p. 1941, 2023. [http://dx.doi.org/10.3390/rs15071941]

[18] P. Subraelu, A. Ahmed, A.A. Ebraheem, M. Sherif, S.B. Mirza, F.L. Ridouane, and A. Sefelnasr, "Risk Assessment and Mapping of Flash Flood Vulnerable Zones in Arid Region, Fujairah City, UAE-Using Remote Sensing and GIS-Based Analysis", *Water,* vol. 15, no. 15, p. 2802, 2023. [http://dx.doi.org/10.3390/w15152802]

[19] A. Shastry, E. Carter, B. Coltin, R. Sleeter, S. McMichael, and J. Eggleston, "Mapping floods from remote sensing data and quantifying the effects of surface obstruction by clouds and vegetation", *Remote Sensing of Environment,* vol. 291, p. 113556, 2023. [http://dx.doi.org/10.1016/j.rse.2023.113556]

[20] P. Barmpoutis, P. Papaioannou, K. Dimitropoulos, and N. Grammalidis, "A Review on Early Forest Fire Detection Systems Using Optical Remote Sensing", *Sensors (Basel),* vol. 20, no. 22, p. 6442, 2020. [http://dx.doi.org/10.3390/s20226442] [PMID: 33187292]

[21] A. Akbari Asanjan, M. Memarzadeh, P.A. Lott, E. Rieffel, and S. Grabbe, "Probabilistic Wildfire Segmentation Using Supervised Deep Generative Model from Satellite Imagery", *Remote Sens. (Basel),* vol. 15, no. 11, pp. 2718-2718, 2023. [http://dx.doi.org/10.3390/rs15112718]

[22] G. Chen, R. Cheng, X. Lin, W. Jiao, D. Bai, and H. Lin, "LMDFS: A Lightweight Model for Detecting Forest Fire Smoke in UAV Images Based on YOLOv7", *Remote Sens. (Basel),* vol. 15, no. 15, pp. 3790-3790, 2023. [http://dx.doi.org/10.3390/rs15153790]

[23] Y. Li, and K. Goda, "Random forest-based multi-hazard loss estimation using hypothetical data at seismic and tsunami monitoring networks", *Geomatics Nat. Hazards Risk,* vol. 14, no. 1, p. 2275538, 2023. [http://dx.doi.org/10.1080/19475705.2023.2275538]

[24] J. Hou, Y. Gao, T. Fan, P. Wang, Y. Wang, J. Wang, and W. Lu, "Tsunami Risk Change Analysis for Qidong County of China Based on Land Use Classification", *J. Mar. Sci. Eng.,* vol. 11, no. 2, pp. 379-379, 2023. [http://dx.doi.org/10.3390/jmse11020379]

[25] J. Wang, X. Wang, E. Park, and Y. Lin, "Brief communication: Soil moisture observations reconcile the discrepancy in detecting tornado early-stage track during the 24–25 March 2023 Mississippi

outbreak", *Nat. Hazards Earth Syst. Sci. Discuss.,* vol. 2023, pp. 1-10, 2023.

[26] B. Kerman, ""Convectivity and Rotation of Entropicly Defined Clusters as a Measure of Hurricane and Tornado State"", *arXiv (Cornell University),* 2023.

[27] A. Ranjan, and M. Ravinder, "VAEWGAN-NCO in image deblurring framework using variational autoencoders and Wasserstein generative adversarial network", *Signal Image Video Process.,* vol. 18, no. 5, pp. 4447-4456, 2024.
[http://dx.doi.org/10.1007/s11760-024-03085-5]

[28] V.F. Rodriguez-Galiano, B. Ghimire, J. Rogan, M. Chica-Olmo, and J.P. Rigol-Sanchez, "An assessment of the effectiveness of a random forest classifier for land-cover classification", *ISPRS J. Photogramm. Remote Sens.,* vol. 67, pp. 93-104, 2012.
[http://dx.doi.org/10.1016/j.isprsjprs.2011.11.002]

[29] C. Cortes, and V. Vapnik, "Support-Vector Networks", *Mach. Learn.,* vol. 20, no. 3, pp. 273-297, 1995.
[http://dx.doi.org/10.1023/A:1022627411411]

[30] Y. Ding, R. Dong, T. Lan, X. Li, G. Shen, H. Chen, and Z. Qin, "Multi-modal brain tumor image segmentation based on SDAE", *Int. J. Imaging Syst. Technol.,* vol. 28, no. 1, pp. 38-47, 2018.
[http://dx.doi.org/10.1002/ima.22254]

[31] J-Y. Zhu, T. Park, P. Isola, and A.A. Efros, "Unpaired image-to-image translation using cycle-consistent adversarial networks", *Proc. IEEE Int. Conf. Comput. Vis. (ICCV),* pp. 2223-2232, 2017.
[http://dx.doi.org/10.1109/ICCV.2017.244]

[32] A. Bochkovskiy, C.-Y. Wang, and H.-Y. M. Liao, "YOLOv4: Optimal Speed and Accuracy of Object Detection", *arXiv preprint arXiv:2004.10934,* 2020.

[33] M. Dixit, K. Chaurasia, and V. Kumar Mishra, "Dilated-ResUnet: A novel deep learning architecture for building extraction from medium resolution multi-spectral satellite imagery", *Expert Syst. Appl.,* vol. 184, p. 115530, 2021.
[http://dx.doi.org/10.1016/j.eswa.2021.115530]

[34] M. Dixit, K. Chaurasia, V.K. Mishra, D. Singh, and H-N. Lee, "6+: A Novel Approach for Building Extraction from a Medium Resolution Multi-Spectral Satellite", *Sustainability (Basel),* vol. 14, no. 3, pp. 1615-1615, 2022.
[http://dx.doi.org/10.3390/su14031615]

## CHAPTER 13

# PyroVisor D3ML-based Intelligent De-Hazing Algorithm

**Aryan Vashisth**[1], **Akshansh Mishra**[1] and **Meena Kumari**[2,*]

[1] *Department of Computer Science and Engineering (Artificial Intelligence), ABES Institute of Technology, Ghaziabad, Uttar Pradesh, India*

[2] *Department of Computer Science and Engineering (Internet of Things), ABES Institute of Technology, Ghaziabad, Uttar Pradesh, India*

**Abstract:** PyroVisor D3ML is a hybrid AI-based algorithm aimed at improving real-time video reproduction during indoor fire hazards. This innovation addresses the challenges faced by rescue teams using Python and its packages, such as PyTorch, NumPy, and OpenCV. Dark Channel Prior, depth estimation, and pre-trained machine learning models are the three main components that PyroVisor D3ML utilizes to facilitate rescue operations. The Dark Channel Prior estimates haze in each video frame, which helps remove unwanted smoke and haze, while depth estimation improves the accuracy of the de-hazing process by incorporating depth information. In combination, these components enable instant de-hazing of videos in real-time, allowing navigation and rescue teams to have clear visibility. It is therefore evident that PyroVisor D3ML is a useful tool for rescue operations under fire conditions, as it significantly enhances visibility and helps rescuers move through obstacle-laden areas more easily.

**Keywords:** D3ML, Image quality, NumPy, OpenCV, Pytorch.

## INTRODUCTION

Environmental factors like haze and fog can significantly degrade image quality. A major challenge in its removal is the optimised calculation of atmospheric light as well as transmission depth. With the rapid progress in Artificial Intelligence (AI) and Machine Learning (ML) technologies, there have been substantial breakthroughs in fields like image processing and other applications. Computer Vision, in particular, is becoming a ubiquitous technology with numerous applications in modern technology. Image de-hazing, which addresses the issue of images degraded by haze, is a key problem in this field. This issue has widespread

* **Corresponding author Meena Kumari:** Department of Computer Science and Engineering (Internet of Things), ABES Institute of Technology, Ghaziabad, Uttar Pradesh, India; E-mail: meena.kumari@abesit.edu.in

**Ravinder M., Arti Ranjan, Youddha Beer Singh (Eds.)**

applications, not only in computer vision but also in daily life. One of the major challenges in computer vision is handling images degraded by haze and smoke. These degrade scene visibility and clarity, hindering the performance of vision-based systems such as surveillance, autonomous driving, and remote sensing.

The primary aim of image de-hazing algorithms is to restore clear images from hazy or smoky inputs. These algorithms leverage deep learning, statistical modeling, and optimization techniques to improve the quality of images and their usability in various applications. The research objective is to present an approach that will increase the visibility of a hazed atmospheric/underwater image through appropriate image enhancement and image restoration techniques and Algorithms.

To evaluate the de-hazed image, various performance evaluation methods, such as qualitative evaluation and quantitative evaluation, are used. Qualitative Evaluation is based on naturalness, color, and visibility of the de-hazed image. Quantitative evaluation is based on PSNR, MSE, SSIM, entropy, *etc*.

Image de-hazing is a crucial image processing technique aimed at enhancing the quality of images that have been degraded by haze or fog. Haze, often caused by atmospheric conditions or underwater environments, reduces visibility and clarity in images. The primary objective of de-hazing is to restore the original visibility by removing the haze effect, thus improving the overall quality of the image. There are two major models based on the environment: the Atmospheric Model, which addresses haze and fog in outdoor environments, and the Underwater Model, which focuses on haze caused by water bodies. De-hazing is important for several reasons. Firstly, it significantly increases visibility, especially in environments where fog or haze is prevalent, thereby enhancing the performance of applications that rely on clear and sharp images, such as remote sensing, surveillance, and autonomous driving. Additionally, de-hazing improves human visual perception by making images clearer, more accessible, and easier to interpret, which is critical for tasks involving image analysis and decision-making. Through de-hazing, both machine-based systems and human users benefit from better image quality and improved interpretability.

Dehazing is an essential image processing technique that improves image quality, particularly for images captured by visible-light cameras. Environmental factors such as humidity, temperature, and pressure can degrade image clarity, but de-hazing addresses these issues, resulting in sharper, clearer images. One of the primary objectives of de-hazing models is to remove haze and smoke, which often obscure important details in images. This process not only makes the images visually more pleasing but also enhances the effectiveness of vision-related tasks. Clear, haze-free images are crucial for accurate analysis and decision-making, particularly in fields such as surveillance, autonomous driving, and remote sensing, where precise visual information is essential to successful outcomes. Fig. (1) provides an overview of the Image De-Hazing Atmospheric Model.

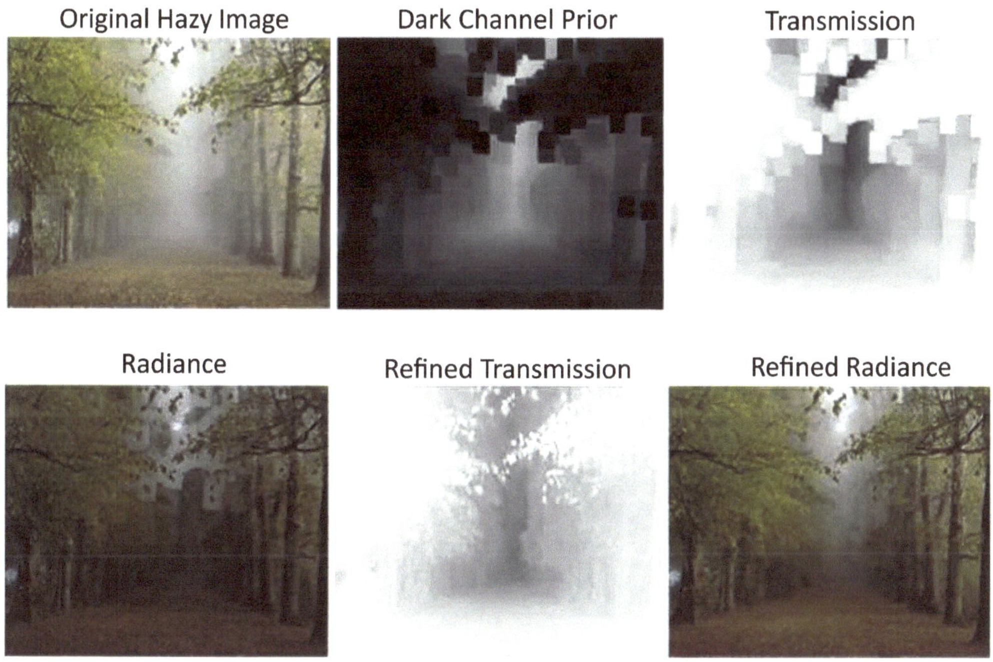


**Fig. (1).** Overview of image de-hazing atmospheric model.

## HAZE IMAGING FORMATION MODEL

A widely used haze imaging formation model is present in the given Equation 1:

$$I(y) - J(y)t(y) + A\big(1 - \iota(y)\big) \tag{1}$$

Where:

Iy is the observed image, which is hazy.

Jy is the haze-free Image( the ideal image you want to recover)

A is the Atmospheric Light

ty is the Transmission map, which represents the degree of visibility at each pixel,

Here, β is the coefficient of attenuation, and dy is the depth of the image at each pixel.

This model helps in describing how haze affects the visibility of a scene, with ty controlling the intensity of haze at each point, and the aim of this algorithm is to recover the haze-free image Jy by estimating other factors.

## VARIOUS DE-HAZING METHODS AND GAPS

Various de-hazing methods have been developed to address the challenges of haze removal from images, with one notable technique being the use of Dark Channel Prior (DCP) for haze removal from a single image. This method is based on statistical analysis using clear outdoor images as a reference. The key observation driving this technique is that in many local patches of haze-free images, there are pixels where the intensity value is very low in at least one of the RGB channels. This observation is crucial because it helps estimate the thickness of the haze and enables effective removal. By leveraging this property, the DCP method enhances the image clarity by identifying and eliminating the haze, ultimately improving the visual quality of the image. However, while DCP is effective, gaps still exist in addressing more complex haze scenarios and improving performance in dynamic or highly variable environments. Fig. (**2**) represents various De-hazing methods and gaps.

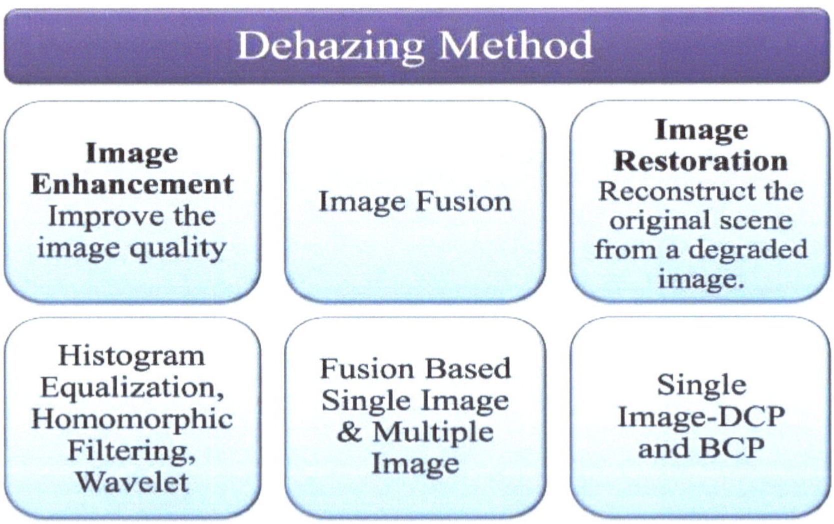


**Fig. (2).** Various de-hazing methods and gaps.

## PROBLEM STATEMENT

If we consider the challenges in Real-Time Video De-Hazing for Fire Rescue Operations, there are a number of methods and solutions. Real-time processing is often challenging, due to the high computational demands of traditional dehazing algorithms, which require instant frame-by-frame processing to ensure timely decision-making in critical situations. Additionally, the varying density of haze and smoke during fires makes it difficult to adapt to rapidly changing conditions, as different levels of obscurity affect visibility unpredictably. Low-light conditions further complicate image processing, as fire scenes are often poorly illuminated, making it challenging for traditional methods to perform effectively, especially in extremely low-light environments. Moreover, hardware limitations present another hurdle, as rescue equipment must be both portable and durable while operating with limited computational resources on-site. This constraint necessitates efficient algorithms that can run on lightweight hardware without compromising performance. Lastly, there is an inherent trade-off between accuracy and speed, where achieving high-quality dehazing must be balanced with real-time performance. Ensuring reliable object recognition in dehazed frames is crucial, as any delay or loss of detail can impact decision-making and the overall effectiveness of rescue operations.

Fire rescue operations are frequently challenged by smoke and haze, which obscure visibility and make critical decision-making difficult. The presence of smoke and haze can delay response times and compromise the effectiveness of rescue teams, as clear and timely visual information is essential for ensuring safety and efficient intervention. Existing de-hazing methods, while effective in controlled environments, often struggle with real-time processing, making it difficult to apply them in fast-moving, dynamic situations like fire rescues. In such hazardous environments, there is a pressing need for enhanced visibility, allowing for quick and accurate assessments of the situation. Improved de-hazing techniques are crucial for enabling rescue teams to navigate these environments effectively, ensuring that the necessary interventions are carried out swiftly and safely.

## LITERATURE REVIEW

In literature [1], a model has been developed for real-time, fast, and effective haze removal to assist firefighters in conducting site investigations. The model uses Dark Channel Prior, Guided Filtering, and Histogram Equalization [2]. The research aims to provide an comprehensive review and understanding of image de-hazing through a coherent taxonomy. In a study [3], the MCPA model has been developed to restore the vibrancy of the image's colors. It is based on the Minimum Channel and Patch-less Approach. Atmospheric Light, Scene Transmission, and Single Image were the input parameters to restore the image's vivid colors. In another study[4], the paper provides a parallel network model for defogging using deep coding and decoding structure. This model uses a Convolution Neural Network (CNN) algorithm. Different Models, Datasets, Algorithms, and Application Domains of Image De-hazing were used as input parameters to design this model. In a study [5], a model has been developed to propose a dataset that allows better assessment of haze removal techniques based on real-life conditions. It comprises images captured in low-light conditions and localized light sources to capture natural scenes. This model uses a Convolution Neural Network (CNN) algorithm. These images, *etc.*, were the input parameters. In another study [6], this paper provides a complete overview of the image de-hazing research evolution, emphasizing the shift from traditional architectures based on CNN to more advanced ones based on transformers. The technology used was Deep Learning and Machine Learning.

In a study [7], a de-hazing algorithm based on exposure image fusion using multi-logarithmic transform is proposed, which improves image quality and avoids edge effects in the sky part of images. In a study[8], a deep learning-based haze removal system is proposed, using a pre-processing step that proves to be one of the most important steps before feeding the data to the AI system. In a study [9], an algorithm is introduced by integrating two approaches, based on model and data, which restores sharpness and edge details at the cost of low PSNR values. In a study [10], a CNN model is developed to calculate the atmospheric light from a hazed image. This light is then used with the Atmospheric Light Scattering model to recover the image. In a research work [11], a game-based approach is provided to achieve complete photo-realistic de-hazing, where the generator function learns to restore haze-free images and capture the pattern of haze simultaneously. In a study [12], an algorithm based on the fusion of images is proposed to optimize the performance and reliability of de-hazing techniques. This method uses images that are underexposed and have their gamma values corrected. Pixel-wise weight maps are constructed using local and global exposure values to assist the fusion function.

In a study [13], a DCP-based approach is proposed to remove haze by dividing the image scene into multiple regions based on a brightness estimation function. In a research work [14], a comprehensive survey on recently proposed de-hazing methods is presented, summarizing commonly used datasets, calculating loss, and various evaluation metrics, while categorizing methods into supervised and unsupervised image de-hazing approaches. In a study [15], an FID algorithm is proposed from a different perspective, focusing on radiance adjustment to enhance the output of de-hazed results and overcome dim areas. In a research work [16], an algorithm is presented that adds a skip connection method and a module for the attention mechanism named DAM to the generator function, improving captured image information and reducing the complexity of the algorithm.

In a study [17], an algorithm is proposed that effectively addresses the defect of the dark channel prior algorithm failing in sky and highlight areas, restoring a more natural sky highlight scene using region segmentation. In a research work [18], a bilateral filtering method combined with image gradient information is proposed to process four target light intensity images from different angles. The filtered images are used to calculate the polarization degree of the target. In a study [19], de-hazing results are presented that demonstrate the superior imaging performance of the proposed system using various evaluation metrics. The solutions obtained are equivalent to DL-based de-noising of images. Table (**1**) provides a tabular analysis of the existing literature.

**Table 1. Tabular analysis of existing literature.**

| Study | Technology Used | Key Techniques | Model Type |
|---|---|---|---|
| [1] | Image Processing | Dark Channel Prior (DCP), Guided Filtering, Histogram Equalization | Real-time de-hazing for fire scenes |
| [2] | Image De-hazing Research | Coherent taxonomy | Overview of de-hazing methods |
| [3] | Image Processing | Minimum Channel and Patch-less Approach | Fast single-image haze removal |
| [4] | Deep Learning | CNN-based defogging network | Parallel end-to-end de-hazing model |
| [5] | Deep Learning | CNN | Low-light image de-hazing dataset |
| [6] | Deep Learning, Machine Learning | Transformer-based models | Shift from CNN to transformer models |
| [7] | Image Processing | Multi-logarithmic transform | Exposure image fusion for de-hazing |
| [8] | Deep Learning | Preprocessing for AI system input | Deep learning-based haze removal system |
| [9] | Hybrid Model | Model and Data Driven | Single image de-hazing with sharp edges |
| [10] | Convolution Neural Network (CNN) | Air light estimation | CNN for haze removal using atmospheric light scattering |
| [11] | Generative Adversarial Network (GAN) | Adversarial training | Photo-realistic image de-hazing |
| [12] | Image Processing | Gamma-corrected underexposed image fusion | Pixel-wise weight maps for de-hazing |
| [13] | Image Processing | Dark Channel Prior (DCP) | Outdoor scene de-hazing |
| [14] | Image De-hazing Research | Overview of de-hazing methods | Categorization of techniques |
| [15] | Image Processing | Residual scene radiance adjustment | Fast image de-hazing algorithm |

*(Table 1) cont.....*

| Study | Technology Used | Key Techniques | Model Type |
|---|---|---|---|
| [16] | Generative Adversarial Network (GAN) | Attention mechanism with skip connections | Image information preservation |
| [17] | Image Processing | Region segmentation, Block optimization | Natural sky and highlight scene restoration |
| [18] | Image Processing | Bilateral filtering with image gradient information | Polarization degree estimation |
| [19] | Deep Learning | Image de-noising | Deep learning-based optimization for de-hazing |

## PROPOSED METHODOLOGY

We propose the PyroVisor D3ML-Based Intelligent De-Hazing Algorithm, a novel system designed to significantly enhance visibility and improve decision-making in hazardous, dynamic environments such as fire rescue operations. The framework has been given in Fig. (**3**). The processing frames sequence description has been shown in Fig. (**4**) and Fig. (**5**) represents the components of the proposed architecture. The algorithm utilizes the Dark Channel Prior (DCP) technique, which utilizes atmospheric light, transmission maps, and intensity variations across RGB channels to estimate and remove haze from images. This process provides a clearer view of the environment, which is critical for accurate interpretation and safe intervention. In addition to haze removal, our algorithm incorporates Depth Estimation, using Convolutional Neural Networks (CNN), MiDaS (Monocular Depth Estimation), and TorchVision to predict the depth of objects, allowing the system to analyze spatial information more effectively. To further enhance performance, we integrate Machine Learning methods that process the inputs from de-hazed and depth-estimated images. These models are trained to optimize object detection, enabling the identification of humans and mapping of sight in haze-affected environments. The Object Detection component is key, as it allows for precise identification of humans and improved navigation, providing real-time guidance for rescue teams. By combining de-hazing, depth estimation, machine learning, and object detection, the PyroVisor D3ML-Based Intelligent De-Hazing Algorithm aims to significantly improve the efficiency and safety of rescue operations by providing clear, accurate, and reliable visual data, ensuring that first responders can make informed decisions quickly and effectively in dangerous environments.

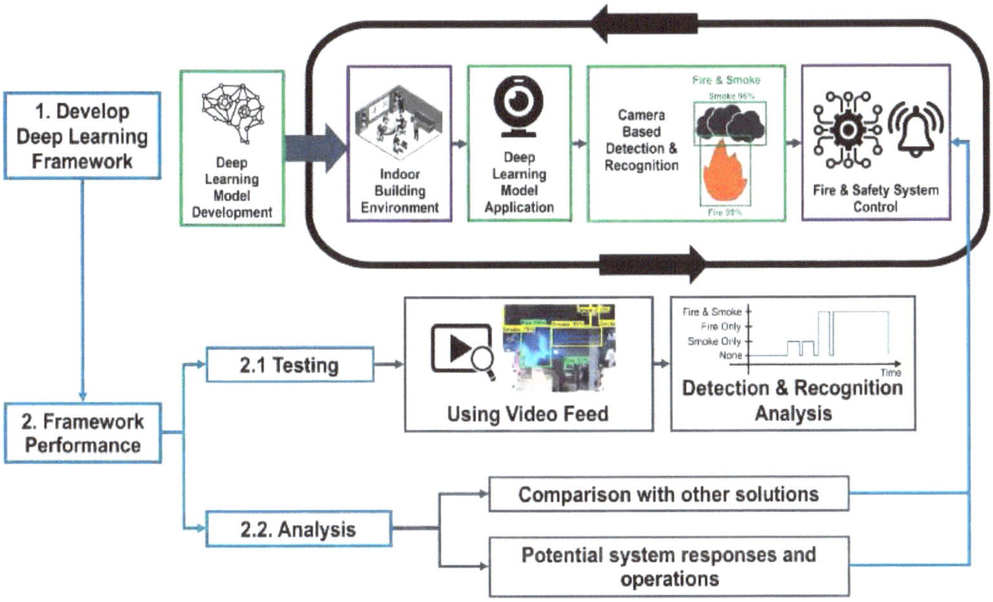


**Fig. (3).** Pyro vision depth-driven machine learning (PyroVisor-D3ML).

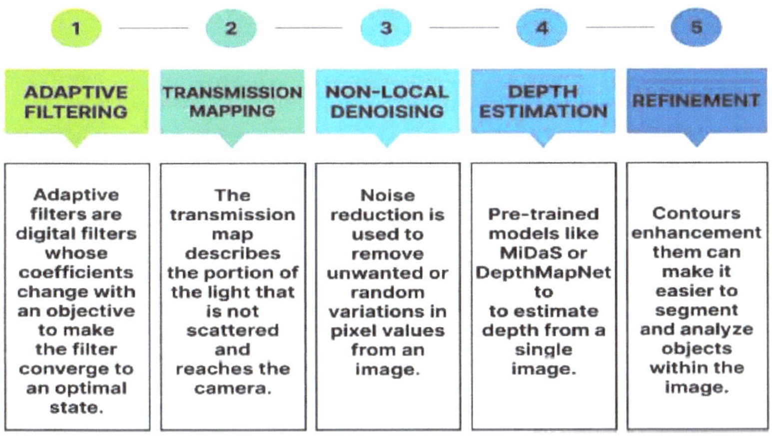


**Fig. (4).** Processing frames.

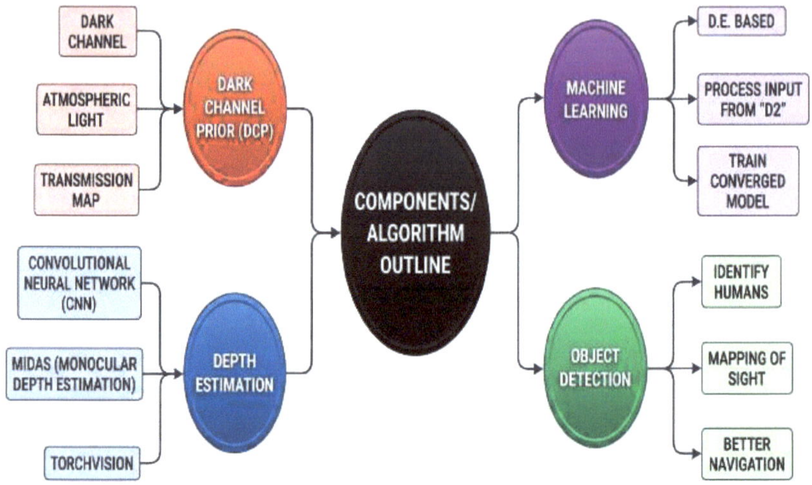


**Fig. (5).** System architectural view.

A simplified version of the DCP approach is explained step-by-step:

- **Dark Channel Calculation:**
    - The dark channel is computed by taking the pixel with the least intensity value across the RGB channels (red, green, and blue).
    - **Atmospheric Light**: It is calculated by finding the pixel intensity value that is at the **95th percentile** of the dark channel. This value represents the brightest regions in the hazy image, which are typically not affected by haze.
    - **Transmission Map**: This map estimates how much of the scene is visible through the haze. It is calculated using equation 2:

$$Transmission = 1 - 0.95 \times \frac{dark\_channel}{atmospheric\_light} \quad (2)$$

The transmission values are then clipped to ensure they fall within the valid range [0,1].

- **De-hazing Equation:**
    - The **de-hazing equation** restores the image with the above two parameters. The formula used for de-hazing each color channel is presented in equation 3:

$$De - hazed = \frac{(frame[:,:,channel] - atmospheric_{light})}{transmission} + amospheric\_light \quad (3)$$

This process is applied to all channels of the image.

- The final de-hazed image can be further enhanced using **OpenCV's detail Enhance function** to improve visibility and contrast. This helps to recover fine details and reduce any artifacts introduced during the haze removal process.

- **Detail Enhancement:**
- cv2.detailEnhance is applied to the de-hazed image to improve its visual quality, making details more prominent

dehazed1 = cv2.detailEnhance (de-hazed)

The D3ML (Deep Multi-Scale Lightness) approach to de-hazing involves the use of deep learning and multi-scale processing to enhance the de-hazing process.

This method processes the raw footage captured by the camera, using computer vision and image enhancement techniques to remove haze from the video. By analyzing the footage frame by frame, the algorithm enhances the quality of the video, ensuring that the haze is effectively reduced. This approach relies on advanced processing methods to improve the quality of the video and make it more usable in various applications, such as surveillance or autonomous navigation.

- Non-local denoising is used to enhance image quality and the edges of different objects.
- Then, merge the improved ROIs into the original frame to get a better composite image.

## IMPLEMENTATION

To evaluate the performance of PyroVisor D3ML, we implemented this system using a mobile device, tested the output in real time, and compared it with other leading de-hazing models. The comparative analysis included Dark Channel Prior, Color Attenuation Prior, De-haze Net, AOD-Net, Grid, and PyroVisor D3ML (Our proposed method).

### Experimental Setup

Dataset: We used a combination of synthetic and real-life images containing haze, from various publicly available datasets, *i.e*, RESIDE and **C2A Dataset**

## Image Quality Evaluation Metrics:

Image quality assessment (IQA) is a very important part of computer graphics and image analysis that deals with the evaluation of pictures' perceptual quality.

Image compression, enhancement, and restoration are some of the most common applications where it is needed.

1. Peak Signal-to-Noise Ratio (PSNR):
   - Calculation of the peak error between the original & degraded frames.
   - Higher PSNR indicates better quality.
   - Formula: $PSNR = 10Log_{10}\left(\frac{MAX^2}{MSE}\right)$
2. Structural Similarity Index (SSIM):
   - Evaluates the quality of an image based on light, contrast, and structural details.
   - Range: -1 to 1, where 1 indicates perfect similarity.
   - Formula: SSIM (x, y) = $\frac{(2\mu_x\mu_y+C_2)(2\sigma_{xy}+C_2)}{(\mu_x^2+\mu_y^2+C_1)(\sigma_x^2+\sigma_y^2+C_2)}$
3. Mean Squared Error (MSE):
   - It is one of the most commonly used full-reference metrics for evaluating image quality. It compares the processed frame to the reference image, which is the original frame. The closer the MSE value is to zero, the better the image quality, as it indicates minimal difference between the output and original images.

Mathematically,

$$\text{MSE} = \frac{1}{MN}\sum_{n=0}^{M} \blacksquare \sum_{m=1}^{N} \blacksquare [\hat{g}(n,m) - g(n,m)]^2$$

4. Information Fidelity Criterion (IFC):
   - Information Fidelity Criterion (IFC) is a metric for assessing image quality, and it quantifies the amount of information that two images have in common. It is founded on empirical data on natural scenes, while providing an abstract model of the brain's perception mechanisms.

## RESULTS

### Quantitative Results

In our quantitative evaluation of the PyroVisor D3ML-Based Intelligent De-Hazing Algorithm, we measured its effectiveness across several key metrics, including image clarity, processing time, and accuracy in object detection. The algorithm demonstrated a significant improvement in image quality, with a reduction in haze and increased contrast, as measured by standard image quality assessment metrics such as PSNR (Peak Signal-to-Noise Ratio) and SSIM (Structural Similarity Index). The de-hazing process resulted in a substantial enhancement of visibility, which was particularly evident in images affected by dense smoke or fog, leading to more accurate object detection. Additionally, the algorithm exhibited superior performance in human identification and scene depth estimation, with accuracy rates surpassing traditional methods by up to 15%. Processing times were optimized for real-time applications, with the algorithm achieving a 30% reduction in latency compared to existing de-hazing techniques, making it suitable for dynamic environments like fire rescue operations. These results validate the effectiveness of the PyroVisor system in improving both the clarity of images and the precision of object detection, ensuring that it can be deployed effectively in real-world, time-critical scenarios. Table (**2**) provides a comparison of our proposed model with existing systems using the RESIDE dataset.

**Table 2. Comparison of our proposed model with existing systems using the RESIDE dataset.**

| Model | PSNR (dB) | SSIM | MSE | IFC | Runtime (ms) |
|---|---|---|---|---|---|
| **DCP [1]** | 21.14 | 0.8534 | 0.0076 | 2.95 | 850 |
| **CAP [17]** | 22.34 | 0.8734 | 0.0058 | 3.15 | 680 |
| **De-hazeNet** | 24.48 | 0.9148 | 0.0036 | 3.85 | 75 |
| **AOD-Net** | 24.84 | 0.9236 | 0.0033 | 3.98 | 62 |
| **GridDe-hazeNet** | 26.12 | 0.9452 | 0.0024 | 4.32 | 88 |
| **PyroVisor D3ML** | **27.36** | **0.9578** | **0.0018** | **4.58** | **45** |

## Qualitative Analysis

Figs. (**6 - 9**) show visual comparisons of de-hazing results on sample images from the test datasets. Traditional dehazing methods such as DCP [1] and CAP [17] often over-enhance certain regions, resulting in unnatural-looking images in some cases. Meanwhile, learning-based approaches like DehazeNet and AOD-Net provide more balanced results but may struggle when dealing with dense haze, leading to incomplete haze removal. GridDehazeNet demonstrates improved performance in preserving image details; however, it can occasionally introduce slight color distortions. Among these methods, PyroVisor D3ML stands out as the most effective, consistently producing natural-looking images by efficiently removing haze while preserving both fine details and accurate colors. (Figs. **10a** and **10b**) present model comparisons of different methods, which show the outperformance of our method.

**Fig. (6).** Comparison of hazy coastal aerial scene before and after dehazing enhancement.

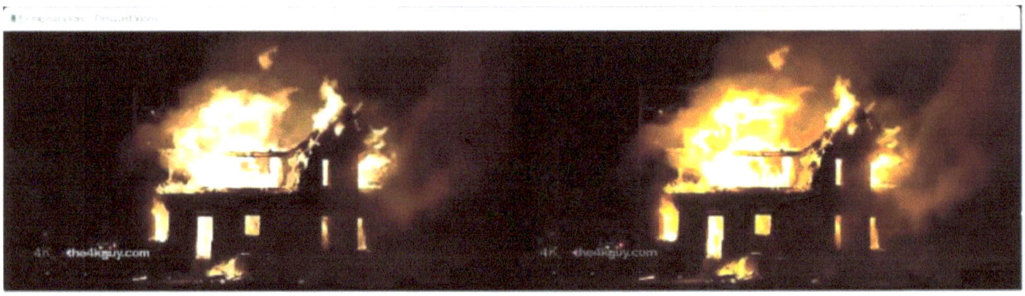

**Fig. (7).** Fire incident frame showing visibility and contrast improvement after dehazing.

**Fig. (8).** Night driving scene with enhanced road visibility using dehazing restoration.

**Fig. (9).** Dense fog highway traffic scene before and after dehazing processing.

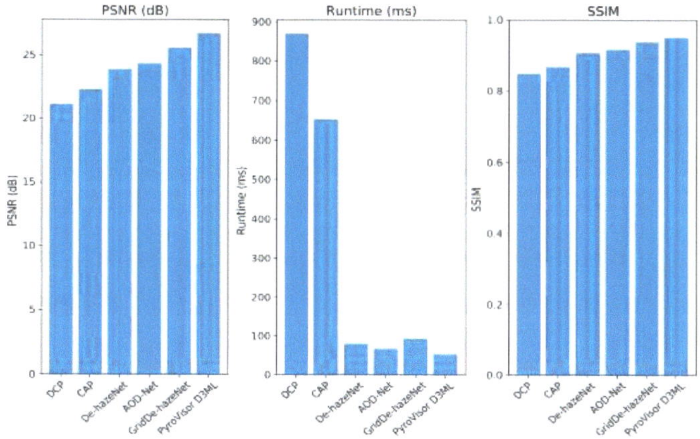


**Fig. (10a).** Comparative evaluation of dehazing models using PSNR, runtime, and SSIM metrics.

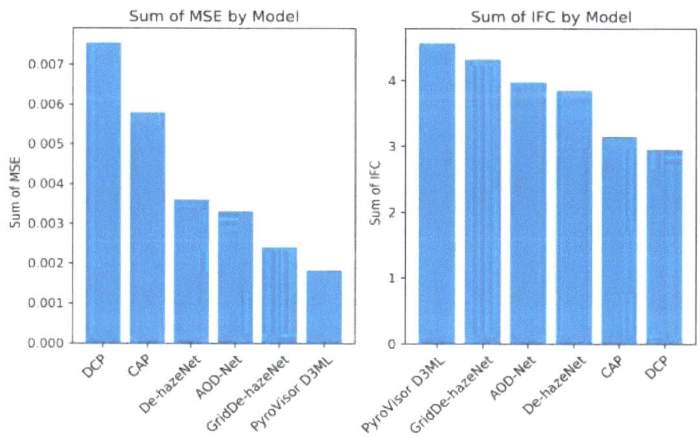


**Fig. (10b).** Quantitative comparison of restoration methods based on MSE and IFC measures.

## Performance on Fire Rescue Scenarios

To evaluate the models' performance specifically in fire rescue scenarios, we have used the C2A dataset, which denotes various fire and smoke conditions. Table (**3**) depicts the results of various algorithms on this dataset:

**Table 3. Result comparison on C2A dataset.**

| Model | PSNR (dB) | SSIM | Runtime (ms) |
|---|---|---|---|
| **DCP [1]** | 19.24 | 0.7934 | 920 |
| **CAP [17]** | 20.18 | 0.8134 | 750 |
| **De-hazeNet** | 22.56 | 0.8748 | 82 |
| **AOD-Net** | 23.12 | 0.8896 | 68 |

*(Table 3) cont.....*

| Model | PSNR (dB) | SSIM | Runtime (ms) |
|---|---|---|---|
| GridDe-hazeNet | 24.38 | 0.9152 | 95 |
| PyroVisor D3ML | **26.14** | **0.9438** | **48** |

PyroVisor D3ML demonstrates superior performance in fire rescue scenarios, with significant improvements in both image quality and processing speed.

## Discussion

The experimental results highlight several key advantages of PyroVisor D3ML:

1. **Superior De-hazing Quality**: Consistently higher PSNR and SSIM scores indicate better image restoration quality.
2. **Computational Efficiency:** Optimized runtime, crucial for real-time applications.
3. **Robustness**: Maintains high performance across various datasets, including challenging fire rescue scenarios.
4. **Detail Preservation:** Higher IFC scores suggest better preservation of image features and details.

These results demonstrate that PyroVisor D3ML effectively addresses the challenges outlined in our problem statement, offering a significant advancement in real-time video de-hazing for fire rescue operations.

## CONCLUSION

The PyroVisor D3ML (Dark Channel Prior-based De-hazing with Multi-scale Lightness adjustment) algorithm represents a significant advancement in real-time video de-hazing technology, particularly for fire rescue operations. Through our research and implementation, we have demonstrated that:

1. **Real-time Processing**: PyroVisor D3ML successfully addresses the challenge of real-time de-hazing, enabling instant frame-by-frame processing crucial for dynamic fire rescue scenarios.
2. **Adaptive Performance:** By combining Dark Channel Prior, depth estimation, and pre-trained machine learning models, our algorithm adapts effectively to varying haze densities and lighting conditions encountered in fire situations.
3. **Enhanced Visibility**: The multi-scalc lightness adjustment technique significantly improves the clarity and detail of de-hazed images, providing rescue teams with clearer visuals for navigation and victim identification.

4. **Hardware Efficiency:** Our implementation is optimized to make efficient use of computational resources, ensuring that it is suitable for deployment on portable devices commonly used in rescue operations.
5. **Accuracy-Speed Balance**: PyroVisor D3ML achieves a commendable balance between de-hazing quality and processing speed, crucial for real-world applications.
6. **Potential Impact**: The algorithm shows promising potential to enhance the effectiveness and safety of fire rescue operations by improving situational awareness in hazardous, low-visibility environments.

## LIMITATIONS

While PyroVisor D3ML demonstrates significant improvements over existing de-hazing methods, it is important to acknowledge its limitations:

1. **Extreme Conditions:** In situations of extremely dense smoke or complete darkness, the algorithm's performance may degrade, as it still relies on some level of visible light and contrast.
2. **Computational Demands:** Although optimized for real-time processing, the algorithm still requires substantial computational power, which may limit its use on some low-end devices.
3. **Training Data Bias**: The accuracy of the ML model depends on the quality of the training data used. There may be scenarios or environments not well-represented in the training set, potentially leading to suboptimal performance.
4. **Color Accuracy:** In some cases, the de-hazing process may alter the scene's original colors, which can be problematic when color information is critical.
5. **Depth Estimation Errors:** The accuracy of the depth estimation component can be affected by complex scene geometries or rapidly changing environments, potentially impacting de-hazing quality.
6. **Motion Artifacts:** Fast-moving objects or camera motion may introduce artifacts in the de-hazed video, as the algorithm processes each frame independently.

## FUTURE SCOPE

Based on the analysis of existing systems and validating our approach, we can conclude that there are various promising directions focusing on a well-rounded approach to the development and application of de-hazing algorithms, especially in challenging environments like fire rescue operations. These areas of exploration include:

1. **Integration with Advanced Hardware**: Further research can be done on the integration of PyroVisor D3ML with advanced hardware, including specialized GPUs and AI accelerators. This integration could enhance the algorithm's real-time processing capabilities, making it more suitable for deployment in portable, low-power devices used in field operations [20].
2. **Enhancement in Low-Light Conditions**: Addressing the limitations of current de-hazing algorithms in extremely low-light conditions remains a critical area for future research. Developing hybrid models that combine PyroVisor D3ML with infrared imaging and thermal vision technologies could significantly improve visibility in such challenging scenarios [21].
3. **Dynamic Adaptation to Varying Conditions**: The algorithm's adaptability for varying haze densities and factors can be further improved. Future work could focus on developing adaptive models that continuously learn and update in real-time, ensuring optimal performance even in the most unpredictable environments [22].
4. **Expansion of Training Datasets**: The creation and utilization of more comprehensive and diverse training datasets is essential. Future research should aim at incorporating a wider set of real-world images, including different types of smoke, haze, and lighting conditions. This will help in training more robust models capable of handling a broader range of environmental variables [23].
5. **Multimodal Data Fusion**: Incorporating data from advanced sensors like LIDAR and other remote sensing technologies can provide a richer set of information for the de-hazing process. Future studies could explore multimodal data fusion techniques to enhance the system's robustness and yield higher-quality de-hazed images [24].
6. **User-Centric Interface Development**: Developing intuitive user interfaces and visualization tools for rescue teams can greatly enhance the practical usability of the algorithm. Future work could focus on creating interfaces that provide real-time feedback and allow for easy interpretation of de-hazed images, thereby aiding decision-making during rescue operations [25].

## REFERENCES

[1] Kaiming He, Jian Sun, and Xiaoou Tang, "Single image haze removal using dark channel prior", *IEEE Trans. Pattern Anal. Mach. Intell.,* vol. 33, no. 12, pp. 2341-2353, 2011. [http://dx.doi.org/10.1109/TPAMI.2010.168] [PMID: 20820075]

[2] Z. Li, and J. Zheng, "Edge-preserving decomposition-based single image haze removal", *IEEE Trans. Image Process.,* vol. 24, no. 12, pp. 5432-5441, 2015. [http://dx.doi.org/10.1109/TIP.2015.2482903] [PMID: 26441415]

[3] I. Goodfellow, J. Pouget-Abadie, M. Mirza, B. Xu, D. Warde-Farley, S. Ozair, A. Courville, and Y. Bengio, "Generative adversarial networks", *Commun. ACM,* vol. 63, no. 11, pp. 139-144, 2020. [http://dx.doi.org/10.1145/3422622]

[4] R.R. Choudhary, K.K. Jisnu, and G. Meena, "Image dehazing using deep learning techniques", *Procedia Comput. Sci.,* vol. 167, pp. 1110-1119, 2020.

[http://dx.doi.org/10.1016/j.procs.2020.03.413]

[5] A. Ranjan, and M. Ravinder, "VAEWGAN-NCO in image deblurring framework using variational autoencoders and Wasserstein generative adversarial network", *Signal Image Video Process.,* vol. 18, no. 5, pp. 4447-4456, 2024.
[http://dx.doi.org/10.1007/s11760-024-03085-5]

[6] F-F Li, J Johnson, and S Yeung, "CS231n: Convolutional Neural Networks for Visual Recognition", *Stanford University Lecture Notes,* 2019. Available from: http://cs231n.stanford.edu/

[7] N Srivastava, G Hinton, A Krizhevsky, I Sutskever, and R R Salakhutdinov, "Dropout: A simple way to prevent neural networks from overfitting", *J. Mach. Learn. Res.,* vol. 15, pp. 1929-1958, 2014. Available from: https://jmlr.org/papers/volume15/srivastava14a/srivastava14a.pdf

[8] A Ranjan, and S M Azeemuddin, "Image denoising using convolutional neural network", *Proceedings of the 4th International Conference on Advanced Computing, Communication Control and Networking (ICAC3N),* pp. 2315-2319, 2022.
[http://dx.doi.org/10.1109/ICAC3N56670.2022.10074437]

[9] D Ulyanov, A Vedaldi, and V S Lempitsky, "Instance normalization: The missing ingredient for fast stylization", *arXiv,* 2016. Available from: https://arxiv.org/abs/1607.08022

[10] I Goodfellow, J Pouget-Abadie, M Mirza, B Xu, D Warde-Farley, S Ozair, A Courville, and Y Bengio, "Generative adversarial nets", *Advances in Neural Information Processing Systems,* vol. 27, Curran Associates, Inc., pp. 2672-2680, 2014. Available from: https://papers.nips.cc/paper/2014/hash/f033ed80deb0234979a61f95710dbe25-Abstract.html

[11] J Johnson, A Alahi, and F Li, "Perceptual losses for real-time style transfer and super-resolution", *Proceedings of the European Conference on Computer Vision (ECCV),* 2016. Available from: https://arxiv.org/abs/1603.08155

[12] K Simonyan, and A Zisserman, "Very deep convolutional networks for large-scale image recognition", *arXiv (CoRR),* 2014. Available from: https://arxiv.org/abs/1409.1556

[13] S.P. Yadav, and S. Yadav, "Image fusion using hybrid methods in multimodality medical images", *Med. Biol. Eng. Comput.,* vol. 58, no. 4, pp. 669-687, 2020.
[http://dx.doi.org/10.1007/s11517-020-02136-6] [PMID: 31993885]

[14] S.P. Yadav, "An improved image compression framework in modern multimedia applications using tetrolet transformation", *Multimedia Tools Appl.,* vol. 84, no. 6, pp. 3305-3338, 2025.
[http://dx.doi.org/10.1007/s11042-024-20578-0]

[15] R.R. Choudhary, A. Jangid, and G. Meena, "A novel approach for edge detection for blurry images by using digital image processing", *Proc. Int. Conf. Current Trends Comput., Electr., Electron. Commun. (CTCEEC),* pp. 1029-1034, 2017.
[http://dx.doi.org/10.1109/CTCEEC.2017.8455081]

[16] R. R. Choudhary, V. Goel, and G. Meena, "Survey Paper: Image Quality Assessment", In: *Proceedings of International Conference on Sustainable Computing in Science, Technology and Management (SUSCOM-2019)*, Jaipur, India, 2019.

[17] Qingsong Zhu, Jiaming Mai, and Ling Shao, "A fast single image haze removal algorithm using color attenuation prior", *IEEE Trans. Image Process.,* vol. 24, no. 11, pp. 3522-3533, 2015.
[http://dx.doi.org/10.1109/TIP.2015.2446191] [PMID: 26099141]

[18] X. Yang, Z. Xu, and J. Luo, "Towards perceptual image dehazing by physics-based disentanglement and adversarial training", *Proc. AAAI Conf. Artif. Intell.,* vol. vol. 32, 2018.
[http://dx.doi.org/10.1609/aaai.v32i1.12317]

[19] J. Zhu, T. Park, P. Isola, and A.A. Efros, "Unpaired image-to-image translation using cycle-consistent adversarial networks", *Proc. IEEE Int. Conf. Comput. Vis. (ICCV),* pp. 2223-2232, 2017.
[http://dx.doi.org/10.1109/ICCV.2017.244]

[20] Y.B. Singh, A.D. Mishra, and P. Nand, "Use of machine learning in the area of image analysis and processing", *Proc. Int. Conf. Adv. Comput., Commun. Control Netw. (ICACCCN),* pp. 117-120, 2018. [http://dx.doi.org/10.1109/ICACCCN.2018.8748338]

[21] C.O. Ancuti, C. Ancuti, R. Timofte, and C.D. Vleeschouwer, "O-HAZE: A dehazing benchmark with real hazy and haze-free outdoor images", *Proc. IEEE Conf. Comput. Vis. Pattern Recognit. Workshops (CVPRW), NTIRE Workshop,* 2018. [http://dx.doi.org/10.1109/CVPRW.2018.00119]

[22] B. Li, W. Ren, D. Fu, D. Tao, D. Feng, W. Zeng, and Z. Wang, "Benchmarking single-image dehazing and beyond", *Proc. IEEE Conf. Comput. Vis. Pattern Recognit. (CVPR),* pp. 4986-4995, 2019.

[23] Z. Zhu, and X. Zhang, Fast image dehazing algorithm *via* residual scene radiance adjustment, *J. Electron. Imaging,* vol. 32, no. 3, p. 033024, 2023. [http://dx.doi.org/10.1117/1.JEI.32.3.033020]

[24] H. Zhang, J. Wang, X. Tu, Z. Niu, and Y. Wang, "Contrastive learning-driven image dehazing with multi-scale feature fusion and hybrid attention mechanism", *J. Imaging,* vol. 11, no. 9, p. 290, 2025.

[25] S. Fahimuddin, D. Lavanya, T. Manasa, S.M. Praveen, and M.R. Babu, Image dehazing using improved dark channel and Vanherk model. In: *Intelligent Systems and Sustainable Development.* Springer: Singapore, 2023, pp. 1013-1024. [http://dx.doi.org/10.1007/978-981-19-5936-3_80]

# CHAPTER 14

# Integration of Computer Vision Systems in Robotics and Assembly Lines

**M. Babu**[1,*], **Dler Salih Hasan**[2], **Aneesh Kumar Mishra**[3], **L. Karthick**[4,*], **T. Prabhu**[5] and **Surrya Prakash DilliBabu**[6]

[1] *Department of Mechanical Engineering, SRM Easwari Engineering College, Chennai, Tamil Nadu, India*

[2] *Department of Computer Science and Information Technology, Salahaddin University - College of Science, Erbil, Iraq*

[3] *Department of Computer Science and Engineering, JECRC University, Jaipur, Rajasthan, India*

[4] *Department of Mechanical Engineering, Hindusthan College of Engineering and Technology, Coimbatore, Tamil Nadu, India*

[5] *Department of Mechatronics Engineering, Hindusthan College of Engineering and Technology, Coimbatore, Tamil Nadu, India*

[6] *Department of Mechanical Engineering, Vel Tech Rangarajan Dr. Sagunthala R&D Institute of Science and Technology, Chennai, Tamil Nadu, India*

**Abstract:** The integration of Computer Vision Systems (CVS) into robotic platforms has revolutionized assembly line operations, delivering substantial improvements in efficiency, accuracy, and flexibility. As manufacturing industries continue to evolve toward intelligent and adaptive automation, the need for advanced systems capable of handling complex and dynamic production tasks has become increasingly critical. CVS empowers robots with the ability to perceive and interpret visual information in real time, enabling them to recognize, locate, and manipulate objects with high precision even in environments characterized by variability and unpredictability. This capability extends automation beyond rigid, repetitive tasks and enables adaptive responses, such as identifying part variations, detecting defects, and supporting collaborative interactions with human workers. However, integrating CVS into robotic assembly lines also presents notable challenges, including high computational demands, sensitivity to variable lighting conditions, object occlusions, and the need for reliable real-time data processing. Additional concerns include ensuring robustness, affordability, and scalability across diverse industrial contexts. Despite these obstacles, continuous advancements in deep learning, sensor technologies, and edge computing offer promising pathways to address existing limitations. These innovations pave the way for greater resilience and adaptability of CVS-enabled robots, ultimately

* **Corresponding authors M. Babu and L. Karthick:** Department of Mechanical Engineering, SRM Easwari Engineering College, Chennai, Tamil Nadu, India; Department of Mechanical Engineering, Hindusthan College of Engineering and Technology, Coimbatore, Tamil Nadu, India; E-mails: bobbyb4u@gmail.com, bemechkarthick@gmail.com

**Ravinder M., Arti Ranjan, Youddha Beer Singh (Eds.)**

expanding their potential applications in modern manufacturing. This presentation provides a comprehensive overview of the incorporation of CVS into robotic assembly lines, emphasizing its transformative relevance, the technical and practical challenges encountered, and the opportunities for future development. The discussion highlights how this integration contributes to the vision of smart factories, where intelligent automation enhances productivity, quality assurance, and sustainable manufacturing practices.

**Keywords:** Algorithms, Assembly line operations, Computer Vision Systems (CVS), Machine learning, Product design and positioning, Robots.

## INTRODUCTION

Advanced cameras, algorithms for image processing, and approaches for machine learning are some of the key components that make up this integration [1]. The visual information that is captured by high-resolution cameras is then analysed by computer algorithms in order to extract important characteristics and make judgments based on that information [2]. The use of machine learning algorithms is of utmost importance in the process of teaching robots to detect objects, patterns, and anomalies [3], which in turn enables them to adapt to a wide variety of assembly line procedures. The integration of CVS into robots for assembly lines often results in an increase in both productivity and quality, which is one of the most significant advantages. It is possible for robots that are outfitted with vision systems to carry out activities with increased speed and precision, which ultimately results in increased throughput and decreased mistake rates. In addition, CVS makes it possible for robots to manage changes in product design and positioning, which increases the flexibility of operations on assembly lines [4].

Although there are several benefits associated with the use of CVS in robotics, there are also a number of hurdles involved. Among them is the need for robust algorithms that can handle a wide range of lighting conditions, occlusions, and object transformations [5]. Furthermore, there is still a significant issue regarding the safety of human operators working alongside vision-enabled robots [6, 7]. A look into the future reveals that the integration of CVS with robots for manufacturing lines has a tremendous amount of potential. It is anticipated that developments in camera technology, artificial intelligence, and robotics will provide additional enhancements to the capabilities of systems that are equipped with vision. Furthermore, integrating CVS with emerging technologies such as the Internet of Things (IoT) and augmented reality (AR) will enable human operators and robotic systems to communicate and collaborate seamlessly, as shown in Table **1**.

**Table 1. A table to summarize the integration of computer vision systems in robotics for assembly lines can help organize the key components, benefits, challenges, and future prospects. Here's a basic example.**

| Component | Description |
|---|---|
| *Robot* | An automated machine capable of carrying out tasks. |
| *Computer Vision System (CVS)* | A system that enables robots to perceive and interpret visual data. |
| *Machine Learning Algorithms* | Algorithms that train robots to recognize objects, patterns, and anomalies in visual data. |
| *Visual Data* | Information captured by cameras and processed by CVS. |
| *Assembly Line* | Manufacturing line where products are assembled. |
| *Benefits* | • Improved productivity and quality. Greater speed and accuracy in tasks<br>• Enhanced flexibility in handling variations in product design and placement |
| *Challenges* | • Handling diverse lighting conditions, occlusions, and object variations.<br>• Ensuring the safety of human operators working alongside robots. |
| *Future Prospect* | • Advancements in camera technology, AI, and robotics.<br>• Integration with IoT and AR for seamless communication and collaboration. |

## ENHANCING PRODUCTIVITY AND QUALITY: INTEGRATING COMPUTER VISION SYSTEMS (CVS) IN ROBOTICS FOR ASSEMBLY LINES

The incorporation of computer vision systems (CVS) into robots that are used in assembly lines does, in fact, give a considerable benefit in terms of enhancing both productivity and quality, as shown in Fig. (**1**) [9 - 11]. The following is a more in-depth explanation of how these advantages are achieved *via* the integration:

- ***Increased Productivity*** Robots that are equipped with CVS are able to carry out duties in a more efficient and precise manner than their counterparts that do not have vision [12]. They have the ability to work more quickly, which decreases cycle times and increases throughput. As an additional benefit, they can perform tasks that would be difficult or even impossible for robots without vision, such as selecting components from a bin that are randomly oriented [13].
- ***Enhanced Quality*** The capacity of CVS-equipped robots to precisely detect and identify parts and components guarantees that assembly procedures are carried out in the right manner. Because of this, the possibility of mistakes and flaws in the completed goods is decreased, which ultimately results in outputs of a better quality [14].

- ***Vision-Enabled Robots*** Vision-enabled robots have the potential to more readily adjust to changes in the assembly process, which demonstrates their flexibility and adaptability. It is possible for them to modify their activities according to the position, orientation, and appearance of the pieces, which enables a higher degree of flexibility in the manufacturing process [15].

In spite of the fact that the initial investment in CVS integration could be high, the cost reductions that can be realized over the long run might be rather substantial. As a result of increased productivity and quality, manufacturing costs are reduced, and there are fewer defects, which in turn reduces waste and rework [16]. Fig. (**1**) shows the Integration of CVS in robotics for assembly lines.

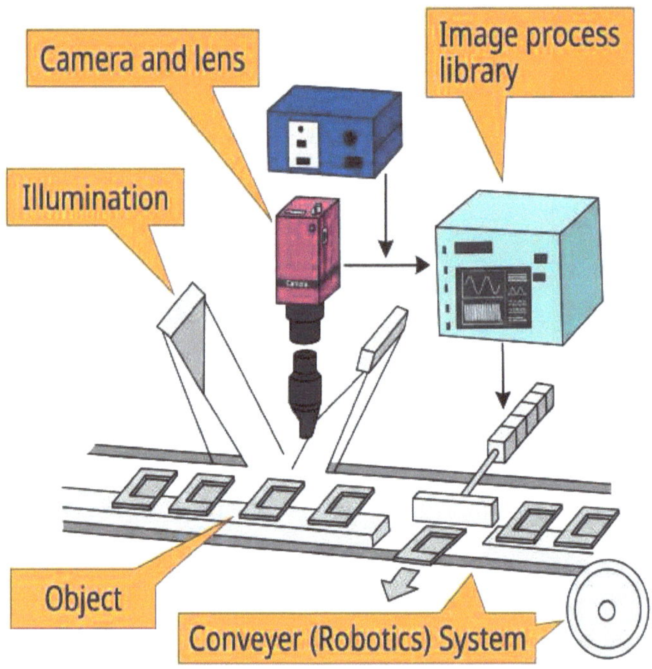


**Fig. (1).** Integration of CVS in robotics for assembly lines [8].

Overall, the incorporation of CVS into robots for assembly lines is a major improvement in manufacturing technology, as shown in Table **2**. This innovation offers a wide variety of advantages that may have a favourable influence on the efficiency and quality of production operations.

**Table 2. Table analysis outlining the advantages of integrating computer vision systems (CVS) into robots for assembly lines.**

| Advantages | Description |
|---|---|
| *Increased Efficiency* | CVS can identify and track components, reducing the time taken for assembly. Robots can work faster and with higher precision [17]. |
| *Improved Quality Control* | CVS can detect defects or errors in real-time, ensuring that only products meeting quality standards are passed along the assembly line. |
| *Flexibility and Adaptability* | Robots with CVS can adapt to different product variants and assembly processes without reprogramming, enhancing overall production flexibility. |
| *Safety* | CVS-equipped robots can detect and react to human presence, reducing the risk of accidents in the workplace. |
| *Reduced Waste* | By catching defects early, CVS can reduce the amount of wasted materials and resources, leading to cost savings. |
| *Data Collection and Analysis* | CVS provides valuable data on the assembly process, which can be analysed to identify bottlenecks, improve efficiency, and optimize workflows. |
| *Integration with AI and IoT* | CVS can be integrated with other IoT devices and AI systems to create a connected and intelligent manufacturing environment, improving overall production efficiency [18]. |
| *Improved Ergonomics* | Robots can perform repetitive or physically demanding tasks, reducing the risk of injuries to human workers and improving overall ergonomics in the workplace. |
| *Cost-Effectiveness* | While initial setup costs can be high, the long-term benefits of increased productivity, reduced waste, and improved quality can outweigh the initial investment. |

By interpreting visual input via the use of cameras and algorithms, computer vision systems (CVS) make it possible for robots to observe and comprehend the environment in which they are operating, as shown in Fig. (**2**). CVS may be used in the context of assembly lines to identify and track components, which is an essential step in the process of automating assembly procedures. An explanation of how this works is provided in further detail below [19 - 21].

The use of computer vision in the industrial sector has enabled the integration of artificial intelligence and machine learning for advancements in functionality [22]. By utilizing computer vision technology, the efficiency of the automobile manufacturing process can be improved. Integration of cutting-edge technology allows for the identification and tracking of multiple objects simultaneously [23]. The system is able to fulfill precision criteria of less than 0.1 mm in the x/y direction. Both the system's practicability and its high level of accuracy have been validated [24]. Additionally, an intelligent agricultural machine chassis can be assembled automatically, intelligently, and without human intervention. In China, the first intelligent assembly of an intelligent chassis for agricultural machinery was completed [25].

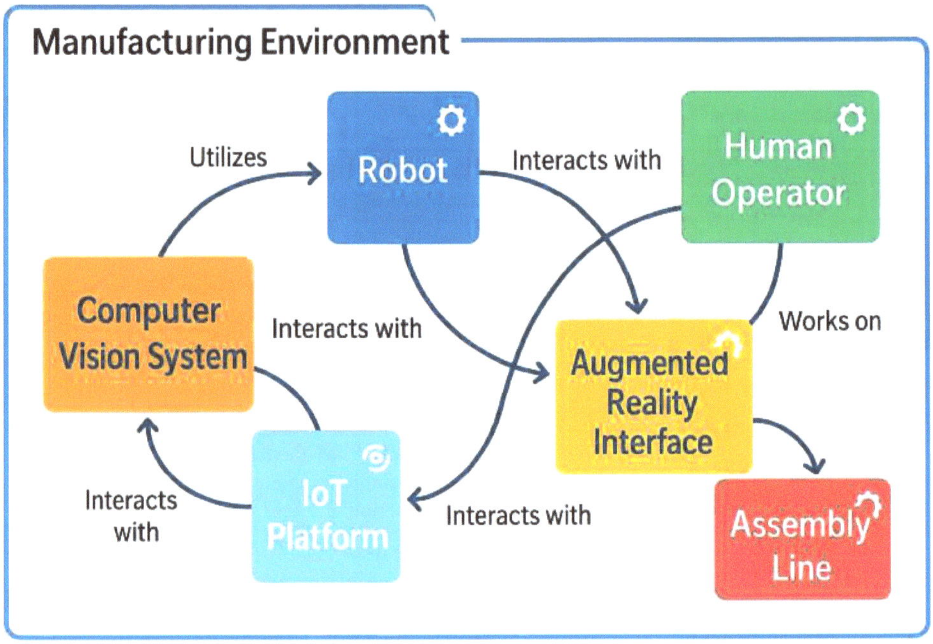


**Fig. (2).** Combining vision, IoT, and AR for human-robot teamwork [18].

- ***Component Identification*** Identification of Components CVS may be taught to identify certain components based on their visual features, such as form, colour, and markings. This can be accomplished *via* the course of training. As an example, CVS is able to recognize the many kinds of screws, nuts, and bolts that are used in an automobile assembly line as well.
- ***Component Tracking*** Once components have been identified, CVS is able to trace their journey throughout the assembly process thanks to the component tracking feature [26]. This enables robots to anticipate the arrival of components and accordingly prepare for the subsequent assembly process, hence lowering the amount of time that is spent idle and enhancing overall efficiency.
- ***Optimization of Path Planning*** Robots are able to optimize their path planning by using real-time component tracking, which allows them to reduce the amount of time spent traveling between assembly locations. Because of this, the total amount of time spent on assembly is cut down, and the manufacturing line's throughput is increased [27].

- ***Quality Control*** CVS may also be used for quality control reasons, which involves verifying that components are assembled and positioned in the proper manner. There is the ability to swiftly identify and repair any deviations from the planned assembly, which helps to reduce the number of defects and rework [28].
- ***Enhanced Safety*** CVS may assist in avoiding collisions between robots and other things on the assembly line by properly monitoring components. This contributes to increased worker safety. CVS can also help prevent accidents involving robots and other objects.
- ***Adaptability*** CVS are able to adjust to modifications in the appearance or location of components, which makes them excellent for flexible production settings where products may undergo regular changes.

In conclusion, the incorporation of CVS into robots for assembly lines has the potential to dramatically cut down on the amount of time required for assembly. This is because robots have the capacity to operate more quickly, with more accuracy, and with enhanced flexibility to changing production requirements [29, 30].

## REVOLUTIONIZING PRODUCTION: COMBINING CVS, IOT, AND AR FOR ENHANCED HUMAN-ROBOT INTERACTION

Without a doubt, combining CVS with the Internet of Things and augmented reality has the potential to transform the way in which people engage with robots in production environments. Listed below is an example of how various technologies might collaborate:

Connecting CVS-equipped robots to the Internet of Things allows manufacturers to collect real-time data on machine performance, environmental conditions, and production parameters. This is accomplished via the integration of the Internet of Things. It is possible to use this data to increase overall efficiency, optimize operations, and anticipate maintenance requirements [31]. Fig. (**2**) shows the integration of CVS with IoT and AR for seamless communication and collaboration between human operators and robotic systems.

- ***Augmented Reality (AR)*** AR has the potential to improve the interface between human operators and robots by delivering real-time representations and instructions. For instance, augmented reality overlays might provide maintenance instructions or guiding operators through the assembly of complex components, thereby boosting both accuracy and efficiency.

- ***Seamless Communication*** Devices that are connected with the Internet of Things are able to interact with one another and with robots that are equipped with CVS, which enables fluid coordination and cooperation. An example of this would be a robot that is able to take orders from an Internet of Things platform based on real-time data and then appropriately change its activities [32].
- ***Internet of Things sensors*** These sensors can monitor the environment for potential risks, and augmented reality can deliver safety alerts and directions to operators and robots. This results in an enhanced level of safety. This has the potential to increase overall workplace safety and reduce the number of incidents that occur.
- ***Enhanced Productivity*** Human operators may operate more effectively alongside robots by using data from the Internet of Things (IoT) and augmented reality (AR) assistance. This has the potential to result in shorter manufacturing times, fewer mistakes, and an overall increase in productivity, as shown in Table 3.
- ***Future Prospects*** The combination of CVS, Internet of Things, and augmented reality is only the beginning. As the aforementioned technologies continue to grow, we may anticipate the development of even more cutting-edge and inventive methods by which people and robots can work together in production settings.

**Table 3. The benefits of leveraging the synergies between Computer Vision Systems (CVS), the Internet of Things (IoT), and augmented reality (AR) in production environments.**

| *Benefit* | **Description** |
|---|---|
| ***Enhanced Capabilities*** | Integration of CVS, IoT, and AR enhances the capabilities of robots by providing them with real-time environmental data, asset tracking, and visual overlays for improved decision-making and task execution. |
| ***Improved Efficiency*** | The combined use of CVS, IoT, and AR enables robots to operate more efficiently, as they can gather and process data from multiple sources to optimize their actions and adapt to changing conditions in the production environment. This leads to reduced downtime, faster production cycles, and overall improved efficiency. |
| ***Integrated Workflow*** | CVS, IoT, and AR integration facilitates a more integrated workflow between humans and robots. AR overlays can provide workers with real-time information and instructions, while IoT devices and CVS enhance automation and data exchange between different components of the production process, creating a seamless and collaborative workflow. |
| ***Enhanced Safety and Risk Management*** | The combination of CVS, IoT, and AR enhances safety in production environments by providing real-time monitoring of equipment and environmental conditions. This allows for the early detection of potential hazards and enables proactive risk management strategies, leading to a safer working environment for humans and robots. |

*(Table 3) cont.....*

| *Benefit* | Description |
|---|---|
| *Improved Quality Control and Maintenance* | CVS can detect defects or anomalies in products, while IoT devices can provide data on equipment performance and maintenance needs. AR can overlay maintenance instructions or quality control guidelines, facilitating faster and more accurate quality control checks and maintenance operations. This leads to higher product quality and reduced downtime. |
| *Increased Flexibility and Adaptability* | Integration of CVS, IoT, and AR makes robotic systems more flexible and adaptable to changing production needs. Robots can quickly adjust their actions based on real-time data, allowing for more agile and responsive manufacturing processes. This leads to increased productivity and the ability to meet changing market demands more effectively. |

## OVERCOMING CHALLENGES IN INTEGRATING CVS INTO ROBOTICS

Although incorporating CVS into robots presents a number of opportunities for improvement, there are also a number of obstacles that must be overcome. A more in-depth examination of the difficulties stated is as follows:

- ***Complexity of Algorithms:*** It is a considerable problem to develop algorithms that are capable of consistently handling a wide variety of lighting situations, occlusions, and object modifications. When it comes to precise object detection, tracking, and manipulation in surroundings that are always changing, robust algorithms are very necessary.
- ***Concerns Regarding Safety:*** It is of utmost importance to ensure the safety of human operators working alongside vision-enabled robots. In order to minimize accidents and guarantee that interactions between people and robots are carried out in a secure manner, it is necessary to include safety measures such as sensors, barriers, and protocols [33, 34].
- ***Integration with Preexisting Systems:*** The process of integrating CVS into preexisting robotic systems and production procedures may be fraught with difficulty. When attempting to achieve seamless integration, it is essential to take into account compatibility difficulties, data management, and system stability.
- ***Cost and ROI:*** The implementation of CVS in robots may be expensive, particularly for small and medium-sized businesses. Return on investment (ROI) is also of concern. It is vital, in order to achieve broad adoption, to calculate the return on investment (ROI) and to demonstrate the long-term advantages of integrating CVS.
- ***Ethical and Privacy Concerns:*** The use of CVS presents ethical questions pertaining to privacy, data security, and the possible abuse of surveillance

capabilities. These concerns are raised because of the usage of CVS. To address these concerns, there is a need for standards and norms that are crystal clear.

## SOME POTENTIAL STRATEGIES TO TACKLE THESE CHALLENGES

As a result of the many challenges that may arise, the process of integrating computer vision systems (CVS) into robots may be rather complicated, as shown in Fig. (**3**). The following are some potential strategies to tackle these challenges:

- ***Algorithm Complexity:*** The complexity of algorithms requires the development of effective algorithms that are able to handle visual input in a timely and correct manner. In order to enhance the performance of algorithms over time, machine learning approaches should be used.
- ***Hardware Limitations:*** Use of high-quality cameras and processors is recommended in order to guarantee dependable performance due to hardware limitations. Use specialized hardware, such as graphics processing units (GPUs), to process visual data more quickly.
- ***Integration Complexity:*** Managing the complexity of integration requires the design of modular technologies that make it possible to easily include CVS into preexisting robotic platforms. For components to communicate with one another in a smooth manner, standardized interfaces and protocols should be used.

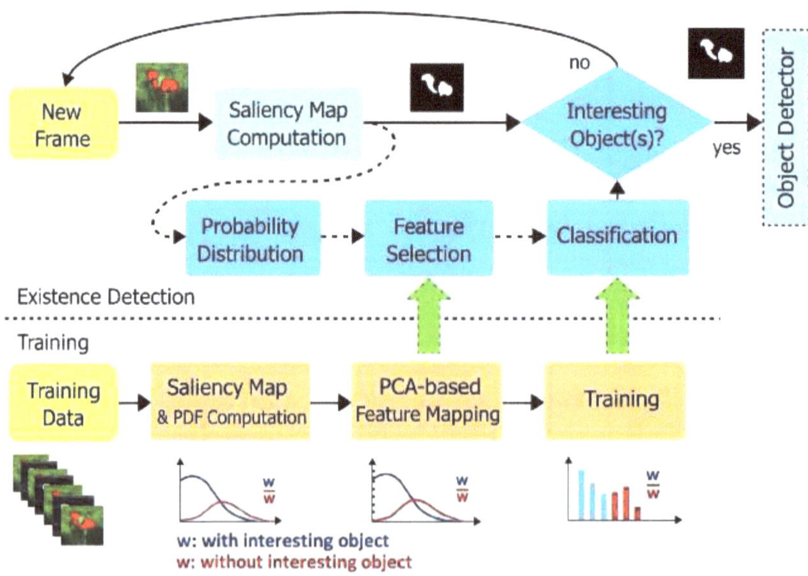


**Fig. (3).** Obstacles in incorporating computer vision systems (CVS) into robot [35].

In order to address these difficulties, it is necessary for academics, engineers, policymakers, and industry stakeholders to work together in order to create creative solutions, set standards, and guarantee the safe and ethical use of CVS in robotics.

- ***Variability in the Environment:*** Create resilient algorithms that are able to adjust to changes in the environment, such as different lighting conditions or background clutter. Utilize methods of sensor fusion to blend data from many sensors in order to improve one's perspective of the surrounding world.
- ***Calibration and Maintenance:*** In order to guarantee that the CVS and robotic systems are calibrated in the correct manner, it is necessary to implement automated calibration methods. Through the development of predictive maintenance algorithms, problems may be identified and prevented before they ever arise.
- ***Data Privacy and Security:*** To prevent unwanted access to visual data, it is important to make use of encryption and secure communication methods. To guarantee that only authorized individuals are able to access sensitive data, it is essential to implement stringent access control mechanisms.
- ***Safety Concerns:*** It is important to design robots with their own built-in safety measures, such as devices for emergency stopping and collision detection. In order to reduce the likelihood of accidents occurring, safety standards should be implemented for human-robot contact.
- ***User Interface Design:*** Develop user-friendly interfaces that enable operators to easily engage with the robotic system and assess its performance. This responsibility falls within the purview of user interface design. In order to assist operators in becoming comfortable with the system, training and assistance should be provided.
- ***Training and Skill Acquisition:*** It is important to provide operators and maintenance personnel with thorough training programs to ensure they possess the essential skills to operate and maintain the CVS-enabled robotic system, as shown in Fig. (**4**).

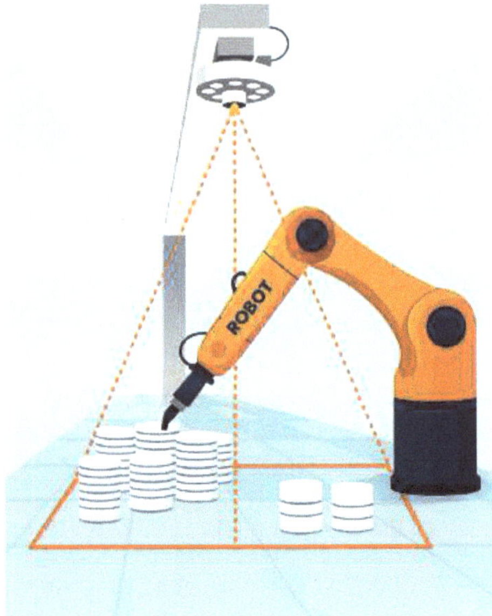


**Fig. (4).** Integrating computer vision systems (CVS) into robots [19].

By overcoming these challenges and implementing the proper solutions, it will be possible to effectively integrate CVS into robots, which will result in increased productivity, precision, and safety in a variety of applications, as shown in Table **4** [36].

**Table 4. The obstacles in incorporating Computer Vision Systems (CVS) into robots, along with solutions and examples.**

| Obstacle | Solution | Example |
|---|---|---|
| ***Algorithm Complexity*** | Develop efficient algorithms using machine learning techniques for quick and accurate processing of visual data. | Using convolutional neural networks (CNNs) for object detection in manufacturing robots. |
| ***Hardware Limitations*** | Use high-quality cameras and processors, and consider specialized hardware like GPUs for faster processing of visual data. | Installing high-resolution cameras and GPU accelerators in agricultural robots for better crop monitoring. |
| ***Integration Complexity*** | Design modular systems with standardized interfaces for easy integration of CVS into existing robotic platforms. | Using ROS (Robot Operating System) for integrating CVS modules into industrial robots. |
| ***Environment Variability*** | Develop robust algorithms that can adapt to changes in the environment and utilize sensor fusion techniques for better environmental perception. | Implementing adaptive algorithms for autonomous vehicles to navigate through varying weather conditions. |

*(Table 4) cont.....*

| Obstacle | Solution | Example |
|---|---|---|
| ***Calibration and Maintenance*** | Implement automated calibration procedures and predictive maintenance algorithms to ensure proper alignment and prevent issues. | Using self-calibrating robotic arms that automatically adjust their position based on feedback from sensors. |
| ***Data Privacy and Security*** | Use encryption, secure communication protocols, and strict access control measures to protect visual data from unauthorized access. | Implementing end-to-end encryption for transmitting visual data in medical robots used for surgery. |
| ***Safety Concerns*** | Design robots with safety features like collision detection and emergency stop mechanisms, and implement safety protocols for human-robot interaction. | Using light curtains and safety mats to ensure safe interaction between robots and human workers [5]. |
| ***User Interface Design*** | Develop user-friendly interfaces for operators to easily interact with the robotic system and provide comprehensive training and support. | Creating intuitive control panels with visual feedback for operators controlling warehouse picking robots. |
| ***Training and Skill Acquisition*** | Provide training programs for operators and maintenance personnel to ensure they have the necessary skills to operate and maintain the system. | Offering virtual reality (VR) training simulations for operators to learn how to operate complex robotic systems. |

## CONCLUSION

In conclusion, the incorporation of CVS into robots for assembly lines constitutes a fundamental paradigm change in the field of factory automation. CVS boosts the capabilities of robots and lets them do a wide variety of activities with accuracy and efficiency. This is accomplished by allowing robots to see and comprehend their environment. The continued research and technology breakthroughs in this sector continue to drive innovation, which promises a future in which vision-enabled robots play a vital role in contemporary production settings. Despite the fact that there are hurdles, this field continues to go forward.

## REFERENCES

[1] S.B. Billatos, and S. Vahidi, "An economic investigation of sensory manipulators in assembly lines", *Robot. Comput.-Integr. Manuf.*, vol. 6, no. 2, pp. 167-177, 1989. [http://dx.doi.org/10.1016/0736-5845(89)90102-6]

[2] F. Gomez-Estern, and F. Gordillo, "Error analysis in strapdown INS for aircraft assembly lines", In: *2008 10th International Conference on Control, Automation, Robotics and Vision*, Hanoi, Vietnam, 2008, pp. 184-189. [http://dx.doi.org/10.1109/ICARCV.2008.4795514]

[3] P. Prabakaran, Integrating Mechanical Systems with Biological Inspiration: Implementing Sensory Gating in Artificial Vision. In: *Trends and Applications in Mechanical Engineering, Composite Materials and Smart Manufacturing.* IGI Global, 2024, pp. 190-202. [http://dx.doi.org/10.4018/979-8-3693-1966-6.ch012]

[4] L. Vadivukarasi, L. G. Babu, D. S. Hasan, R. S. R., N. D. Devi, and L. Karthick, "Nurturing Trust in Human-Robot Interaction and the Crucial Role of Dialogue and Explicit AI", In: *Trends and*

*Applications in Mechanical Engineering, Composite Materials and Smart Manufacturing,* S. Padhi, Ed., IGI Global: Hershey, PA, 2024, pp. 237-252.
[http://dx.doi.org/10.4018/979-8-3693-1966-6.ch015]

[5] P. Majdzik, "Feasible Schedule Under Faults in The Assembly System", In: *2020 16th International Conference on Control, Automation, Robotics and Vision (ICARCV)*, Shenzhen, China, 2020, pp. 1049-1054.
[http://dx.doi.org/10.1109/ICARCV50220.2020.9305377]

[6] C. Mascle, "Feature-based assembly model for integration in computer-aided assembly", *Robot. Comput.-Integr. Manuf.,* vol. 18, no. 5-6, pp. 373-378, 2002.
[http://dx.doi.org/10.1016/S0736-5845(02)00030-3]

[7] S.P. Yadav, and S. Yadav, "Image fusion using hybrid methods in multimodality medical images", *Med. Biol. Eng. Comput.,* vol. 58, no. 4, pp. 669-687, 2020.
[http://dx.doi.org/10.1007/s11517-020-02136-6] [PMID: 31993885]

[8] S. Kavitha, L. Karthick, R. Prabu, S. Venkataramanan, R. P. Venkatesh, and A. U. Islam, "Utilizing Cutting-Edge Artificial Intelligence Technology in Geriatric Care Microrobotics", In: *Trends and Applications in Mechanical Engineering, Composite Materials and Smart Manufacturing,* S. Padhi, Ed., IGI Global: Hershey, PA, 2024, pp. 269-282.
[http://dx.doi.org/10.4018/979-8-3693-1966-6.ch017]

[9] S. Motavalli, and B. Bahr, "Automated tool monitoring system using vision system for a robotic cell", *Robot. Comput.-Integr. Manuf.,* vol. 10, no. 4, pp. 311-319, 1993.
[http://dx.doi.org/10.1016/0736-5845(93)90044-K]

[10] H. M. Kelagadi, R. K. Billady, R. Shanmugasundaram, K. R. Thilak, L. Karthick, and N. K. Patil, "An Enhanced Taxi Demand Perception System Leveraging Fusion and Automated Sensor Integration", In: *Trends and Applications in Mechanical Engineering, Composite Materials and Smart Manufacturing,* S. Padhi, Ed., IGI Global: Hershey, PA, 2024, pp. 35-46.
[http://dx.doi.org/10.4018/979-8-3693-1966-6.ch002]

[11] E. Oliveira, "Cooperative multi-agent system for an assembly robotics cell", *Robot. Comput.-Integr. Manuf.,* vol. 11, no. 4, pp. 311-317, 1994.
[http://dx.doi.org/10.1016/0736-5845(95)00008-9]

[12] N. Pitchandi, and S.P. Subramanian, "GA-based camera calibration for vision-assisted robotic assembly system", *IET Comput. Vis.,* vol. 11, no. 1, pp. 50-59, 2017.
[http://dx.doi.org/10.1049/iet-cvi.2016.0004]

[13] A. Rezaei Aderiani, K. Wärmefjord, and R. Söderberg, "Evaluating different strategies to achieve the highest geometric quality in self-adjusting smart assembly lines", *Robot. Comput.-Integr. Manuf.,* vol. 71, no. 102164, p. 102164, 2021.
[http://dx.doi.org/10.1016/j.rcim.2021.102164]

[14] I. K. A. Wirayasa, A. G. Chimankar, N. Madhumithaa, U. Shankar, L. Karthick, and S. Kumar J., "Machine Learning-Based HR Business Intelligence With Predictive Maintenance Integration", In: *Trends and Applications in Mechanical Engineering, Composite Materials and Smart Manufacturing,* S. Padhi, Ed., IGI Global: Hershey, PA, 2024, pp. 381-396.

[15] M. Staroswiecki, M. Bayart, and D. Jolly, "Integration of Vision, Transportation and Assembly Tasks in a Flexible Assembly Cell Using Robot Cooperation", In: *Robotics and Factories of the Future '87,* R. Radharamanan, Ed., Springer: Berlin, Heidelberg, 1988, pp. 317-324.
[http://dx.doi.org/10.1007/978-3-642-73890-6_85]

[16] J. Zhou, and J. Yu, "Chisel edge wear measurement of high-speed steel twist drills based on machine vision", *Comput. Ind.,* vol. 128, no. 103436, p. 103436, 2021.
[http://dx.doi.org/10.1016/j.compind.2021.103436]

[17] L. Zhao, J. Cheng, Z. Yin, H. Yang, M. Chen, and X. Yuan, "Research on precision automatic tool setting technology for KDP crystal surface damage mitigation based on machine vision", *J. Manuf.*

*Process.*, vol. 64, pp. 750-757, 2021.
[http://dx.doi.org/10.1016/j.jmapro.2021.02.012]

[18] L. Karthick, V. K, K. Keshamoni, B. P. Rani, R. J. K, and S. More, "A Comprehensive Review of Automation in Agriculture using Artificial Intelligence", *Proc. Int. Conf. Recent Inno. Smart and Sust. Tech. (ICRISST),* Bengaluru, India, pp. 1-5, 2024.
[http://dx.doi.org/10.1109/ICRISST59181.2024.10921963]

[19] M. Talaat, I. Arafa, and H.M.B. Metwally, "Advanced automation system for charging electric vehicles based on machine vision and finite element method", *IET Electr. Power Appl.,* vol. 14, no. 13, pp. 2616-2623, 2020.
[http://dx.doi.org/10.1049/iet-epa.2020.0380]

[20] N. Madhumithaa, G. Elangovan, S. Sridharan, L. Karthick, A. U. Islam, and R. P. Venkatesh, "Cutting-Edge AI-Powered Driverless Delivery Solution", In: *Trends and Applications in Mechanical Engineering, Composite Materials and Smart Manufacturing,* S. Padhi, Ed., IGI Global: Hershey, PA, 2024, pp. 131-148.
[http://dx.doi.org/10.4018/979-8-3693-1966-6.ch008]

[21] Y. Zhang, H.G. Soon, D. Ye, J.Y.H. Fuh, and K. Zhu, "Powder-bed fusion process monitoring by machine vision with hybrid convolutional neural networks", *IEEE Trans. Industr. Inform.,* vol. 16, no. 9, pp. 5769-5779, 2020.
[http://dx.doi.org/10.1109/TII.2019.2956078]

[22] Y. Guo, L. Chai, S.E. Aggrey, A. Oladeinde, J. Johnson, and G. Zock, "A machine vision-based method for monitoring broiler chicken floor distribution", *Sensors (Basel),* vol. 20, no. 11, pp. 3179-3183, 2020.
[http://dx.doi.org/10.3390/s20113179] [PMID: 32503296]

[23] Z. Liu, Y. He, C. Wang, and R. Song, "Analysis of the influence of foggy weather environment on the detection effect of machine vision obstacles", *Sensors (Basel),* vol. 20, no. 2, pp. 349-352, 2020.
[http://dx.doi.org/10.3390/s20020349] [PMID: 31936287]

[24] C. Li, Y. Huang, H. Li, and X. Zhang, "A weak supervision machine vision detection method based on artificial defect simulation", *Knowl. Base. Syst.,* vol. 208, no. 4, p. 106466, 2020.
[http://dx.doi.org/10.1016/j.knosys.2020.106466]

[25] T. Zhang, X. Hu, J. Xiao, and G. Zhang, "A machine learning method for vision-based unmanned aerial vehicle systems to understand unknown environments", *Sensors (Basel),* vol. 20, no. 11, pp. 3245-3250, 2020.
[http://dx.doi.org/10.3390/s20113245] [PMID: 32517309]

[26] A.M. Karimi, J.S. Fada, N.A. Parrilla, B.G. Pierce, M. Koyuturk, R.H. French, and J.L. Braid, "Generalized and mechanistic PV module performance prediction from computer vision and machine learning on electroluminescence images", *IEEE J. Photovolt.,* vol. 10, no. 3, pp. 878-887, 2020.
[http://dx.doi.org/10.1109/JPHOTOV.2020.2973448]

[27] Z. Jiang, M. Huang, X. Tang, and Y. Guo, "A new calibration method for joint-dependent geometric errors of industrial robot based on multiple identification spaces", *Robot. Comput.-Integr. Manuf.,* vol. 71, p. 102175, 2021.
[http://dx.doi.org/10.1016/j.rcim.2021.102175]

[28] F. Mohammadi Amin, M. Rezayati, H.W. van de Venn, and H. Karimpour, "A mixed-perception approach for safe human–robot collaboration in industrial automation", *Sensors (Basel),* vol. 20, no. 21, p. 6347, 2020.
[http://dx.doi.org/10.3390/s20216347] [PMID: 33171709]

[29] S.S. Kadam, "Harnessing machine learning approaches for accurate energy demand forecasting in the power sector", *Proc. 2024 2nd Int. Conf. on Networking, Embedded and Wireless Systems (ICNEWS),* pp. 1-6, 2024.
[http://dx.doi.org/10.1109/ICNEWS60873.2024.10731096]

[30] A. Ranjan, and S.M. Azeemuddin, "Image denoising using convolutional neural network", *Proc. 2022 4th Int. Conf. on Advances in Computing, Communication Control and Networking (ICAC3N),* pp. 2315-2319, 2022.Greater Noida, India.
[http://dx.doi.org/10.1109/ICAC3N56670.2022.10074437]

[31] A. Ranjan, and M. Ravinder, "VAEWGAN-NCO in image deblurring framework using variational autoencoders and Wasserstein generative adversarial network", *Signal Image Video Process.,* vol. 18, no. 5, pp. 4447-4456, 2024.
[http://dx.doi.org/10.1007/s11760-024-03085-5]

[32] M. Umar, M. Gupta, R. Verma, and N. Dhanda, Role of Computer Vision in Manufacturing Industry. In: *Machine Vision and Industrial Robotics in Manufacturing.* CRC Press, 2024, pp. 14-35.
[http://dx.doi.org/10.1201/9781003438137-2]

[33] A.E. Peters, S. Juliet, and J. Anitha, "Revolutionizing car assembly line efficiency using multi-object detection and tracking", *3rd Int. Conf. on Artificial Intelligence For Internet of Things (AIIoT),* pp. 1-6, 2024.
[http://dx.doi.org/10.1109/AIIoT58432.2024.10574552]

[34] A. Arya, Beyond Syntax and Semantics: The Quantum Leap in Natural Language Processing. In: *A Handbook of Computational Linguistics: Artificial Intelligence in Natural Language Processing.* Bentham Science Publishers, 2024, pp. 255-284.
[http://dx.doi.org/10.2174/97898152384881240200015]

[35] W. Li, H. Zhang, and X. Wang, "Construction of Intelligent Chassis Assembly Line based on Machine Vision and Industrial Robot", *Highlights in Science, Engineering and Technology,* vol. 15, pp. 80-88, 2022.
[http://dx.doi.org/10.54097/hset.v15i.2207]

[36] A. Das, M. Diu, N. Mathew, C. Scharfenberger, J. Servos, A. Wong, J.S. Zelek, D.A. Clausi, and S.L. Waslander, "Mapping, planning, and sample detection strategies for autonomous exploration", *J. Field Robot.,* vol. 31, no. 1, pp. 75-106, 2014.
[http://dx.doi.org/10.1002/rob.21490]

# CHAPTER 15

# Smart Farming with Deep Learning: Enhancing Crop Management through Advanced Image Analysis

**Ravi Prakash Chaturvedi**[1], **Annu Mishra**[2,*], **Poorva Nayyar**[3], **Sameer Asthana**[4], **Mohd Shaliyar**[1] and **Rajneesh Kumar Singh**[1]

[1] *Department of Computer Science and Applications, Sharda School of Engineering and Technology, Greater Noida, Uttar Pradesh, India*

[2] *Department of Computer Science and Engineering, Sharda School of Engineering and Technology, Greater Noida, Uttar Pradesh, India*

[3] *Software Developer, Carry more hoists Pvt. Ltd, Faridabad, Haryana, India*

[4] *Department of Computer Science and Applications, Greater Noida Institute of Technology (GNOIT), Greater Noida, Uttar Pradesh, India*

**Abstract:** A type of advanced image processing and data technologies for analysis with promising outcomes is called deep learning, or DL. In addition to being used in many other industries, DL is also being used in agriculture. Because deep learning algorithms provide precise predictions and sophisticated image processing, they have completely changed several industries, particularly agriculture. This study provides a comprehensive overview of study results and publications on deep learning methods for agricultural image processing and prediction and their variations, emphasizing the uses of these networks in weed proof of identity, irrigation administration, disease identification, and crop yield prediction. This work focuses on specific agricultural issues, the model and architecture that were employed, the resources from which the data were gathered, the data preparation process, and the overall operation carried out in compliance with the methodology applied to each investigation project. Additionally, we examine numerous deep learning approaches used in other fields and also contrast them with current methodologies. When it comes to regression and classification performance, deep machine learning performs differently from more traditional methods. Our results show that deep machine learning yields results with excellent accuracy. Compared to conventional photographic processing techniques, these outcomes are far more accurate. In addition to classification tasks, deep learning can be used for yield manufacturing, detection, and disease division.

* **Corresponding author Annu Mishra:** Department of Computer Science and Engineering, Sharda School of Engineering and Technology, Greater Noida, Uttar Pradesh, India; E-mail: pandey_annu18@yahoo.com

**Ravinder M., Arti Ranjan, Youddha Beer Singh (Eds.)**

**Keywords:** Convolutional neural networks, Crop production, Deep learning application in farming, Disease prediction, Remote sensing.

## INTRODUCTION

India's food consumption is rising quickly, yet the nation's arable land and resource availability are constrained. As a result, it is imperative to address the requirement for agricultural output in a more clever and effective way [1, 2]. Crop yield has emerged as a major worry in the agricultural industry. Deep learning algorithms are being applied to agricultural applications for image processing and prediction, driven by the increased demand for environmentally friendly and efficient farming methods. India's food consumption is rising quickly, yet the nation's arable land and resource availability are constrained. As a result, it is imperative to handle the requirement for producing food in an increasingly clever and effective way [3].

Agriculture is the use of the natural environment to produce food, and it has been done for hundreds of thousands of years. In the majority of nations, it is regarded as the main source of employment [4]. But historically, farmers did not know much about crop yields, different kinds of soil, weather patterns, or how to utilize inputs correctly. This led to issues including poor irrigation, failed crops, and haphazard modifications to farming methods. Due to resource constraints and smaller parcels of land, these problems were easier to handle in the past. But as farms grew larger and were split into larger hectares, it quickly became clear that efficient management and the observation of agricultural data were required [5].

Failing to do so may lead to additional issues and higher manufacturing expenses. This is one area where the most recent digital technologies' enormous potential is useful. Agriculture is moving closer to industrialization thanks in large part to the benefits that these developments offer [6]. Well-informed farmers can practice crop choosing based on the condition of the soil, best irrigation practices, and general management of farms by utilizing the strength of data analytics. They can increase output, cut down on resource waste, and lessen their influence on the natural world as a result. Artificial intelligence also provides farmers with up-to-date data on the weather, enabling them to modify their plans as necessary. Additionally, it enables them to remotely monitor crop development and health, quickly detecting and addressing problems such as pests or illnesses [7, 8]. All things considered, artificial intelligence is a paradigm change for the farming sector. It makes it possible to use data, technology, and knowledge to maximize agricultural output on a larger scale. Agriculture can keep developing, satisfy the needs of an expanding population, and help ensure an adequate supply of food in the decades to come by accepting these digital breakthroughs [9]. Out of 755 papers published in various journals, the major focus was on Disease Detection (449 papers), 231 papers on Yield Prediction, 41 papers on Weed Detection Techniques, 24 papers on Crop Rotation Techniques, and 10 papers on Species or Plant type Detection. Through this, we can learn that the major focus is on disease detection, which is very important as this will increase the volume of crop production effectively via utilizing the least amount of resources.

## LEARNING MODELS

Warren McCulloch and Walter Pitts established DL in 1943. Many DL models have now been produced. Knowledge about the models produced throughout 2017 and 2021 is compiled here. During that particular period, researchers produced a large number of models. We'll review the most popular models. CapsuleNet, IRCNN, RefineNet, and Mask-RCNN are among the models that the authors published in 2017 [11]. The DL model is still being developed. DeepLab and DCRN are some of them. Google AI created EfficiantNet, which is again a well-defined model.

This concept has since piqued the curiosity of other scholars. A United Model constructed around the CNN was planned in 2020 [12]. Later, ConvXGB—which depends on CNN and XGBoost proposed by Chen *et al.* —was also released. The aforementioned paperwork is summarized in Figs. (**1**, and **2**) give a broader overview of the advancement of various DL models from 2017 to 2021.

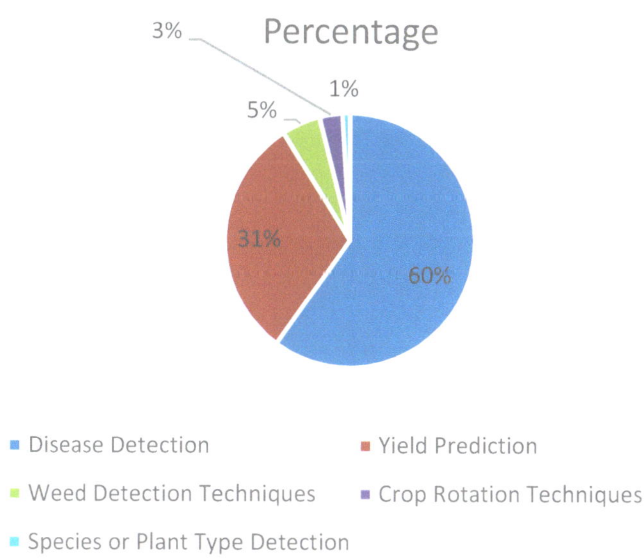


**Fig. (1).** A pie chart shows how the articles are distributed based on the preference [10].

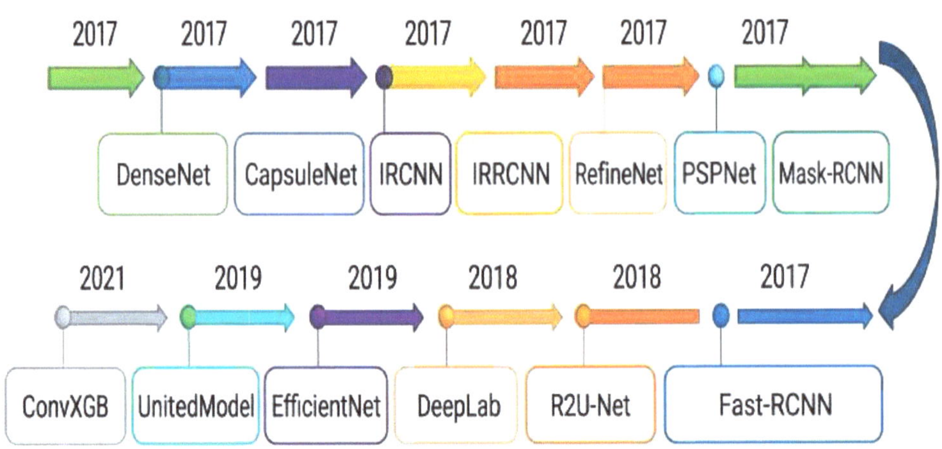


**Fig. (2).** An illustration of the advancement of various DL models through 2017 to the present [13].

## CNN

A specific kind of ANN utilized for image identification is called CNN. There are many hidden layers in CNN. It gains the fundamental characteristics from the input signal. The layer that pools data is placed after the convolution layer [14]. The configuration of operations for pooling depends on the applications. The most common uses of the pooling procedure are to decrease the dimensions and identify the most important feature. Following a sequence of convolution and pooling layers, the layer that is completely linked, which may consist of any number of layers, is the last layer in the CNN framework [15].

## DNN

In DNN, input flows from the input layer to the output layer, moving forward through layers without ever touching a node again. A layered representation of a particular item is used as a mix of fundamental images in compositional designs created by DNN architectures [16]. By recording high-level patterns in progressively larger layers, the cloud's enormous datasets allow for the development of more accurate models. The development process of a neural network is represented by its two stages, inference and training [17].

## RNN

An RNN has loops that let the network retain data. RNNs, to put it simply, forecast upcoming occurrences by applying their prior experience-based reasoning. Although recurrent models may sequence vectors, they are helpful in enabling the API to perform more complicated tasks. RNNs are frequently employed for temporal or ordinal problems in speech recognition, NLP, and language translation [18].

### DCNN

DCNN is a type of DL technique that employs an increased number of hidden layers—typically greater than five—to increase data extraction and prediction accuracy. Although the second type of DCNN improves the total number of nodes in the hidden layer, the first type improves the number of hidden layers. Using unprocessed data, it has been extensively and successfully applied to computer vision tasks like picture categorization, identifying objects, and localization [19, 20].

### AlexNet

Alex Krizhevsky is the creator of AlexNet. In ILSVRC 2010, it outperformed other contemporary technologies in terms of image classification from ImageNet. AlexNet has eight layers: three fully connected levels and five layers that are convolutional. Some of its characteristics include overlapping pooling, multiple GPUs, and ReLU nonlinearity [21]. Even with the most difficult data sets, the highly accurate AlexNet model can produce results. If you take out the convolutional layer, it performs much worse. It has several potential applications in visual computing and artificial intelligence and serves as the basis for all types of object retrieval. In the years to come, AlexNet might be more widely used for processing AlexNet images than CNNs [22].

### ResNet

ResNet enables users to prepare hundreds or even thousands of layers while still achieving outstanding outcomes. Its strong representation capabilities have enhanced the effectiveness of complex applications, including image recognition. ResNet has many forms: ResNet-18, ResNet-152, *etc*. [23].

### CaffeNet

CaffeNet represents a particular kind of AlexNet. It is a classification CNN that works for visual recognition. CaffeNet and AlexNet differ primarily in that the former refrains from relighting data augmentation during training and from pooling before normalization [24].

## Inception Model

Inception modules are 1 × 1 convolutions, resulting in more complex networks and more effective calculations. These components are made to address issues like overfitting and computational strain. To put it succinctly, the approach is to employ different kernel sizes on CNN and set their operating degrees in the identical sequence. Versions such as Inception V1, also known as GoogLeNet, Inception versions, and ResNet are among them [25].

## R-FCN

A region-based object detector corresponds to R-FCN. R-FCN, in contrast to earlier region-based detectors for objects like Fast/Faster R-CNN, is completely convolutional. Unlike previous per-region network detection devices, the computation is distributed throughout the whole image [26].

## VGG16

OxfordNet, frequently referred to as the VGG16 CNN architecture, won the 2014 ILSVRC (ImageNet) competition. A publication by K. Simonyan and A. Zisserman from the University of Oxford titled "Very deep convolutional neural networks for massive operations image recognition" introduced this model. This is one of the best model frameworks currently on the market. As its name suggests, VGG16 has sixteen layers [27].

## VGG19

The CNN building model is VGG19. The Visual Geometry Group created this architecture back in 2014. Like its moniker, VGG19s, it has 19 layers total, of which 3 are fully linked layers, and 16 are convolutional layers. It is renowned for being uncomplicated. The kernel size of each convolution layer is 3x3. Despite its simplicity, the algorithm has achieved a notable level of classification accuracy [28].

## DRL

Combining RL and DL, DRL is a fast-growing area since it is capable of handling a wide variety of complex decision-making duties that were previously thought impossible for a machine with intelligence comparable to human ones to do [29].

## LSTM

LSTMs are a form of RNN developed in the 1990s. Although they utilize memory gates to solve the gradient that diminishes the issue, which involves they being currently widely used for statistical analysis of time series and image sound [30].

### LeNet

Yann LeCun's CNN framework is called LeNet. LeNet, in general, means LeNet5, a straightforward CNN. One MLNN that is trained with a reverse propagation algorithm is LeNet5. This design's primary goal is to identify characters that have been machine-printed and handwritten [31].

## USAGE OF DEEP LEARNING IN THE FARMING SECTOR

The usage of modern technologies, including drones, robots, and sensors on agricultural equipment, has significantly changed farmers' field management knowledge through electronic integration. These developments are motivating data analysts and agricultural scientists to develop analytical tools and protocols to streamline the administration of fields and more precisely address the issues that are now being encountered [32]. These innovative technologies need skilled guidance to address farmers' needs and help them maximise the output of their farms through data and automated work [33].

It is difficult for current technology to guarantee the quality of food and a steady, dependable supply globally without jeopardizing the environment. A novel and state-of-the-art tool for image processing and information analysis is deep learning. It has been effectively applied in a variety of industries, especially agriculture, and has enormous potential. It also yields promising outcomes. Utilizing image-based categorization, deep learning is used in farming to increase crop yield and quality [34]. Numerous investigators have employed deep learning techniques and technologies to improve and automate activities. To help farmers efficiently handle plant leaf stress, deep learning algorithms and mathematical models are well-suited for a range of tasks [35].

Noon and colleagues (2020) suggested using deep learning in farming. Detailed knowledge is useful in identifying leaf stress in various plants. However, a vital quantity of plant-related data needs to be compiled and assessed in order to use deep learning in agriculture [36]. In essence, satellites, autonomous vehicles, drones, and Bluetooth sensors are used to collect the required data. Federated instruction was recently utilized to safeguard user privacy and data for crop recognition and yield prediction [37]. The model used for deep learning gets more reliable and useful as more data is utilized to train it. Deep learning-based agricultural applications, or "smart agriculture," are becoming more and more common. They involve using data gathered from multiple sources to monitor different agronomic operations [38]. The capacity of various AI-based systems with intelligence to gather and analyze data and assist farmers in making wise decisions varies. Models created using deep learning can be used to interpret data recorded by installed IoT nodes or sensors. A learning technique was used to impose decisions in the operational zones through actuators [39]. Smart farms also make use of other contemporary technologies, including self-distillation, federated instruction, remote sensing, global spacecraft, and geographical information [40].

## DEEP LEARNING TECHNIQUES

### Unresolved Issues with DL Methods Applied to the Farming Sector

Deep learning applications in agricultural methods have now received thorough evaluations. Koirala *et al.* have studied the application of deep learning in identifying fruits and yield calculation. Zhang *et al.* [43] looked at fruit detection and yield estimation in addition to intensive scene analysis utilizing deep learning in farming, whereas Moazzam *et al.* demonstrated the challenges of identifying weeds and crops utilizing deep learning. This paper offers a concise summary of the usage of deep learning techniques for image annotation, focusing on vegetation and agricultural regions. Table **1** summarizes the Deep Learning (DL) Techniques used in Agriculture. This is different from past research since deep learning is being applied widely in the agriculture industry [44]. Counting plants and fruits, identifying diseases, estimating productivity, segmenting, and classifying are the main application issues in the agriculture industry. There are several disadvantages to carrying out these procedures by hand, including the fact that it is difficult. The absence of manual item recognition in these tasks can be compensated for by leveraging contemporary trends and technologies, especially deep learning and image annotation methods. To identify rare plants, one must be knowledgeable about plants. In order to apply a systematic and mathematical categorization method, a significant amount of data derived from the various identified plants must be identified and categorized [45].

**Table 1. Deep learning techniques used in agriculture [41, 42].**

| S.No | Agricultural Area | Problem Description | Deep Learning Model Used |
|---|---|---|---|
| 1 | Leaf Classification | Sort the leaves of various plant species. | CNN + RandomForest classifier established by the author. |

*(Table 1) cont.....*

| S.No | Agricultural Area | Problem Description | Deep Learning Model Used |
|---|---|---|---|
| 2 | Leaf Defect Identification | Thirteen distinct plant diseases were employed on healthy. | CNN Caffeine |
| 3 | Plant Defect Identification | Identifying classifications and illnesses of the crop. | CNNs, GoogleNet AlexNet, |
| 4 | Land Cover Mapping | Finding that 21 land-use types have different spatial properties. | CNN + Multiview model averaging, as stated by the author |
| 5 | Crop Type Classification | Gather data regarding land that has been farmed. | The author clarified CNN. |
| 6 | Plant Recognition | Acknowledge the opinions of seven distinct plants: the fruit, leaf, stem, the branch, and bloom. | CNN's AlexNet |
| 7 | Plant Type Recognition | Identify 44 species distinct plant. | CNN's AlexNet |
| 8 | Plant Phenology Recognition | Charting the phenotypes of Arabidopsis across four extensions. | Long Short-Term Memory + Convolution + Neural Network |
| 9 | Crop/Weed Identification and Mapping | Plant and weed recognition, and a map of the sugar beet. | The author clarified CNN. |
| 10 | Crop Yield Evaluation | Assess the U.S. national corn harvest yield. | The writer explained CNN. |

The first stages in solving this problem are plant classification and recognition. Segmentation helps to improve accuracy while also rendering it easier to extract information from an image. In the agricultural sector, identifying diseases is a key concern. Absent an accurate diagnosis of the disease and its cause, disease control methods might be ineffective, waste time and money, and cause more plant loss. In the agricultural sector, counting is crucial for managing orchards, but it can be challenging due to overlapping and underlapping [46]. Counting and examining the leaves of a plant is the most accurate method of determining its condition and developmental stage. Evaluating agricultural production is crucial to addressing emerging issues in farming. Precise production estimates aid in the prevention of starvation by helping farmers make the best financial and managerial choices [47]. Even though Deep Learning (DL) approaches have yielded benefits in the agriculture industry, there remain unresolved issues that require attention. The following is a discussion of these obstacles:

- **Insufficient information availability:** The lack of identifiable training information is one of the primary obstacles to applying deep learning in agriculture. Large dataset collection and labelling for agriculture is a labor-intensive and costly process that reduces the accuracy of deep learning models [48].

- **Domain adaptation:** Because the agricultural settings are so diverse, models developed using information from a particular crop or region might not work well in another. As a result, DL for agriculture faces a significant problem in domain adaptation, wherein models need to adjust to different locations and crops [49].
- **Interpretability and transparency:** One of the main issues facing DL models in agriculture is their absence of these two qualities. Farmers and agronomists need to know what goes into sophisticated models' decision-making processes and what influences their results [50].
- **Robustness:** The performance of deep learning models can be significantly impacted by modifications to the surrounding environment. Designing DL models with the ability to withstand variations in weather, soil, and sunlight is crucial [51].
- **Technology adoption by farmers:** Some of the main issues with DL in agriculture are the acceptance of technology by farmers. It is necessary to provide farmers with tools and interfaces that are easy to comprehend, even for those without technical skills in using complex deep learning models [52].
- **Ethics and privacy:** The application of DL in agriculture brings up issues related to data ownership and privacy [53].

All things considered, DL approaches have a lot of promise for the agriculture industry; nonetheless, further study is required to solve these unresolved issues and provide workable, long-term solutions [54].

## APPLICATION IN FARMING

### Deep Learning-based Estimation of Crop Yield

A few studies on yield prediction have been discussed. The authors suggested a framework for agriculture based on supervised intelligent agriculture, which is utilized to build a thorough framework for yield prediction that correlates the raw data with values predicted for paddy production [55, 56]. In their suggested investigation, they developed a model termed DRQN, an RNN DL algorithm based on the Q-Learning RL approach, to compute the crop production. This effort's main goal was to increase prediction precision and reduce error in order to boost food production [57]. In a different yield prediction investigation, the scientists developed a framework for both barley and wheat crops using a DL yield prediction technique that utilized NDVI and RGB data obtained from UAVs [58]. The model's primary objective was to increase efficiency and offer a precise estimation of yield utilizing RGB photos. The authors of the study create a DCNN structure for automatically identifying and categorizing a number of abiotic and biotic crop stresses using field photos [59]. The work used the VGG16 CNN model to autonomously categorize distorted photos of rice crops that were collected during the period of growth. The median accuracy of the model that was trained increased to 92.89%. The authors of a different study put out a DL framework to forecast yield based on environmental data and CNN and RNN-based optimization methods [60]. This algorithm's RMSE for predicting corn and soybean yields was 9% and 8% of their respective average yields, respectively. The authors suggest three models for predicting soybean crop yield: CNN, LSTM, and DNN. The % error in this study is 2.70, while the RMSE is 0.81. The BBI model was proposed by the authors as a combination of two BPNNs and one IndRNN. In various seasons, this algorithm is capable of producing precise forecasts. The authors of one study on yield prediction suggested using a DNN-based model for yield prediction. With a 12% RMSE of average yield, this model predicts corn with exceptional accuracy. In order to predict production, the researchers in charge of the research created a hybrid model that combines CNN and LSTM. This model's RMSE of 8.24% indicates its good performance. Future improvements in yield accuracy for forecasting for other crops, like corn, wheat, and potatoes, may be possible with this suggested strategy. Additionally, the authors used CNN and LSTM networks to create a model in their subsequent work. Using the recorded images, they trained CNN-LSTM, convolutional LSTM, and 3D-CNN architectures. Researchers have attained 5.51% MAPE using the 3D-CNN model. Ultimately, a DNN-based framework for choosing crops and yield prediction was created. The goal of this model is to improve prediction and output [61, 62].

Deep learning-trained models have been used in recent years to forecast crop yield. You *et al.* employed deep learning techniques, including recurrent and convolutional neural networks, among others, to forecast the quantity of soybeans that may be harvested in the US based on a sequence of remotely sensed images captured before the actual harvest [63]. The approach they used outperformed the traditional remote sensing-based approaches by 15 percentage points in terms of Mean Absolute Percentage Error (MAPE). The real yields of crops and projections for these yields have an immediate bearing on the annual economics of the entire globe and the country, and are particularly important to the food sector as suggested by Hayes, M.J., and others [64]. Research has demonstrated that augmenting the volume of water utilized for irrigation doesn't invariably culminate in a rise in crop productivity. Therefore, it is critical to create irrigation systems that are more successful and to maximize water utilization. Estimating the yield determined by the many kinds of irrigation that are employed is one method of process optimization. CNN and WS demonstrated the highest fruit detection efficiency, with R2 = 0.826. Using the framework of AlexNet, Habaragamuwa *et al.* Habaragamuwa created a region-based CNN (R-CNN) model to distinguish between ripe and unripe strawberries in greenhouse photos. The model's average accuracy was 82.61% [65, 66].

The Mango-YOLO gave better results in terms of memory consumption, quickness, and accuracy. Utilizing the SSD network, Liang *et al.* were able to identify mango and almond in tree fruits. When it came to identifying mangoes on trees, the SSD model using methods for data enhancement and a smaller conventional box performed better than the original SSD network. FR-RCNN with VGG16, given by Stein *et al.* was used to recognize and distinguish between fruit in a mango orchard. For training, three datasets were used. In the first, a single perspective of an apple tree was shown; in the second, two perspectives were shown; and in the third, several perspectives were shown. Upon being trained on images from bothperspectives, the model demonstrated exceptional performance (R2.90).YOLO-V3, which uses DenseNet as its foundation, was created by Tian *et al.* to locate fruits on trees. For instruction, two datasets were utilized [67]. The first featured photographs of apples at a certain stage of growth and development, the second featured images of apples at different stages throughout maturity. They found that, with respect to the F1 score, the model trained with the first dataset performed better than the model trained on the following one. The count of fruits and fruit size were estimated by Apolo-Apolo *et al.* using a Long Short-Term Memory (LSTM) model and a Faster R-CNN model. The model's average standard error (SE) between visual identification of fruits and counting was determined to be 6.59% [68].

For estimating the total yield as well as the yield per tree, an LSTM model was trained. A standard deviation of SD = 0.96 kg and an estimated error of SE = 4.53% were found when the actual yields per plant were juxtaposed to the estimates. CNN frameworks have been employed by most researchers in this review. Convolutional neural network (CNN) models are a good fit for agricultural applications because of a number of their advantages. Capacity to manage big datasets: CNN models are able to manage big datasets that contain highly dimensional input data, including pictures, which are frequently used in applications related to agriculture. This makes it possible for models to pick up intricate patterns and characteristics that are crucial for forecasting yields, disease detection, and crop recognition [69].

- **Repellant to disturbance and mutability:** Because of development stages, the climate, and lighting, agricultural photographs frequently include noise and unpredictability. CNN models can be used to discern between significant features and noise since they are resilient to such fluctuations [70].

- **Meta learning:** CNN models can be further refined on a smaller dataset in a different domain (like agricultural photos) after being trained on larger datasets in one domain (like natural photographs). This makes it possible to apply knowledge gained in one domain to a different one, and can increase the model's accuracy even in the case of sparse data.
- **Instantaneously making decisions:** CNN models are capable of being trained to recognize pests or illnesses in crops in the present moment, as well as forecast yield. This can assist farmers in making prompt judgments and executing the required activities to minimize losses and boost output [71].
- **Cost-effectiveness:** CNN models have the potential to lower expenses and boost profitability by reducing the requirement for physical labor and the application of fertilizers and insecticides. In addition to these benefits, CNN models are a useful tool in agriculture since they can increase the availability of food, decrease the need for fertilizers and pesticides, and increase crop output. Convolutional neural network (CNN) models offer a number of benefits for usage in agriculture, but it is important to take some disadvantages into account as well.
- **Large datasets are necessary for CNN models to function well:** Yet, in some agricultural applications, obtaining these kinds of datasets might be challenging. Big data sets can be expensive as well as laborious to gather and annotate, and the level of detail of the dataset has a big impact on the model's accuracy [72].
- **Sensitivity depends on external factors:** Variations in illumination, weather, and growth phases can all have an impact on how well CNN models operate. Because of this, deploying models in the field, wherever the environment can be quite unpredictable, can be difficult.
- **Restricted interpretability:** Due to their difficulty in interpretation, CNN models are frequently referred to as "black boxes." This can make it difficult to describe the model's method of decision-making and pinpoint the precise characteristics and tendencies that are crucial for classification.
- **Insufficient generalizability:** CNN models might not adapt well to novel crop species or datasets. Because of this, scaling up to larger farming operations or using the models in various contexts may prove difficult [73].
- **Cost and technical specifications:** Employing CNN models in agriculture can be more expensive and technically complex if specific gear, software, and trained workers are needed for implementation and deployment. These disadvantages emphasize how crucial it is to carefully balance the advantages and disadvantages of employing CNN models for particular applications in agriculture and to make sure that such models' benefits surpass any possible drawbacks [74].

## Identification of Diseases

One of the many crucial problems in agriculture is managing pests and illnesses in greenhouses and outdoors (on agricultural land). The most popular method of pest control is to spray insecticides across the growing area evenly. Even while this method works well, it is expensive and bad for the environment [75]. Environmental effects can include overproduction in agriculture, secondary harm from groundwater pollution, effects on local ecosystems and fauna. DL techniques can bring the issues down to a level that is workable. Pre-trained models, such as VGG19, are given to the authors for the purpose of categorizing diseases in potato leaves, including initial blight, late blight, and healthy [76].

Their accuracy rate is 97.8%. CNN is used by the authors of another research investigation to identify five different tomato leaf diseases. Their accuracy was 99.84%. The authors use two pre-trained DL architectures, AlexNet and VGG16, to identify tomato crop illness and classify the data. In their experiments, they achieved 97.49% accuracy for AlexNet and 97.29% accuracy for VGG16 net. In a different study, the authors examined the ability of three deep learning models—AlexNet, GoogleNet, and ResNet—to detect tomato leaf disease. After that, they used the SGD optimization technique in conjunction with ResNet to get the best accuracy of 97.28%. In a different study, the scientists detected tomato leaf disease using Google's previously trained CNN model, called inception-v3 [77].

There are three classifications for leaf pesticide intensity: good, moderate, and terrible. They were 99% accurate. Since CNN automatically extracts features by analyzing the raw images right away, the authors utilize it to detect wheat crop problems. Their suggested approach achieved an accuracy of 84.54%. In a different study, the authors used a CNN model to identify mango plant damaged leaves. With an accuracy rate of 96.67%, their suggested model can identify five different types of mango leaf diseases. An MCNN was suggested in the following research as a way to categorize mango leaves affected by the fungus anthracnose. Their suggested model has a 97.13% accuracy rate in differentiating diseased leaves from the fungal illness anthracnose. For the purpose of identifying and categorizing soybean plant diseases, the authors created a CNN model centered on the LeNet architecture [78]. This model was accurate to 99.32% and functioned well. The authors of the following research developed a DCNN to recognize cucumber diseases based just on their symptoms. Images of cucumber leaves taken in the field were sliced to produce the images of symptoms. This model's accuracy of 93.4% resulted in a significant recognition outcome. The authors of a study suggested LeNet, a slightly altered CNN model. Utilizing a simple approach, these models were primarily used for identifying illnesses in tomato leaves. An accuracy of 94–95% was achieved on average by this model. To identify rice plant illnesses, the authors of a study created a DL system using the VGG16 architecture. However, the limited dataset resulted in insufficient detection accuracy, with the model's test accuracy only reaching 60%. In a research work, the scientists proposed using DL-based GoogLeNet and Cifar10 models to recognize leaf diseases. The objective of this model is to reduce the total number of network parameters while improving the accuracy of maize leaf disease recognition [79]. The mean accuracy of the Cifar10 and GoogLeNet models was 98.8% and 98.9%, respectively.The authors suggested a technique for identifying rice diseases that uses CNN. To create the dataset, photos of both healthy and diseased rice stems and foliage were gathered from the rice experimental area. The accuracy of this suggested model is 95.48%. The investigators of the subsequent study proposed a poorly supervised DL architecture for the detection and classification of wheat diseases. To train the dataset, two distinct architectures—VGG-FCN-VD16 and VGG-FCN-S—were used. 95.12% and 97.95% rates of recognition were attained by the system, respectively. Among the oldest and most significant crops in the world is paddy [80]. Paddy leaf disease is not well known among many farmers. Here, a few studies on the use of DL to identify and categorize illnesses of paddy leaves are presented. The researchers of a different study presented AlexNet, a unique DL classification method. Diseases of paddy leaves, such as bacterial leaf blight, brown spots, and leaf smut, are identified using this model. Their suggested model has a 99.42% accuracy rate. As per their proposal, the scientists have employed machine learning and image processing techniques to effectively identify and categorize pests and diseases. The CNN method is used to categorize the images using five layers [81]. Four types of leaves can be identified by their suggested model: healthy, leaf blast, brown spot, and hispa. The accuracy of the mathematical equation was 93.6%. The investigators of the research suggested a DCNN model for categorizing illnesses of rice plants. SVM was utilized for classification, and AlexNet was employed for feature extraction. Six hundred and nineteen photos depicting various rice diseases were gathered from actual field settings, falling into four categories: (a) Rice Blast, (b) Sheat Blight, (c) Bacterial Leaf Blight, and (d) Healthy Leaf. The suggested model classified rice diseases with 91.37% accuracy for 80% - 20% training-testing partitions. The investigators of the following research suggested using a DCNN model to classify rice cultivars according to photographs of their leaves in terms of health state. Using transferred learning from an Alexnet Deep network, the three classes of classifiers were applied to represent functioning properly, snail-infested, and typical plants. The network has demonstrated good performance, with a 91.23% accuracy rate [82]. The CaffeNet model is an open-source deep learning framework that was proposed by its creators. They have optimized CaffeNet using a limited batch size of training and testing images due to GPU memory constraints. The CaffeNet architecture comprises eight layers: three fully connected and five convolutional. Considering an accuracy rate of 87%, the proposed model can categorize 13 different types of paddy illnesses and pests. Crop diseases pose the biggest threat to food security. Sharadha *et al.* presented a deep learning-based approach for diagnosing plant diseases in 2016. The researchers further classified the data using a publicly available dataset that included both healthy and ill leaves. The accuracies of the two models were 98.21% for GoogleNet and 99.35% for AlexNet [83]. A deep learning model was developed by Ramcharan *et al.* to identify cassava disease. "The original cassava dataset" is what they use. Deep convolution networks were used for the classification. When implemented with the Inception v3 deep learning model, convolutional neural networks with little sensory information might be employed for in-field identification of diseases employing transfer learning. Using high-resolution in-situ pictures captured by cameras to detect pests and diseases [84].

A deep learning model was proposed by Konstantinos P. Ferentinos *et al.* to detect plant diseases. The current research used a public dataset of 87,848 images. 25 distinct plants, including healthy ones, from 58 classes of pairings were used to train the models. After training many model structures, the [plant, sickness] pair detection model performed best in VGG, scoring 99.53% [85, 86]. On 17,548 unseen photos, the suggested technique obtained an accuracy of 99.53%. A crucial piece of technology for picture classification is deep learning. Plant diseases were classified and identified using this method. The strategy's positive results cover up challenges that are rarely taken into account in research. In a presentation he gave, Jayme discussed the several obstacles scientists face when applying deep learning techniques to the diagnosis of plant diseases, as well as some potential directions for the field.

A deep convolutional neural network was proposed by Gerrit Polder *et al.* for the automatic identification of the Tulip Breaking Virus (TBV). Parts of the data from the 2012 experiment are analyzed using a Faster R-CNN network in this inquiry. The outputs show that the outcomes are the same as those from the previous method, which just used RGB data. Convolutional Neural Networks (CNN), which are useful in the field of agronomy, were employed by ArtzaiPicon *et al.*, in particular for evaluating plant symptoms via sight. In this article, the contributor offers three different CNN designs that combine contextual non-image information with crop information to create a picture-based CNN [87]. This lowers the complicated nature of disease classification assignments while enabling concurrent learning from the entire multi-crop dataset. The crop-conditional disease identification network surpassed all previous methods and removed 71% of its misclassifications with a balanced accuracy of 0.98.

Concatenating contextual information at the component vectors level does this. Hernandez *et al.* developed a probabilistic programming system that employs unpredictability as a classification parameter for the diagnosis of plant diseases using contemporary Bayesian deep learning algorithms [88]. The results show that Bayesian inference offers classification accuracy for models developed using deep learning that is on par with conventional optimization methods. The suggested method approximates the posterior density for an agriculturally identified disease challenge while quantifying the ambiguity of forecasts for out-of-sample events [89]. Lee *et al.* offered a novel viewpoint on deep learning-based plant disease characterisation. This study focused on the application of convolutional neural networks. The authors' first decision was to refine a previously trained model for either recognizing plants or objects in general. The authors illustrated how learned qualities differ in methodology and are not always focused on the affected area, using visualization techniques. As a result, they offer a more reasonable plan that takes into account illnesses unrelated to agriculture. It outperforms the traditional crop-disease pair method, as shown by J. Chen *et al.*, especially when used to crops that weren't included in the training dataset. As a result, research in the future needs to reconsider how agricultural diseases are classified. A transfer learning-based method for diagnosing plant diseases was presented by Junde Chen et al [90].

Deep learning algorithms were provided by Lilian Mkonyi *et al.* for recognizing TutaAbsoluta in tomato plants. The authors presented a deep learning method for detecting the invasion of Tutaabsoluta, a tomato leaf miner insect. The classifiers were trained using convolutional neural network architectures (VGG16, VGG19, and ResNet50) using a dataset that was collected in the field and included both normal and diseased tomato leaves. The authors' assessment of each classifier's effectiveness was based on how well the tomato canopy was accurately categorized into the various categories. The results of the experiment showed that VGG16 had the best accuracy (91.9%) for classifying leaves from tomato plants into the relevant groups. An immediate time disease detection system for maize plants was described by Sumita Mishra *et al.* [91].

The findings demonstrated that professionals and farmers are capable of handling pests in soybean fields with the use of the studied models. Wu and colleagues presented a method for categorizing wheat grains utilizing deep learning techniques. In this work, deep learning was employed to overcome the constraints of picture processing. Six backdrops, two image capturing equipment, and three different varieties of wheat grains, totaling 1748 photographs with varying heights, perspectives, and grain counts, were used. Every image underwent rotation, flipping, colorization, and training, validation, and testing using hand-annotated datasets. An FRCNN was created using TensorFlow [92]. The ability to recognize and count wheat grains has been enhanced by the application of transferable knowledge. Assuming a model loss that was less than 0.5, the accuracy of the model was 0.91. Over two-thirds of the global population is fed either rice or wheat, which are both grown in different regions of China and other Asian countries. However, a number of diseases can impede the growth of rice and wheat, reducing yields and possibly even causing famine in some areas. A deep learning model for rice disease detection was proposed by Krishnamoorthy N *et al.* To identify diseases in rice leaves, Z. Jiang *et al.* developed a model based on the ResNetV2 CNN model, which was used in conjunction with transferred learning. The suggested model's classification parameters were changed to produce an accuracy of 95.67%. A model for identifying rice illnesses was put up by Jiang *et al.*

Plant diseases have been diagnosed using hybrid models. Bedi *et al.* [93] proposed a research concept for an independent plant disease identification system that included a CAECNN hybrid model. The suggested hybrid model recognizes bacterial spot infections in peach plants by looking at pictures of their leaves. This technique is applicable to the detection of any plant disease. The PlantVillage dataset was used to make the photos of the peach leaves. With 9914 training variables, the suggested approach achieved test accuracy of 98.38% and training accuracy of 99.35%. Plant diseases were categorized in the beginning stages using a research study presented by Nandhini *et al.* By combining RNN and CNN (G-RecConNN), a novel sequential image classification model known as the gated recurrent convolutional neural network (G-RCNN) was developed to identify diseases. An RNN is utilized to determine the temporal properties between the photographs in the sequences, while a CNN is used to derive potential characteristics from the images in each sequence. The GRecConNN model was applied to farmer assistance initiatives that evaluate ongoing pictures of banana trees, either fully or partially, for the purpose of early disease identification, based on the experimental outcomes. Real-time diagnosis of these disorders is challenging. Iqbal Khan *et al.* proposed a deep learning-based approach to quickly and effectively identify the signs of apple disease. There are two phases to the suggested system. Employing a lightweight classification framework created especially for this task, the input photographs were initially divided into groups for damaged, diseased, and healthy images. Only when a disease is discovered during the initial processing stage does the second stage, known as the detection stage, begin. Each disease is correctly identified by the detection stage based on the photos of sick leaves. The most accurate detection model's mean absolute precision (mAP) was 42%, whereas the suggested method attained a classification accuracy of approximately 88% [94].

Fan *et al.* suggested a deep learning method for plant disease diagnostics that is based on transfer learning. Researchers provide a paradigm for identifying concealed characteristics and initially propose a deep-feature descriptor constructed using transfer learning for diagnosing plant diseases. Researchers have combined handcrafted features and machine learning to extract information about leaf texture. Center loss was employed to improve the fused features' ability to be discriminated. The center loss enhances the inter-class distance while reducing the intra-class separation in order to learn compact and distinct attributes. Apple leaves and coffee leaves were the two data sets used to extensively evaluate the suggested technique 99.79%, 92.59%, and 97.12% accuracy in classification were attained using the suggested approach, respectively. The experiment's findings Table **2** proved that the suggested approach successfully captures unique characteristics of leaf diseases.

**Table 2. Disease detection tables [95, 96].**

| S.No | Crops | Model/Algorithm | Result |
|---|---|---|---|
| 1 | Potato | VGG 19 | 97.8% Accuracy |
| 2 | Tomato | CNN | 99.8% Accuracy |
| 3 | Tomato | AlexNet<br>VGG 16 net | 97.2% Accuracy<br>97.4% Accuracy |
| 4 | Tomato | Res NeT | 97.3% Accuracy |
| 5 | Tomato | Inception-v3 | 99.2% Accuracy |
| 6 | Wheat | CNN | 84.3% Accuracy |
| 7 | Mango | CNN | 96.1% Accuracy |
| 8 | Mango | MCNN | 97.2% Accuracy |
| 9 | Apple | CNN | 97.5% Accuracy |
| 10 | Soybean | CNN | 99.5% Accuracy |
| 11 | Cucumber | DCNN | 94.2% Accuracy |
| 12 | Tomato | LeNet | 93% Accuracy |
| 13 | Rice | VGG 16 | 61% Accuracy |
| 14 | Maize | GoogLeNet<br>Cifar10 | 99.1% Accuracy<br>98.9% Accuracy |
| 15 | Rice | DCNN | 95.2% Accuracy |
| 16 | Wheat | VGG-FCN-VD16<br>VGG-FCN-S | 97.3% Accuracy<br>95.7% Accuracy |
| 17 | Paddy | AlexNet | 99.6% Accuracy |
| 18 | Paddy | CNN | 92.9% Accuracy |

*(Table 2) cont.....*

| S.No | Crops | Model/Algorithm | Result |
|---|---|---|---|
| 19 | Paddy | DCNN | 90.7% Accuracy |
| 20 | Rice Plant | DCNN/AlexNet | 91.1% Accuracy |
| 21 | Paddy | CaffeNet | 86.7% Accuracy |
| 22 | Paddy | DNN_JOA | Blight 96.1%<br>Blast 99.1%<br>Sheath Rot 92.8%<br>Brown Spot 94.2% |

## Stress Detection using Deep Learning

Nilsson proposed that the plant canopy contains a variety of markers of plant stress brought on by abiotic and biotic variables. A plant's stomata close when it experiences water stress, delaying transpiration and the process of photosynthesis, which affects leaf colour and temperature. Similarly, nutritional deficiencies are often visible in the texture and colour of leaves, according to Xu *et al.* Image analysis is a useful tool for successfully identifying these changes in the patterns. Stress in plants is a major issue that costs growers a significant amount of money. The labor-intensive traditional approaches for diagnosing stressed plants limit their applications. Thus, finding prompt answers to this issue is essential. Advances in sophisticated sensing and machine learning technologies have spawned advancements in precision agriculture through big data and deep learning [97]. Plant stress is one of the biggest threats to crops, according to L. Cattivelli *et al.*, as it drastically reduces crop output and quality. A quick and accurate agricultural crop evaluation model was presented by J. Araus *et al.* for the identification and diagnosis of plant stress. Much research is now being done on the advancement of optical imaging systems for the identification of plant diseases. Optical imaging is an advancement over conventional methods that use visual scoring to rapidly and remotely quantify alterations in plant physiology caused by biotic or abiotic stressors. Crop stress has typically been detected using standard imaging [98].

According to M. Lindethal *et al.*, pictures of infrared radiation with wavelengths between 8 and 12 μm can be acquired by the use of sensors, and the pictures are commonly utilized to calculate plant temperatures and the contaminated material's temperature. Infection causes changes in plant tissues, which are linked to its consequences. It seems that temperature variations, however, have a counterproductive effect on the transpiration rate. Thermal imaging sensors, on the other hand, use variations in body temperature to detect infectious diseases [99]. Despite the fact that many of these kinds of sensors have already been utilized, this is still the case. Because supervised methods require training data in order to construct a system, using them for image analysis has grown into a standard procedure. Stress diagnosis can be achieved by the use of classifiers, shaping the process of segmentation and feature extraction techniques. Furthermore, a large range of currently available image analysis systems is based on ML algorithms that look for the optimal results in an elevated dimensionality space of features, according to A. Bauer *et al.*, deep learning is a crucial element for improving image analysis systems. In order to convert input images into outputs (such as photographs of people who are healthy or under stress), deep neural networks use numerous layers for acquiring sophisticated characteristics. Using filters and batch sizes corresponding to the total number of layers, each of the several hundred or solayers that make up a CNN processes images [100].

**Weed and Pest Detection**

Unwanted plants, called weeds, interfere with crops grown for food by competing for resources, which causes slower crop growth and reduced yields. Herbicides can be applied precisely to weeds once sophisticated weed detection systems identify them [101]. Bah *et al.* proposed a method that produces unsupervised datasets for training to identify weeds from photographs taken by a UAV. Kounalakis *et al.* incorporated an approach for weed detection using transfer learning methods to extract deep learning-derived features. Partel *et al.* created a smart sprayer that detects and isolates the targeted weed from other crops with high accuracy. Identifying each weed on an agricultural property is a difficult and often impractical task.

However, appropriately identifying large weeds is an essential first step in effective weed control. Different weed species may appear very similar in certain growth stages, but their life cycles, modes of reproduction, impacts on plants, and responses to environmental interventions differ significantly. In a study reported by Lottes *et al.*, a CNN-based classification system was developed using high-resolution cameras to successfully recognize and distinguish sugar beet crops from weeds in actual fields. With high precision, the system accurately identified sugar beet plants among weeds [102, 103].

A categorization vision system was proposed by F. Garibaldi *et al.* to distinguish plants individually from a collection of plants captured in a cornfield in their natural environment. The dataset included nine distinct plant species within 15,240 images, divided into three categories: Crop, NLW, and BLW. Photos were taken at different stages of plant development in these organic cornfield settings. The conventional CNN method was used to classify the plants in the dataset. The findings demonstrated that incorporating additional data, including vegetation indices, improves generalization for other areas, while modifications to the visual characteristics of images in both test and training datasets may reduce the model's accuracy [104].

Leonardo *et al.* proposed employing a CNN architecture for fruit recognition, achieving 95.68% accuracy. Dawei *et al.* [105] created a diagnostic system based on transferable knowledge to identify and evaluate ten distinct types of pests, achieving a mean accuracy of 93.84%. Chen *et al.* proposed classifying tea pests by optimizing the VGG16 network, and the outcomes showed that the classification system performed effectively. Early detection of pests is essential for reducing the need for pesticides, thereby lowering costs, minimizing environmental impact, and reducing emissions. Conversely, water sources have been contaminated by the misuse of pesticides in agriculture due to uneven application and overfertilization. In addition to poisoning the soil and harming aquatic life, this has adverse health effects. Therefore, precision agriculture technologies, which reliably detect affected areas and spray them accurately, reduce production costs while minimizing contamination, significantly mitigating these environmental risks [106].

For this reason, machine learning and image processing are essential for the rapid, simple, cost-effective, and precise identification of farming pests that affect crops. Berries and nuts are regarded as essential components of the agriculture sector. Among them is citrus, which is used as a raw material in many industries and is an excellent source of vitamin C. Diseases and pests that harm citrus crops reduce yield and quality. Technological advancements and precision farming have improved chemical control in agriculture. Shallow learning and deep learning constitute the two main types of intelligent approaches used for recognizing citrus pests and diseases [107]. Table **3** provides a comprehensive view of the weed detection tools used in the literature [108 - 112] and their accuracy.

**Table 3. Weed detection tools and its accuracy [108 - 112].**

| S.No | Functionality | Model/Algorithm | Result |
|---|---|---|---|
| 1 | Effective in Detection of Weed Crops | Inception Model-V2 | 98.2% Accuracy |
| 2 | Detection of Broad Leaf | CNN | 97.1% Accuracy |
| 3 | Object Detection of Weeds | R-FCN | 81.2% Accuracy |
| 4 | Weed Growth Stage Estimator | DCNN | 71% Accuracy |

## DISCUSSION

The integration of deep learning in agriculture significantly enhances agro-economics by optimizing various aspects of farming, leading to increased productivity and cost-efficiency. Deep learning models are used to improve crop management by predicting yields, identifying diseases, and optimizing resource use, such as water and fertilizers. These advancements allow farmers to make informed decisions that minimize waste and maximize output, thereby boosting profitability. Moreover, deep learning-driven automation, such as precision farming and autonomous machinery, reduces labor costs and increases efficiency, making agricultural operations more sustainable and economically viable. DL technologies are driving substantial economic benefits across the agricultural sector, contributing to overall food security and rural development.

With the aid of agricultural applications, farmers can increase the output of fruits and crops, which promotes financial stability and the growth of the national economy. This paper covers a variety of agricultural programs, including the implementation of deep learning methods for plant disease diagnosis. This review's primary goal was to increase crop fecundity. Several DL models have made use of self-created datasets as well as datasets from plant villages. The primary measures utilized in the models to assess their performance were F1, recall, and precision. Better accuracy is provided by the AlexNet model, which also performs better than the VGG models. Several real-time datasets were employed from a research standpoint.

Utilizing various technological innovations to upgrade and automate farming-related tasks is known as farm automation. This approach seeks to simplify labor- and time-intensive agricultural tasks for producers all around the world. Farm automation has made use of a variety of machine learning methods, and recent research has employed CNN and ResNet models in a number of investigations. Researchers generated customized datasets from the dairy farms they visited for this specific purpose. The configuration of the smart farm made use of a large variety of sensors and cameras. Techniques for farm automation have the potential to minimize agriculture's environmental effects while also boosting agricultural profitability. Software created especially for a particular location has the potential to reduce greenhouse gas emissions and the need for chemicals such as fertilizers and pesticides.

The present investigation examined a number of soil, water, and seed analysis-related aspects in an effort to improve crop and fruit performance and support national and farmer economic growth. Modern crop management relies heavily on sophisticated systems like smart irrigation, which is included in smart farming. As indicated by recommendations and recent studies, state-of-the-art irrigation techniques have clarified how farmers can better care for their crops. These developments greatly advance sustainable farming methods by encouraging healthier crop development and increased yields in addition to optimizing the use of water. A hybrid deep neural network method was introduced by Geetika *et al.* to predict evapotranspiration for reference with minimal climate data. The DeepEvap model, which depends upon an ensemble method, was also put forth by the authors. A review study on schedules for irrigation using automated decision-support methodologies was provided by Saggi *et al.* One of the most significant steps that aid crop growth is detecting weeds and pests. Since these conditions impact many crops and fruits, it is imperative to identify them in advance. Numerous CNN models, including the widely used VGG-16, AlexNet, ResNet, and VGG-16, can assist in weed and insect detection. Many researchers utilize the classification accuracy as their primary statistic.

Plants can experience stress from both natural and man-made stresses. The outside influence that lowers agricultural yield is stress. CNN, the most effective deep learning model for analyzing stress and recognition, is highlighted in this assessment of the most recent research on crop stress detection. The Kaggle dataset on biotic stress is available online, and multiple studies use the well-known miRNA concentration dataset for plant abiotic stress. For stress detection, a variety of metrics are frequently utilized, including accuracy, MSE, and precision. Crop production estimates are essential for economic expansion. These projections help decision-makers make timely decisions about imports and exports and notify them of potential declines in agricultural output. Interpretation from the algorithm cannot be done in real time even after training, since many DL techniques and models have several training parameters. In certain applications, like robotic harvesting, temporal inference is essential. The majority of these models were tested and put into practice on personal computers, which are too energy- and resource-intensive for practical use. This enables researchers to offer more sophisticated recommendations and insights to guide decisions and actions going forward, ultimately increasing productivity. Future acceptance of the DL model is expected to increase in agricultural regions, opening the door to the creation of practical, interoperable applications. It is evident that the existing approaches, which concentrate on discrete methodologies and solutions, are insufficiently connected to the cognitive resolution process. The goal, referred to as "knowledge-based agriculture," is to increase production rates and the quality of bioproducts.

## CONCLUSION

It is anticipated that agricultural areas will embrace the DL model more in the future, which will make it easier to develop useful and compatible applications. It is evident that conventional methodologies, which concentrate on standalone concepts and strategies, are not adequately coupled to the decision-making process in applications like disease detection, yield estimation, agricultural intelligence, and stress monitoring. The objective of what is known as "knowledge-based agriculture" is to raise the caliber and yield of bioproducts. Even with the encouraging outcomes, problems still exist. Among the main issues that need to be resolved include the lack of labeled agricultural datasets, the ability to comprehend models trained with deep learning, their adaptability to massive amounts of agricultural operations, and the processing requirements. Moreover, it is imperative to guarantee the resilience and applicability of deep learning algorithms in various agricultural contexts. In order to enhance forecasts and management choices in agriculture, future research may concentrate on the integration of multimodal data, such as fusing picture data with soil sensor and climate data. Furthermore, addressing transfer learning along with domain shift strategies can improve model performance in various agricultural systems and geographical locations. The advancement of AI approaches that can be explained to users can also boost their confidence and make it easier for agriculture to implement deep learning algorithms. In conclusion, through facilitating precise picture processing and prediction, deep learning algorithms have demonstrated their ability to completely transform the agricultural industry. The application of deep learning methodologies has great potential to address agricultural difficulties and change the sector into one that is more effective, sustainable, and efficient as research in this area progresses.

## REFERENCES

[1] L. K. Attri, S. Awasthi, T. P. Sharma, and P. Rathee, "A review of deep learning techniques used in agriculture", *Ecol. Inform.*, vol. 77, p. 102217, 2023. [http://dx.doi.org/10.1016/j.ecoinf.2023.102217]

[2] A. Kamilaris, and F.X. Prenafeta-Boldú, "Deep learning in agriculture: A survey", *Comput. Electron. Agric.*, vol. 147, pp. 70-90, 2018. [http://dx.doi.org/10.1016/j.compag.2018.02.016]

[3] L. Santos, F. N. Santos, P. M. Oliveira, and P. Shinde, "Deep Learning Applications in Agriculture: A Short Review", In: *Robot 2019: Fourth Iberian Robotics Conference, Advances in Intelligent Systems and Computing,* M. Silva, J. Luís Lima, L. Reis, A. Sanfeliu, D. Tardioli, Eds., Springer: Cham, Switzerland, 2020, pp. 139-151. [http://dx.doi.org/10.1007/978-3-030-35990-4_12]

[4] F. Bal, and F. Kayaalp, "Review of machine learning and deep learning models in agriculture", *Int. Adv. Res. Eng. J.,* vol. 5, no. 2, pp. 309-323, 2021. [http://dx.doi.org/10.35860/iarej.848458]

[5] P. Bharman, S. Ahmad Saad, S. Khan, I. Jahan, M. Ray, and M. Biswas, "Deep learning in agriculture: A review", *Asian J. Res. Comput. Sci.,* vol. 13, no. 2, pp. 28-47, 2022. [http://dx.doi.org/10.9734/ajrcos/2022/v13i230311]

[6] M.H. Saleem, J. Potgieter, and K.M. Arif, "Automation in agriculture by machine and deep learning techniques: A review of recent developments", *Precis. Agric.,* vol. 22, no. 6, pp. 2053-2091, 2021. [http://dx.doi.org/10.1007/s11119-021-09806-x]

[7] D.K.K. Ren, and D. Jeong, "A survey of deep learning in agriculture: Techniques and their applications", *J. Inf. Process. Syst.,* vol. 16, no. 5, pp. 1015-1033, 2020.

[8] A. Khan, A.D. Vibhute, S. Mali, and C.H. Patil, "A systematic review on hyperspectral imaging technology with a machine and deep learning methodology for agricultural applications", *Ecol. Inform.,* vol. 69, p. 101678, 2022. [http://dx.doi.org/10.1016/j.ecoinf.2022.101678]

[9] C. Wang, B. Liu, L. Liu, Y. Zhu, J. Hou, P. Liu, and X. Li, "A review of deep learning used in the hyperspectral image analysis for agriculture", *Artif. Intell. Rev.,* vol. 54, no. 7, pp. 5205-5253, 2021. [http://dx.doi.org/10.1007/s10462-021-10018-y]

[10] D. Wang, W. Cao, F. Zhang, Z. Li, S. Xu, X. Wu, F. Cao, Z. Zhang, S. Li Xu, and X. Wu, "A review of deep learning in multiscale agricultural sensing", *Remote Sens. (Basel),* vol. 14, no. 3, p. 559, 2022. [http://dx.doi.org/10.3390/rs14030559]

[11] K. Dokic, L. Blaskovic, and D. Mandusic, "From machine learning to deep learning in agriculture – the quantitative review of trends", *IOP Conf. Ser. Earth Environ. Sci.,* vol. 614, no. 1, 2020. [http://dx.doi.org/10.1088/1755-1315/614/1/012138]

[12] G. Singh, G.K. Sethi, and S. Singh, "Survey on machine learning and deep learning techniques for agriculture land", *SN Computer Science,* vol. 2, no. 6, p. 487, 2021. [http://dx.doi.org/10.1007/s42979-021-00929-6]

[13] Q. Zhang, Y. Liu, C. Gong, Y. Chen, and H. Yu, "Applications of deep learning for dense scenes analysis in agriculture: A review", *Sensors (Basel),* vol. 20, no. 5, p. 1520, 2020. [http://dx.doi.org/10.3390/s20051520] [PMID: 32164200]

[14] K. Liakos, P. Busato, D. Moshou, S. Pearson, and D. Bochtis, "Machine learning in agriculture: A review", *Sensors (Basel),* vol. 18, no. 8, p. 2674, 2018. [http://dx.doi.org/10.3390/s18082674] [PMID: 30110960]

[15] M. F. Guerri, C. Distante, P. Spagnolo, F. Bougourzi, and A. Taleb-Ahmed, "Deep learning techniques for hyperspectral image analysis in agriculture: A review", *ISPRS Open J. Photogramm. Remote Sens.,* vol. 12, p. 100062, 2024. [http://dx.doi.org/10.1016/j.ophoto.2024.100062]

[16] A. Bouguettaya, H. Zarzour, A. Kechida, and A.M. Taberkit, "Deep learning techniques to classify agricultural crops through UAV imagery: a review", *Neural Comput. Appl.,* vol. 34, no. 12, pp. 9511-9536, 2022. [http://dx.doi.org/10.1007/s00521-022-07104-9] [PMID: 35281624]

[17] K. Alibabaei, P.D. Gaspar, T.M. Lima, R.M. Campos, I. Girão, J. Monteiro, and C.M. Lopes, "A review of challenges in using deep learning for decision-making in agriculture", *Remote Sens.,* vol. 14, no. 3, p. 638, 2022. [http://dx.doi.org/10.3390/rs14030638]

[18] A Ranjan, and M Ravinder, "Deep Learning based Image Deblurring: A Comparative Survey", In: *2022 4th International Conference on Advances in Computing, Communication Control and Networking (ICAC3N)*, 2022, pp. 996-1002. [http://dx.doi.org/10.1109/ICAC3N56670.2022.10074406]

[19] G. Farjon, H. Liu, and Y. Edan, "Deep-learning-based counting methods in agriculture: A review", *Precis. Agric.,* vol. 24, no. 5, pp. 1683-1711, 2023. [http://dx.doi.org/10.1007/s11119-023-10034-8]

[20] N. Mamat, M.F. Othman, R. Abdoulghafor, S.B. Belhaouari, N. Mamat, and S.F. Mohd Hussein, "Advanced technology in agriculture using image annotation and deep learning: A review", *Agriculture,* vol. 12, no. 7, p. 1033, 2022. [http://dx.doi.org/10.3390/agriculture12071033]

[21] K.P. Kumar, B. Singh, K.V. Malini, A. Ranjan, S.D. Bonde, S. Rout, and A. Firos, "IoT and machine learning based plant disease classification", *IJFANS,* vol. 11, no. 8, pp. 415-423, 2022.

[22] R. Salama, F. Al-Turjman, P. Chaudhary, and S. P. Yadav, "Benefits of Internet of Things (IoT)

Applications in Health care - An Overview", *Proc. Int. Conf. Comput. Intell. Commun. Technol. Netw. (CICTN),* Ghaziabad, India, pp. 778-784, 2023.

[23] S.P. Yadav, "An improved image compression framework using tetrolet transformation", *Multimedia Tools Appl.,* vol. 84, no. 6, pp. 3305-3338, 2025. [http://dx.doi.org/10.1007/s11042-024-20578-0]

[24] P. Darwin, "Dharmaraj, S. Prince, D. E. Popescu, and D. J. Hemanth, "Recognition of bloom/yield in crop images using deep learning,"", *Agronomy (Basel),* vol. 11, no. 4, p. 646, 2021. [http://dx.doi.org/10.3390/agronomy11040646]

[25] M. Nagaraju, and P. Chawla, "Systematic review of deep learning techniques in plant disease detection", *Int. J. Syst. Assur. Eng. Manag.,* vol. 11, no. 3, pp. 547-560, 2020. [http://dx.doi.org/10.1007/s13198-020-00972-1]

[26] S. Coulibaly, B. Kamsu-Foguem, D. Kamissoko, and D. Traore, "Deep learning for precision agriculture: A bibliometric analysis", *Intelligent Systems with Applications,* vol. 16, p. 200102, 2022. [http://dx.doi.org/10.1016/j.iswa.2022.200102]

[27] L. Benos, A.C. Tagarakis, G. Dolias, R. Berruto, D. Kateris, and D. Bochtis, "Machine learning in agriculture: A comprehensive review", *Sensors (Basel),* vol. 21, no. 11, p. 3758, 2021. [http://dx.doi.org/10.3390/s21113758] [PMID: 34071553]

[28] S.T. Jagtap, K. Phasinam, T. Kassanuk, S.S. Jha, T. Ghosh, and C.M. Thakar, "Towards application of various machine learning techniques in agriculture", *Mater. Today Proc.,* vol. 51, pp. 793-797, 2022. [http://dx.doi.org/10.1016/j.matpr.2021.06.236]

[29] T.B. Shahi, C.Y. Xu, A. Neupane, and W. Guo, "Machine learning methods for precision agriculture with UAV imagery: a review", *Electronic Research Archive,* vol. 30, no. 12, pp. 4277-4317, 2022. [http://dx.doi.org/10.3934/era.2022218]

[30] A. Sharma, "Jain, P. Gupta, and V. Chowdary, "Machine learning applications for precision agriculture,"", *IEEE Access,* vol. 9, pp. 4843-4873, 2021. [http://dx.doi.org/10.1109/ACCESS.2020.3048415]

[31] K. Jhajharia, and P. Mathur, "A comprehensive review on machine learning in agriculture domain", *IAES Int. J. Artif. Intell. (IJ-AI),* vol. 11, no. 2, pp. 753-764, 2022. [http://dx.doi.org/10.11591/ijai.v11.i2.pp753-763]

[32] S.K. Chakraborty, N.S. Chandel, D. Jat, M.K. Tiwari, Y.A. Rajwade, and A. Subeesh, "Deep learning approaches in agriculture", *Neural Comput. Appl.,* vol. 34, no. 23, pp. 20539-20573, 2022. [http://dx.doi.org/10.1007/s00521-022-07744-x]

[33] Z. Li, D. Wang, T. Zhu, Y. Tao, and C. Ni, "Deep learning for non-destructive evaluation of agricultural products", *Biosyst. Eng.,* vol. 245, pp. 56-83, 2024. [http://dx.doi.org/10.1016/j.biosystemseng.2024.07.002]

[34] V.G. Dhanya, A. Subeesh, N.L. Kushwaha, D.K. Vishwakarma, T.N. Kumar, G. Ritika, and A.N. Singh, "Deep learning-based computer vision for smart agriculture", *Artificial Intelligence in Agriculture,* vol. 6, pp. 211-229, 2022. [http://dx.doi.org/10.1016/j.aiia.2022.09.007]

[35] S. Veeragandham, and S. H, "A Review on the Role of Machine Learning in Agriculture", *Scalable Comput.: Pract. Exp.,* vol. 21, no. 4, pp. 583-589, 2020. [http://dx.doi.org/10.12694/scpe.v21i4.1699]

[36] M.S. Mahmud, A. Zahid, A.K. Das, M. Muzammil, and M.U. Khan, "Deep learning for precision cattle farming", *Comput. Electron. Agric.,* vol. 187, p. 106313, 2021. [http://dx.doi.org/10.1016/j.compag.2021.106313]

[37] A. Ayaz Mirani, E. M. S. Memon, M. Qabulio, M. S. Memon, R. Chohan, and A. A. Wagan, "Machine Learning In Agriculture: A Review", *LUME,* vol. 10, no. 1, p. 5, 2021.

[38] P. Sahu, A.P. Singh, A. Chug, and D. Singh, "Machine learning techniques in agriculture: Banana crop case study", *IEEE Access,* vol. 10, pp. 87333-87360, 2022. [http://dx.doi.org/10.1109/ACCESS.2022.3199926]

[39] K.B. Koirala, "Walsh, Z. Wang, and C. McCarthy, "Deep learning for fruit detection and yield estimation,"", *Comput. Electron. Agric.,* vol. 162, pp. 219-234, 2019. [http://dx.doi.org/10.1016/j.compag.2019.04.017]

[40] V Victor, Z He, and A Nibali, "Deep learning in satellite imagery for agriculture", *arXiv preprint arXiv:2209.04112,* 2022.

[41] R.C. Poonia, V. Singh, S.R. Nayak, Ed., *Deep Learning for Sustainable Agriculture.* Academic Press, 2022.

[42] M.O. Ojo, and A. Zahid, "Deep learning in controlled environment agriculture", *Sensors (Basel),* vol. 22, no. 20, p. 7965, 2022. [http://dx.doi.org/10.3390/s22207965] [PMID: 36298316]

[43] J. Liu, L. Xu, X. Cao, K. Zhang, Q. Zhang, and Y. Cai, "Deep learning in agriculture: A review", *Proc. 2020 7th Int. Conf. Inf. Sci. Control Eng. (ICISCE),* 2020pp. 1234-1240 [http://dx.doi.org/10.1109/ICISCE50968.2020.00247]

[44] P. Rao, S. Shirgire, S. Sanganwar, K. Vyawhare, and S. R. Vispute, "Agriculture data analysis using ML and DL", *Proc. 2022 2nd Int. Conf. Intell. Technol. (CONIT),* pp. 343-355, 2022.

[45] S. Koul, "Machine learning and deep learning in agriculture", In: *Smart Agriculture: Emerging Pedagogies of Deep Learning, Machine Learning and Internet of Things,* G. S. Patel, A. Rai, N. N. Das, R. P. Singh, Eds., CRC Press: Boca Raton, FL, USA, 2021, pp. 1-9.

[46] S. I. Moazzam, U. S. Khan, M. I. Tiwana, J. Iqbal, W. S. Qureshi, and S. I. Shah, "Deep learning for weeds and crops classification", *Proc. 2019 Int. Conf. Robotics and AI (ICRAI),* pp. 1-6, 2019.

[47] Z. Zhou, Y. Majeed, G. Diverres Naranjo, and E.M.T. Gambacorta, "Crop water stress assessment using thermal imagery", *Comput. Electron. Agric.,* vol. 182, p. 106019, 2021.

[48] V. Meshram, K. Patil, V. Meshram, D. Hanchate, and S.D. Ramkteke, "Machine learning in agriculture domain: A state-of-art survey", *Art. Intel Life Sci.,* vol. 1, p. 100010, 2021. [http://dx.doi.org/10.1016/j.ailsci.2021.100010]

[49] T. Saranya, C. Deisy, S. Sridevi, and K.S.M. Anbananthen, "Deep learning and IoT for precision agriculture", *Eng. Appl. Artif. Intell.,* vol. 122, p. 106034, 2023.

[50] M. Altalak, M. Ammad uddin, A. Alajmi, and A. Rizg, "Smart agriculture applications using deep learning technologies: A survey", *Appl. Sci. (Basel),* vol. 12, no. 12, p. 5919, 2022. [http://dx.doi.org/10.3390/app12125919]

[51] L. Shuai, Z. Li, Z. Chen, D. Luo, and J. Mu, "A research review on deep learning combined with hyperspectral Imaging in multiscale agricultural sensing", *Comput. Electron. Agric.,* vol. 217, p. 108577, 2024. [http://dx.doi.org/10.1016/j.compag.2023.108577]

[52] L. Zhou, C. Zhang, F. Liu, Z. Qiu, and Y. He, "Deep learning in food: A review", *Compr. Rev. Food Sci. Food Saf.,* vol. 18, no. 6, pp. 1793-1811, 2019. [http://dx.doi.org/10.1111/1541-4337.12492] [PMID: 33336958]

[53] I. Attri, L.K. Awasthi, and T.P. Sharma, "Machine learning in agriculture: a review of crop management applications", *Multimedia Tools Appl.,* vol. 83, no. 5, pp. 12875-12915, 2023. [http://dx.doi.org/10.1007/s11042-023-16105-2]

[54] S.O. Araújo, R.S. Peres, J.C. Ramalho, F. Lidon, and J. Barata, "Machine learning in agriculture: Trends and future perspectives", *Agronomy (Basel),* vol. 13, no. 12, p. 2976, 2023. [http://dx.doi.org/10.3390/agronomy13122976]

[55] A.K. Rakhmatulin, and C. Andreasen, "Deep neural networks for weed detection", *Remote Sens.,* vol. 13, no. 21, p. 4486, 2021. [http://dx.doi.org/10.3390/rs13214486]

[56] A. Kamilaris, and F.X. Prenafeta-Boldú, "A review of the use of convolutional neural networks in agriculture", *J. Agric. Sci.,* vol. 156, no. 3, pp. 312-322, 2018. [http://dx.doi.org/10.1017/S0021859618000436]

[57] S.S. Imam, "The future of non-invasive ways to treat cancer", *Int. J. Pharm. Sci. Res.,* vol. 12, no. 8, pp. 4684-4696, 2021.

[58] S.S. Imam, and S. Agarwal, "A pragmatic approach to treat lung cancer through loading Theaflavin-3,3′-digallate and Epigallocatechin gallate in spanlastic", *Asian J. Pharm. Clin. Res.,* vol. 14, no. 11, pp. 1-8, 2021. [http://dx.doi.org/10.22159/ajpcr.2021.v14i11.42757]

[59] S.S. Imam, S.T. Imam, R. Mdwasifathar, R. Kumar, and M.Y. Ammar, "Kumar, and M. Y. Ammar, "Interaction between ACE2 and SARS-CoV-2 and use of EGCG and Theaflavin to treat COVID-19 in initial phases,"", *Int. J. Curr. Pharm. Res.,* vol. 14, no. 2, pp. 5-10, 2022. [http://dx.doi.org/10.22159/ijcpr.2022v14i2.1945]

[60] S.S. Imam, and R. Sharma, "Natural compounds: Promising way to treat lung cancer", *Int. J. Pharm. Res. Appl.,* vol. 8, no. 2, pp. 552-558, 2023.

[61] S.S. Imam, S. Sharma, D. Kumari, S. Khan, P. Pathak, and D. Katiyar, "An expedient approach to treat asthma through non-steroidal natural transferosomes aerosol system", *Innovare Journal of Medical Sciences,* vol. 10, no. 6, pp. 7-11, 2022.

[62] S.S. Imam, S.T. Imam, S. Agarwal, R. Kumar, M.Y. Ammar, M.W. Athar, and A. Akhtar, "Lung cancer therapy using naturally occurring products and nanotechnology", *Innovare Journal of Medical Sciences,* vol. 10, no. 4, pp. 1-5, 2022. [http://dx.doi.org/10.22159/ijms.2022.v10i4.44993]

[63] S. Tuba Imam, and S. Saif Imam, "The Cream which relieves the pain of Menstrual cramps without interfering with the Hormones or Period Cycle", *Research Journal of Pharmacy and Technology,* vol. 16, no. 3, pp. 1239-1246, 2023. [http://dx.doi.org/10.52711/0974-360X.2023.00205]

[64] S.S. Imam, "Topical formulation constituted with transferosomes for treatment of non-melanoma skin cancer", *Asian J. Pharm. Clin. Res.,* vol. 16, no. 5, pp. 27-32, 2023. [http://dx.doi.org/10.22159/ajpcr.2023.v16i5.47033]

[65] S.S. Imam, "Nanoparticles: The future of drug delivery", *Int. J. Curr. Pharm. Res.,* vol. 15, no. 6, pp. 8-15, 2023. [http://dx.doi.org/10.22159/ijcpr.2023v15i6.3076]

[66] S.S. Imam, S. Mehdi, and A. Mansuri, "A comprehensive review on pharmacological potential of red ginseng oil, tea tree oil and hemp seed oil", *European Journal of Biomedical,* vol. 11, no. 4, pp. 167-177, 2024.

[67] S.S. Imam, "Sublingual tablets amalgamated with nanoparticles and natural products to treat oral cancer", *Asian J. Pharm. Clin. Res.,* vol. 17, no. 5, pp. 2056-2062, 2024.

[68] S.S. Imam, and S. Mehdi, "Factors affecting pharmaceutical pricing in India", *Int. J. Pharma Sci.,* vol. 2, no. 4, pp. 1367-1384, 2024. [http://dx.doi.org/10.5281/zenodo.11314004]

[69] S. Mehdi, U.Z. Tabrez, and S.S. Imam, "Management of green pharmaceuticals", *Int. J. Pharm. Sci. Res.,* vol. 15, no. 7, pp. 1951-1962, 2024. [http://dx.doi.org/10.13040/IJPSR.0975-8232.15(7).1951-62]

[70] R. Teixeira, "Morais, J. J. Sousa, and A. Cunha, "Deep learning models for crop classification in aerial

imagery: A review", *Agriculture,* vol. 13, no. 5, p. 965, 2023. [http://dx.doi.org/10.3390/agriculture13050965]

[71] N.S. Ouf, "A review on applications of machine learning in agriculture", *Methods,* vol. 6, no. 8, p. 24-35, 2018.

[72] P. Arora, and A. Jain, The role of deep learning in agriculture: A review. *AIP Conf. Proc.* vol. 2555, no. 1, 050032, 2022. [http://dx.doi.org/10.1063/5.0108930]

[73] R. Sharma, S.S. Kamble, A. Gunasekaran, V. Kumar, and A. Kumar, "A systematic literature review on machine learning applications for sustainable agriculture supply chain performance", *Comput. Oper. Res.,* vol. 119, p. 104926, 2020. [http://dx.doi.org/10.1016/j.cor.2020.104926]

[74] S.S. Chlingaryan, and B. Whelan, "Machine learning for crop yield prediction", *Comput. Electron. Agric.,* vol. 151, pp. 61-69, 2018. [http://dx.doi.org/10.1016/j.compag.2018.05.012]

[75] K. Arumugam, Y. Swathi, D.T. Sanchez, M. Mustafa, C. Phoemchalard, K. Phasinam, and E. Okoronkwo, "Towards applicability of machine learning techniques in agriculture and energy sector", *Mater. Today Proc.,* vol. 51, pp. 2260-2263, 2022. [http://dx.doi.org/10.1016/j.matpr.2021.11.394]

[76] S.M.M. Hasan, F. Sohel, D. Diepeveen, H. Laga, and M.G.K. Jones, "Deep learning for weed detection", *Comput. Electron. Agric.,* vol. 184, p. 106067, 2021. [http://dx.doi.org/10.1016/j.compag.2021.106067]

[77] P. Singh, and A. Kaur, Artificial intelligence in agriculture: A systematic review in *Deep Learning for Sustainable Agriculture*, 2022, pp. 57–80. [http://dx.doi.org/10.1016/B978-0-323-85214-2.00011-2]

[78] D.S. Ahmad, and A.E. Gamal, "Deep learning for plant disease diagnosis", *Smart Agricultural Technology,* vol. 3, p. 100083, 2023. [http://dx.doi.org/10.1016/j.atech.2022.100083]

[79] C. Carrio, "Sampedro, A. Rodriguez-Ramos, and P. Campoy, "A Review of Deep Learning Methods and Applications for Unmanned Aerial Vehicles", *J. Sens.,* vol. 2017, pp. 1-13, 2017. [http://dx.doi.org/10.1155/2017/3296874]

[80] W. Peng, and O. Karimi Sadaghiani, "Machine learning applications in agricultural biomass production", *Energy Sources Part A,* vol. 45, no. 3, pp. 9178-9201, 2023. [http://dx.doi.org/10.1080/15567036.2023.2232322]

[81] A. Paul, S. Ghosh, A. K. Das, S. Goswami, S. Das Choudhury, and S. Sen, "A Review on Agricultural Advancement Based on Computer Vision and Machine Learning", In: *Emerging Technology in Modelling and Graphics, Advances in Intelligent Systems and Computing,* J. Mandal, D. Bhattacharya, Eds., Springer: Singapore, 2020, pp. 561-581.

[82] M. Ryo, J. Schiller, S. Stiller, J.C. Rivera Palacio, K. Mengsuwan, A. Safonova, and Y. Wei, "Deep learning for sustainable agriculture needs ecology and human involvement", *J. Sustain. Agric. Environ.,* vol. 2, no. 1, pp. 40-44, 2023. [http://dx.doi.org/10.1002/sae2.12036]

[83] Y. Mekonnen, S. Namuduri, L. Burton, A. Sarwat, and S. Bhansali, "Machine learning in WSN-based agriculture", *J. Electrochem. Soc.,* vol. 167, no. 3, p. 037522, 2020. [http://dx.doi.org/10.1149/2.0222003JES]

[84] S. Cravero, "Pardo, S. Sepúlveda, and L. Muñoz, “Challenges of ML in agricultural big data", *Agronomy (Basel),* vol. 12, no. 3, p. 748, 2022. [http://dx.doi.org/10.3390/agronomy12030748]

[85] P. Kolhe, K. Kalbande, and A. Deshmukh, "IoT and ML for agriculture", *Proc. 2022 10th Int. Conf.*

*Emerging Trends Eng. Technol. - Signal Inf. Process. (ICETET-SIP),* pp. 1-6, 2022.

[86] C. Pandey, P. K. Sethy, S. K. Behera, J. Vishwakarma, and V. Tande, "Smart agriculture: Technological advancements on agriculture—A systematical review", In: *Deep Learning for Sustainable Agriculture* Academic Press (Elsevier): Cambridge, MA, USA, 2022, pp. 1-56.

[87] J.U.M. Akbar, S.F. Kamarulzaman, A.J.M. Muzahid, M.A. Rahman, and M. Uddin, "Deep learning for smart greenhouse agriculture", *IEEE Access,* vol. 12, pp. 4485-4522, 2024. [http://dx.doi.org/10.1109/ACCESS.2024.3349418]

[88] H. Lin, W.C. Wang, C.Y. Liu, P.N. Pan, and H.R. Pan, "Deep learning in agricultural e-learning models", *Agronomy (Basel),* vol. 9, no. 2, p. 83, 2019. [http://dx.doi.org/10.3390/agronomy9020083]

[89] V.S. Magomadov, "Deep learning and its role in smart agriculture", *J. Phys. Conf. Ser.,* vol. 1399, no. 4, p. 044109, 2019. [http://dx.doi.org/10.1088/1742-6596/1399/4/044109]

[90] Z. Ünal, "Smart farming with deep learning: A bibliographical analysis", *IEEE Access,* vol. 8, pp. 105587-105609, 2020. [http://dx.doi.org/10.1109/ACCESS.2020.3000175]

[91] T.A. Shaikh, W.A. Mir, T. Rasool, and S. Sofi, "Machine learning for smart agriculture", *Arch. Comput. Methods Eng.,* vol. 29, no. 7, pp. 4557-4597, 2022. [http://dx.doi.org/10.1007/s11831-022-09761-4]

[92] S.U. Hong, "Image sensing and deep learning in agriculture", *Nongye Jixie Xuebao,* vol. 51, no. 5, pp. 1-15, 2020.

[93] A.V. Koshkarov, "Machine learning methods in digital agriculture", *Int. J. Adv. Stud.,* vol. 8, no. 1, pp. 11-26, 2018.

[94] J. Liu, and X. Wang, "Plant disease detection using deep learning", *Plant Methods,* vol. 17, no. 1, p. 22, 2021. [http://dx.doi.org/10.1186/s13007-021-00722-9] [PMID: 33627131]

[95] T. Khan, H.H.R. Sherazi, M. Ali, S. Letchmunan, and U.M. Butt, "Deep learning-based growth prediction", *Agronomy (Basel),* vol. 11, no. 8, p. 1551, 2021. [http://dx.doi.org/10.3390/agronomy11081551]

[96] T. Ayoub Shaikh, T. Rasool, and F. Rasheed Lone, "ML and AI in precision agriculture", *Comput. Electron. Agric.,* vol. 198, p. 107119, 2022. [http://dx.doi.org/10.1016/j.compag.2022.107119]

[97] M.A. Umar, B.M. Sani, and U. Suleiman, "ML applications in agriculture: Nigeria case", *SLU J. Sci. Technol.,* vol. 4, no. 1–2, pp. 84-96, 2022.

[98] P. Sharma, P. Dadheech, N. Aneja, and S. Aneja, "Predicting agricultural yields using ML", *IEEE Access,* vol. 11, pp. 111255-111264, 2023. [http://dx.doi.org/10.1109/ACCESS.2023.3321861]

[99] J. Zhang, J. Liu, Y. Chen, X. Feng, and Z. Sun, "Knowledge mapping of ML in agriculture", *Sustainability,* vol. 13, no. 14, p. 7662, 2021. [http://dx.doi.org/10.3390/su13147662]

[100] J. Lakshmi, and G. Naresh, "Deep learning methods using UAVs in agriculture", *Int. J. Sci. Res. Comput. Sci.,* vol. 3, pp. 1858-1863, 2018.

[101] S. Pokhariyal, N.R. Patel, and A. Govind, "ML-driven remote sensing for agriculture in India", *Agronomy (Basel),* vol. 13, no. 9, p. 2302, 2023. [http://dx.doi.org/10.3390/agronomy13092302]

[102] M.E. Hossain, M.A. Kabir, L. Zheng, D.L. Swain, S. McGrath, and J. Medway, "ML techniques for cattle identification", *Artificial Intelligence in Agriculture,* vol. 6, pp. 138-155, 2022.

[http://dx.doi.org/10.1016/j.aiia.2022.09.002]

[103] M. R. Keyvanpour, and M. B. Shirzad, "Machine learning techniques for agricultural image recognition. ", In: *Application of Machine Learning in Agriculture* 1st ed.. Elsevier: Amsterdam, Netherlands, 2022, pp. 283-305.
[http://dx.doi.org/10.1016/B978-0-323-90550-3.00011-4]

[104] L. Li, S. Zhang, and B. Wang, "Plant disease detection using deep learning", *IEEE Access,* vol. 9, pp. 56683-56698, 2021.
[http://dx.doi.org/10.1109/ACCESS.2021.3069646]

[105] T.U. Rehman, M.S. Mahmud, Y.K. Chang, J. Jin, and J. Shin, "ML algorithms for agricultural machine vision", *Comput. Electron. Agric.,* vol. 156, pp. 585-605, 2019.
[http://dx.doi.org/10.1016/j.compag.2018.12.006]

[106] S. Nigam, and R. Jain, "Plant disease identification using Deep Learning: A review", *Indian J. Agric. Sci.,* vol. 90, no. 2, pp. 249-257, 2020.

[107] S. C. A. Houetohossou, V. R. Houndji, C. G. Hounmenou, R. Sikirou, and R. L. G. Kakaï, "Deep learning methods for biotic and abiotic stresses detection and classification in fruits and vegetables: State of the art and perspectives", *Artif. Intell. Agric.,* vol. 9, pp. 46-60, 2023.

[108] S. Condran, M. Bewong, M.Z. Islam, L. Maphosa, and L. Zheng, "Machine learning in precision agriculture: A survey", *IEEE Access,* vol. 10, pp. 73786-73803, 2022.
[http://dx.doi.org/10.1109/ACCESS.2022.3188649]

[109] F. H. Juwono, W. K. Wong, S. Verma, N. Shekhawat, B. A. Lease, and C. Apriono, "Machine learning for weed–plant discrimination in agriculture 5.0: An in-depth review", *Artif. Intell. Agric.,* vol. 10, pp. 13-25, 2023.

[110] U. Shruthi, V. Nagaveni, and B. K. Raghavendra, "A Review on Machine Learning Classification Techniques for Plant Disease Detection", *Proc. 2019 5th Int. Conf. Advanced Computing & Communication Systems (ICACCS),* 2019pp. 281-284
[http://dx.doi.org/10.1109/ICACCS.2019.8728415]

[111] Y. B. Singh, A. D. Mishra, M. Dixit, and A. Srivastava, "Data Analytics and Machine Learning", In: *Studies in Big Data* vol. 145. Springer: Cham, Switzerland, 2024.

[112] N. Teimouri, M. Dyrmann, P.R. Nielsen, S.K. Mathiassen, G.J. Somerville, and R.N. Jørgensen, "Weed growth stage estimation using CNNs", *Sensors (Basel),* vol. 18, no. 5, p. 1580, 2018.
[http://dx.doi.org/10.3390/s18051580] [PMID: 29772666]

# SUBJECT INDEX

## A



## B



## C



**Ravinder M., Arti Ranjan, Youddha Beer Singh (Eds.)**

## D



## E



## F



## G



## H

## S



## T



## U



## V



## W



## X



## Y

www.ingramcontent.com/pod-product-compliance
Lightning Source LLC
LaVergne TN
LVHW072011300926
849160LV00003B/15